Teaching Cues for Sport Skills for Secondary School Students

SIXTH EDITION

Hilda A. Fronske

UTAH STATE UNIVERSITY

Edward M. Heath

UTAH STATE UNIVERSITY

PEARSON

Boston   Columbus   Indianapolis   New York   San Francisco   Upper Saddle River
Amsterdam   Cape Town   Dubai   London   Madrid   Milan   Munich   Paris   Montréal   Toronto
Delhi   Mexico City   São Paulo   Sydney   Hong Kong   Seoul   Singapore   Taipei   Tokyo

Executive Editor: Sandra Lindelof
Assistant Editor: Meghan Zolnay
Editorial Assistant: Tu-Anh Dang-Tran
Editorial Development Manager: Barbara Yien
Senior Development Editor: Susan Malloy
Managing Editor: Mike Early
Production Project Managers: Dorothy Cox and Michael Penne
Production Management and Composition: Integra Software Services, Inc.
Interior Designer: Marilyn Perry
Cover Designer: Tandem Creative
Executive Marketing Manager: Neena Bali
Front Cover Photo Credits: Top to bottom: Shutterstock/Corbis; Shutterstock;
   Shutterstock/Getty Images
Back Cover Photo Credit: Shutterstock

Library of Congress Cataloging-in-Publication Data

Fronske, Hilda Ann.
   Teaching cues for sport skills for secondary school students / Hilda Ann Fronske, Utah State
   University, Edward M Heath, Utah State University, Benjamin Cummings.—Sixth edition.
      pages cm.
   Includes bibliographical references and index.
   ISBN-10: 0-321-93515-2
   ISBN-13: 978-0-321-93515-1
   1. Sports—Study and teaching (Secondary)   2. School sports—Coaching.   I. Title.
   GV361.F66 2014
   796.077—dc23

                                                                    2014000891

                                                ISBN-10:   0-321-93515-2
                                                ISBN-13: 978-0-321-93515-1

www.pearsonhighered.com

I would like to dedicate this book to my good friend Wasel Lambert,
Karl Lambert (husband), and her 5 children: Melissa, (husband) Bo Oldroyd
and Ruby Gene (daughter), Amy, Jared, Jefferson, and Daniel.

—Hilda Fronske

This book is dedicated to all of those teachers and coaches who, like Dr. Fronske,
have a passion for their job to instill their same enthusiasm for physical activity and sport in
students. These teachers truly realize the joy that comes from a lifetime of physical activity
and the important role physical activity plays in the quality of our lives.

—Edward Heath

Contents

Preface

Have you ever dreamed of a book that covered teaching cues, equipment tips, safety, etiquette, teaching progressions, mini-games, rules, strategy, scoring, and assessment for a wide variety of sports and activities? The wait for dedicated teachers who want to expose their students to a host of physical activities is over! Featured in this unique and exciting book are teaching cues and other helpful information to enhance the teaching of 29 different sports and activities.

Teaching Cues for Sport Skills for Secondary School Students, Sixth Edition, will save teachers and coaches hours of planning time with this user-friendly format. The cues will also establish your credibility with students because you can tell them why a particular cue works and you can better analyze skills and accelerate student learning. Teachers can make use of the authors' and sport consultants' years of experience to enhance their ability to teach these activities.

WHAT'S NEW TO THIS EDITION?

Students will benefit from a variety of new content in this edition, including:

- Additions and reorganization of each activity chapter to include, in order, equipment tips, safety, etiquette, teaching progressions, mini-games, updated rules, strategies, updated scoring, and assessment ideas.
- Chapter 22 on Strength Training with Free Weights has been completely rewritten.
- New pictures and extensive revisions to Chapter 26 on Track and Field Events.
- Addition of several diagrams of fields and courts.
- Consistent additions to the cues tables throughout the book, filling in the Why? and Common Error sections for nearly every activity.

ACKNOWLEDGMENTS

My thanks to the incredible crew at Pearson Education, Benjamin Cummings. Susan Malloy, Tu-Anh Dang-Tran, and Sandra Lindelof; thank you for all your time, insights, editing skills, and making this whole process fun.

Edward Heath and his family, wife Megan and children Daniel, McKinley, and Emma. Thank you Ed for all of the time and detail you put into this book and to your family to support you in this endeavor.

I would like to thank our President of our university, Stan Albrecht, for the outstanding leader he is at Utah State University.

Additionally, I would like to thank Carolyn Brittain and Debbie Phippen, our staff assistants, for their time and talents that went into the process of this book.

Lastly, I appreciate the time, effort, and suggestions of the reviewers for this edition: Brian Culp, Indiana University-Purdue University Indianapolis; Ferman Konukman, State University of New York; Ellen Martin, Columbus State University; Bennie Prince, University of Arkansas at Little Rock; Peter Rattigan, Rowan University; Thomas Roberge, Norwich University; and Katelyn Smither, Old Dominion University.

Sport Consultants

Teaching Physical Education Is Fun with the Right Tools: Ed Heath, professor in HPER, Utah State University, Logan, Utah.

Aerobic Kickboxing: Chris Erickson, certified aerobic kickboxing instructor, second-degree black belt, elementary physical education teacher, Adams Elementary School, Logan, Utah. Shelley Dawson, Sports Academy and USU Aerobic Kick Boxing Instructor, Utah State University, Logan, Utah. Chandra Salmon, soccer player, Utah State University, Logan, Utah.

Archery: Joyce Harrison, associate dean, Brigham Young University, Provo, Utah. Derek Lindley, archery manager at pro shop, Al's Sporting Goods, Logan, Utah. Val Spillet, vice president of Al's Sporting Inc., Logan, Utah.

Badminton: Peggy Savosik, Jim Leete, and Jim Stabler, USA Badminton, Colorado Springs, Colorado. Gord Smith, Badminton Canada, Gloucester, Ontario, Canada. Richard Jones, Brigham Young University, Provo, Utah. Edward Heath, professor in physical education, Utah State University, Logan, Utah. Benji Skinner, graduate student, Utah State University, Logan, Utah.

Baseball: Justin Jensen, associate scout for Milwaukee Brewers, Rocky Mountain School of Baseball, Logan, Utah. Jonathan Howell, Health, Physical Education, and Recreation Department, Utah State University, Logan, Utah. Rick Thorne, Skyview High School head baseball coach, Smithfield, Utah. Ryan Zimmerman, pitcher for AA baseball, Tampa Bay Rays, assistant football coach, Utah State University, Logan, Utah.

Basketball: Coach Al Brown, assistant basketball coach for Lady Volunteers, University of Tennessee, Knoxville. Shanna Stevens, Utah State University club basketball coach, Logan, Utah. Jacob Smith, Student, Utah State University, Logan, Utah. Jaycee Carroll, basketball player, Utah State University, Logan Utah. Kyle Straatman, basketball coach, Mt. Crest High, Hyrum, Utah. Casey Richardson, undergraduate student, Utah State University, Logan, Utah.

Bowling: Richard Jones, professor in pedagogy and sports, Brigham Young University, Provo, Utah. Russell Boyer, undergraduate student, Utah State University, Logan, Utah.

Cycling—Mountain Biking: Quinn Bingham, bicycle technician, Al's Sporting Goods, Logan, Utah. Jeff Keller, Sunrise Cycle, Logan, Utah. Steven Gudmundson, graduate student, Utah State University, Logan, Utah. Emily Watkins, graduate student, Utah State University, Logan, Utah. Gerald Smith, professor in HPER, Utah State University, Logan, Utah. Eadric Bressel, Professor in HPER, Utah State University, Logan, Utah.

Cycling—Road Biking: Jeff Keller, Sunrise Cycle, Logan, Utah. Steven Gudmunson, graduate student, Utah State University, Logan, Utah. State Stowers, bicycle technician, Al's Sporting Goods, Logan, Utah. Emily Watking, undergraduate student, Utah State University, Logan, Utah. Gerald Smith, Professor in HPER, Utah State University, Logan, Utah. Eadric Bressel, Professor in HPER, Utah State University, Logan, Utah.

Field Hockey: Laura Darling, United States Field Hockey Association, Colorado Springs, Colorado. Katie Harris and Deanie Stetson, Falmouth

High School, Falmouth, Maine. Lauren Eichenberger, SUNY, Cortland Field Hockey, New York.

Fitness Equipment Workout: Edward Heath, professor in physical education, Utah State University, Logan, Utah. Rod Hammer, MS, Icon Health and Fitness, Logan, Utah. Dayna Barrett, Assistant Wellness Coordinator, Utah State University, Logan, Utah.

Floor Hockey: Ross Keys, physical education undergraduate student, and Michael Burggraf, physical education undergraduate student, Utah State University, Logan, Utah. Gianni Maddalozzo, instructor in physical education, Department of Exercise and Sport Science, Oregon State University, Corvallis, Oregon.

Football: Bill Bauer, facility coordinator, Utah State University, Logan, Utah. Jeff Berg, football player, Utah State University, Logan, Utah. Art Erickson, player and coach, Utah State University, Logan, Utah. Ryan Allred, undergraduate physical education, Utah State University, Logan, Utah. Jacob Smith, student, Utah State University, Logan, Utah. Jesse Parker, Intramural Supervisor, Utah State University, Logan, Utah. Jarett Tauiliili, Utah State University Football, Logan, Utah. Kyle Strattman, physical education major, Utah State University, Logan, UT. Casey Richardson, physical education major, Utah State University, Logan, UT.

The Foundation of Sport Skills: Dominque Gaisie, football player, Utah State University, Logan, Utah. Paul Igboeli, football player, Utah State University, Logan, Utah. Anthony Porras, soccer player and student, Utah State University, Logan, Utah. Julie Douglas, student, Utah State University, Logan, Utah. Dayna Barrett, Assistant Wellness Coordinator, Utah State University, Logan, Utah. Jacob Smith, student, Utah State University, Logan, Utah. Christopher Curtis, student, Utah State University, Logan, Utah.

Golf: Robert Fronske, amateur golf player, Tempe, Arizona. Dan Roskelley, golf professional, Logan Golf and Country Club, Logan, Utah. Brett Wayment, assistant professional, Logan Golf and Country Club, Logan, Utah. Ed Heath, Professor in HPER, Utah State University, Logan, Utah.

Lacrosse: Roger Allen, lacrosse coach, Logan, Utah. Mason Goodhand, Utah Lacrosse Association, Salt Lake City, Utah. Heriberto "Eddie" Vega, head lacrosse coach, Utah State University, Logan, Utah. Erin Smith, US Lacrosse, Baltimore, Maryland. Nick Baker, Lacrosse Player, Utah State University, Logan, Utah. Lauren Eichenberger, Suffern High School lacrosse, New York. Photography: Erin Smith.

Pickleball: Sarah Lowe, Angela Kimball, Amy Thatcher, and Jackie Ellis, tennis team at Utah State University, Logan, Utah. Tedi Searle, physical education undergraduate student, Utah State University, Logan, Utah. Doug Smith, general manager, Pickle-Ball Inc., Seattle, Washington.

Racquetball: Chris Atkins, head racquetball club coach, Utah State University, Logan, Utah. Jim Hiser, American Amateur Racquetball Association, Colorado Springs, Colorado. Susan Hill, graduate student, Health Department, Southern Illinois University, Carbondale, Illinois. Benji Skinner, graduate student, Utah State University, Logan, Utah.

Recreational Walking, Running, and Hiking: Patrick Shane, head women's cross-country/distance coach, Brigham Young University, Provo, Utah. Kevin Prusak, assistant professor, elementary physical education, Brigham Young University, Provo, Utah. Sue Vincent, assistant professor, elementary physical education,

Brigham Young University, Provo, Utah. Jesse Nelson, undergraduate student, Utah State University, Logan, Utah. Loretta Cide, undergraduate student of physical education, Utah State University, Logan, Utah.

Soccer: Chris Agnello, men's soccer coach, Department of Exercise and Sport Science, University of Utah, Salt Lake City, Utah. Brent Anderson, assistant soccer coach, Heather Carins, head women's soccer coach, Utah State University, Logan, Utah. Charles Dudschus, Health, Physical Education, and Recreation Department, Utah State University, Logan, Utah. Kelli Brooke Parsons, undergraduate physical education student, Utah State University, Logan, Utah. Jin Wang, men's soccer coach, Rockford College, Rockford, Illinois. Brian Hopkinson, student, Utah State University, Logan, Utah.

Softball, Fast-Pitch and Slow-Pitch: Lloydene Searle, women's fast-pitch head softball coach, Utah State University, Logan, Utah. Ann Schulz, softball coach, Sandridge Junior High School, Layton, Utah. Emily Watkins, graduate student; Stephanie Vasarhely, graduate teaching assistant; Nicole Downs, physical education undergraduate student; Kelly Warner, physical education undergraduate student, Utah State University, Logan, Utah. Hailey Fronton, Dakota Monarrez, Ambur Orozeo, Jo Koons, Utah State University Softball, Logan Utah.

Strength Training with Free Weights: Evan Simon, Head Strength Coach, University of Wisconsin, Madison, Wisconsin.

Swimming and Water Polo: Katrina Bingham, swimming and water aerobics instructor, Utah State University, Logan, Utah. Lisa Klarich and Steven Dunn, Health, Physical Education and Recreation Department, Utah State University, Logan, Utah. Christopher Hudson, Assistant Aquatics Coordinator, Utah State University, Logan, Utah. Zachary Miller, Head Water Polo Coach, Bear River High School, Tremonton, Utah. Danny Espin, Head Water Polo Coach, Bear River High School, Tremonton, Utah. Breanna Studenka, Health, Physical Education and Recreation, Utah State University, Logan, Utah.

Team Handball and Indoor Hybrid Ball: Mary Phyl Dwight, cochair, Coaching and Methods Committee, United States Team Handball Federation, Kansas City, Missouri. Reita Clanton, assistant coach for women's team handball, Atlanta, Georgia. Peter Mathesius, physical education instructor, Utah State University, Logan, Utah. Randy Webb, helps with Police Athletic League (PAL), former teacher, coach, parks and recreation for 30 years, Knoxville, Tennessee. Lauren Eichenberger, SUNY Cortland Team Handball, New York.

Tennis: Janet Carey, tennis professional, Neversink, New York. Dan Clifton, tennis instructor for campus recreation instructional program, Utah State University, Logan, Utah. Steven Dunn, former assistant professor in physical education; Rolayne Wilson, associate professor of physical education; Joy Hartung, tennis athlete and undergraduate student; Tedi Searle, physical education undergraduate student; and Clay Stevens, former graduate student, Utah State University, Logan, Utah. Sarah Lowe, Angela Kimball, Amy Thatcher, and Jackie Ellis, tennis team at Utah State University, Logan, Utah. Christian Wright, head tennis coach, Utah State University, Logan, Utah. Edward Heath, professor of physical education, Utah State University, Logan, Utah.

Track and Field Events: Curtis Collier, track technician, Utah State University, Logan, Utah. Dayna Barrett, track and field heptathlete, and Jamie Bennion, heptathlete and graduate student, Utah State University, Logan, Utah. Jon Goble, Utah State University Track, Logan, Utah.

Ultimate Frisbee: Ann Asbell, activity specialist, Department of Exercise and Sport Science, Oregon State University, Corvallis, Oregon. Janenne Graff, player/coach, Ultimate Frisbee Club, Utah State University, Logan, Utah. Steven Noorda, student, Utah State University.

Volleyball: Carl McGown, Department of Physical Education, Brigham Young University, Provo, Utah. Lana Moser, head volleyball coach, Preston High School, Preston, Idaho. David Cuthbert, head coach for Wessex Volleyball Club Junior Women, Poole, UK. Stormy Schuler, Volleyball Player, assistant coach, Utah State University, Logan, Utah. Lori Karaghouli, head women's volleyball coach for 20 years, Mountain Crest High School, Hyrum, Utah. Paige Neves, Utah State University Volleyball, Logan, Utah. Jacob Christofferson, student, Utah State University.

Yoga: Rachel Hebert, yoga practitioner and model, San Francisco, California. Denise "Deni" Preston, certified group exercise fitness instructor for American Council on Exercise, Brigham Young University, Provo, Utah. Jennifer Fallon, M.S., yoga instructor, Utah State University, Logan, Utah. Kylie Cardon, student, Utah State University, Logan, Utah. Julie Christenn, student, Utah State University, Logan, Utah. Photography: Christina Pierson.

Teaching Physical Education Is Fun with the Right Tools

Have you ever found yourself asking these questions: How can I do a good job teaching physical education and have fun at the same time? What is the quickest and most efficient way to teach sport skills? What tools do I have available to provide a positive learning environment in the sports arena and to build lasting relationships with my students?

This book answers these questions and provides a wealth of teaching cues for physical education activities in your curriculum. The benefits of this book are distinct from the skills text.

- The text answers *why* a cue is appropriate for a skill.
- The text includes photographs of students and athletes, with each cue labeled.
- The text provides cues for successfully teaching fundamental sport skills that are developmentally appropriate.
- The text reinforces the National Standards for Physical Education (AAHPERD, 2013).
- The text provides a resource for enrichment of the state core curricula.
- Using teaching cues addresses the three learning domains: psychomotor, cognitive, and affective.
- The cues are broken down by components and are easily modified for students with disabilities.
- The cues provide a framework for authentic assessment by teachers and students.
- The cues provide an opportunity to integrate other curricular areas.

NATIONAL STANDARDS & GRADE-LEVEL OUTCOMES FOR K-12 PHYSICAL EDUCATION

The goal of physical education is to develop physically literate individuals who have the knowledge, skills and confidence to enjoy a lifetime of healthful physical activity.

To pursue a lifetime of healthful physical activity, *a physically literate individual*:

- Has learned the skills necessary to participate in a variety of physical activities.
- Knows the implications of and the benefits from involvement in various types of physical activities.
- Participates regularly in physical activity.
- Is physically fit.
- Values physical activity and its contributions to a healthful lifestyle.

Standard 1–The physically literate individual demonstrates competency in a variety of motor skills and movement patterns.

Standard 2–The physically literate individual applies knowledge of concepts, principles, strategies and tactics related to movement and performance.

Standard 3–The physically literate individual demonstrates the knowledge and skills to achieve and maintain a health-enhancing level of physical activity and fitness.

Standard 4–The physically literate individual exhibits responsible personal and social behavior that respects self and others.

Standard 5–The physically literate individual recognizes the value of physical activity for health, enjoyment, challenge, self-expression and/or social interaction.

The AAHPERD, 2013 content standards and your state core curriculum provide a curricular foundation for teaching physical education.

TOOL 2: WHAT ARE TEACHING CUES?

A *cue* is defined as a guiding suggestion or a stimulus that excites the imagination to action. Cues are short, catchy phrases that call the student's attention to key components of a skill. A cue projects a clear description of a skill component into the student's mind.

Cues may be verbal, serving as a short reminder of more complete information presented about a skill. A cue developed around rich visual imagery, or related to the student's previous experience, remains in cognition much longer than a lengthy discourse on the fine points of technique. A mind cluttered with many technical concepts cannot direct the muscles to achieve flawless coordination. At best, a mind concentrating on one visual or kinesthetic prompt may direct that one body part to obey the command. For example, a verbal cue for shooting a basketball is "palm up." Phrases may be more visual, with the intent of creating a picture in the learner's mind that results in correct skill performance. The "palm up" cue could be followed by "like holding a waiter's tray." These are prompts that provide a rich, visual imagery for students to identify the skill component. By visualizing these familiar patterns, students are able to develop skill patterns, and if they begin to show poor form, a cue serves as a quick reminder of proper form.

Often when teaching sport skills, the teacher overloads the student with too much information and technical jargon, which may make little sense to the student. Motor learning specialists have long noted that the simpler the instructions, the easier it is for the student to concentrate on the skill at hand. The KISS principle, "keep it short and simple," is applied.

TOOL 3: WHY DO STUDENTS NEED TO GET A CUE?

Cues are used to motivate students. Research has determined that students who receive cues appear to be more motivated to improve their performance than students who do not receive them. The self-confidence of the cued students seems to increase steadily with improved skill ability, as they work to improve each day. Students who do not receive cues appear to be frustrated and bored and have a difficult time staying on task (Fronske, Abendroth-Smith, & Blakemore, 1997).

Cues can help students set higher goals in skill performance. Cues arouse students to direct their efforts toward improving their performance and provide a foundation for setting goals. When students feel the success of learning one cue at a time, you can introduce other cues without intimidation until they become proficient at the complete skill component. Mastering one cue at a time gives students opportunities to work toward specific goals. By providing a cue, or a few alternative cues, students are able to choose one and work at their own pace. Create cues posters and display them in your facility for your students to refer to as they practice the skills (Figure 1.1). Cues help all students experience success with sport skills.

Physical education teachers have students for a short period of time during the week. It is imperative that this time be utilized to the fullest. The use of material in this book on short, accurate, qualitative teaching cues can save teachers hours of preparation. Research indicates that the combination of accurate, qualitative cues; appropriate numbers of cues; and use of visual demonstrations along with verbal explanations seems to produce greater skill development gains (Rink, 1993). The cues in this book have been developed by experts in their respective areas to help teachers give accurate, qualitative cues regarding a specific sport skill. These cues *work*!

FIGURE 1.1 Cues Poster

Cues also address the psychomotor, cognitive, and affective learning domains. They:

- Enhance the learner's memory (cognitive).
- Compress information and reduce words (cognitive).
- Encourage focus on one specific component of a skill (psychomotor).
- Help teachers and students analyze a skill performance by helping them focus on a particular component of the skill (psychomotor).
- Strengthen correct performance (psychomotor).
- Help teachers give positive, corrective feedback (affective and cognitive).
- Help peers give positive, corrective feedback (affective and cognitive).
- Motivate students to develop and refine skills (affective and cognitive).

TOOL 4: HOW DO STUDENTS GET A CUE?

Students are visual learners and need three to five demonstrations. The use of demonstrations is the best way to teach with cues. Cues used with demonstrations help students develop a strong visual image of the skill. When demonstrating a skill, the teacher focuses the students' attention on one specific component of the skill through the use of a good verbal or visual cue. To avoid confusing students, it is important to keep verbalization to a minimum. For example, having students make an upside-down L when performing skipping A's gives them a picture upon which to base their skill. By picturing the correct pattern movements, they are able to develop the correct skipping patterns. If they begin to show improper form, a cue, a demonstration, or both can serve as a quick reminder of proper form.

Do not overload students with too many cues. Here are some helpful tips when teaching with cues:

- Research in motor learning indicates that students can best learn with a limited amount of new material.
- Giving students too much information or progressing to new information before students have grasped a concept may hinder the learning process.
- Too much information is worse than no information at all.
- For each component of a skill, practice the whole skill, but focus on each part in turn.
- Give students no more than one to three cues at a time.
- Following the acquisition of the motor pattern targeted to the first cue (e.g., in the football punt, "kick the fish in the belly"), teachers then move to the next phase of the motor skill.
- Additional cues should build on the previously learned skills, with no more than three cues for each teaching episode.
- Students need short bits of information that they can quickly apply to their skill.
- Practice, practice, practice; repetition, repetition, repetition.

Provide students with lots of opportunities to respond (OTRs), such as touching the ball. You want maximum activity with minimum wait time. Each student or pair is provided with a piece of equipment. This increases a student's OTRs. This book provides great drill progressions and mini-games to assist you when teaching sport skills and games that offer lots of OTRs.

Providing feedback to your students is a critical tool to help them learn sport skills. To earn your credibility as an educator, you must work hard during each class session. Giving appropriate feedback is the "heartbeat" of the class. Is it tough to give feedback in each class session? Yes. Why? Because it takes focus, intensity, time, and effort to pay attention to the performance of the students. When teachers are in tune and give appropriate corrective feedback, it helps to maintain the supportive climate. When teachers pay attention to students, students feel important, and when teachers give feedback, students feel appreciated.

Teachers need to notice details about their students. "What kind of details?" you might ask. Start with the effort the individual is giving when performing a skill or participating in a game. Study each student's face and body language. This takes hard work on your part, but if the students know you are paying attention to them and that you notice the small details, they will develop trust in you because they sense you care about them as individuals.

But this tool is not enough for you to earn credibility with your students. You must know the correct movement patterns to analyze the skills of your students and give technical feedback. Using the cues in this book will give you a jump start in earning credibility with your students. Teaching sport skills is easier and more effective when you focus on one to three cues and then give feedback on those cues.

Just as important as technical feedback is positive communication between you and a student. Eighty percent of what a teacher communicates to students is through nonverbal behaviors, such as body language: for example, thumbs up or down, clapping, the "yes" arm pump, the raise-the-roof motion, the OK sign, facial expressions, "The Look," raising the eyebrow, a wink, the with-it-ness body stance, avoid hands in pockets or folded arms.

Another communication technique is appropriate touch, such as high fives, low fives, side fives, backward fives, and a jump with two-handed fives. Appropriate places to touch students may be the arms, shoulders, and back. Be sensitive to other cultural customs regarding appropriate touch.

There is one more tool that works when giving feedback: The Challenge. This tool is rarely discussed in the literature. The best coaches in the United States—John Wooden, Pat Summit, Phil Jackson, and many others—challenge their athletes. A Challenge is stimulating and thought-provoking; something that incites or quickens actions, feelings, and thoughts; and it arouses action or effort by encouragement. The Challenge is usually disguised. It comes with risk, but it can become a major tool for taking your students beyond what they think is their potential.

The Challenge happens only after you have built positive relationships with your students. To issue a challenge, you must know the student's backgrounds, dreams, and goals. Then and only then will The Challenge be effective.

To review, the following are five examples of feedback:

- *Effort:* "Abby, great effort on trying to throw the ball left-handed. Try making a better L for me." Or, "Great effort running the bases."
- *Technical:* Give positive, specific feedback on a cue, and then correct an error. "Amanda, great L throwing on the ball. Now try to take a longer step on the target." (Figure 1.2).
- *Nonverbal:* Clear across the gym, you notice that Adam is practicing making an L with her left arm. Give her a thumbs-up and a big smile. (Figure 1.3).
- *Appropriate touch:* "Amanda, I like your long step to the target." You give Amanda a high five (Figure 1.4).
- *Challenge:* John already knows how to throw. You say to John, "Is that the hardest or farthest you can throw the ball?" Another example might be found in a game situation. You notice John jogging around the bases.

FIGURE 1.2 Technical Feedback

FIGURE 1.3 Nonverbal Feedback

You might say, "John, is that the fastest you can go around the bases? I noticed you are quite a sprinter and you outrun everyone in class. Show me how fast you can run."

If you use these specific feedback tools, will it help you become a better teacher? Absolutely! Start today.

Mini-Games Increase Feedback Opportunities

Mini-games with three to six students on each team are recommended so that students have an opportunity to respond. Feedback is easier to give when your class is divided into smaller groups. More is better! More students with

FIGURE 1.4 Appropriate Touch

FIGURE 1.5 Mini-Game

their own equipment. More opportunities to practice. More feedback gives the students more skill development and more confidence to succeed (Figure 1.5).

Feedback on the cues should be given during these games. Teachers usually do not give technical feedback in the game situation but get caught up watching the game, or if they do give feedback, it is in the form of "nags" (negative feedback). Mini-games provide a great opportunity to gain credibility with your students. Remember: it takes effort, hard work, observation, focus, and timing to give precisely the right feedback. Try to use a variety of feedback techniques, and always give the students something to work on. Your class will be full of exciting options to help your students learn skills, have fun playing games, and develop lifetime sport skills. You will also be so absorbed in the class that time will pass very quickly, and your passion for your work will increase. The students will feel your fervor, enthusiasm, and passion when you teach. Watch the best teachers and see what *they* do.

Using Technology

Using PowerPoint Presentations and YouTube videos to teach sport skills can be a valuable teaching tool for teachers and coaches. Students and athletes can be highly motivated by PowerPoints and YouTube. Virtually anyone can make a PowerPoint presentation and access a YouTube clip to help teach sport skills since the information on the Internet is vast. Utilize these technologies in the classroom when students are fatigued or on rainy days before competition. The following is a link to view examples of PowerPoint presentations: https://hper. usu.edu/htm/faculty-resources. The PowerPoints provide the instructor with ideas to supplement and improve future classes and teams. Using technology in this way has effectively enriched the learning experience of students, athletes, teachers, and coaches.

TOOL 5: HOW DO I ORGANIZE A SUCCESSFUL CLASS?

Develop a Supportive Climate on the First Day

On the first day of class, the teacher needs to get to know each student—and the students need to get to know each other—before anything else is done (Figure 1.6). How do you set the stage for the first hour of class? The first rule is that no one talks when a student or teacher is "onstage." Ask each student to stand and talk about something they carry with them each day, or perhaps to imagine some piece of sports equipment they would like to be. Why is this activity critical on the first day? It breaks the ice between the students and the

FIGURE 1.6 Supportive Climate on the First Day

teacher. The students begin to feel comfortable with each other. They begin relating to each other's experiences. First impressions and judgments—good or bad—are replaced by feelings of warmth for the individual. The students feel more comfortable talking with each other, and they learn specific facts about their classmates. They can use this information to open a conversation. Walls come down. Relationships start to form. The teacher also benefits and has information with which to spark a later conversation.

Another reason this activity is so effective is that all students must be quiet when not onstage. This teaches respect for each other, and the teacher can begin to work on management skills, setting the tone for the rest of the year.

On the second day, have students network with a partner for about five minutes. Each student stands with a partner, and they share with the group what they have learned about each other. Once again, emphasize the rule that no one else is to talk when partners are sharing their experiences about their new friend. Respect is reinforced. You will be amazed at how well the students listen during this time. Perform this type of activity throughout the year whenever you feel a need to bond with your class. Remember, the first few days are critical in terms of what you will do the rest of your year. The benefits of a supportive climate (Patton & Griffin, 1981) include the following:

- Group members more easily accept others' influence.
- Members of the group are less suspicious of the motives of others.
- A greater degree of tolerance of deviant behavior occurs.
- When conflicts arise, the group is able to focus on the group goals rather than on defending egos.
- The group develops trust, which allows more freedom for group risk-taking.
- Members of the group feel better about themselves.

Establish a Supportive Climate When Teaching Sport Skills

Teachers need to establish a framework of support in order to implement teaching cues successfully. Students need to feel safe in order to reach out and try new behaviors. Creating a supportive climate promotes a safe learning environment for students. The supportive climate happens verbally, with positive, clear cues and reinforcing phrases. It also happens in a safe, nonverbal physical environment.

Nonverbal behaviors, which accompany verbal cues, also communicate to students. A teacher who says, "Nice dive," accompanied by a harsh tone of voice and disapproving facial expression, communicates, "Bad dive." The way teachers present cues—the tone of their voice, their body language, their manner of touch, or the way they dress (such as a teacher not wearing a swimsuit in a swim class)—can enhance or detract from a positive comment.

Great teachers and coaches are skillful at giving the most appropriate cue at the appropriate time, using verbal and/or nonverbal signals. Combining verbal cues and positive nonverbal cues becomes a powerful tool for providing feedback from the teacher. By creating a supportive climate, you can help students feel comfortable and become motivated to explore and learn a variety of sports.

Build Relationships and Still Get the Work Done

Hunter (1998) states this about building relationships: "If we focus only on tasks and not on the relationship, we may experience turnover, rebellion, poor quality, low commitment, low trust and other undesirable symptoms" (40). Being an excellent leader maximizes the teacher's effectiveness. The first thing one must do is value those leading and strive to develop healthy and mutually respectful relationships. Hunter continues, "The key then to leadership is accomplishing the tasks at hand while building relationships" (41).

How does a teacher continue to build relationships (Figure 1.7) and still get the work done? Teachers have many opportunities to learn each day about students' lives and what they treasure. Here are some options to think about: Take time before school, at lunch, and after school to visit with your students. Interview them about their interests, dreams, and goals. Attend school functions to let them know you care about them. Let them talk about what they did over the weekend, on spring break, or during their summer vacations.

Expending the effort to build relationships with your students develops their respect and trust. They will be more willing to work for you, so work on building relationships daily. The best teachers do, and the work gets done in a supportive climate.

Establish Protocols and Use Management Skills

Protocols are necessary to provide a safe learning environment and to provide structure for your students. Just like any other sport skill, the protocols need to be practiced repeatedly. For further information, refer to Graham, Holt/Hale, and Parker (2000) and Pangrazi (2007a, 2007b). The following protocols are just a few to get you started:

1. Establish start and stop signals. The signals need to be different from each other. They can be auditory or visual, or a combination of both—for example, one whistle blow to start and two whistle blows to stop.

FIGURE 1.7 Building Relationships

FIGURE 1.8 Establishing Protocols

FIGURE 1.9 Everyone Has a Piece of Equipment

2. Establish protocols; for example (Figure 1.8):
   - Proper dress: tee shirt, shorts, tennis shoes, and socks
   - No talking while others are talking
   - A gathering place for giving instruction and talking to the entire class
   - Distributing and collecting of equipment
   - Grouping students: partners, teams, and so forth
   - Off-task behavior; for example, three strikes, you're out—one strike is a warning; second strike, the student sits out for 5 minutes and observes the class; third strike, the student sits out for the entire class

3. Provide a piece of developmentally appropriate equipment for each student; this is key so students have many opportunities to practice sport skills. Teachers (Figure 1.9) need to be creative in finding ways to work their budget to buy safe, age-appropriate equipment. For example, good, inexpensive leather volleyballs can be purchased from college volleyball teams. Old tennis balls can be purchased from tennis teams or tennis clubs. Send home a letter with students at the beginning of the school year indicating your equipment needs. Enlist the help of the high school shop or an applied technology school to make equipment. Use your creativity to find solutions.

4. Establish a "home" for the equipment when giving directions: for example, students can place a basketball or softball between their feet (Figure 1.10).

5. Move around the perimeter of the area with your back to the wall during activities. You can observe the entire class, give instruction, and offer feedback to students.

6. Maximize activity time and minimize wait time. Mini-games are very effective in increasing OTRs and minimizing wait time.

FIGURE 1.10 Establish a Home for the Equipment

7. Avoid having lines of students wait for their turn.

8. See Woods and Langley's concerns (1997, 8–9) below about circle formations which are not game like:

   • Lack of practice time
   • Requirement for complex use of the skill
   • Organizational pattern that does not match game requirements
   • Potential to embarrass and discourage
   • No clear goals for success
   • Potential to increase management problems

The authors then list six suggestions for effective student learning:

   • Adequate practice time
   • Requirement for less-complex use of skill
   • Organizational patterns that match game requirements
   • Development of student self-confidence
   • Clear goals for success
   • Effective management of student practice

Use a Successful Teaching Model

How does a teacher correctly teach a motor skill? What is a correct and successful teaching model? How do teaching cues fit into this model? The following are components of a good teaching model, with suggestions for implementing cues:

   • Get the students' attention! Use anticipatory sets (attention-getters) to motivate the students to perform the skill. Make sure they pay attention to the instructions. Be enthusiastic!
   • Organize the group so that everyone can see and hear. State the lesson objective by describing what is to be learned and why it is important. Your objective should be brief, simple, and direct. This should lead to a demonstration (Figure 1.11).
   • Preassess your students by asking how many of them know how to perform the skill, or ask the students to perform the skill if it is relatively safe.
   • Demonstrate the entire skill three to five times. Show the skill from front, side, and back angles. Demonstrations should be performed as they

FIGURE 1.11 Demonstrate So All Can See and Hear

would appear in a game situation. Move the class around so they can see the demonstration from different angles. The students should see a correct demonstration of the skill. Remember, a picture is worth a thousand words when learning a sport skill.

- After the demonstration, have the students practice the skill. This will give you time to assess their proficiency.

- Have the students practice the skill. You provide feedback on the cue words used in the demonstration. Use a systematic approach to giving feedback to all of your students during the class.

- Use one teaching cue at a time. This directs the students' attention to the specific area of focus.

- Provide additional demonstrations and new cues when students have mastered the previous ones.

- Review and/or demonstrate the cues during class closure. Provide the students with an opportunity to ask questions.

- Have students repeat aloud the cues for the skill. The cues will be fresh in their memories.

Develop Cues for Students with Disabilities

You might have the opportunity to teach students with disabilities. Be creative in developing cues and activities for these students. For example, you could put a bell around a ball for a blind student, integrate brightly colored equipment for the hearing impaired, and use balloons for the student in a wheelchair. The cues presented in the following chapters can be used and adapted for students with disabilities. Include all of the other students. Let them participate on their own levels, see their excitement in being able to participate, and feel the emotional bonding with your students.

TOOL 6: AUTHENTIC ASSESSMENT: HOW DO I KNOW THE CUES ARE WORKING?

Cues Help Instructors Analyze a Skill

Some physical education teachers tend to analyze skills excessively and tell all they know (Lockhart, 1996). Cues are short and to the point, and they focus the assessment process on giving specific feedback.

Teaching cues provide students with valuable information to accompany demonstrations. Cues aid you in focusing on correct skill performance so that appropriate feedback can be given. Incorporating cues in the teaching process makes it possible for you to identify major errors quickly. For example, when the students are performing the forehand stroke in tennis, and the cue is "swing racket low to high," it is easy to observe whether the racket head is high at the end of the stroke. It is also important to explain why it is necessary to perform a particular cue accurately.

Cues Strengthen Correct Performance

A critical component of skill acquisition is identifying the parts of the skill that are being performed correctly. You can have the students work in pairs or in small groups; in this way, they can analyze their performance and give feedback to each other on one specific cue. For example, the following three cues for throwing a ball are used: 1. Take the ball straight down and graze your shorts, 2. stretch your arm way back, and 3. make an L. Student responses might include the following:

- "Hey, I like the way you brought your arm down and grazed your shorts. That action will give you more distance."
- "Way to make an L shape with your arm! You're keeping the ball away from your head."
- "Wow! Way to stretch your arm way back! That was a great stretch. It looks like Barry Bonds's or Dale Murphy's."

This type of specific feedback increases the likelihood that the student will repeat the correct response in the near future.

Cues Help Correct Errors in Technique

"Coach, how can I get over the hurdles faster?" "How do I improve my sprint time?" "What is the best way to exchange the baton?" These are questions students might ask about track skills. Are you ready to answer these questions without criticizing or giving the student too much information?

Your challenge is to identify the cause of the problem and look for solutions. The effective use of cues avoids judgment and criticism. Cues are used to correct errors constructively. Cues help you identify the problem and provide accurate feedback to the student: for example, "Stacie, I really liked how you made a 'banana shape' when performing the long jump. This time, work on the 'jackknife position' when you land."

Cues Help Peers Correct Errors in Technique

When students are provided with correct teaching cues, they can help give feedback to other peers. Pair students and have them observe their partner's performance. For example, if the cue given on throwing is, "Stand sideways and take a long step toward the target," a student can watch his or her partner and assess whether he or she is standing sideways and taking the long step. If his or her partner steps too high or takes a short step, but is standing sideways, he or she can provide him or her partner with the following feedback: "Hey, Stacie, you stood sideways. Now remember to take a long step with your foot toward the target." This feedback emphasizes a student's correct performance, notifies him or her of the error, and suggests a specific way to correct it, providing a more positive interaction.

CONCLUSION

The tools outlined in this chapter help make teaching fun and exciting. Students will appreciate your expertise and retain knowledge in a fun and caring environment. This book is intended to widen your vision about teaching. The cues in this book can be effective, motivating, and life-altering when students are successful. To establish credibility quickly, incorporate the teaching cues in subsequent chapters to obtain the edge that is necessary to connect with your students. Have fun!

FYI

PUBLICATIONS

American Alliance for Health, Physical Education, Recreation, and Dance (AAHPERD). (2013). http://www.aahperd.org/naspe/standards/nationalStandards/index.cfm

Fronske, H., Abendroth-Smith, J., & Blakemore, C. (1997). The effect of critical cues on throwing efficiency of elementary school children. *The Physical Educator, 54*(2), 88–95.

Graham, G., Holt/Hale S., & Parker, M. (2000). *Children moving: A reflective approach to teaching physical education* (5th ed.). Mountain View, CA: Mayfield.

Hunter, J. C. (1998). *The servant: A simple story about the true essence of leadership.* Roseville, CA: Prima.

Lockhart, A. (1996, May). Communicating with the learner. *Quest, VI,* 57–67.

Pangrazi, R. (2007a). *Dynamic physical education for elementary school children* (15th ed.). San Francisco: Benjamin Cummings.

Pangrazi, R. (2007b). *Dynamic physical education curriculum guide: Lesson plans for implementation* (15th ed.). San Francisco: Benjamin Cummings.

Patton, B. R., & Griffin, K. (1981). *Interpersonal communication in action: Basic text and readings* (3rd ed.). New York: Harper & Row.

Rink, J. (1993). *Teaching physical education for learning.* St. Louis: Times Mirror/Mosby.

Woods, A., & Langley, D. (1997). Circle drills: Do they accomplish your goals? *Journal of Physical Education, Recreation, and Dance, 68*(3), 8–9.

2

The Foundation of Sport Skills

INTRODUCTION

Creating a solid foundation of sport skills involves the basics of dynamic stretching, developing a strong core, and learning the correct technique of fundamental sport skills which sets an athlete up for success in more complex motor skills. Spending time learning these essential techniques will help to avoid bad habits down the road, which are extremely hard to fix once they've been practiced for lengthy periods of time. Therefore, taking time to develop and hone these fundamental skills will hasten the learning of the more complicated sport skills. For example, if an athlete knows how to jog and sprint correctly, he or she conserves energy and is faster and more efficient in the sport he or she plays. If an athlete has the proper technique in throwing a ball, he or she will have the skill needed to serve a ball in volleyball or tennis. Working on the skills of punting and kicking can help an athlete better adjust to football, soccer, and indoor hybrid ball. If an athlete knows how to jump correctly, the spike in volleyball or the rebound in basketball will be easier to master.

SKILLS LISTED WITH CUES

The following skills are included in this chapter: dynamic stretches, exercises to develop the core, jogging, sprinting, throwing overhand, throwing underhand, catching, punting, kicking, athletic stance, vertical jump, horizontal jump, stopping, and changing directions. All cues in this chapter can be used to teach for the left or right sides. When there is a difference between right- and left-handed cues, cues specific to each side will be noted.

EQUIPMENT TIPS

Use 12" Extra Soft Clincher Gymballs and 8" Gripper Volleyballs (see FYI to order these balls) for throwing and catching and measuring tape to measure jumps. Medicine balls and stability balls can be used to develop the core.

TEACHING IDEAS

Before teaching different sports, the teacher or coach should focus on teaching proper technique in the different sport skills discussed in this chapter. The following is a sequence of skills and drills:

1. Begin teaching dynamic stretches and core exercises. Dynamic stretches send blood to the muscles and nerves faster than static stretches and warm the body so that the muscles and nerves are ready to fire much more efficiently.

2. Teach that a strong core is critical for all sports. For example, one can throw a ball faster, hit a golf ball farther, and swim and sprint more efficiently with a strong core. Core exercises include a variety of exercises, like sit-ups and push-ups, that develop muscles from the rib cage down to the thigh, on the front, sides, and back of the body (see Chapters 22 and 27 for more exercises).

3. Teach good posture and cues for jogging and sprinting. Sprinting drills include the following:
   - Walking A's
   - Skipping A's
   - Running A's
   - Running C's

   Have students partner up and give feedback to each other (see Chapter 27). It usually takes two to four weeks to begin seeing improvement in sprinting. Good mechanics of sprinting can take years to develop.

4. Teach overhand throw: right side, left side. The reason to learn to throw with both hands is to develop skills on both sides of the body. Throwing on both sides gives balance to the body and equalizes the strength on both sides. For example, a football quarterback trains by throwing medicine balls both right side and left side, not just one side. Likewise, a tennis player chooses to serve both right side and left side. Both of these athletes have the advantage over an athlete who is trained on only one side. Have students throw soft softballs against a gym wall. Add speed to the ball. Have students partner up and give feedback on overhand throwing cues.

5. Teach underhand throw: right side, left side. The underhand throwing pattern is similar to a golf swing and a topspin in tennis. Have students throw soft softballs against a gym wall. Add speed to the ball. Have students partner up and give feedback on underhand throwing cues.

6. Teach catching. Catching is a skill that is vital to many sports, but it is sometimes neglected. One cannot overemphasize the importance of teaching correct techniques in catching. Always keep your eyes on the ball from start to finish. The eyes catch the ball. Spend time practicing catching with all sizes of balls.

   Throwing and catching drills include the following:
   - Throwing 8" Extra Soft Clincher Gymballs against a wall (right side and left side). Have students partner up and give cues to each other.
   - Add speed.
   - Throwing and catching to a partner using 12" Extra Soft Clincher Gymballs and 8" Gripper Volleyballs for underhand and overhand throws (right side and left side).

- Throwing and catching high and low balls underhand and overhand.
- Throwing and catching and getting rid of the ball fast with a two-step hop using softballs.

7. Teach the skills of punting and kicking to help develop better coordination between the hip, knee, and ankle and to improve coordination to increase foot velocity at contact. Students will experience greater success in popular games like soccer and football because they have practiced these two skills that require foot and ball coordination.

   Punting and kicking drills include the following:
   - Kick against a wall or to a partner.
   - Punt to each other outside.

8. Teach athletic stance, vertical jump (jumps measured with tape measure), horizontal jump, stopping, and changing directions.

Mastering these fundamental skills is critical before moving on to teaching sports. Spend time practicing these skills. The rewards are worth it!

IDEAS FOR SKILL ASSESSMENT

Mini Skills Meet: Students choose 3 to 5 of the following skills for competition.

1. Jog 1 mile or 5K (timed)
2. Sprint 40 yards or 100 yards (timed)
3. Throw right side/left for speed using a radar gun or throw for distance
4. Underhand throw right side/left side for speed using a radar gun
5. Punt for distance or use goals posts for accuracy 10-25 yards
6. Kick into a soccer goal from 12 to 25 yards, 5-10 balls
7. Standing vertical jump
8. Standing horizontal jump

FYI

For further information regarding equipment discussed in this chapter, please consult the following organization.

ORGANIZATION

GOPHER
2525 Lemond St. SW, P.O. Box 998
Owatonna, MN 55060-0998
Phone: 1-800-533-0446

WEBSITE

www.gophersport.com

SKILL	CUE	WHY	COMMON ERROR
Body Posture	Head over shoulders Shoulders over hips Hips over heels	More efficient to have foot strike underneath body	
	Run tall	More efficient at landing	Leaning too far forward or backward
	Pull chin in	Helps stabilize the head position and keeps body erect	Chin up or down
	Pull both shoulders up and back	Helps stabilize the core	Shoulders slumped
Foot Placement	Land on ball of foot first then gently let heel touch	More efficient when foot strikes under hip	Striking on heel first causes breaking action
	Ball heel or just ball of foot strikes ground	More efficient and faster to push off ground	
Eyes	Eyes looking forward searching for a spot to run to	Eyes focused forward keeps the body erect and foot strikes under the hip	Eyes looking down causes poor body posture while running
	Pick another spot when you reach that spot	Provides focus using goals; the brain can get lazy without goals, especially for long runs	Running speed decreases and runner becomes lazy and bored
Core	Tighten your core muscles while being tall in posture	Strong core will help foot come off the ground quicker; helps with posture	Slouching the core muscles
Hands	Brush side of shorts with thumbs	Conserves energy Keeps body in tight package	Hands and arms straight or crossing midline of body
Tempo	Each foot strikes lightly on ground; goal is to barely hear footsteps	Conserves energy	The foot strikes loud or heavy

Words to Cue in While Jogging

Run tall
Run light
Eyes look straight ahead and pick a spot

Technique Cues

Land ball heel, strike under hip
Brush shorts with thumbs
Tighten core

SKILL	CUE	WHY	COMMON ERROR
Posture	Run tall as if being picked up by the hair	Keeps body erect and in tight package	Leaning forward or backward
	Pull chin in		
Arm Action	Hold arms at 90° angle	The faster you pump your arms, the quicker you go	Arms are straight
	Swing comes from shoulders		Using elbow action, not shoulders
Thumb Action	Hands "Cheek to Cheek"		
Core	Core is flat and tight	Striking the ground is faster with a strong core	Core is slouched
	Tuck buttock in		Hips are down
	Hips up, core tight	Foot comes off the ground faster, higher and more powerful knee drive	
Sprinting Action	Toe up Heel up Knee up	Leg cycle more efficient	Toe and heel point to ground causing breaking action
Thigh	Thigh is parallel to ground	Leg cycle more efficient	Thigh is too high or too low
	Snap leg down		
Foot Placement	Ball of foot lands under hip	Moves the body forward more efficiently	Heel strikes first causing breaking action
	Let the foot touch quickly on the ground as if hot coals or broken glass is on the ground		Slows you down
Heel of Foot	Heel is tight, package comes up and under buttocks after ball of foot strikes the ground		
Eyes	Eyes look forward and pick a spot	Keeps body erect and increases confidence	Eyes looking down results in poor posture
	Keep eyes level	Helps maintain a faster pace	Slows sprinter down mentally and physically
Tight Package	Be a tight package with legs and arms	Striking ground faster is more energy efficient	Dangling limbs and arms

Words to Cue in Sprinting

Run tall/pick a spot with eyes
Cheek to cheek
Run like hot coals are on the ground

THROWING CUES

SKILL	CUE	WHY	COMMON ERROR
Grip (Figure 2.1)	Hold ball on finger pads	Better control	Holding ball in palm of hand
Stance (Figure 2.1)	Stand sideways, point free arm to target	More power	Standing forward with free arm at side
Leg Action (Figures 2.1 and 2.2)	Right-handed: Point left toe to target Left-handed: Point right toe to target	Accuracy	Toes pointing sideways
	Take a medium step to target	More power and balance	Too short of step or too long of step
Throwing Arm (Figures 2.1 and 2.2)	Stretch arm way back, make an L-shape	More power	Bends arm behind head
Throwing Wrist	Make a C-shape with hand and keep ball in line with ear and shoulder—ball to wall	Increases accuracy	Ball not in line with ear and shoulder
Release	Right-handed: At 2 o'clock Left-handed: At 10 o'clock	Better accuracy	Release at noon is too high, release at 6 o'clock is too low, and anywhere in between is either too high or too low
Non-Throwing Arm (Figure 2.2)	Pull elbow up and back; tight package with core, arm, and elbow	The non-throwing arm brings the core around to get more speed	Non-throwing arm is straight at side
Follow Through Throwing Arm, Opposite Foot	Follow through with throwing arm across the body	More speed	No follow-through with throwing arm or opposite foot
	Step forward with opposite foot		
Core Action (Figure 2.2)	Be tall through core and shoulders when you throw	More power; being a tall package is more efficient	Losing speed because shoulders are slumped
	Rotate the core around		No core action

FIGURE 2.1 Stance and Set Up for Throwing (right side)

FIGURE 2.2 Throwing Action (right side)

Words to Cue in While Throwing Right Side

Stretch your arm way back, make an L-shape

Release at 2 o'clock

Pull left elbow up and back; tight package with core, left shoulder, and left elbow

Words to Cue in While Throwing Left Side

Stretch your arm way back, make an L-shape

Release at 10 o'clock

Pull right elbow up and back; tight package with core, right shoulder, and right elbow

UNDERHAND THROWING CUES

SKILL	CUE	WHY	COMMON ERROR
Start Position *Hands*	Hold ball in finger pads	Better release	Holding ball in palm of hand
	Hold ball in front of chest		
Opposite Foot (from throwing arm)	Take a medium step with opposite foot	More control	Taking a short step or too long of step
Core Action	Turn core sideways	More power on the ball	Keeping core straight
	Rotate core around		
Throwing Arm Action	Swing arm straight back to shoulder height	Faster, more efficient	Swinging arm sideways
Release Point	Release at hip	More accuracy	Releasing before or after hip
Throwing Arm Follow-Through Action *Straight Ball*	Swing straight through	Creates more speed on the ball	Stopping hand short of shoulder

continued

SKILL	CUE	WHY	COMMON ERROR
Curve Ball	Swing low to high across the body to opposite shoulder		Swinging in front of same shoulder
Non-Throwing Arm Action	Bring elbow up and back	Help rotates the core around	Dangling non-throwing arm

Words to Cue in Throwing Underhand Curve Ball Right Side

Rotate core
Release at hip
Swing low to high at release point across body

The curveball follow through action will help you with a tennis top spin and right side, and right arm for a golf swing

Words to Cue in Throwing Underhand Curve Ball Left Side

Rotate core
Release at hip
Swing low to high at release point across body

The curveball follow through action will help you with a tennis top spin and left side, and left arm for a golf swing

CATCHING CUES

SKILL	CUE	WHY	COMMON ERROR
Eyes (Figure 2.3)	Keep eyes always on the ball from start to finish	Helps you make adjustments on the ball while it is thrown	Without your eyes on the ball you will not know where the ball is thrown, makes it difficult to catch
	See it to the tuck		
Hands	Keep hands in ready position, fingers spread to make big hands, to receive the catch out in front of the body	Helps you react to the throw quicker, in every direction in front of you	Not having your hands ready gives you a slower reaching time to catch the ball
	Catch first, move second	Helps you hold onto the ball	Dropping the ball
Arms	Reach out	The ball will not hit your body and the bend in your arms gives the hands more room to absorb the catch	Having arms too close to the body when the ball is caught causes ball to bounce off of the chest

continued

SKILL	CUE	WHY	COMMON ERROR
Arms, *continued*	Absorb the ball like a sponge by bending the arms		
Finger Pads (Figure 2.4)	Always use the pads of your fingers to catch the ball with fingers spread to make big hands	The pads of the fingers are the softest part of your hands, which absorb the catch more efficiently	If you use your palms rather than your finger pads, the ball is more likely to drop because of the lack of reinforcement provided by the palms
	Use soft hands		
Low Balls (Figure 2.3)	Keep thumbs up and palms together side by side	Allows you to adjust how low you need to go to catch the ball	Having a straight leg and not bending the knees give less ability to reach to the ball
	Keep knees bent	Hands help reaction time	
High Balls (Figure 2.4)	Keep thumbs down and together when catching the ball above the waist	With thumbs down, more fingers are used to catch the ball and thumbs help secure the ball	Without the diamond and thumbs touching the ball, the ball is most likely to go through the hands
	Form a diamond with hands	Allows you to have full extension of your arms	
Catching Ball (Figure 2.4)	Always catch the ball with two hands	More surface area to hold onto the ball	Catching the ball with one hand
	Catch the ball with your eyes; locate the ball with eyes as soon as the player releases the ball	Avoid dropping the ball	Eyes wandering and not focused on the ball

Eyes always on the ball from start to finish

Absorb the ball with finger pads and bring arms in like a shock absorber

Thumbs up and palms together side by side

FIGURE 2.3 Catching Low Balls

Catch the ball with two hands

Use finger pads to catch the ball

Always catch the ball with your eyes; catch first, move second

FIGURE 2.4 Catching High Balls

Words to Cue in While Catching

Eyes catch the ball and see it to the tuck
Reach out, draw the ball in, and absorb it like a sponge
Catching with your finger pads
Big hands—fingers spread

KICKING CUES

SKILL	CUE	WHY	COMMON ERROR
Approaching the Ball	Approach the ball at an angle	Gains momentum for the kick	Approaching straight in
	Run at an angle		Approaching at angle and last few steps change to straight
Eyes (Figure 2.5)	Look at the destination of where you want the ball to go	Helps put your hips in place to direct the ball	Head is down, eyes looking at the ball
Non-Kicking Foot (Figure 2.5)	Place standing foot to the side and middle of ball	Stabilizes the body for the kick	Losing momentum because standing foot is behind the ball
	Put weight on standing foot; plant foot, toes point to the target where your eyes are looking	Better balance; helps with accuracy	
Kicking Knee	Bend knee over the ball	Gets the core involved in the kick	Keeping kicking knee back and straight
Kicking Foot Action (Figure 2.5)	Draw leg back and cock the leg	Creates more speed and power to the ball	Having a straight leg
	Point toe to ground Ankle locked; kick with laces	More control and speed	Kicking with toes and getting hurt
High Ball	Kick lower one-third of the ball	Kicking under the ball brings it up	Not following through with leg and kicking the ground
Low Ball	Kick middle of ball	Ball will stay at lower level	Missing the ball
Arms and Hands (Figure 2.5)	Arms and hands out	Keeps balance	Arms dangling at the side
Follow-Through Action	Land on standing foot	Keeps balance	Not following through
			Not using core momentum
			Landing on kicking leg

FIGURE 2.5 Kicking

Words to Cue in While Kicking Right Side

Approach the ball at an angle
Ankle locked
Plant left foot and point toes to the target where your eyes are looking
Follow through on left foot

Words to Cue in While Kicking Left Side

Approach the ball at an angle
Ankle locked
Plant left foot and eyes point to where you want the ball to go
Follow through on right foot

PUNTING CUES			
SKILL	**CUE**	**WHY**	**COMMON ERROR**
Starting Position	Hold ball with two hands	Better accuracy for the ball to land on foot	Holding ball with one hand Holding ball for too long Throwing ball up in the air
Hand Action	Push ball out in front of you	Better accuracy to hit foot	Letting go of the ball too soon
	Drop the ball	Greater chance for the ball to land on foot	Throwing the ball up or to the side
Kicking Leg Action	Bring leg back	More power	Kicking with straight leg, foot dorsi flex, and hurting foot
Kicking Foot Action	Contact ball on right foot's shoe laces; ankle firm	More control of ball	Making contact on shin, leg, or completely missing the ball

continued

SKILL	CUE	WHY	COMMON ERROR
To Kick Ball High	Kick bottom of ball	Gives height to the ball	Contacting the ball too close to ground
	Kick ball at knee height		Having poor timing
To Kick Ball Low	Kick middle of ball	Gives distance and the ball travels lower to the ground	Contacting the ball too high Having poor timing
Follow Through with Kicking Leg	Follow through high with kicking leg	Ball will go higher and farther	Stopping leg at contact
	Follow through forward and land on left leg	Get full momentum of core through the kick	Following through too high
Non-Kicking Foot Action	Put all weight on non-kicking foot	Foot balances the rest of the body	Collapsing non-kicking leg and foot
Core Action	Rotate core up and around	Core action drives the ball	Being stiff or too loose

Words to Cue in Punting Right Side

Drop ball
Bring right leg back, cock right leg
With pointed toe, kick ball on shoe laces
Follow through with core action

Words to Cue in Punting Left Side

Drop ball
Bring left leg back, cock left leg
With pointed toe, kick ball on shoe laces
Follow through with core action

ATHLETIC STANCE CUES

SKILL	CUE	WHY	COMMON ERROR
Feet	Stand with feet shoulder width apart	Balance	Having feet too close together or too far apart
	Shift weight evenly onto the balls of your feet	Change direction quicker	Putting weight on the heels
Back	Keep back straight	In order to have vision to see what is going on	Back bent like an L-shape
Knees	Bend knees Stay low to the ground	Easier to move from one spot to the next and more explosive action	Keeping legs straight

continued

SKILL	CUE	WHY	COMMON ERROR
Buttocks	Keep butt down	Able to move faster	Standing up
		Keeps one low to the ground and good center of balance	
Hand and Arms	Hands and arms out	Helps body move faster	Dangling hands at the side
Eyes	Keep eyes looking forward	More control	Looking at floor
	Keep eyes focused on player's ball, etc.	Faster reaction time to ball or player	
Head	Keep head on a swivel	Always aware of your environment	Having a non-mobile head
Shoulders	Keep shoulders back	Strengthens core and faster reaction time	Rounding shoulders inward

Words to Cue in for an Athletic Stance

Butt down/knees bent
Back straight
Eyes looking for action

	VERTICAL JUMP CUES		
SKILL	**CUE**	**WHY**	**COMMON ERROR**
Stance	Keep feet shoulder width apart	Better balance Solid base	Keeping feet too close or too far apart
Back	Keep back straight	Avoids bad posture	Bending the back
Legs	Bend the knees down as far as possible	To store power for the jump	Having straight legs
Feet	Power starts in toes and works up until it explodes through fingers	Engages the power in the legs and helps give explosion	Having weight on heels
Arms (Figure 2.6)	Keep arms 90° angle before explosion	Drives momentum	Keeping arms straight
	Keep hands at eye level		
	Have big hands and big arms	Allows you to get momentum in arms	Having little arm swing
	Swing arms back to hip		Not getting hands back to hip
	Reach for the sky		Not getting full reach

continued

SKILL	CUE	WHY	COMMON ERROR
Head/Eyes (Figure 2.6)	Connect eyes with hands	Creates max velocity	Looking ahead instead of at hands stops your momentum
	Have eyes follow the hands down, and then look up and extend the arms as eyes come up		
	Throw all your momentum up hands	Keeps momentum going	
	Look up beyond target	Allows you to jump higher	
Jumping Action (Figure 2.6)	Push off with balls of feet		Pushing off with heels
	Go down, load, and come back up in one fluid motion	Helps to get the most energy you have created in muscles and nerves	Having jerky motions
	Be explosive; don't get stuck at the bottom	Doesn't stall your momentum	Spending too much time at the bottom
Landing	Land lightly on your feet; bend knees like a shock absorber	Softens landing	Landing heavy and loud
		Prevents injury	Landing stiff legged

FIGURE 2.6 Vertical Jump

Words to Cue in When Jumping Vertical

Eyes follow hands
Go down, load, come right back up
Eyes look up beyond target

HORIZONTAL JUMP CUES			
SKILL	**CUE**	**WHY**	**COMMON ERROR**
Stance (Figure 2.7)	Keep feet shoulder width apart	Better balance Solid base	Feet too close or too far apart
Back	Keep back straight	Avoids bad posture	Back bent
Legs	Bend the knees down as far as possible	Stores power for the jump	Not bending the knees enough
Feet (Figure 2.7)	Power starts in toes and works up until it explodes through fingers	Engages the power in the legs and helps give explosion	Having weight on the heels
Arms (Figure 2.8)	Keep arms at 90° angle before explosion	Drives momentum	Keeping arms straight
	Keep hands at eye level	Allows you to get momentum in arms	Having little arm swing
	Have big hands and big arms		
	Swing arms back to hip		Not getting arms back to shoulder height
	Reach out and forward to shoulder level		Arms keep going up
Head/Eyes (Figure 2.8)	Connect eyes with hands	Creates max velocity	Having eyes looking forward or up
	Have eyes follow the hands down, then look forward and extend the arms forward	Helps you go out instead of up	
	Throw all your momentum through hands	Keeps momentum going forward	
	Look beyond target	Allows you to jump farther	Having eyes not focused on target
Landing	Land softly on your feet; bend knees like a shock absorber	Absorbs the weight of the jump and prevents injury	Landing heavy or with a stiff leg

FIGURE 2.7   Jumping Horizontal Stance

FIGURE 2.8   Horizontal Jump

Words to Cue in When Jumping Horizontally

Bend knees
Push with balls of the feet
Arms swing back and forward; arms stop at shoulder level

STOPPING CUES

SKILL	CUE	WHY	COMMON ERROR
Running	Run fast	To gain momentum	
Stopping	Stop on front foot	Maintain balance	Stopping with both feet together
	Put right leg forward, left leg back, and have legs shoulder width apart	Stop on the leg that feels comfortable to stop with	
	Put left leg forward, right leg back, and have legs shoulder width apart		
	Bend knees to absorb the shock	Absorbs the shock of the knees	Stopping stiff legged
	Keep back straight	Maintains good posture	Bending back
	Keep eyes looking forward	Gives vision for the next play	Eyes down

Words to Cue in When Stopping

Stop on front foot
Bend knees like shock absorber
Eyes forward

CHANGING DIRECTION CUES

SKILL	CUE	WHY	COMMON ERROR
Run Stop Change Directions	Pivot on back foot		
	Put weight on the ball of back foot	Balance	Putting weight on heels
	Move front foot forward and to the side, back, and side	To fake opponent	Staying in one spot
	Bend knees	Absorbs the shock of knees from stopping	Keeping legs straight
	Focus eyes in different directions	Gives vision of playing area	Keeping eyes down

Words to Cue in While Changing Direction

Pivot on back foot
Keep knees bent
Keep eyes focused

3

Aerobic Kickboxing

INTRODUCTION

Taebo, CardioKarate, Karabo, Cardio Kickboxing, or even kickboxercise all refer to the same thing: the rhythmic repetitions of traditional fighting techniques combined with elements from aerobic dance. This blending of martial-arts–based techniques, such as punches, kicks, and knee and elbow strikes, with aerobic dance music and choreography produces aerobic kickboxing.

Currently, aerobic kickboxing is one of the fastest-growing additions to the health and fitness craze in the United States. As its name implies, aerobic kickboxing is really a type of cross-training workout. An aerobic kickboxing workout incorporates all the muscles of the body and can include anaerobic components through the use of burnout drills: muscular endurance with prolonged repetition of techniques. Although aerobic kickboxing works well as a solo activity, it is a good supplement for other sports or physical activities.

Why Should Physical Educators Teach Aerobic Kickboxing?

In an effort to motivate more kids to participate in physical education classes (particularly in school districts where PE is an elective), some schools are currently experimenting with activities that high school students already choose to do in their free time. The current success of aerobic kickboxing in the health and fitness clubs and the massive media hype on aerobic kickboxing due to the success of Billy Blank's Taebo video series has made it an obvious choice for such an activity. Aerobic kickboxing is already now being offered either as a unit or as a regular class in some public schools. In both cases it is generally the regular physical education staff that ends up teaching it. It is for you, the physical education teachers of the third millennium, who will likely find yourselves teaching aerobic kickboxing at some point in your career, that this chapter has been written.

What Do I Need to Get Started?

Contrary to what many current fitness clubs and martial-arts studios advertise, you don't need experience with either aerobics or martial arts, just a basic knowledge of the techniques you plan to incorporate, an ability to keep a steady beat, and tons of energy and enthusiasm. Nevertheless, expertise with either of these activities would enhance the quality of your program.

SKILLS LISTED WITH CUES

Aerobic kickboxing involves a plethora of skills that can be used and therefore taught, which makes it impossible to cover all of them in just a few short pages. But wait! Don't panic just yet. There are a few basic skills that, once learned and performed correctly, can make any instructor look good in front of a class regardless of a lack of experience with aerobic kickboxing. What's more exciting is that not only will your class get an incredible workout, but they will more than likely have fun doing it,...and you will too! The techniques covered in this chapter along with their cues are the boxer's stance, center position, Roc Hop step, step-and-touch step, bob and weave, jab punch, cross punch, uppercut punch, aerobic uppercut punch, hook punch, speed bag punch, back fist strike, front kick, side kick, roundhouse kick, and back kick. Once learned, these techniques can be used as a strong backbone of any aerobic kickboxing program for all experience levels.

Tips

1. The best way to learn to teach any aerobic class, including aerobic kickboxing, is to attend classes taught by a variety of instructors to get a feel for their teaching styles until you develop your own class.

2. If you find particular instructors or teaching formats you like, imitate them (don't directly copy them) for a while until you feel comfortable teaching with your own style.

3. Videos can be an invaluable resource for new ideas. But remember that many of your students may also have the same video, so you'll still need your own creativity to keep the combinations from the videos fresh.

4. A good rule of thumb to use when preparing an aerobic kickboxing class is to mirror your routine on both sides of the body (i.e., what you do on one side, you have to do on the other side). This will keep your classes feeling balanced.

5. A good idea, especially for beginning aerobic kickboxing instructors, is to write out the entire workout from warm-ups to cool-downs. List the specific techniques you want to teach, in the order you want, with the approximate amount of time needed for each activity. Remember, if you do jab punches with the left hand, you'll have to do them on the right side as well.

6. It is *never* a good idea when teaching aerobic kickboxing (or any other type of aerobics class) just to roll in the video cart, plug in an aerobics video, and expect the class to follow along. Watching a video for class is boring and looks unprofessional. Either make up a routine using techniques you know, or find someone else with more experience to teach that unit.

Equipment Tips

1. Equipment needed to teach aerobic kickboxing includes a quality stereo system, kickboxing targets or punching bags, bag gloves or hand wraps to protect the knuckles and wrists from injury, jump ropes, regular hand weights, and music. Good, clean, high-energy music and a decent sound system are critical to the overall quality of the class. If the music flops, so will your class.

2. Aerobic kickboxing requires no special clothes or equipment—just a pair of secure shorts (remember you will be bouncing on the balls of your feet a lot, so things can fall off) and a cool tee shirt.

3. Hand wraps, if used, should secure the wrist enough so that the range of motion is limited but should not restrict blood flow in the hand or forearm. Many boxing and martial-arts supplies now include wrap instructions.

4. Equipment such as bags, jump ropes, and hand weights should be in place before class begins so that students can get to it in a matter of seconds, but it should also be out of the way so that it doesn't become a safety hazard.

5. If you decide to incorporate bags into your class, it is suggested that a portable heavy bag, such as the Century Wavemaster bag, be used rather than smaller bags such as handheld focus mitts or kicking shields. This way students can work alone if need be, and time will not be wasted in showing new students how to hold the smaller bags.

6. When focus mitts are used, be sure everyone knows how to hold the bag correctly for their partner. If students don't know how to hold a bag, safety problems can arise.

7. Be sure to match students of equal size and power when using focus mitts and kicking shields in order to reduce the chance that a student holding the pad will be injured by a technique too powerful for him.

8. Smaller pads can be a lot of fun. Use some creativity on how you have the class hold the smaller bags, so that both students are getting a great workout. For example, to keep students' heart rates up, have one student punch the focus mitts as many times as he or she can until tired; then have the pad holder do squat thrusts until tired while the puncher bounces in place. This can be done several times, in two-minute periods, with students exchanging pads.

Safety

One of the scariest things about the current media push for aerobic kickboxing is the notion that aerobic kickboxing teaches self-defense. Aerobic kickboxing does not teach self-defense. While the techniques may be the same, and even technically correct, aerobic kickboxing is intended more to improve overall fitness than to learn self-defense. Techniques such as hook punches or roundhouse kicks may be the same as in self-defense class, but aerobic kickboxing does not teach students how or when to use these techniques. It would be just as fair to say that by shooting free throws, a person can learn how to play basketball. Aerobic kickboxing instructors should explain this principle to students right from the beginning.

TEACHING IDEAS

1. Teaching aerobic kickboxing is slightly different from aerobic dance classes. Aerobic kickboxing classes do not have to be taught using the standard 32-count system used in aerobic dance. (The 32-count system

has students performing combinations in exactly 32 counts of music.) Aerobic kickboxing techniques are different from the dance techniques used in dance aerobics, and therefore timing is less important. If you know how to stay on count, this ability will help your classes. However, simply staying on beat (listen to the bass for help) with correct technique, lots of energy, and enthusiasm is sufficient for aerobic kickboxing.

2. Do not shortcut techniques to stay on beat with the music. If the music seems too fast, either simplify the combinations or pick slower music.

3. If you're familiar with professionally produced aerobics music, step music works really well for aerobic kickboxing. It's about a 128-count system.

4. Write your entire routine on a 3 × 5 index card so that it can be taped to a mirror, a nearby desk, or some other convenient place. If you should forget a combination, you can glance at your note card.

5. Aerobic kickboxing is aerobic in nature, meaning it is continuous. Keep the class in their target heart rate range of about 70–80 percent of their maximum heart rate. *All feedback and corrections should be done while the class stays moving.*

6. The old adage "Fake it until you make it" definitely applies to aerobic kickboxing. If you forget what comes next in your routine, fake it until you remember. Doing so will keep the class on task and their heart rates up.

ASSESSMENT IDEAS

All students come in at different fitness levels.

1. The objective of aerobic kickboxing is to elevate each student's heart rate by providing a great work out. Heart rates taken every 10 minutes motivates the students to set goals (Box 3.1) of 120 beats to 180 beats per minutes

2. Another objective is to see how long they can keep their heart rate up: 10, 20, 30, 40, 50 minutes.

3. If the student can complete the workout, 5 points for each workout.

BOX 3.1 Computing Target Heart Rate

For Karvonen's HR reserve method (60-90% of maximal HR reserve) a student should use closer to 60% if they are on the low end of fitness and a higher percentage for those who are more fit. Compute the target heart rate as in the example for a 14-year-old student who is in the middle range of fitness (75% of HR reserve is used).

Resting HR <u>66</u> bpm (take before getting out of bed)

Maximal HR = 220 − age → 220 − <u>14</u> = <u>206</u> bpm

HR reserve = max HR − rest HR → <u>206</u> − <u>66</u> = <u>140</u> bpm

$THR_{75\%}$ = (.75 * HR reserve) + rest HR → (.75 * <u>140</u>) + <u>66</u> = <u>171</u> bpm

Karvonen M, Kentala K, Mustala O. The effects of training on heart rate: a longitudinal study. *Annales Medicinae Esperimentalis et Biologiae Fenniae* 1957; 35:307-315.

For further information about aerobic kickboxing, consult the following organizations and resources.

ORGANIZATIONS

Promise Enterprises
P.O. Box 7654
Jackson, MS 39284
Phone: (601) 372-8313

EQUIPMENT SUPPLIES

Century Martial Supply
1705 National Boulevard
Midwest City, OK 73110-7942
Phone: (800) 626-2787
Website: http://www.centurymartialarts.com/

Asian World of Martial Arts
917 Arch Street
Philadelphia, PA 19154-2117
Phone: (215) 969-3500
Website: http://www.awma.com

PROFESSIONAL MIXED AEROBIC WORKOUT MUSIC

Aerobic and Fitness Association of America
15250 Ventura Blvd., #200
Sherman Oaks, CA 91403

Power Music
P.O. Box 27927
Salt Lake City, UT 84127-0927

Dynamix: (800) 843-6499
In-Lytes Productions: (800) 243-7867
Muscle Mixes Music: (800) 52-Mixes
Musicflex: (718) 738-6839
Sports Music, Inc.: (800) 391-7692
The Work Out Source: (800) 552-4552

PUBLICATION

Thiboutot, F., & Croteau, K. (2001, January 1). *Cardio kickboxing elite*. Roslindale, MA: YMAA Publications.

WEBSITE

www.artofcombat.com/aerobic2.htm

FIGURE 3.1 Boxer's Shuffle or Fighting Stance

FIGURE 3.2 Center Position

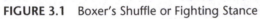

STANCES AND STEPS			
SKILL	**CUE**	**WHY**	**COMMON ERROR**
Boxer's Stance	Shoulders and hips face straight ahead	Allows boxer to hit target with maximum power and reach	Shoulders turn inward
Boxer's Shuffle (Figure 3.1)	Dominant leg steps back		
	Fists by cheeks; knuckles scrape cheeks	Develops good technique that protects face and ribs	Hands drop below chin
	On balls of feet	Keeps body moving and light on feet; allows boxer to move quickly	Feet flat on floor
	Shoulders and hips face straight ahead		Shoulders turn inward
Center Boxing Stance Position (Figure 3.2)	Feet shoulder width apart with slight bend in knees	Allows for maximum lateral movement	Feet too close or wide
	Fists by cheeks; knuckles scrape cheeks, shoulders square	Protects face	Hands drop below chin

continued

SKILL	CUE	WHY	COMMON ERROR
Roc Hop Step	Bring lead leg knee up (or kick)		
	Feet return to side-by-side		
	Rear leg steps back		
	Feet return to side-by-side	Step is more of a dance step that is used in conjunction with punches and kicks	Not returning feet to side-by-side
Step and Touch	Move point foot of trailing leg laterally		
	Step and touch		
Bob and Weave	Drop body, bending at knees	Allows the boxer to drop under a punch, come up chambered to center a punch	Bending over at the waist
		Can be used with or without a partner	
	Move upper body side to side		Whole body rising up all at once
	Lead with shoulder coming up		
	Keep hands and eyes up		Looking down during bob

Note: Cues for all punches except one are to be executed while in the boxer's stance. The one exception is the aerobic uppercut punch, which is always done from the center position. This punch is not intended to create any power. It is used as a burnout exercise for the arms and shoulders and should not be practiced on pads.

Here are a couple of cues to remember that apply to any punch: Hands always start and end by the cheeks; the wrists should always be locked straight out; and the nonpunching hand should be kept up by the cheek at all times. A common error that many people make while learning to punch is to use only their arms and shoulders to punch. A correct punch actually uses the entire body beginning with a slight turn of the pivot foot, continued by a slight turn of the hips and shoulder, and ending when the force is finally released through the arm and fist to the target.

		PUNCHES	
SKILL	**CUE**	**WHY**	**COMMON ERROR**
Jab	Extend lead arm straight out		Arm not fully extended
	Fist tight with wrist straight		Fingers loose Wrist bent
Cross Reverse	Extend rear arm straight out		Arm not fully extended
	Rear leg pivots onto ball of foot	Pivot creates power and distance for punch	Foot stays flat on ground
	Shoulders turn inward, leading with punching shoulder		Shoulders stay square
Uppercut Punch	Knees dip	Power for punch comes from hip as knees push on return back	Punch uses only shoulders
	Punching hand chambers back, held in tight 45° angle		Arm kept too vertical
	Explode off feet, pushing fist and navel through target		Punch stops at target Shoulders stay squared
Aerobic Uppercut Flutter Punch	Feet and shoulders square up		One leg stays back
	Both arms held in tight 45° angle		
	Rapid punch using just the shoulders and arms	Rapid punches are designed to burn out arms and shoulders	Arm kept too vertical
	Elbows are brushing sides		Elbows point outward
Lead Arm Hook	Lead arm drops to make a tight L between shoulder, elbow, arms, and wrist	Arm drops to be able to strike to sides of bag or partners	Wrist slightly bent
	Lead hand generally at rib or head level		
	Lead foot lifts up onto ball of foot		Foot stays flat
	Lead foot, hips, and lead shoulder pivot inward through target	Creates power punch	Only leg turns Punch stops at target

continued

SKILL	CUE	WHY	COMMON ERROR
Back Fist Strike	Lead arm drops to make a tight L between shoulder, elbow, and wrist with palms facing you		Wrist slightly bent
	"Open the gate"	Arm extended for open gate in order to align back of hand with target	
	Extend arm and shoulder through target	Push through target with fist to create power	
Speed Bag Punch	One or both arms turn inward 45° so elbows point out		Arm(s) drop to make L
	Move arms in circling motion		
	First two knuckles should lead punch		Pinkie finger leads punch
	"Hit the back of the hand"		

Note: All kicks can be broken down into four basic parts. These parts are the *chamber* when the knee lifts up, the *extension* or kick, the *recoil* where the knee returns to the chambered position, and the *recovery* when the kicking leg returns to the ground. Be sure to watch for all four parts in your students' kicks.

As beginning kickers get excited, they tend to kick faster by shortcutting one or more of these four parts. By shortcutting a kick, students develop poor technique and will not be able to generate much power. They may also injure themselves in classes that incorporate the use of kicking bags. So watch for it!

KICKS			
SKILL	CUE	WHY	COMMON ERROR
Front Kick	Bring up knee of kicking leg	Tight chamber and recoil creates power	Kicking with foot dorsiflexed
	Flex the ankle	Flex ankle to allow kick to make contact with ball of foot	
	Extend kick out		
Side Kick	Bring knee to chest, heel pointed out	Tight chamber creates power	Kick not locked out
	Extend kick straight out		Kicking with entire bottom of foot

continued

SKILL	CUE	WHY	COMMON ERROR
	Push heel through target	Power for kick is maintained when sent through target rather than bouncing off target	
	Stomp your target		
Roundhouse (Figure 3.3)	Bring kicking knee up at 45° angle		
	Planted foot pivots 180°	Power from kick is created when hips are in line with target; pivoting the hips will turn them to align with target	Foot doesn't pivot
	Extend kick with toes pointed		Kicking with foot dorsiflexed
Back Kick	Pick up kicking knee		Kicking with entire bottom of foot
			Knee points out
	Kick straight back, hit with heel		
	Brush knees together "like a cricket"		

Kicking leg chambered at knee

Fists by cheeks

Bottom foot planted Toes pivoted

FIGURE 3.3 Chamber for Roundhouse Kick

4

Archery

INTRODUCTION

Are you looking for a new way to have fun or a new sport to add to your curricula? Archery is one of the oldest sports participated in today. Why is archery still being enjoyed by many? Young and old alike enjoy the challenge of hitting a target. Archery can be enjoyed year-round—indoors during inclement weather and outdoors in the fresh air. Archery provides opportunities for physical activity and competition. Those who join archery clubs or leagues can participate with archers of their own age and abilities. In many high schools and universities, students can join archery teams and perhaps even receive scholarships.

If students are taught the fundamental archery skills, display an interest, and experience success, teachers could then suggest they pursue related sports, which include field archery, bow hunting, bow fishing, and target archery.

By providing these archery cues, teachers might incorporate archery into their curricula. Consequently, students of all ages can learn a new sport and "be on target for fun."

SKILLS LISTED WITH CUES

In this chapter we have designed equipment cues for selecting a bow, arrows, arm guard, and finger tab. Cues are given for safety techniques and retrieving arrows from a target. The other cues cover beginning skills for the stance address, bow arm, nock, draw, anchor (target shooting), aim, release, follow-through, and adjusting the sight pin.

Tips

1. Purchasing a peep sight (a tiny aperture the archer looks through to align the arrow with the target) and stabilizer makes the archery experience more enjoyable and successful.

2. A frequent archery error is dropping the bow arm to see where the arrow is going. This is called *peeking*. An archer gets in a hurry and peeks to see where the arrow is going, and consequently the arrow drops. Keep the arrow on the string by not peeking. Have patience and wait until the arrow is off the string.

3. If an archer has a problem with inconsistency in accuracy, go to an archery pro shop for suggestions or check for consistent anchor point and consistent draw length. If everything is done the same way each time, accuracy will result.

Equipment Tips

1. There are a variety of bows: long bows, recurve bows, and compound bows. They can be manual or automatic.

2. Carbon graphite arrows, although more expensive than aluminum arrows, are lighter, faster, stronger, and straighter.

3. The peep sight is a tiny aperture the archer looks through to align the arrow with the target. The peep sight will force the archer to anchor in the same place for each shot. Anchoring in the same place time after time increases accuracy.

4. The stabilizer assists the archer by quieting the bow and placing the pin on target. The stabilizer also prevents the archer from shaking.

5. An archery pro shop is the best place to purchase a bow because the personnel can set up the bow for proper shooting and give specific instruction.

6. The mechanical release is a pull trigger that releases the strings on a bow. The trigger provides a quicker, smoother, and more accurate release.

7. Field archers shoot in rough terrain, with three-dimensional targets, from a variety of distances.

8. Bow hunting requires arrows with different points—broad heads for larger game and blunt heads for smaller game. To hunt game birds such as quail, use flu flu arrows that have larger and more feathers to reduce the distance the arrow travels.

9. Bow fishing is another unique option, requiring solid fiberglass arrows that have fish points. A bow-fishing reel is another good idea.

10. Targets, bows, and arrows can be purchased at Gopher – see FYI for website.

Safety and Etiquette

1. Use archery equipment only in places especially designed for shooting arrows. Allow plenty of room behind the targets and to the sides.

2. Students should always point the bow and arrow downrange and never at another person.

3. Students should never shoot an arrow to where they cannot see the landing area, and they should never shoot an arrow straight up.

4. Students should not draw a bow without an arrow on it, and they should never dry-fire (release without an arrow) a bow.

5. Students should not overdraw bows.

6. Students should never shoot an arrow when someone is downrange.

7. Students should not draw or shoot a bow unless they are shooting on a line.

8. Students should wait for the teacher's verbal command (or whistle) to shoot, and they should wait for a different command to walk beyond the shooting line and collect arrows.

9. Students should prop their bows on the target while looking for arrows behind the target.

10. All equipment should be regularly inspected by the teacher and students for damage.

TEACHING IDEAS

1. Practice without shooting and to check the proper skill cues.
2. Have partners check cues.
3. Start students with large targets that are easy to hit.

Mini-Games

1. Use balloons for some fun targets and noise when they are popped.
2. Use cooperative groups and keep score in a group at first for a nonthreatening and fun learning environment.
3. Shoot at paper targets with a bull's-eye. Keep score. Use this idea when fundamentals are mastered.
4. Shoot to a variety of paper targets. Target shooting during the winter months maintains correct form and technique, thus increasing the archer's ability to hit the game during hunting season.
5. Getting involved in an archery club provides an opportunity to learn from the experience of other archers and to improve techniques.
6. To hunt game, an archer needs correct equipment, an in-depth knowledge of the ethical principles and laws of hunting game, and correct techniques to harvest the game as well as camouflage, scent-masking, and tracking skills.

GAME PLAY

Rules

1. Six arrows (an end) are usually shot at one time.
2. An arrow hitting the wrong target counts as a shot but not a score.
3. The arrow that cuts two colors is always given the higher value of the two.
4. If the arrow hits the petticoat, it counts for neither score nor hit.

Scoring

Each ring on target has its own scoring (Figure 4.1):

1. Yellow = 9 points
2. Red = 7 points
3. Blue = 5 points
4. Black = 3 points
5. White = 1 point

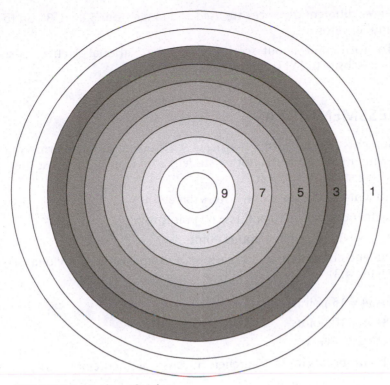

FIGURE 4.1 Archery Scoring

National Archery Association (NAA) Rounds Scoring

1. The 5 color, 10 ring face is used and scores are counted from the center out: 10, 9, 8, 7, 6, 5, 4, 3, 2, 1 (Figure 4.2).

2. Number of arrows can range from 20 to 36 (an end) at each distance seen below.

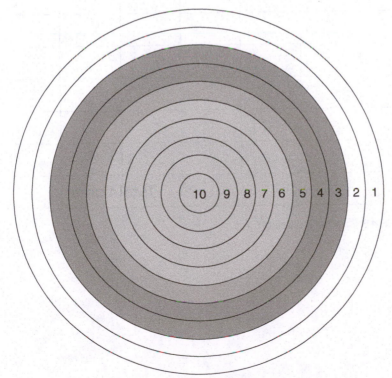

FIGURE 4.2 National Archery Association (NAA) Rounds Scoring

3. Three different distances are used and range from 50, 40, 30 up to 90, 70, and 50 yards.

4. To learn more about scoring go to the National Archery Association (see website in FYI below).

ASSESSMENT IDEAS

1. Students pair up with a partner. Each student shoots 6 arrows (an end). Winner pairs up with another student who won. If they lost they pair up with a student who lost.

2. Students need 6 ends of 6 arrows (an end).

3. Each end is worth 10 points = 60 points total.

4. If they win, they get 1 bonus point.

5. Student's best (end score) 6 arrows. Example of an individual score card (Figure 4.3):

   36–54 = 15 points

   18–35 = 10 points

   1–17 = 5 points

   5 bonus points for top 3 archers in class (total score of 6 ends)

Name: _____   Best End Score: _____

1	2	3	4	5	6	End Score
					Total Score	

FIGURE 4.3 Archery Scoring Card

For further information and special help, consult the following organizations and resources.

ORGANIZATIONS

Provides archery videos

National Archery Association
One Olympic Plaza
Colorado Springs, CO 80909
Phone: (719) 866-4576
Fax: (719) 632-4733

The Athletic Institute
200 Castlewood Drive,
North Palm Beach, FL 33408

Gopher
2525 Lemond St. SW, P.O. Box 998
Owatonna, MN 55060
Phone: (800) 533-0446

Go to the local pro archery shop for lessons and proper equipment setup.

WEBSITES

www.usarchery.org
www.BearGoldenEagle.com
www.gophersport.com

EQUIPMENT

SKILL	CUE	WHY	COMMON ERROR
Selecting Bow	Choose a bow that you can draw comfortably and hold for 10 seconds	Reduces straining	Bow too heavy
Selecting Arrow	Place nock against chest; reach with fingers; arrow should be 1 inch past fingertips (or draw a marked arrow)	Less chance of injury and better projectory	Arrow too short or too long
	Partner stands to the side and reads marking even with bow		
	Hunters add 1 inch		
Arm Guard	String should divide the arm guard in half; this varies with modern compound bows	Protection	

continued

SKILL	CUE	WHY	COMMON ERROR
Finger Tab or Glove or Release	Protect fingers with tab or glove	Shoot for a longer duration and more comfortably	String hurts fingers
Retrieving Arrows	Stand to side of arrow; check position of other archers		Bending arrow Injuring students
	With one hand: fingers straddle arrow; press against target	Safety; for example, by pulling an arrow straight out, a student poked himself in the eye	
	With the other hand: grasp arrow close to target; rotate and pull straight back		

FINDING THE DOMINANT EYE

Hold arms straight out, make a triangle with both hands.
Center a small object in the triangle, keeping the object certain.
Close one eye, and if the object does not move, you have found your dominant eye.

SHOOTING AN ARROW			
SKILL	**CUE**	**WHY**	**COMMON ERROR**
Stance Address	Straddle the shooting line (one foot on each side)	Consistency	Standing behind the line
	Weight even		Leaning forward or backward
	Good posture		
	Feet shoulder width apart		
Bow Arm	Grip bow as if holding a soda can	More accuracy	Gripping bow too tightly
	Thumb and index finger touch	Smoother release	
	Push bow toward target		Gripping bow too lightly
	Elbow points outward at shoulder level		

continued

SKILL	CUE	WHY	COMMON ERROR
Nock	Nock arrow at 90° angle	Consistency	Arrow too high or low on string
	Snap nock on bow string under nock locator		
	Index finger points away from bow		
Draw (Figure 4.4)	Make a scout sign (three fingers up)	Consistency	More or less than three fingers on string
	String in first groove of index finger		String on fingertips or hand wraps around fingers
	Keep back of hand flat		
	Elbow level with hand		Elbow too low
	Squeeze shoulder blades together		Drawing with arm only
Anchor (Target Shooting) (Figure 4.5)	Touch string to center of chin and center of nose; index finger pushes against jawbone	Consistency; doing everything the same ensures accuracy	Failing to anchor
Anchor (in Bows Without Sights)	Touch corner of mouth with index finger of draw hand	Consistency; also allows archers to aim down the path of the arrow	Failing to adjust anchor for use of bows without sights

continued

String in first groove of index finger

Make scout sign (Three Fingers Up)

FIGURE 4.4 Draw the Arrow

Close dominant left eye when shooting right-handed

Touch string to center of nose and chin

Shoulder level

FIGURE 4.5 Anchor (Target Shooting)

SKILL	CUE	WHY	COMMON ERROR
Aim	Look through pin to center of gold sight pen		Looking at target instead of pin
	Aim for 3–5 seconds before releasing		Releasing while drawing
	Close dominant left eye when shooting right-handed		Leaving dominant left eye open when shooting right-handed
Release	Relax fingers; string "slips" off fingers	Arrow performance; prevents left-to-right wobble	Jerking string hand back or allowing the string to "creep" forward before releasing it
Follow-Through (Hold) (Figure 4.6)	Fingers move back along side of face		Moving string hand
	Hold position until arrow hits target	Increases accuracy; prevents peeking	Moving bow arm
Adjust Sight Pin	Choose arrow with sight pin		Moving sight after each arrow or failing to adjust sight
	If arrows go high, move pin up		
	If arrows go low, move pin down		
	If arrows go left, move pin left		
	If arrows go right, move pin right		

FIGURE 4.6 Follow-Through (Hold)

5

Badminton

INTRODUCTION

Badminton is a physically demanding sport that provides players with a good measure of aerobic and anaerobic power, flexibility, strength, and speed. The skill of badminton can be relatively easy to learn, especially with the correct teaching cues. When designing these cues we consulted the USA Badminton Association in Colorado Springs, Colorado, and the Canadian Badminton Association for their expertise and suggestions. For example, the cue for the wrist action when teaching the badminton overhead clear is "pronate the wrist," which describes clockwise forearm rotation. Snapping the wrist would be the common error. This cue and others will provide the teacher with correct teaching techniques.

Jim Stabler, a member of Pikes Peak Badminton Club, Colorado Springs, CO, likes to think of the grip in terms of "shaking hands with the racquet." Hold the racquet with the racquet head perpendicular to the floor. Now shake hands with it. Hold it loosely with the index finger open along the handle. Do not grip it like you would a baseball bat. If your index finger is open, it is possible to use your wrist and internally pronate your arm when hitting the shuttles. If you grip it like a bat, you can't bend your wrist. The tendon to your index finger is all tied up in the grip, so you won't have the flexibility to bend your wrist and utilize the power you can generate that way. How does a baseball pitcher throw a baseball at 90 miles an hour? He uses his legs, back, arm, and wrist as he hurls the ball to the catcher. If he used only his arm, he'd have very little velocity. It is the same whip of the wrist and internal rotation of the arm that allow an advanced badminton player to hit a shuttle at 150 miles per hour or more. The shuttle weighs one-sixteenth of an ounce, so you are not hitting an object that weighs very much. You can utilize the action of your wrist and arm to hit the shuttle very hard.

Badminton is unique in that the object you're playing with can fly at 150 miles an hour or more by hard hits, or you can use a drop shot and just dink it ever so slowly over the net. No other sport employs this wide range of speed in its game.

SKILLS LISTED WITH CUES

A recommended teaching progression of skills before the strokes are taught is as follows: grips, flick-up, feeding, ready position, and court position. Teachers should take extra time to teach flick-up and feeding skills. The cues for the badminton skills in this chapter include this teaching progression as well as forehand/backhand underhand clear, forehand/backhand overhead clear, forehand/backhand smash, forehand/backhand drive, net shots (finesse shot), long singles serve, short doubles serve, and singles/doubles boundaries, scoring, and strategies. After each skill, we have added some drills to work students' skills.

Tips

1. Remember...correct grip, ready position.
2. Get into the habit of hit-move, hit-move, hit-move.
3. Move to hit the shuttle; don't wait for it.
4. Court sense for singles: after each shot, the singles player should attempt to return to base position, which is midcourt. Remember to get in ready position regardless of court position.
5. Court sense for doubles is different. Partners adopt an "up-back" arrangement and, when attacking, a "sides" arrangement. Communicating with and supporting each other is the key to playing a good doubles game.

Equipment Tips

1. Shuttles may be made from feathers or nylon. The flight of a shuttle is what makes the game unique, since it does not soar in an arc as a ball does. Very often, cheap nylon shuttles do not "catch" the air very well and are too fast. To test the speed of a shuttle, strike it underhand as hard as possible, hitting it the length of the court fairly close to parallel to the floor. If the shuttle is moving at the correct speed, it should land on or near the doubles service line at the other end. Purchase yellow shuttles. They are easier to see, especially in poor lighting.
2. Court shoes are recommended.
3. You will need 100 to 200 shuttles for a class.
4. Purchase quality rackets to prevent string breakage (see FYI).

Etiquette

1. The server calls out his or her score first, then opponent's score before he or she serves the shuttle cock. For example, 5 points for server, 1 point for opponent.
2. It is the responsibility of badminton players to call all faults on their own side of the net.
3. Players should respect opponents' calls without argument.
4. Lightly hit the shuttle underhand to the opponent if they are serving.
5. Players should signal if a shuttlecock lands in or out of the court. Pointing the hand to the ground with the fingers spread means that the shuttlecock landed "in." Making an L with the thumb and index finger and pointing it up means that the shuttlecock landed "out."

TEACHING IDEAS

1. Partners feed to each other.

2. *Partner feed drill:* One partner feeds the shuttle by hand to the receiver. The receiver hits and then attempts to assume set position and after each return. Cue words: feed–hit–set position. The instructor should specify the type of hand feed.

3. *Racket feed drill:* same as above, but the feeder racket feeds to the receiver. The feeder gradually sends the shuttle to more challenging positions: farther right, farther left, in front, and behind, and he or she specifies the type of feed and type of return.

4. *High Clear Tip Drill 1:* Don't let the shuttle get behind you when you hit high clears. Take a step back so that you can hit it well in front of you. If you swing and miss, the shuttle should fall against the front of your body and not over your head.

5. *Clears Drill 2:* One, two, or three feeders. Feeders have at least 25 shuttles. One player hits underhand and overhead clears, and then rotates. Spend lots of time hitting clears. Three or four days can be spent having students practice feeding and clears, forehand and backhand, underhand and overhead.

6. *Smash Drill:* Three feeders and one hitter. Feeders have at least 25 shuttles. Feeders hit high clears; hitter smash shuttles. Rotate hitters, and switch to backhand smashes. Then feeders can feed to forehand and backhand, with the hitter smashing both sides.

7. Three feeders (have at least 25–30 shuttles) and one hitter. Hitter hits forehand and backhand drive shots; then rotate.

8. Three feeders (have at least 25–30 shuttles) and one hitter. Hitter hits forehand and backhand finesse shots; then rotate.

9. *Rapid fire drill:* Three feeders and one hitter. Each feeder needs 25–30 shuttles. All three feeders feed one hitter. Feeders mix up shots: long short, high low side; the hitter moves all over court. Rotate hitters. Great work out!

10. Partners serve long and short serves to each. Spend lots of time serving. The serve can win matches.

11. *Serve tape drill:* Put court tape in center of service box (4 feet diameter, 2 feet radius). Have players practice serving outside the circle.

12. *Rally tape drill:* Players try to hit corners and avoid rally circle (4–4 1/2 meter diameter circle outlined with tape in the middle of court).

Mini-Games

1. Game-like drill: This drill can be done with clears, clears and smashes, or all the skill of badminton; this is a good drill to use with large classes. Assign three to four players per court. One player hits, gets off the court to back, and the partner comes on court and plays next shot. Rotate hits.

2. Quick scoring game: One player feeds the shuttle. Play it out. Whoever wins the rally, wins the point. Whoever has a shuttle feeds the bird. The player feeds inside the single boundaries. Play single boundaries. Play to 11 points and rotate students in games. Winners play each other. A player who lost plays a player who lost.

3. Play a quick scoring game. Players can hit the shuttlecock off the ground on the bounce.

4. Kings/Queens Court: The top player stands on the rally tape side of the court. The players on the opposite court try to hit the player out of the rally circle and score one point to get kings/queens spot. Have a line of people to rotate into the challenger court. This drill can be used when playing tournaments. Keep one court open for this game. When a player finishes a tournament game, they can rotate into this game.

RULES, STRATEGIES, AND SCORING

The rules, strategies, and scoring for badminton are best described in table form. They can be found in the cue tables at the end of the chapter.

ASSESSMENT IDEAS

Teach skills and drills, then let students have as much opportunity to play different students. Playing lots of games develops their skill level. A student who wins a game is paired up with another student who wins; a student who lost is paired up with a student who lost.

1. Students play 6–12 singles games; each game is worth five points.
   Total 30–60 points.
2. Students play 6–12 doubles games; each game is worth 5 points.
   Total 30–60 points.
3. Each game they win is worth one bonus point.
4. Short serve: Serve 12 inches from short line. Place two cones 12 inches past the short service line—one on each side of the service court. Do 10 short serves. Serves must land between the cone and the short line, or hit the cone.
5. Long serve: Serve 12 inches from the baseline and place two cones on each side. Do 10 long serves. Serves must land between the cone and base line, or hit the cone. Because the serve is so important, each student should be tested on both the short and long serve at weeks 1, 3, and 5.

FYI

For further information and special help, consult the following organizations and resources.

ORGANIZATION

Provides information on instructor manuals, videotapes, drills, skill progressions, program materials, awards, and pictures. Check websites for new coaching programs, new umpire clinics, etc.

USA Badminton
One Olympic Plaza
Colorado Springs, CO 80909
Phone: (719) 866-4808
Fax: (719) 866-4507
Email: usab@usabadminton.org
Website: www.usabadminton.org

VIDEO AND MANUAL

Badminton 2000 plus guide to teaching badminton. Can be purchased through USA Badminton. $39.99 plus shipping.

PUBLICATIONS

Golds, M. (2002). *Badminton (skills of the game)*. Ramsbury, Wiltshire, England: Crowood Press.

USA Badminton. *Badminton official rule book*. (2007). Colorado Springs, CO: USA Badminton.

EQUIPMENT COMPANY

Yonex, World Leader in Golf, Tennis and Badminton
Website: Yonex.com
Phone: (310) 793-3800

BASIC GRIPS AND STANCE

SKILL	CUE	WHY?	COMMON ERROR
Forehand Grip	Heel of hand at butt of racquet		Choking up on racket
	V on top bevel		Grip too tight
	Index finger positioned to pull trigger		Incorrect placement of index finger
	Squeeze trigger finger on impact		
Backhand Grip	Turn racquet clockwise		Failure to rotate grip from forehand to backhand
	Make V on left bevel		
	Knuckle on top		
Ready Position (Figure 5.1)	Hold racquet up	If racquet is down at your ankle, it takes a good part of a second to get it back up. That part of a second is all it may take for you to be late in making a good shot.	
	Knees bent		Standing upright
	Weight on balls of feet		Weight on heels
Correct Order of Play	1. Be ready to hit the shuttle 2. See the shuttle 3. Hit the shuttle	Make sure you do this in order. If step 2 comes before step 1, you might be late in hitting the shuttle.	Fall backward/fall away

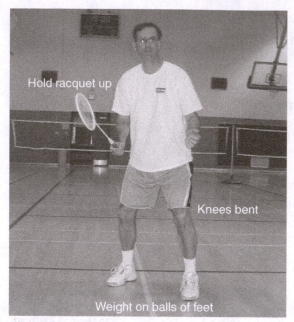

Hold racquet up

Knees bent

Weight on balls of feet

FIGURE 5.1 Ready Position

Reach up and contact shuttle high

Pronate forearm through contact with whipping action

FIGURE 5.2 Forehand Overhead Clear

FLICK-UP AND FEEDING			
SKILL	**CUE**	**WHY?**	**COMMON ERROR**
Flick-Up *Definition*	Flick move using the racquet to scoop the shuttle from the floor (speeds game up); players must employ proper grip to do this move	Speeds up the game	
Action	Side scooping action, feel snap of wrist as racquet head turns	Speeds up the game	Forward and up action
	Raise shuttle to land on strings		Improper grip
Feeding *Definition* (Figure 5.5)	Serving the shuttle by racquet so that receiver has a good chance to return it		

CLEARS

SKILL	CUE	WHY?	COMMON ERROR
Forehand Underhand Clear	Whip wrist and brush shorts	More power	Snapping wrist
	Contact shuttle below waist	Rule	Contacting too soon, lack of height
	Swing up over opposite shoulder	More distance	Not following through, lack of depth
Forehand Overhead Clear	Right hand	More distance and power	Snapping wrist, not extending elbow
	Left hand	More power and distance	Snapping wrist
	Reach up and contact shuttle high in front of body, like throwing something on roof		
	Whip!		
	Push from back to forward foot (Figure 5.2)	More power	Weight forward

SMASH—DRIVES—NET SHOTS

SKILL	CUE	WHY?	COMMON ERROR
Forehand Smash (Figure 5.3)	Lean into the net		
	Contact shuttle high and in front of body	To hit shuttle down	Contacting shuttle behind head
	Pronate hand	Shuttle will go downward	Snapping wrists
	Pronate hand	Power	
	Wrist starts cocked, finishes in pronated position	Power	
	Whip action	Faster	
	Swing is half-moon with face of racquet pointing down at contact	Control	Swinging too long or too short
Forehand Drive	Pivot on racquet foot and move other foot toward shuttle		Feet are stationary
	Contact more to the side of body, like throwing a ball sidearm	Control and accuracy	Contact too high or too low

continued

Wrist starts cocked and finishes pronated

Contact shuttle high and in front of body

Whip action

FIGURE 5.3 Forehand Smash

Loosen grip

Slide racquet under shuttle

Be gentle

FIGURE 5.4 Net Shot (Finesse Shot)

SMASH—DRIVES—NET SHOTS, continued

SKILL	CUE	WHY?	COMMON ERROR
Backhand Drive	Same as forehand; change grip		
Net Shot (Finesse Shot) (Figure 5.4)	Loosen grip	More control	Firm grip
	Be gentle; slide racquet under shuttle		Swinging at shuttle
	Focus on palm of hand; lift shuttle over, use arm only, not racquet		Hitting hard
	Push/lift/nudge/caress		

SERVING

SKILL	CUE	WHY?	COMMON ERROR
Long Singles Service	Bend knees and swing under and up	More power	Side swing
	Contact out in front of body	See better and control of shuttle	Contact behind body
	Swing under shuttle	For better aim	Swing to the side or over
	Follow through straight up to hit face with biceps	More power and accuracy	No follow-through
Short Doubles Service (Figures 5.5 and 5.6)	Stand 12–18 inches behind T	To be in proper starting position	Stand more to one side
	Pinch shuttle at tip of feathers	Easier to drop with control	Hold ball of shuttle
	Drop shuttle	Better contact for serve	Throw shuttle in the air

continued

SKILL	CUE	WHY?	COMMON ERROR
Short Doubles Service, *continued*	Gently stroke the shuttle into opponent's court with backhand or forehand motion	Control speed of racquet easier	Not controlling racquet speed
	Stand up straight		Leaning over holding the shuttle close to the floor

Note: The serve is a defensive shot, not an offensive shot as in tennis, for example. Remember the quote of the great doubles champion Don Paup: "The serve and return of serve are the two most important shots in any rally."

SINGLES—RULES, STRATEGIES, SCORING

SKILL	CUE	WHY?	COMMON ERROR
Basic Rules	You can hit the bird one time on your side only		
	Your body or racquet cannot touch the net		
	The bird touches the sideline or end line, bird is in		
	The racquet cannot hit the shuttlecock on the opponent's side of the net		Player hits shuttlecock on receiver's side
	If the shuttlecock hits you, the opponent receives the point		

continued

FIGURE 5.5 Service

Pinch shuttle at tip of feathers

Stand 12–18 inches behind T

FIGURE 5.6 Short Doubles Service

Drop shuttle

Gently stroke the shuttle

SKILL	CUE	WHY?	COMMON ERROR
Strategies	Play opponent's weak side	Keep opponents on the defensive	Playing opponent's forehand side
	Be unpredictable	Make your opponent run	Using same shot
	Use deception, and disguise shots		Giving away your shot
	Use clears to force opponent deep in court and on the move	Keep out of the center court position	Hitting shuttle to middle of court
	After hitting, get back to the center court position	Stay center court	Staying out of position or not moving feet
	Mix shots, then take advantage of the weak return with a well-placed, powerful smash	Make your opponent run to weaken his or her return	Hitting right to opponent
	The patient, aggressive player wins points	To control the game	Not being in control
4 Square Approach	Hit to one of the four corners of the court. Next shot to opposite corner. Repeat through rally.	Take opponent out of center court position.	Hitting right to the opponent.
Scoring	At the beginning of the game (0–0) and when the server's score is even, the server serves from the right service court. When the server's score is odd, the server serves from the left service court.		
	Every time there is a serve, there is a point	New rally scoring rules	Using traditional scoring system (setting, etc.)
	The side winning a rally adds a point to their score		
	Rally scoring		
	A game consists of 21 points		
	At 20–20 win by 2		
	At 29–29 the first one to 30 points wins the game		
	The side winning the game serves first in the next game		The side who did not serve first serves

continued

SINGLES—RULES, STRATEGIES, SCORING, continued

SKILL	CUE	WHY?	COMMON ERROR
Match	A match consists of two out of three games of 21 points		
Singles Service Area	Tall and narrow man (Figure 5.7)		

DOUBLES—RULES AND STRATEGIES

SKILL	CUE	WHY?	COMMON ERROR
Doubles Service Area	Short and wide man (See Figure 5.7)		
Strategy *Front/Back* (Figure 5.8)	"Up/back" formation in attack mode after a smash or drop	Best offensive position	Staying side to side Not getting to up and back position
	Front player is halfway between service line and net	Good attack position	Backing up to center position
	Back player is shadow to front player	Staying in position	Moving up to center position

continued

Singles service boundaries

Tall and narrow man

Net

Doubles service boundaries

Short and wide man

FIGURE 5.7 Service Boundaries for Singles and Doubles

Shadow to front player

Front player halfway between service line and net

FIGURE 5.8 Doubles Formation for Attack Mode After a Smash or Drop

If one partner moves to side of court, the other goes to the opposite side to cover court area

FIGURE 5.9 Doubles Formation When Defending or in Trouble

SKILL	CUE	WHY?	COMMON ERROR
Side to Side (Figure 5.9)	If one partner moves to side of court, the other goes to the opposite side of court to cover court area	Only as needed to cover more ground	Staying side to side Not getting to up and back position
	When defending or in trouble, use side position that is parallel to partner	To cover more ground	Staying out of position
	Each player covers own property	To stay balanced	Reach into partner's area
	Stay within property line	To stay balanced	Crossing over line
Basic Guidelines	Support partner in every way possible	Teamwork Communication is essential	Playing your own game
	Always be ready to cover for partner	Shot can pull partner out of position	Not paying attention to partner
	Don't get in each other's way; let partner take his or her own shots	Communication is very important	Not communicating
Shots Approach	Hit shuttle to sides and corners with accuracy	Get either/both opponent(s) out of up and back positions	Hitting right to the person in their up and back position

DOUBLES SCORING

SKILL	CUE	WHY?
Scoring Doubles Game	Rally point scoring	In the traditional scoring system, each side has serves except at the start of the game
	A side has only one serve	In rally scoring, a side has only one serve
	The server serves from the right service court at the beginning of the game when the score is even	
	When it is an odd score, the server serves from the left service court	
	If serving side wins a rally, the serving side scores one point and the same server serves from alternate court	
	If receiving side wins a rally, the receiving side wins a point	

continued

SKILL	CUE	WHY?
Scoring Doubles Game, *continued*	The receiving side becomes the new serving side	
	The players do not change their respective service courts until they win a point when the side is serving	Guarantees alternate servers
	If players commit an error in the service court, the error is corrected when the mistake is discovered	
Scoring	A game consists of 21 points	
	At 20–20 win by 2	
	At 29–29 the first side to 30 points wins the game	
Match	A match consists of two out of three games of 21 points	A two-minute interval between each game
		In the third game, players change ends when the leading score reaches 11 points

6

Baseball

"There is no joy in Mudville: mighty Casey has struck out."
(Ernest Lawrence Thayer)

INTRODUCTION

What the fans in joyless Mudville never knew about their mighty slugger Casey is that after striking out, Casey decided to ask his coach how to improve his batting skills. Casey's coaches now face the challenge of correcting Casey's swing and restoring joy to Mudville. Was there really anything wrong with Casey's swing, or was the pitcher just better that day?

Selecting critical errors and giving the right cue is not an easy task for the coach. The cues in this chapter were designed to help coaches analyze skills and provide effective cues. For example, the cue, "See the ball, hit the bat," helps the batter focus on the ball all the way into the hitting zone as the bat head makes contact with the ball.

SKILLS LISTED WITH CUES

This chapter presents cues for the following baseball skills: hitting, throwing, fielding ground balls and fly balls, bunting, pitching (fastball, curveball, slider, knuckleball, forkball, screwball), catching, and sliding (feet first, head first).

Tips

1. Warm up with a fungo bat (lighter than a normal bat). This drill teaches quick hands, which increases bat speed. Warming up with heavy bats teaches your hands to drag the bat through the strike zone.

2. Run a couple of laps around the bases or the park before stretching out and warming up the arm. This activity warms the arm up a little faster and helps circulate the blood.

3. Start with short-distance throwing and move into a long toss. A long toss is defined as throwing the ball as far as possible but still keeping it on the line. The long toss is the only true way to increase arm strength, and it also feels good. Stay away from the rainbow toss (a toss that goes too high).

4. Using the fungo bat in a drill with Wiffle golf balls is ideal. "See the ball, hit the bat" helps with a quick wrist to develop bat speed.

5. Regular bats can be used for batting tees and soft-toss drills, as well as live batting practice.

Equipment Tips

1. Gloves: Infielders need short-pocket gloves for quick access and release, and outfielders need large-pocket gloves for fly balls and fielding ground balls on the run. A first baseman uses a first-base glove.

2. Bats: Pick a bat that is comfortable in the hands; it should not be too heavy or too long. The key to hitting is bat speed.

3. A fungo bat is used to hit infield balls. These bats are not made for hitting pitched balls. The bat will break when hitting a pitched ball.

4. Batting gloves protect the hands when hitting. They also provide protection under the mitt and protection for baserunning. The runner should hold the batting gloves in clenched fists to protect fingers when sliding.

5. Wiffle balls can be used for soft-toss drills. They can also be used for batting practice in a very small area if a cage is not available. A player can use Wiffle balls for batting practice before games. The use of Wiffle balls avoids damage to fences. Baseballs have a tendency to bend a chain-link fence.

6. Catcher equipment, including shin guards, a chest protector, a helmet, a cup, a mask, and a throat guard, is needed for protection.

7. Baseball caps are critical to help block the sun.

8. Shoes with plastic cleats or spikes are recommended because they help with traction.

Safety

Most injuries occur from wild pitches, batted balls, and collisions in the field. Below is a list to help keep players safe.

1. Batting helmets should be worn properly (low on the forehead) when a player is at bat, running bases, and warming up to bat.

2. The catcher should wear all the gear.

3. Players need to wear molded plastic cleats, not metal cleats.

4. Install breakaway bases. These bases can be dislodged when a runner slides into base.

5. After warming up, make sure all extra bats, balls, etc. are safely put away before the game begins.

6. Have players practice calling for the ball to avoid collisions.

7. If a batter sees a pitch that might hit them, they should duck and turn away from the pitch, exposing the back and rear end to the pitch.

8. Players should practice running bases with heads up to look for other players and the ball.

9. Teach players to slide correctly. No head first slides.

10. Never throw a bat.

Pitching Safety

1. There are rules regarding the number of pitches players can throw in a game. Below are the pitch count limits recommended by U.S.A. Little League and the American Sports Medicine Institute:

   11–12 years old: 85 pitches in one day or 115 pitches a week

   13–16 years old: 95 pitches in one day

   17–18 years old: 105 pitches in one day

2. 4 to 10 innings is recommended per week to pitch. Pitchers should take three months off per year.

3. Caution should be used for 9–16 year olds throwing breaking balls (curve balls and sliders)—poor mechanics may cause injuries.

Etiquette

1. Umpires are the ones who control the game and make all of the deciding factors that are involved in calling the game.

2. If a coach disagrees with a specific call, it is appropriate to call "time" and go discuss it with the umpire who made the call.

3. "Trash talk" is not allowed between opposing players and/or coaches.

4. After the game is finished, both teams will line up at home plate to shake hands and show good sportsmanship.

TEACHING IDEAS

1. *Batting drill stations:* To develop the necessary techniques and rhythm to hit a live pitch, many repetitions of a correct swing are necessary. The emphasis in these drills should be on hand position at setup, hand action during the swing, and hip rotation.

   a. *Soft-toss drill:* The batter hits into a fence or net. The partner kneels at a 45-degree angle from the batter, a short distance from the batter's front foot, and tosses underhand. The batter cocks the bat as the partner takes the ball back to tossing position and swings upon delivery.

   b. *Batting tee:* A tee is used. The ball is rotated to different positions to give the batter a variety of areas to hit.

   c. *Hip drill:* Place the bat behind the back, cradling it in the crook of the elbows. Now rotate back and forth and feel how the body weight is naturally transferred from back to front foot as the hips rotate. Make sure the back foot comes up at the heel (squash the bug) as the weight is transferred forward.

2. *Four-corners drill:* 4 to 12 players on the four bases throw the ball around the bases. The goal is to catch the ball in the catching zone. (The catching zone is the top left-hand side toward the glove side, to the left of the heart for a right-handed player.) This drill teaches players to shuffle feet and have a quick ball exchange. Modifications of four-corners drill: catch, shuffle, throw, hop, chase. Go clockwise, then counterclockwise.

GAME PLAY

Rules

1. Innings differ depending on the level of baseball. Little League Baseball usually consists of either 6–7 innings with each inning being divided in half (top of the inning is when the visiting team is hitting and the bottom of the inning is when the home team is hitting).

2. Only 9 defensive players should be on the field.

3. Play begins when the batter has both feet in the batter's box and the umpire motions to begin play, either verbally by saying "play" or physically by "hand movement."

4. If a batter hits the ball in play (between the lines that run from home plate to foul poles on both the left and right side), he or she must run to first, which is located down the foul line on the right side of the field.

5. The batter now becomes the base-runner and is required to touch first base before second base, second base before third base, and third base before home plate.

6. The batter gets three strikes (a swing and a miss or a ball that crosses the strike zone) before he or she is considered out. If there are four balls (any pitch that does not cross the strike zone) the batter gets to take first base.

7. Each team is allowed three outs before switching roles from hitting to defense. You are considered out as a batter/base-runner if you strikeout (three strikes), force out (if the defensive player reaches the designated base before the batter/base-runner), tagged out (defensive player tags the base-runner with the ball in his or her hand, or the glove with the ball in it), and a fly out (defensive player catches the ball in the air that the batter hit).

8. If a batter reaches all the bases before touching home plate, the hitting team scores one run.

9. The visiting team always starts the game as the hitting team, and the home team always starts on defense.

10. At the end of the regulated innings (6 for Little League), the team with the most runs wins the game. In the event of a tie, the teams will continue play until one of the teams is winning after one full inning.

Strategies

1. Batting order should depend on the specific qualities of each player (speed, power, situational hitter).

2. Use the bunt (situational hitter) to move a base-runner from first base to second base to put the runner in scoring position. (A runner at second base is considered in scoring position because the runner will have a high chance of scoring if the batter gets a hit.)

3. As a base runner, you want to steal bases (run to the next base without the batter hitting the ball) if the defense is giving you the following base. This will remove the chance of a double play, as well as put the base-runner in scoring position.

4. Defensive strategy revolves around the pitcher. The pitcher is considered the most important position on the field. He or she starts play, as well as creates difficulty for the batter to hit the ball by using different types of pitches with different speeds and spins.

5. Fielders are the ones who catch fly balls, receive ground balls, and produce "outs."

ASSESSMENT IDEAS

1. Throw right side/left side for speed using a radar gun, or throw for distance.
2. Time a player around the bases.

FYI

For further information and special help, consult the following resources.

PUBLICATIONS

Delmonico, R. (1995). *Defensive baseball*. Chicago, IL: Masters Press.

Delmonico, R. (1996). *Offensive baseball drill*. Champaign, IL: Human Kinetics.

Petrack, C. (1998). *Complete guide to outfield play*. Haworth, NJ: Harding Press.

WEBSITES

www.howtoplay.com/ht_p/baseball/essentials.html

www.educationworld.com/a_sites/sites082.shtml

BATTING

SKILL	CUE	WHY?	COMMON ERROR
Hitting *Stance* (Figure 6.1a)	Stand sideways with eyes focused on pitcher	Creates more torque in your core – more power	Standing forward, head tilted
	Feet slightly wider than shoulder width, knees slightly bent	Proper balance	Feet too far apart or too close together
	Weight over balls of feet, heels lightly touching the ground, more weight on back leg		Weight on heels
Arm Swing	Hitter should think "shoulder to shoulder" (start with chin on front shoulder; finish swing with chin on back shoulder)	Keeps the head in proper position; head should stay still	Moving head during the swing; head too tense
Hip Rotation (Figure 6.1b)	Back hip snaps or rotates at pitcher; drives body through ball; take photograph of pitcher with belly button		No hip rotation
	Throw hands through baseball; "slow feet, quick hands"		Using arms instead of wrists

continued

SKILL	CUE	WHY?	COMMON ERROR
Hitting, *continued* *Focus of Eyes*	See the bat, hit the ball	Gets the barrel of the bat to the ball and not the handle	Not seeing the ball hit the bat
	Watch ball all the way into catcher's mitt	Helps the batter to see the ball all the way into the hitting zone	
Step	Step 3–6 inches (stride should be more of a glide)	You do not want to transfer your weight all on front foot; stay back and pop hips	Overstriding causes bat to drop during swing (jarring step)
			Also causes head to drop, which causes eyes to drop, obscuring vision on the ball
	Short stride, quick swing		Hitter "steps and then hits"
Follow-Through (Figure 6.2)	Top hand rolls over bottom hand; bat goes around the body on follow-through		
Recommended Progression	Teach cues in order listed; when first three are mastered, add others		

(a) Batter's Stance

(b) Hip Rotation

FIGURE 6.1 Hitting

FIGURE 6.2 Hitting (Follow-Through)

	HITTING—INEXPERIENCED BATTERS		
SKILL	**CUE**	**WHY?**	**COMMON ERROR**
Bunting	Pivot toward pitcher; square body to pitcher, but do not square 6–5 feet	Both eyes focused on the ball	Hitter or bunter does not get his or her body properly squared around in position to bunt
	Slide top hand up bat; keep bat head slightly above the handle; keep fingers behind bat or protect fingers from ball; bat head higher than knob	Less chance to hit ball in air; direct the ball down to ground	Hands remain together (bat is not kept level if pitch is either high or low); wrapping hand around bat
	Catch ball with bat—imagine a net in the barrel of the bat; catch the ball in the net	Deadens the ball	Pushing bat at ball, swiping at ball
Checkpoint for Coaches	If the batter is not gripping, standing, or holding the bat correctly, coach could correct the player individually		Don't use these cues unless a player needs assistance; give one at a time
Grip	Hold bat in base of fingers (this allows wrist to roll freely and generates bat speed)	Enables wrists to turn freely during the swing	Bat held in palm of hand, squeezing bat slows the swing
	Align knuckles "Eight middle knuckles, all in a row"	Proper grip beginning of proper swing	1st knuckles are aligned
Closed Stance	Feet are shoulder-width apart; then front foot is placed toward plate	Helps untrained hitter step toward the pitcher	Stepping back or stepping into the bucket

continued

SKILL	CUE	WHY?	COMMON ERROR
Bat Position	Bat held armpit high and far enough away from the body that both fists of player could fit between the chest and bat	Allows for proper starting position	Bat held too close to shoulder
	Back elbow held away from body at about an 8:00 position; front elbow should be closer to body	Creates a shorter swing	Back elbow drops, creating an upswing and a fly-ball swing
Bat Angle	Straight up in air or up and angled slightly back over shoulder	Helps make a short, quick swing	Cradling bat around head; bat is pointing back toward pitcher

THROWING

SKILL	CUE	WHY?	COMMON ERROR
Grip	Get a seam, either across the seams or with the seams	Makes ball spin backward, allowing it to travel farther and straighter	Not getting a seam; poor control of ball
	Hold ball with fingertips: first 2 fingers on top of ball, second 2 underneath to the side, thumb opposite side	The more loose you are, the more rotation, which causes ball to travel farther	Holding baseball in palm or placing more fingers on top of ball
Stance	Stand sideways; instep of back foot faces target	Everything is in line with the target	Standing facing the target
Throwing Action	Point glove-hand shoulder at target	Increase consistency	Staying square to target (no shoulder or hip rotation is possible)
	Take a long step toward target	Help increase torque in core	Stepping across body, no step at all, or a step that is too high
	Stretch arm way back	To create velocity	
	Make L-shape with throwing arm		Taking the ball directly behind head with bent elbow
	Let glove fall into armpit; pull glove arm down, and replace glove arm with throwing arm	Prevents over rotation	Pulling glove arm will open up shoulders too far and cause arm problems

continued

THROWING, continued

SKILL	CUE	WHY?	COMMON ERROR
Throwing Action, *continued*	Whip the arm through; snap wrist	Creates slingshot action for more velocity	No wrist action; all arm
	Follow through; wrist goes to opposite knee; slap knee	Decreases injury Allows for more accurate throwing	No follow-through

FIELDING—GROUND BALLS

SKILL	CUE	WHY?	COMMON ERROR
Stance	Feet shoulder-width apart, weight on balls of feet (right-handers lead slightly with left foot because the slight lead of the left foot means that less time is needed to rotate body to throw); butt low to ground	Proper balance	Weight on heels; feet too close or too far apart
	Create a triangle with both feet and glove; the glove is the apex (top) of the triangle	Allows to field ball in front of the body	Glove inside or behind knees, fielding ball directly between the legs
	Bend at knees; bend slightly at waist; butt low to ground	Better balance – more consistent fielding	Bending over from waist
Catching Action	Field ball out in front	Allows missed balls to most likely stay in front of body	Trying to play ball behind the legs
	Keep glove close to ground		Starting with glove waist high and trying to go down at ball
	Keep the glove lower than the ball	Allows missed balls to stay in front	Scared to stay low because ball may hit face
	Elbows inside knees act as shock absorber to cushion the impact of a ground ball	Creates soft hands	
	Put your nose on the ball; follow the ball into glove with eyes	More control of ball	Pulling head up; not seeing ball into glove for fear of being hit in the face
	Secure ball with both hands; alligator jaws	Keep throwing hand close for quick release	Fielding ball with only the glove

continued

FIELDING—GROUND BALLS, continued

SKILL	CUE	WHY?	COMMON ERROR
Catching Action, *continued*	Read a hop; read the path of the baseball; try to field ball on big or long hop; after a big hop, ball will usually stay low	Decrease chance of creating an error	Letting ball dictate how to play it (letting ball play fielder)

FIELDING—FLY BALLS

SKILL	CUE	WHY?	COMMON ERROR
Stance	Comfortable stance, weight on balls of feet	Running with weight on the heels makes it difficult to track a fly ball	Rigid, fight stance; weight on back of heels like a boxer
Catching Position	Position body underneath flight of baseball (the path should be coming down to the eyes)	Having to catch ball behind your head or below your waist	
Catching Action	Place glove slightly out from and above head; reach for the sky with fingers just before the ball arrives	Minimize catching errors	Catching ball to side of body; fingers stretched out rather than up
	Always use both hands	To secure ball and quicken transfer to hand	One-handed "showboat"
	Follow ball into glove with eyes	For a quick release	Not watching ball all the way into the glove

PITCHING FUNDAMENTAL CUES

SKILL	CUE	WHY?	COMMON ERROR
Nose	Nose over toes at all times in the wind up	Too many movements of the head or body will waste energy and cause inaccuracy	Wild and crazy pitches
Balance	Balance is key to shifting weight from back to front	Creates more power and velocity	Not using upper body as one
Chest	Chest should end over the front knee when releasing ball	More power on top of the ball; best finish	Knee too far out in front without good strong upper body finish
Finish the Pitch	Finish the pitch with your whole body falling toward your target	Want all your energy and power focused on a single point	Leg swings around and body twists

SKILL	CUE	WHY?	COMMON ERROR
Delivery	Step directly toward home plate	Stay on midline to be accurate	Foot goes too far one way or the other
	Use normal throwing motion, nice and easy (loosey-goosey)	Don't try to throw across body	Overthrowing, trying to throw the ball too hard; avoid sidearming
	Simply play catch with catcher, throwing strikes	Narrow focus – aim small – miss small	Trying to do too much; overthrowing and not throwing any strikes
	Comfortable, smooth delivery	Increase consistency in catch and pitch	No rhythm
	Follow-through: throwing hand should come down and brush against the opposite knee		
Pitches *Fastball*	Grip with two seams for a sink action	More movement to deceive hitter	Wrong grip or simply grabbing ball
	Pressure on fingertips		No pressure points
	Smooth delivery		Rushed motion
	Wrist snap	Quick backspin on ball to create velocity	No wrist action
	Grip across (four seams) for downward angle pitch	Creates more velocity	
Curveball	Grip with seams	Creates a spin on the baseball, causing it to spin or curve	Wrong grip
	Fastball motion		Motion too slow and obvious
	Reduce speed of ball		Too much speed; no rotation or spin
	Tickle ear	Puts topspin on ball so ball will drop	Not cocking wrist
	Karate chop action		Creates more topspin
	Snap fingers		Letting ball simply roll off fingers
Slider	Backward C	Puts more of a side rotation on ball to deceive batter	Wrong grip and placement of fingers
	Off center		Holding ball in center
	Fastball speed and motion		Slow or rushed motion
	Turn wrist over or turn doorknob		Throwing like a curveball, cocking wrist
	Second finger		First finger releases ball

continued

SKILL	CUE	WHY?	COMMON ERROR
Knuckleball	Fingernail grip	Lack of spin causes ball to float and dance	Knuckles on seams
	Dig seams		Not enough pressure on seams
	Extend and push toward plate		Forcing the ball
	Stiff wrist		Snapping the wrist
Forkball	Make a fork shape with fingers	Causes the ball to dip or dive	Fingers not far enough apart
	Fingers outside seams		Fingers directly on seams
	Ball rolls away		Pressure on fingertips
	No wrist action or snap		Too much wrist
Screwball	Grip narrow seams	Causes the ball to spin and break opposite of curveball action	Simply grabbing baseball
	Overhand		Sidearm
	Inside out		Curveball motion
	Reverse snap		Not enough wrist action
	Thumb flip		No thumb

CATCHING			
SKILL	CUE	WHY?	COMMON ERROR
Catcher's Stance (Figure 6.3)	Feet outside shoulders, heels elevated	Balance	Kneeling
	Head up	To focus on ball	Flinching; head down
	Elbows resting outside the knees	Hands in good position to catch ball	Elbow inside the knees
	Place throwing arm behind back	Placing arm directly behind or to the side of the catcher's mitt is more likely to cause injury	Keep throwing arm in front
	Catch the ball using both hands; elbows act as shock absorbers	Two hands helps trap the ball in the glove	Relying solely on catcher's mitt
	Move to ball laterally; allow the ball to get through the hitting zone	Batter may make contact with mitt or hand, causing injury	Reaching for ball
	Be a wall		

FIGURE 6.3 Catcher's Stance

SLIDING			
SKILL	**CUE**	**WHY?**	**COMMON ERROR**
Feet First	Sprint	To beat the throw	Slowing up
	Slide early	To not hit base standing up	Sliding too late (injuries)
	Sit down	Closer to base	Falling and hopping
	Curl leg under, making the number 4 figure	More efficient	Sliding with both legs forward
	Keep hands in front of the body	Faster, keeps the momentum going	Hands behind body breaks momentum
	Roller-coaster ride		Lying down completely

7

Basketball

INTRODUCTION

Ball-handling skills make basketball fun, fast, and a great spectator sport. These skills are the foundation of basketball. Duke, a giant in basketball, and Butler College, an underdog school, had great ball-handling skills in the 2010 NCAA Men's Final Basketball Championship game. Both teams were fundamentally sound and displayed these skills with great finesse; one of the best NCAA Men's Final Championship games ever played with a final score 61–59. It was a thrilling event that will be remembered by all who watched.

Ball handling is sometimes neglected when teaching basketball skills. Instructors are encouraged to teach these skills and the new drills provided in this chapter, as well as spend the time working on the fundamentals of shooting, passing, and defense. The paramount detail for a teacher to remember in teaching basketball is to provide as many opportunities as possible for the students to touch the ball. Ideally, every student should have a basketball.

SKILLS LISTED WITH CUES

Cues are provided for stationary ball handling, speed dribble (right side, left side), ball handling moving skills, crossover, reverse spin, behind the back plant, behind the back running, between the legs, dribbling two balls low, dribbling two balls alternate high/low, defense, one-on-one defense, defender drives past you, drills for ball-handling skills, passing, catching, the set shot, shooting drills, right and left handed layups, ball handling layup drills, triple threat, free throw, jump shot, rebounding, jumping and dunking, blocking out, the pick, offensive footwork, offensive one-on-one moves, spacing defense, and out-of-bounds.

Tips

Equipment Tip

Have a lot of basketballs and baskets available.

Safety

1. No rings, earrings, bracelets, or jewelry of any kind. This increases risk of injury to students wearing the jewelry as well as injury to teammates and opponents.
2. Tie shoe strings in double knots to keep them from coming undone.
3. Make sure socks do not have wrinkles in them to avoid blisters.
4. You need a clean floor. Make sure the floor is swept.
5. Make sure obstacles close to basket are padded.
6. Remove any objects on and around floor.

Etiquette

1. Treat others like you want them to treat you.
2. No trash talk.

TEACHING IDEAS

1. Every player should have a basketball. This is a must.
2. Practice should be 90 percent dribble, pass, shoot, and handling the ball.
3. Practice—practice—practice! How many hours are you willing to practice?
4. Use two basketballs per player to dribble or pass to a partner.
5. Know the feel for the ball and what the ball can do for you.
6. The best players shoot the ball up to 8 hours a day. Recruiters look for 90 percent ball-handling and shooting skills. Tell students that to be good they need the fundamentals: dribble, pass, and shoot.
7. When playing a game, you must boil down teaching to the basic cues of the game, like placing your rebounder under the basket on the right-hand side of the basket. Why? Most of the balls go there.

Mini-Games

1. Play a lot of games: half-court and full-court games.
2. Play dribble tag, relays, passing games, and shooting contests (using right and left hands).
3. Be creative in your games. Use your imagination. Change and modify your rules (e.g., you must find a way to score without dribbling).
4. Time players on dribbling the length of the court, both right- and left-handed.
5. Time the player on rebounding and throwing a baseball pass the length of the court.
6. Direct stretching, footwork, and ball handling at the beginning of each session before activity begins.
7. All jump balls go to the defense.

GAME PLAY

Rules

Fouls

1. Personal fouls. Personal fouls include any type of illegal physical contact: hitting, pushing, slapping, holding, illegal pick/screen (player is moving). When an offensive player sticks out a part of their body and makes contact with a defender in an attempt to block the path of the defender.

2. Flagrant foul. Violent contact with an opponent that includes hitting, kicking, and punching. This type of foul results in free throws, plus possession of the ball after the free throws.

3. Intentional foul. When a player makes contact with another player with no reasonable effort to steal the ball.

4. Technical foul. A player or a coach can commit this type of foul. It does not involve player contact or the ball, but is instead about the etiquette of the game. Foul language, obscene gestures, and excessive arguing can be considered a technical foul, as can technical details, such as filling in the scorebook improperly or dunking during warm-ups.

5. Charging. An offensive foul that happens when a player pushes or runs over a defensive player who hasn't established position. The ball is given to the defensive team.

6. Blocking. Blocking is illegal contact resulting from a defender not establishing position.

Violations

1. Walking/Traveling. Taking more than a step and a half without dribbling or moving the pivot foot once a player stops dribbling.

2. Carrying/palming. When a player dribbles the ball with the hand too far to the side of or under the ball.

3. Double Dribbled. Dribbling the ball with both hands at the same time or picking up the ball and then dribbling again.

4. Held ball. When two or more opposing players gain possession of the ball at the same time.

5. Goaltending. When defensive player interferes with a shot while it's on the way down toward the basket, after it has touched the backboard, or while it's in the cylinder above the rim, it is goaltending and the basket counts. If committed by an offensive player, it's a violation, and the ball is awarded to the opposing team.

6. Backcourt violation. Once the offense moves the ball across the mid-court line, they cannot go back across the line during possession. If they do, the ball is awarded to the other team.

7. Time restrictions. A player passing the ball inbounds has 5 seconds to pass the ball. If that time is exceeded, then the ball is awarded to the other team. Other time restrictions include the rule that a player cannot have the ball for more than 5 seconds when being closely guarded, and shot-clock restrictions requiring a team to attempt a shot within a given time frame are in place at some levels.

Strategies

Strategies for game play are located in the cue sheets at the end of the chapter (see pages 82–98).

Scoring

1 point = a free throw made behind the free throw line
2 points = a basket made in front of the 3-point line or on the 3-point line
3 points = a basket made behind the 3-point line

Game Cues

The author uses the following three cues:

1. Shoot when you are open. (Results in a higher percentage of shots going in).
2. Drive to the basket and find the holes. (Best three point shot, 98 percent close up, and a free throw if fouled).
3. Move when you do not have the ball.

Why?

1. The students feel comfortable to shoot when they are open.
2. The players have fun finding openings and practicing ball-handling skills while driving in to the basket.
3. The players have a specific goal to think about when they do not have the ball.

ASSESSMENT IDEAS

1. Shoot 10 shots with dominant hand 10 feet from the basket.
   7–10 = 15 points
   4–6 = 10 points
   1–3 = 5 points
   (7 or above = 5 bonus points)
   Options: 10 shots right side, right hand, 3 feet from basket
                10 shots left side, left hand, 3 feet from basket
2. Play 6 games, 5 points a game = 30 points total
3. Points awarded for individual baskets made in games:
   5–6 baskets = 15 points
   3–4 baskets = 10 points
   1–2 baskets = 5 points
   Over 6 baskets in one game = 5 bonus points

FYI

For further information and special help, consult the following organizations and resources:

ORGANIZATION	WEBSITE
USA Basketball 5465 Mark Dabling Boulevard Colorado Springs, CO 80918–3842 Telephone: (719) 590-4800 Fax: (719) 590-4811	http://www.basketballworld.com/

Move ball in and out of legs

Stay low

Long stride

FIGURE 7.1 Scissor Walk with Basketball

STATIONARY BALL—BALL HANDLING			
SKILL	**CUE**	**WHY?**	**COMMON ERROR**
Hand Position Drill	Slap the ball with wide fingers	This will develop a feel for the ball and control of the ball	Palm on ball
Around the World	Move the ball around the waist; change directions; then move the ball around your head; then change directions quickly again	To develop quick reaction time with hands and body awareness	Dropping the ball
Figure 8 Around Legs	Move ball in figure 8 formation around the knees and then change directions quickly	Promotes ball control	Loses ball
Scissor Walk with basketball (Crab Walk) (Figure 7.1)	Lunging down the court, move the basketball in and out of your legs, going from baseline to baseline and staying low	Promote basketball position and coordination in ball movement	Standing straight up

FULL- AND HALF-COURT DRIBBLING DRILLS			
SKILL	**CUE**	**WHY?**	**COMMON ERROR**
Hand Placement on Ball When Dribbling	Thumb out, fingers spread wide, ball touching all five finger pads when dribbling; keep eyes up	Develop feel for the ball	Fingers together
Hand Action	Yo-yo action with your hand on the ball; push ball hard toward floor	Develop feel for hand on ball and force in dribbling	Slapping the ball

continued

SKILL	CUE	WHY?	COMMON ERROR
Hand Action, *continued*	Waving action with your hand		Palm touches the ball
	Hand waving down at the ball		Dribble with both hands
	Note: Use left and right hands equally when practicing		
Eyes	Eyes looking up the court for open players and for opportunities to pass, shoot, or drive; see the defenders but don't look at them	To develop court awareness and player positions	Eyes looking down at the ball
Speed Drills *Change of Speed, Crossover*	Emphasize change of direction and change of speed; keep head up	To promote ball-handling skills	
Five-Trip Dribble (Single Ball)	Used to change direction on the court; protect ball with arm guard		
Speed Dribble	Quickly dribble down the court with right hand; dribble back with left hand	Control with speed	Bouncing ball too high

BALL-HANDLING CUES

SKILL	CUE	WHY?	COMMON ERROR
Crossover	Dribble at an angle (right side)	Depends on defense	Dribbling straight
	Keep the ball below the knees	Faster transition; less chance for the opponent to steal the ball	Dribbling higher then knees
	Plant outside foot	So you can drive through and change direction	Planting wrong foot
	Point back foot in new direction	Faster change of direction; deceive opponent quicker	Not pushing off foot
	Explosive push with back foot	Better acceleration and change of speed	Dribbling straight

continued

SKILL	CUE	WHY?	COMMON ERROR
Crossover, *continued*	Change direction, left side dribbles		Dribbling straight
	Keep hands close together for exchange of the ball	To have better ball control, quicker switch	Hands too far apart or too high
Reverse Spin	Spin backward off pivot foot/inside foot	Faster transition	Not having spin
	Keep ball low and close to body	Do not lose control of the ball	Dribbling ball too high
	Dribble ball next to inside foot	Keeps ball protected	Keeping ball on outside, having ball stolen
	Transfer ball to other hand after you spin	Keeps control of ball	Having hand on bottom of ball is considered a carry violation
	Keep hand on top of the ball	Rule	
Behind the Back Plant	Stay low	Helps you protect the ball from defender	Keeping legs straight
	Keep ball low	Controls the ball	Dribbling ball too high out
	Plant your feet; jump stop	Helps protect the ball from defender	Continuing to move, not stopping
	Keep hand on the back of the ball	Pushes ball out in front	Hands slipping to side of ball
	Smack opposite cheek with hand	A way for you to know where the ball is for the new hand	Hand to side
Behind the Back Running Down Court	Stay low and run fast	Helps protect ball from defender	
	Keep ball low	Better ball control; makes it difficult for your defender to steal the ball	Dribbling ball too high
	Keep hand behind back, smack opposite cheek with hand, and push ball forward	To know exactly where ball is for exchange of hands	Pushing ball outside too far
	Have opposite hand out and ready for ball	Better ball control and faster transition	Having hands too high or too far to the side
Between the Legs	Perform a crossover but bounce ball between legs when you change direction with feet		No crossover, dribbling straight

continued

SKILL	CUE	WHY?	COMMON ERROR
Between the Legs, *continued*	Plant foot in the direction you want to go		Not planting foot
	Spread legs	Creates ball space between legs	Having legs too close together
	Point back toe in the direction you want to go	Prepares you to change direction, faster transition	Not changing direction
	Bounce the ball low between the legs and away from the defender	Protects ball from the defender	Bouncing ball high, out of control
	Explode off back foot	Helps change of speed	Weight on back foot
	Keep eyes up	Helps you to see the court and teammates	Keeping eyes down
Dribble Two Balls Low	Focus on non-dominant hand	Helps to dribble ball with weak hand	Not having control of the ball
Dribble Two Balls Alternate High-Low	Have up and down motion	Develops coordination confidence	Not having control of the ball
Two Balls: Crossover, Reverse Spin, Between Legs	For more advance players	Develops more advance skills in dribbling and creativity in ball handling	Not for beginners
Defense Cues	Point back foot back Step back and at angle	Cuts off defender	Stepping sideways
One-on-one	The opponent's stomach never lies, watch the core area of offensive player	Maintains balance and control	Bringing feet together
	Aways keep feet 6" apart	Maintains balance and control	Losing balance with feet together
	Push your shuffle step	Faster transition with feet	Sliding feet
Defender Drives Past You	Turn and sprint two or three steps	Can catch defender	Staying in the same spot and watching defender go to the basket or get an open spot
One-on-one	Do two shuffle steps with feet	Pushes defender from basket	
	Angle defender toward the out of bounds	Protects basket	

Drills

Have students partner up and dribble side-line to sideline of the basketball court.

1. Crossover
2. Reverse spin
3. Behind the back—plant
4. Behind the back—running
5. Between the legs
6. Be creative and choose your own
7. All of the above
8. Add two balls for each of the above (Figure 7.2.)
9. Add a defender

Keep head up

Fingers spread

Concentrate on dribbling ball with non-dominant hand

FIGURE 7.2 Dribbling Two Balls, Ball Handling

PASSING AND CATCHING

SKILL	CUE	WHY?	COMMON ERROR
Passing (Figure 7.3) *Hand Position*	Two thumbs down behind the ball	For proper spin	Thumbs up
Fingers	Spread fingers wide	For control	Fingers narrow on ball
Eyes	Eyes focused on your target	For accuracy	Eyes wandering
Passing Action	Extend your arms like shooting horizontally, following through with thumbs down	For proper speed and accuracy	No follow-through with arms
	Palms out at finish	More consistency	Palms face up or down
Catching (Figure 7.4) *Hand and Finger position*	Big hands, wide fingers	To develop receiving skills	
Catching Action	Reach out, pull the ball in, or suck the ball in like a vacuum	Prevent defense from stealing ball	Moving before catching the ball
Eyes	Smother the ball with your eyes	To assure catching	Eyes look away
Passing and Catching Drills *Partner Passing*	Face each other using one ball; one-hand push pass with your right hand and then your left hand; follow through each time	Like shooting a basketball, only horizontally with right hand	Does not reach out to throw the ball straight
		To pass around a defender; right side/left side	

continued

Eyes focused on target

Follow through with thumbs down

FIGURE 7.3 Two-Hand Chest Pass

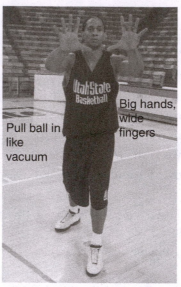

Big hands, wide fingers

Pull ball in like vacuum

FIGURE 7.4 Catching the Pass

PASSING AND CATCHING, continued			
SKILL	**CUE**	**WHY?**	**COMMON ERROR**
Target Passing	Throw to your partner's target (e.g., partner's shoulder, head, or hands); make a target on the wall when practicing by yourself	Like shooting a basketball, only horizontally with the left hand	Partner does not make target with hands
Chest Pass and Bounce Pass Simultaneously	Both partners have a ball; one partner makes two-hand chest pass while the other partner makes bounce pass at the same time; switch after a while	Develop advanced skills in passing	Coordinating the two passes – forgetting which one to pass; failure to communicate
Pass with a Figure 8	Perform a figure 8 around your knees, then pass to your partner off the figure 8; keep the ball moving	Passing while on the move	Being in too big of a hurry and drops ball
Behind the Back Passing	Standing slightly sideways, bring ball behind the back and pass to your partner; use your right hand, then your left hand; learn through error	Alternative pass for advanced players	Hand does not come around the body
Baseball Pass	Throw (as a football quarterback passes a football) to your partner	For long-distance passing with accuracy	Does not follow through with arm

continued

PASSING AND CATCHING, continued			
SKILL	**CUE**	**WHY?**	**COMMON ERROR**
One-Bounce Baseball Pass	Use strong then weak arms to throw your baseball passes with a bounce first	Alternative pass for advanced players	Does not put two hands on ball before release
	Step farther back as needed to throw longer passes		
Buzzer Beater Baseball Pass Length of the Floor	Dribble once, then throw downcourt to partner at the other end of court, counting to self … 3-2-1 BZZ	Develop end-of-game confidence	
Three-Man Player Drills *Three-Man Weave*	Start with three lines, ball in middle line	To include movement in passing as done in game situations	Uneven lines
	Running downcourt, middle passes to player on right side, who passes to the player coming toward him or her		Tries to pass to player behind you
	Pass and go behind; follow your pass. Be ready to receive ball back quickly	So player does not get hit with the ball	Running in front of the player you passing to instead of behind the player
	Person who receives the ball at key drives in for the layup	To score	Tries to make too many passes – ball gets stolen
	Use game speed; go all out	To make it more game–like	Jogs through the motion

SET SHOT CUES			
SKILL	**CUE**	**WHY?**	**COMMON ERROR**
Shooting Hand Set Up (Right) (Figure 7.5)	Spread fingers	More control of ball	Having fingers together
	Keep hand up	Better accuracy	Having hand forward
	Wrinkle wrist	More power	Having wrist straight
	Balance like a waiter's tray	More control	
Non-shooting Hand Set Up (Left)	Make left hand straight; fingers spread on the side of the ball	Left hand used only for balance	Having the ball in the palm of the hand

continued

SKILL	CUE	WHY?	COMMON ERROR
Stance	Have right foot slightly ahead of left foot	More power	Having both feet even
	Have shoulder and body square to the basket	Better accuracy	
	Slightly bend knees with buttocks out	Strength of shot comes from legs	
Sight	Focus on 2 inches above the rim	Eyes need a specific spot to focus on	Not focusing
	Basket looks like a big bin	You need a big target	Basket looks small
Shooting Action *Hand Finger Action*	Roll ball off fingers for a nice backspin	To develop proper backspin	Ball is thrown up
Arm Action (Figure 7.6a)	Finish with arm straight	Projects ball in the air and arch	Moving arm forward
(Figure 7.6b)	Keep elbow above eye	Gives the ball height to get over the rim	Keeping elbow below the chin
(Figure 7.7)	Make a goose neck finish; thumbs pointed at shoes	Accuracy	Keep left hand straight
Non-shooting Hand	Keep left hand straight and fingers spread like a big handprint	Hand used only for balance and accuracy	Pushing the ball with thumb because the player is not strong enough

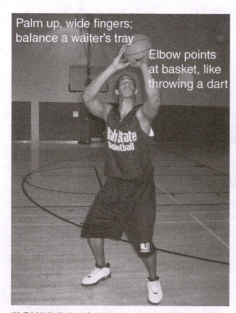

Palm up, wide fingers; balance a waiter's tray

Elbow points at basket, like throwing a dart

FIGURE 7.5 Setup

Gooseneck finish

Freeze hand at top

FIGURE 7.7 Finish Position On Shot For Left-Handed Players

Imagine basket looks like a big bin

Wrist points at rim

Thumb points at shoes

Gooseneck finish

(a) Side View

Gooseneck finish

Thumb points at shoes

Elbow above Eye

(b) Front View for Right-Handed Players

FIGURE 7.6 Set Shot—Finish Position

FUNDAMENTAL SHOOTING DRILLS

SKILL	CUE	WHY?	COMMON ERROR
Fundamentals *Right Hand and Left Hand*	Start close to the basket shooting five on the right side one-handed, then shooting five on the left side one-handed	Develop confidence and form at close distances	Not starting close to basket
Shooting Practice with No Defender	Step back from under the basket, shoot five right-handed and five left-handed	Develop consistency and accuracy	Only working one hand
	Steps back until you are at the free-throw line; shoot five with strong hand only	Repetition creates consistency	
Consecutive Free Throw	Consecutive free-throw shot with no dribble and a partner	Confidence	
	Find a rhythm		

continued

SKILL	CUE	WHY?	COMMON ERROR
Shooter Rebounds Free Throw	Shooter rebounds ball before it touches floor and passes back to partner for the shot; so shooter rebounds own shot and passes to partner on foul line	Shoot and follow shot	Allows ball to hit floor – bad pass to partner
	You want to shoot without a defender because you make more shots when you're open; when you're defended you tend to pass, not shoot	Shoot when open so you make more shots	Shoot with defense close – shot blocked
Body Position for the Shot	Line feet and hands with basket	Extremely important for successful shooting	

LAYUPS

SKILL	CUE	WHY?	COMMON ERROR
Right-Handed *The Approach*	Head up, eyes on top of square	The closer you are to the basket, the more likely you are to make it	Looks down at their feet
	Ball in outside hand with low approach	Player is ready to jump – quick to basket	Shooting ball more likely to be blocked if approach is high
Release of Layup	Bring ball close to chin; chin ball, step, and push off foot with opposite shooting hand	Harder to block	Ball is low and gets stolen
(Figure 7.8)	Extend arm, reach high (ball kisses backboard), release ball at peak of reach	A high, soft shot is more likely to go in	Short arm makes the ball hit bottom of rim
Left-Handed *Footwork*	Step left, right, hop (jump)	Same as right hand	Jumping off wrong foot
Shooting Action (Figure 7.9)	Left hand shoots ball		Using wrong hand on wrong side

Ball handling skills can be used to drive to the basket for layups.
Have two or four lines of students, depending on the number of baskets. Students should rebound their own ball.

FIGURE 7.8 Right-Handed Layup

FIGURE 7.9 Left-Handed Layup

TRIPLE THREAT

SKILL	CUE	WHY?	COMMON ERROR
Triple Threat *Ready Position* (Figure 7.10)	Triple threat	A position that allows player to execute all parts of the game	Not assuming the position
	Purpose: to fake out opponent with the option of shooting, passing, or dribbling	Good way to score or fake out defender	Put ball above the player's head
Hand Position	Shooting position on ball	Shoot if defender backs off	Hands not in shooting position; hands too close together
Holding Ball	Hold ball to side on hip	Keep it away from the defense	Ball held too high or too low
	Keep ball on hip—hold ball to side to pass, dribble, or step into shot	Always ready to quickly do all three	Not ready to pass, dribble, or shoot
	Elbows out	Gives player strength to hang on to ball	Elbows in – ball knocked out of hands

FREE THROW CUES

SKILL	CUE	WHY?	COMMON ERROR
Routine	Find the nail	Routine kept simple	Having a fancy routine that takes attention away from the shot
	Three dribbles	Research states greater percentage of shots are made with simpler routine	

continued

Triple threat—
shoot, pass,
or dribble

Keep ball
on hip

FIGURE 7.10 Ready Position—Triple Threat

Drills

1. Lay Up Crossover
   (right side, left side)
2. Lay Up Reverse Spin
   (right side, left side)
3. Lay Up Behind the Back—Plant
   (right side, left side)
4. Lay Up Behind the Back—Running
   (right side, left side)
5. Lay Up Between the Legs
   (right side, left side)
6. Lay Up Be Creative and Choose Your Own
   (right side, left side)
7. Lay Up Add a Defender to Each of These
   (right side, left side)

Make 10–25 baskets as a class or team and then switch to a new ball-handling skill.

SKILL	CUE	WHY?	COMMON ERROR
FREE THROW CUES, continued			
Routine, *continued*	Wrinkle wrist		
	Keep arm straight above eye	Same release point every time	Different release point – elbow bent
	Gooseneck finish	Gives shot a soft touch	Does not flick the wrist
Leg Action	Bend knees	Bending your knees helps get the ball to the hoop	Keeping legs straight through the shot
		No air balls	

Drill

Practice shooting free throws with the same routine from the nail.

SKILL	CUE	WHY?	COMMON ERROR
JUMP SHOT CUES			
Jump Shot	Jump above the defense, then shoot at the top of the jump	Reduces block shots	Not using the legs to jump high
(Figure 7.11)	Get high	Get above the defense	
	Keep body in a coil ready to jump	Develops consistency	Keeping body straight at take off

continued

SKILL	CUE	WHY?	COMMON ERROR
Jump Shot Technique Drill	Plant inside foot	Power	Not planting foot
	Keep body square to the basket	Accuracy	
	Keep hands open and ready to catch the ball	Better control of ball; ready to shoot	Having hands down and not being ready for the ball
	Take a quick jump shot	Faster release time; won't get the shot blocked	Hanging on to the ball too long and jumping late
	Keep the same shooting fundamental		

REBOUNDING

SKILL	CUE	WHY?	COMMON ERROR
Attacking Basket	Work on blocking out, then attacking the basket	To reduce chance of opponent getting ball	Attack basket first
One Player	Cover the weak side of basket (opposite side of shot)	70 percent of missed shots fall away from side shot on	
	Most shots go long off the back side		

continued

Same finish with hands as set shot

Shoot at top of jump

FIGURE 7.11 Jump Shot

Jump Shot Drill

1. Two balls, two lines
2. Player runs from the end line to the outside key
3. Ball is thrown when the player is set
4. Player plants inside foot
5. Player gets hands ready and catches the ball
6. Quick jump shot

REBOUNDING, continued

SKILL	CUE	WHY?	COMMON ERROR
One Player, *continued*	Rebounding involves contact		Shy away from contact
	Move from side to side and back up into a player; keep contact	Teaches to keep contact	Makes contact and stops moving
	Be active, aggressive, and alert	The more aggressive player gets rebound	
Two Players	Check the player without the ball: if he or she moves to the basket, take him; if not, attack the basket for the ball	To reduce chance of opponent getting ball	Constantly looks for a player instead of grabbing the ball

BLOCKING OUT

SKILL	CUE	WHY?	COMMON ERROR
Action of Body	Find with hands	Develop a routine to keep opponent from getting ball	Does not use hands and arms
Turn Back to Opponent (Figure 7.12)	Put buttocks under opponent's hip or create a stable wall between opponent and ball	Getting lower than the opponent allows you to move them	Not able to hold position
Hands (After Pivot)	Elbows out, palms wide; feel for opponent	Know which way opponent moves	Reach for ball too soon

THE PICK

SKILL	CUE	WHY?	COMMON ERROR
Hustle	Earn your position	To avoid fouling	
Stance	Stand wide	Develop larger target; more effective	Narrow stance
	Weight on balls of feet	Stronger base so you hold your ground	Weight on heels
Arms	Elbows bent and big	To keep defender away	Arms straight
Men	Hands clasped in front	To protect sensitive parts of your body	Hands at side
Women	Arms crossed against body	To protect sensitive parts of your body	Hands at side

continued

Palms wide

Elbows out

Feel for opponent

Put buttocks under opponent's hip

FIGURE 7.12 Blocking Out

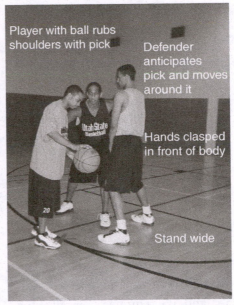

Player with ball rubs shoulders with pick

Defender anticipates pick and moves around it

Hands clasped in front of body

Stand wide

FIGURE 7.13 Player Coming Off the Pick

THE PICK, continued			
SKILL	**CUE**	**WHY?**	**COMMON ERROR**
Coming Off the Pick (Figure 7.13)	Rub shoulder to shoulder	To shake off the defender with the pick	Leave a gap for the defender to go through
	Right to right; left to left		
Pick and Roll	After you pick, you reverse pivot toward basket	Gives a player more opportunity to get open	Forward pivot and lose sight of ball and position
	Hand up high; ask for ball	Ready for a pass	Hands down at side
	Receive pass and go in for layup or shot	To score	
Defender Going Through a Pick	Anticipate taking a hook step around player	To beat the defender to a position	Wait until they are already screened

OFFENSIVE FOOTWORK			
SKILL	**CUE**	**WHY?**	**COMMON ERROR**
Technique	Ready and triple-threat position	To develop advanced skills	
	Two-step stop—emphasis on heel-toe (jump stop to be used for post people only)	Come to a controlled stop	Feet land at different times

continued

SKILL	CUE	WHY?	COMMON ERROR
Technique, *continued*	Change of speed and direction	Keep the defender guessing	
	Fake shot and drive—left and right (without the ball)	To take advantage of an aggressive player	Shoot with a defender in your face

Guards and Wings Drill

1. Catch and shoot
2. Catch and drive
3. Catch and reverse
4. Catch shot, fake, and drive
5. Catch, swing through, and drive
6. Catch, jab, and go (emphasis on heel-toe technique)

Posts Drill

1. Front pivot shot (both ways)
2. Front pivot crossover
3. Drop-step baseline/power shot
4. Drop-step middle, drop hook, jump hook, or power shot
5. Step-back shot
6. Post people can also use perimeter drills

SPACING

SKILL	CUE	WHY?	COMMON ERROR
Teach Spacing When Passing on Offense *Spacing Creates Open Areas*	The perfect passing distance is 15 feet	Put pressure on defense to react	Passing too long – over 15 feet or too short
	Anything beyond 15 feet is a potential stolen pass	Long pass gives defender time to react	Too long of passes – ball gets stolen
	Teach students to play off each other	To create efficient spacing	Player is not aware of teammate
	Use the free-throw line to gauge distance; use lines on the floor to gauge the distance of 15 feet	Better control of ball	Does not know what 15 foot passes are

DEFENSE

SKILL	CUE	WHY?	COMMON ERROR
Man-to-Man Defense	Force opponents from the middle to the sideline; force them to play on one side of the floor	So teammates will know where to help	Running without purpose
On-Ball Defense (Figure 7.14)	One hand mirrors the ball; the other hand is in the passing lane	Prepares defender to block pass or steal ball	Hands lack purpose

continued

The other hand in passing lane

One hand mirrors ball

FIGURE 7.14   On-Ball Defense

One eye on player, one eye on ball

Pistol formation

FIGURE 7.15   Off-Ball Defense—Two Passes Away

DEFENSE, continued			
SKILL	**CUE**	**WHY?**	**COMMON ERROR**
On-Ball Defense, *continued*	Keep palm up	Prevents fouls; able to steal ball easier with hand closer to the ground than the ball	Keeping palm down
Off-Ball Defense (Figure 7.15)	Deny defense is one hand always in the passing lane, palm up close to ball	Develops a team defense concept	Both arms at side
	One eye on your player, the other eye on the ball one pass away	Allows player to help teammate	Eyes wandering
	One eye on your player, one eye on the ball, two passes away in pistol formation	Allows player to help a teammate who got beat	Eyes wandering

The Key to a Zone

1. A key to zone defense: keep them out of the lanes and deny the passing lanes.

2. Run an odd front when playing zone defense: if thay have an offense set at a 1-2-2, you play a 2-3 zone defense; if they have one guard, you have two defenders on their point guard; if they run a 1-3-1 defense, you run a 2-3 offense (two-guard front and three low post).

3. The objective is to take the point guard out of the game; he or she runs the show.

8

Bowling

INTRODUCTION

"Strike!" The crashing of pins fills the air with excitement and anticipation of bowling the perfect game of 300. Families, friends, coworkers, and peers can all join in the fun of bowling. How does one learn to bowl? Many bowlers learn by trial and error. Teachers offering bowling in their curriculum could use the cues in this chapter to explain the skills of bowling, even when a bowling alley is not available. (How do you add bowling but not a bowling alley to your curriculum? See equipment tips.)

SKILLS LISTED WITH CUES

Teachers can use simple instructional cues in this chapter to teach the following bowling skills: grip, stance, arm action and leg action on approach and delivery, delivering a straight ball and hook ball, using the arrows for spares and placement of feet, and finding an eye target for spares, splits, and adjustments. Because scoring the game of bowling can be confusing and frustrating to the beginning bowler, we have added scoring cues.

We hope that these cues will help students be more comfortable with bowling and that they will seek real bowling opportunities. Friends can go bowling and experience success together.

Tips

Equipment Tips

Bowling in Gyms

1. Gym floor.
2. Rubber bowling balls can be ordered, or round soccer Nerf balls can be used.

3. Pins can be made from two-liter pop bottles or empty tennis ball cans, or white plastic pins can be ordered.

4. Scorecards can be obtained from a local bowling alley.

5. Long ropes can be used for lane dividers, or a gym wall can be one side of a lane.

6. Use colored tape for lane arrows and X's to mark the spots where the pins stand.

Bowling Alleys

1. Bowling shoes are used so that dirt and other abrasive particles are not brought onto the lanes.

2. Go to a pro shop to get fitted for a ball.

3. Bowling shoes are designed with soles that allow the bowler to slide.

Etiquette

1. Remain behind the foul line at all times.

2. Never walk in front of another bowler.

3. Give the bowler to your right the right-of-way.

4. Remain quiet while other students are bowling.

5. To avoid injuries, have students cradle the ball when walking with it.

TEACHING IDEAS

1. Have students practice technique and scoring in gym. Have two lines back to back at center court. Pair up in partners (bowl to wall, take turns with balls).

2. Same drill as in #1, except bowl to one pin only, progress to three pins, five pins, and all 10 pins. Work on technique. Scoring options: Set one pin up; if they knock one pin down, award one point. Set three pins up; if they knock three pins down, score one point. Set five pins up; knock five pins down to score one point. Team competition: four on a team; set three pins up; count number of pins knocked down by team, have a five-minute time limit. One student bowls; the other runs the ball down to partner; and the other two set up pins. Rotate after they finish their frame at bowling (Figure 8.1). Work on fitness and bowling skills.

3. Strength Activities: squeeze a tennis ball, do push-ups, and swing a bowling ball.

4. Bowling in a gym is fun. Tournaments can be set up.

5. The best place to bowl is at a bowling alley.

6. Take a trip to a local bowling alley (funded by parents).

GAME PLAY

Rules

1. Foot cannot touch the line.

2. If the ball goes into the gutter, it is a dead ball. No points are scored if the ball hits the gutter and bounces back on the lane and knocks the pins over.

Strategies

1. When a bowler first starts to bowl: Roll the ball and see how the ball is moving. Look to see if it goes straight down or slides to the sides of the lane. Then the bowler can start playing with arrows, dots, etc. Once you get the ball performing the way you want, you can move on.

2. Take a white locker-room towel or a towel used to wipe hands in bowling. Fold the towel and place it by foul line. Make sure ball goes over towel—this prevents the bowler from dropping the ball.

3. For other helpful bowling strategies, see Figure 8.7 at the end of the chapter.

Scoring

Teach scoring with 10 pins in gym. Get bowling cards from local bowling alleys. Create even teams of four. One: student bowls, one student runs the ball down to bowler, one sets up pins, and one keeps score; rotate students' roles after they finish their frame at bowling. These drills and scoring system add fitness to the lesson, and the students enjoy the competition. For additional scoring tips, see the cue sheet at the end of this chapter (pp. 117–118).

Handicapping

Handicapping is used in bowling to create parity between bowlers and stimulate greater competition. The following rules and formulas are used when computing a handicap.

    a. A minimum of nine games must be bowled before students can compute a handicap.

    b. Handicap = (200 − Average score) × 0.8

    c. Average score = total points ÷ number of games

    d. The handicap is added to each player's total score at the end of a game during tournament play, as in the following example:

Rotate counterclockwise after one bowler bowls a frame

Two set pins up

One runs ball back to bowler

One bowls

FIGURE 8.1 Gamelike-Fitness Drill

Joe bowls the following scores for nine games: 107, 113, 121, 115, 135, 101, 112, 115, 140

$$(107 + 113 + 121 + 115 + 135 + 101 \\ + 112 + 115 + 140) \div 9 = 117.7$$

Joe's average number of pins per game is 117.7. To compute his handicap

$$(200 - 117.7) \times 0.8 = 65.84$$

Joe bowls against Frank in the tournament. Joe gets a final score of 132, and Frank's score is 159. Joe's handicap is 66, and Frank's handicap is 63. The final scores are as follows:
Joe: 132 + 66 = 198
Frank: 159 + 63 = 222
Frank wins the tournament.

ASSESSMENT IDEAS

1. Have players bowl 6–10 games. Each game is worth five points, 30–50 total points.

2. Take players' best score of the 6–10 games:

    120 – 140 = 20 points
    100 – 120 = 15 points
    70 – 99 = 10 points
    50 – 69 = 5 points

3. Five bonus points can be awarded to the top three bowlers in the class or to players who score higher than 140 points.

FYI

For further information and special help, consult the following organizations and resources:

ORGANIZATION

American Bowling Congress (ABC) coordinator at local bowling center.
Young American Bowling Alliance (YABA)
5301 South 76th Street
Greendale, WI 53129–1192
Phone: 800-514-2695

PUBLICATIONS

Blassingame, C., & Cross, T. S. (1994). *Success in bowling through practical fundamentals*. Champaign, IL: Kendall/Hunt.
Harrison, M., & Maxey, R. (1987). *Bowling*. Glenview, IL: Scott, Foresman.

WEBSITE

www.amug.org/~a249/pinboy.html

SKILL	CUE	WHY?	COMMON ERROR
Conventional	Thumb on top, handshake position		
	Thumbhole at 12:00, finger holes at 6:00		
	Grip ball with second groove of two middle fingers		Squeezing with thumb
	Ring finger and middle finger		
Fingertip	Cradle opposite hand	Helps balance the ball	
	Grip ball with first groove of two middle fingers		Thumb in first Squeezing, with thumb
Stance (Figure 8.3)	Erect, knees relaxed		Knees locked, shoulders not square to pins
	Stand tall		
	Ball supported by non-delivery hand	Helps balance the ball	Ball hanging from thumb and fingers
	Ball carried on palm of right hand		
	Ball on right side at shirt-pocket level		Ball above or below shirt pocket
	Ball hides right shirt pocket (good place to start); find your comfort zone		
	Lower right shoulder	Helps put bowler on plane with ball	
	Tilt slightly right		
	Feet slightly apart		
	Three boards between feet		
	Left foot slightly advanced		
	One-half foot length ahead		
	Eyes focus on aiming spot	More ball control by looking at spot or arrows	Looking at pins
	Look at second arrow from right	Ball will hit the pocket and blow out the pins	

SKILL	CUE	WHY?	COMMON ERROR
Arm Action (Figure 8.2a)	First step and arms push away together		Stepping before pushing away
	Step away, push away		
	Extend ball arm straight forward to waist level		Pushing ball up or to the right too far
	Long reach but short step, like handing ball to friend		
	Use pendulum swing, like ball on end of string	Accuracy and speed	Applying too much force, changing direction of ball
	Ball falls downward and backward		
(Figure 8.2b)	Ball swings back, shoulder high	Power	Ball goes too high or arcs behind body
	Horizontal in front to horizontal in back		
	Extend left arm outward for balance	Balance	
	Keep ball swinging, arms relaxed		Trying to throw ball too fast
	Gravity and inertia provide main force		
	Release ball as arm passes vertical; ball should land 3–4 feet beyond foul line	Will drop ball and cause it to bounce	Dropping ball or setting it down on boards

continued

Ball swings back, shoulder high

Extend left arm out for balance

(a) Arm Action (Approach)

Wrist straight and firm

Thumb at 12:00 position

(b) Delivery

FIGURE 8.2 Straight Ball—Fourth Step

SKILL	CUE	WHY?	COMMON ERROR
Leg Action	First step very short	Short steps = provide control	First step too long
	Each step is a little longer and faster		
	Second step medium		
	Third step long		
(Figure 8.4)	Fourth step longest	Longer steps = power	
	First step and push away together		Feet finishing before arm swing
	Keep ball swinging and feet walking		
	Second and third steps with down and backswing		
	Fourth step with forward swing and delivery		
How to Avoid Ball Bouncing	Bend at knees	Smooth ball delivery and higher scores	Straight legs
	Release knee high		
	Lean forward at waist		Standing up
Coordination	Push, step, swing, roll		Taking two to three steps

First step and arms push away together

Step away, push away

FIGURE 8.3 Bowling Stance—First Step

Shoulders stay parallel to foul line

Follow through in straight, upward swing

Fourth step longest

FIGURE 8.4 Straight Ball—Fourth Step (Follow-Through)

SKILL	CUE	WHY?	COMMON ERROR
Straight Ball (Figure 8.2b)	Wrist straight and firm		Arm rotation right or left
	Thumb at 12:00		
	Release ball as arm passes vertical and starts upward		Dropping or setting ball on approach before foul line
	Trajectory like airplane, landing 3–4 feet beyond foul line		Holding ball too long causes you to loft ball
(Figure 8.4)	Follow through in straight upward swing		Stopping arm action on release of ball
	Arm points in direction you want ball to go		
	Shoulders stay square (parallel) to foul line		Body rotates clockwise on ball of foot
Hook Ball	Cup the palm		
	Thumb at 10:30		
	Hand stays behind ball		Hand on side of ball
	Thumb comes out first (ball spins counterclockwise)	Control of backspin	Spins like a top
	Deliver ball with finger only		
	On release, flip the fingers and shake hands	Spins the ball	
	Release with the V form		
	Follow through in straight upward swing	Power and accuracy	
Leg Action	Lower the body during third and fourth steps		Bouncy up-and-down action
	Bend knees to smoothly lower body at end of approach		
	Decelerate fourth step		Loss of balance from too quick a stop
	Left foot steps and slides to a stop		

continued

DELIVERY, continued			
SKILL	**CUE**	**WHY?**	**COMMON ERROR**
Leg Action, *continued*	Keep back foot in contact with floor		Poor timing results in picking up back foot and clockwise body rotation
	Don't spin out		
	Left knee and foot point toward pins		Body rotation
	Keep facing target		

USE OF ARROWS			
SKILL	**CUE**	**WHY?**	**COMMON ERROR**
Using Arrows	Easier to hit a target 15 feet away than one 60 feet away		Looking at pins
	Focus eyes and attention on aiming points (arrows)		
Three Basic Positions *Strike*	Second arrow from right (10 boards in from right edge)	More control of ball to hit correct pin	
Right-Side Spare	Third arrow from left (15 boards in from left)		
Left-Side Spare	Third arrow from right (15 boards in from right)		
Aim of Eyes (Strike)	Second arrow from right (10 boards in from right side)		Bowling down center of lane
Placement of Feet (Strike)	Left toe on second dot board from right		
	Third dot from right at foul line		
Use of Arrows (Spare)	Use one of three basic positions; move start position one board left to move ball contact three boards right; move feet one board right to move ball contact three boards left	More control of ball to hit correct pin	

continued

USE OF ARROWS, continued			
SKILL	**CUE**	**WHY?**	**COMMON ERROR**
Use of Arrows (Spare), *continued*	1-inch change in starting position equals 3-inch change in ball contact point		
Aim of Eyes (Spare)	Left-side spares (7 pin, etc.): same starting position as strike ball—aim over third arrow from right		Bowling down left side of lane
	Right-side spares (10 pin): third arrow from right		
Placement of Feet (Spare)	Left-side spares: same as strike starting position; make slight adjustments right or left to change ball contact point		
	Left toe on second dot from right		
	Right-side spares: left foot four boards in from far left edge of lane		
Splits	Use same arrows as spares; adjust starting position slightly right or left to change contact point of ball	More control of ball	
Adjustments Leaving Spares	Are you hitting your target on arrow? If no, hit target	More control of ball hitting correct pins	Not hitting target on arrow

SKILL	CUE		
Open Frame	Count pins you knock over		
	Pin count		
Spares (Figure 8.5)	Score 10, plus pin count from next ball		
	Maximum 20 points		
Strikes (Figure 8.5)	Score 10, plus pin count from next two balls		
	Maximum 30 points		
Tenth Frame	You can score bonus points in the tenth frame by bowling a spare or a strike		
Open	Score like a regular frame		
Strike	Bowl two more balls		
Spare (Figure 8.5)	Bowl one more ball; 10 points plus score from first ball; for example: 8 points plus spare = 18		
Strike Plus Spare	Bowl three balls; add 20 points to total score after ninth frame		
Three Strikes	Bowl three-ball maximum; add 30 points to total after ninth frame		
	To score a 300 game, you must get 3 strikes in the last frame		
	Note: When scoring, mark a spare with a slash (/) and a strike with an X.		

Enclosed are blank score sheets (see Figure 8.6). For helpful bowling strategies, see Figure 8.7.

How to Mark Score

Spare (/) Count 10 plus what you knock down on next ball.
Strike (X) Count 10 plus what you knock down on next two balls.
Immediately after each ball bowled, mark results in proper frame box.

1	2	3	4	5	6	7	8	9	10
7 /	X	6 2	X	X	0 /	3 3	X	X	X X 6
20	38	46	66	86	99	105	135	165	191

FIGURE 8.5 How to Mark Score

Bowling Game Score Sheet

Name	HDCP	1	2	3	4	5	6	7	8	9	10	Total
1												
Name	HDCP	1	2	3	4	5	6	7	8	9	10	Total
2												
Name	HDCP	1	2	3	4	5	6	7	8	9	10	Total
3												
Name	HDCP	1	2	3	4	5	6	7	8	9	10	Total
4												

Bowling Game Score Sheet

Name	HDCP	1	2	3	4	5	6	7	8	9	10	Total
1												
Name	HDCP	1	2	3	4	5	6	7	8	9	10	Total
2												
Name	HDCP	1	2	3	4	5	6	7	8	9	10	Total
3												
Name	HDCP	1	2	3	4	5	6	7	8	9	10	Total
4												

Bowling Game Score Sheet

Name	HDCP	1	2	3	4	5	6	7	8	9	10	Total
1												
Name	HDCP	1	2	3	4	5	6	7	8	9	10	Total
2												
Name	HDCP	1	2	3	4	5	6	7	8	9	10	Total
3												
Name	HDCP	1	2	3	4	5	6	7	8	9	10	Total
4												

FIGURE 8.6 Bowling Game Score Sheet

Helpful Bowling Strategies

- No ball lofting
- Bend at knees
- Thus, smooth ball delivery and higher scores

63-ft. Lane bed

Foul line

16-ft. Approach area

Left hand

Right hand

Four-Step Approach

FIGURE 8.7 Bowling Strategies

9

Cycling—Mountain Biking

INTRODUCTION

Mountain biking has become an increasingly popular activity since its beginning in the early 1980s (see Figure 9.1). It is a great aerobic workout and at times requires anaerobic power as well. It can challenge your technical riding ability, depending on where you ride, and it's also a lot of fun. However, to make it the most fun, bikers should take precautions to prevent personal injury, injury to other trail users (bikers, hikers, and equestrians), and damage to the bicycle or trail.

Mountain biking requires a variety of skills to cope with obstacles, such as rocks, logs, switchbacks, creeks, ditches, holes, tire ruts, animal crossings, washouts, shale, and the like. The cues in this chapter are intended to help the biker ride safely, learn correct biking techniques, have more fun, and experience success more quickly.

One of the most important safety features in mountain biking is a helmet. Wearing a helmet will minimize the risk of serious head injury. Following are two examples where a helmet saved a rider from serious injury and perhaps even death.

One accident involved a friend of mine, Curt, who was riding a trail on his way to work at a hospital. He slid off the trail, and as he landed, he hit his head, shoulder, and ribs. He separated his shoulder and broke a couple of ribs, and his helmet had a huge crack in it. Had he not been wearing his helmet, his skull would have had the crack in it. Curt happens to be a pediatric anesthesiologist, and he sees many children admitted to the hospital with head injuries because they weren't wearing a helmet when riding a bicycle.

The other instance in which a helmet saved the person from injury was perhaps even more serious than Curt's accident. A young woman was pulling her child in a carrier behind her bike. She was crossing a busy street during morning rush hour and was hit by a car. The wheel of the car ran over her head. Had she not been wearing a helmet, she would most likely have died. Fortunately, her child was unharmed, and the woman's helmet kept her alive. Some people may think helmets look silly or that it's too big a hassle to put one on, but a helmet can save your life.

SKILLS LISTED WITH CUES

Included in this chapter are cues for the following techniques: buying the correct size bike, body position (feet/seat/upper body position), body position while climbing/descending, bunny hop, braking (to stop fast, to corner in loose terrain, to ride in rough terrain), pedaling and shifting under a load, riding down curbs, riding up curbs, cleaning the bike, and rules of the trail.

TIPS

1. Statistics show that in most bicycle accidents, the rider, for some reason, simply falls off the bicycle. The remainder of bicycle accidents are collisions with automobiles, fixed objects, and other bicyclists.

2. Check the brakes and pads. There shouldn't be so much play in brakes that you have to completely squeeze them before they'll work. Check the quick releases, which hold the wheels on; make sure they are tight.

3. Check all cables (frayed cables could cause a serious accident).

4. Check the bottom bracket. Grab the crank arms, not the pedal, and move them from side to side. If there is any play, the bike needs adjustment. This procedure should be repeated with the wheels. Any play in these needs to be eliminated immediately.

5. Check the lock on front brake. Rock it forward and backward. If there is any play in the head set, get it adjusted immediately because a repair can become more expensive later.

6. Every bike, no matter how much it is ridden, needs a checkup every year. If something is wrong with your bike, get it checked more often.

7. Check wear and tear on the drivetrain, including the chain, crank set, and cassette.

Equipment Tips

1. The first and most important equipment needed is the *helmet* (Figure 9.2). Different brands fit different heads (see FYI). The biggest problem with wearing a helmet is getting the correct fit. Find one that is the correct size for your head, and then use the supplied pads to make it fit comfortably without any pressure spots. It should be about a finger's width up from your eyebrows and fit squarely on your head. Buckle up the helmet and tighten the strap so that moderate forces won't allow it to slide more than about an inch. You can test the fit by grasping the helmet and moving it from side to side and front to back. It should be tight enough so that you can feel the strap slightly pressing your throat as you swallow. Some helmets have a lower retention system that cradles the lower rear portion of your head. This is the best type of helmet for mountain biking because it creates a more secure fit and will keep the helmet from rattling on a rough trail or dislodging if you have a big crash.

2. Lightweight biking components are suggested.

3. Gears are a matter of personal preference and riding terrain. Consult a local bike dealer for area specifications.

4. Padded biking gloves are best because they provide safety and cushioning during a ride and during a wreck (the palms usually hit first in a wreck); they also provide better friction between hand and grip, especially when hands are moist. Gloves will also keep your hands from getting too sweaty, sore, blistered, or cold.

5. Take two water bottles or a water backpack. Precaution: Hydrate well even when you don't feel like drinking. Bikers are not aware of how much water they lose.

6. Snacks can include hard candies to keep mouth moist. Cut fruit and other foods into bite-size pieces and put in plastic sandwich bags. Carry "gorp" on long rides: raisins, peanuts, M&M's, and so on. Milky Way and 3 Musketeers bars are high in carbohydrates (two-thirds of their calories).

7. Take juice or fruit drinks in aluminum-foil packets.

8. Binoculars improve view and enjoyment of outdoors.

9. Take a lightweight jacket.

10. Padded biking shorts are optional. They not only increase comfort but also improve circulation.

11. On every ride, the following items should be carried in your backpack or bag: tire repair kit and chain breaker, spare tube, portable air pump, patch kit, tire levers, and a cell phone.

12. Toe clips (or clipless pedals) are optional but highly recommended. They will keep the foot in the proper position on the pedal and allow for higher force production (see the body position cue for riding uphill). Toe clips are helpful especially when climbing hills and doing bunny hops.

13. Sunglasses will be helpful when it is sunny, and they will also help keep bugs, rocks, and dirt from entering the eyes. If it isn't sunny, a pair of clear sport glasses will help protect your eyes from debris.

14. Suspension is a feature that adds a lot of comfort to your riding. Having front and/or rear suspension helps absorb the bumps and provides a smoother ride, making your arms and body less tired.

15. Bar ends on your handlebars allow for a change in hand position as a rest from the traditional grip, and they make it easier to lean forward when riding up hills.

Safety and Etiquette

1. *Ride on open trails only.* Respect trail and road closures, private property, and requirements for permits and authorizations.

FIGURE 9.1 Have Fun on the Trail

FIGURE 9.2 Equipment Tips

2. *Leave no trace.* Don't ride when ground will be marred, such as on certain soils after it has rained. Never ride off trail or skid tires. Never discard any object; pack out more than you pack in.

3. *Control your bicycle.* Inattention for even a second can cause disaster. Excessive speed frightens and injures people.

4. *Always yield.* Make your approach well known in advance to hikers, horseback riders, and other bikers. A friendly greeting is considerate and appreciated. Stop and walk when horses are present.

5. *Never spook animals.* Give them extra room and time to adjust to you; running livestock and disturbing wild animals are serious offenses. Leave ranch and farm gates as you find them, or as marked.

6. *Plan ahead.* Know your equipment, your ability, and the area in which you are riding, and prepare accordingly. Be self-sufficient. Keep your bike in good repair. Carry necessary supplies.

7. *No texting, using the internet, or talking on cell phones while riding.* It is just not worth the risk to divert your attention even for a moment.

TEACHING IDEAS

1. Start in a parking lot and have students become familiar with the bike and its gears. Practice shifting; get the feel of what makes pedaling easier and harder. Practice turns and braking; then move to wide, flat dirt roads and then to a wide dirt hill with a gradual incline.

2. Practice braking techniques: Apply the rear brake first. Practice on dirt roads so the transition to the trail is less drastic.

3. Practice smooth transitions while shifting and especially while shifting under a load, such as when ascending a hill.

4. Technical riding: Provide cones and have students ride between them. Create different trails. This drill will teach where the front and rear wheels are on the trail.

5. Practice braking downhill as well as riding downhill.

6. Technical skills can be practiced all the time.

7. Once students adapt to the feeling of the bike on such terrain, move them to a rougher terrain with sharper turns or hills, and other different situations.

8. Practice these basic skills on varying types of terrain.

ASSESSMENT IDEAS

Teach students technique, safety and etiquette of mountain biking.
Students work on fitness on their own time. If they ride:

Daily

  15–30 minutes = 1 point / day
  31–45 minutes = 2 points / day
  46–60 minutes = 3 points / day

Weekly

  If a student rides 4 days a week for 15 minutes per ride, he or she earns 4 points.
  If a student rides 5 days a week for 60 minutes per ride, he or she earns 15 points.

Monthly

> If a student rides 4 days a week for 15 minutes per ride for 4 weeks, he or she earns 16 points.
>
> If a student rides 5 days per week, for 60 minutes per ride for 4 weeks, he or she earns 60 points.

Awards

> Water bottle = 25 points
> School tee shirt = 50 points

FYI

For further information and special help, consult the following organizations and resources.

ORGANIZATIONS

> USA Cycling
> 210 USA Cycling Point, Suite 100
> Colorado Springs, CO 80919-2215
> Phone: (719) 434-4200
> Fax: (719) 434-4300
> Website: www.usacycling.org

USA Cycling provides the rules of the trail and a free 40-page book. This organization is especially useful to newcomers who want to get started right on a bike.

> Bicycling Magazine
> New Rider Network
> Box 6075
> Emmaus, PA 18098

Bicycling Magazine provides information regarding helmets.

> Bell Sports Customer Service
> 1924 County Road 3000 N.
> Rantoul, IL 61866
> Phone: (800) 456-Bell
> Fax: (217) 893-9154

1. Bell will replace your helmet (starting at $40.00) if you write and describe the crash.
2. With this information, Bell can do research on actual crashes.
3. A Bell helmet has many air vents, permitting hot air to be replaced by cool air while riding. This ventilation reduces the risk of heat exhaustion.
4. A Bell helmet goes down lower than most helmets, protecting the occipital lobe of the brain, which is responsible for sight and other critical functions.

PUBLICATION

Sloane, E. (1988). *The complete book of cycling.* New York: Simon & Schuster.

WEBSITE

www.bicyclesource.com

BIKE SIZE

SKILL	CUE	WHY?	COMMON ERROR
Legs (Figure 9.3)	Straddle bike		Bike is too big. When riding up a steep hill, the front wheel comes up. The bike will also corner poorly.
	Pull bike to groin; front tire should be 2 inches off ground	A bike that is too small can be uncomfortable because you bend over too far	
Seat Height	At bottom of stroke knees are slightly bent	More efficient–minimize knee injuries	Too high; knees are hyperextended, or hip rocking occurs

BODY POSITION

SKILL	CUE	WHY?	COMMON ERROR
Feet	Ball of foot over axle of pedal	More efficient	Foot too far forward, pedal under arch
Seat Position	Position seat so that when knees and legs are at 3:00 and 9:00, seat is slightly behind ball of back foot and pedal axle	Minimizes knee injuries	
Upper Body	About 60% of body weight should be over rear wheel and 40% over front wheel	The bicycle will be more stable and will handle better	Too much weight over seat

UPHILL—DOWNHILL—ROUGH TERRAIN RIDING

SKILL	CUE	WHY?	COMMON ERROR
Riding Uphill (Figure 9.4)	Balance weight 60–70% over back wheel and 30–40% over front wheel to keep traction in back	More efficient	Not enough weight on front wheel will cause front wheel to come off ground
	Shift weight to middle	To keep front wheel down so that you do not lose traction in loose dirt	
	Pedal in circles, using a pushing action on each pedal	Less injury	Using only a pushing action

continued

Pull bike to crotch

Straddle bike   Front tire should be 2 inches off the ground

FIGURE 9.3 Fitting Bike

Shift weight to middle

Pedal in circles using both a pulling and pushing action

FIGURE 9.4 Body Position for Riding Uphill

UPHILL—DOWNHILL—ROUGH TERRAIN RIDING, continued

SKILL	CUE	WHY?	COMMON ERROR
Riding Downhill (Figure 9.5)	Move back on seat and down	Won't crash	Sitting too far forward on seat increases the risk of flying over handlebars
	Hold seat with upper thigh	More stable	
	Watch ahead; pick a path	Won't fly over handlebars	
Riding in Rough Terrain (Figure 9.6)	Power through corner		
	Keep rear wheel behind you	More control of bike	
	Relax; go with the flow		Too stiff; cannot let knees, elbows, and body flow to absorb bumps
	Stutter-step; get dominant foot in front toe position		
	Be like a shock absorber	Makes for a smoother ride	
	Soak up the bumps with knees and arms like a sponge	More efficient	
	Let bike float over things		
	Straddle saddle; stand on pedals		
	Avoid hitting obstacles with pedal	Won't crash	

FIGURE 9.5 Body Position for Riding Downhill

FIGURE 9.6 Riding in Rough Terrain

PEDALING—BRAKING—SHIFTING			
SKILL	**CUE**	**WHY?**	**COMMON ERROR**
Pedaling	Maintain cadence at a spin of about 80 rpm	Don't get tired as fast	Usually too slow, which lugs your motor
	Ride smarter, not harder		
Braking *To Stop Fast*	Scoot buttocks back	Very efficient in stop	Sitting too far forward, weight shifts forward
	Pedal at 3:00 and 9:00 position		
	Squeeze both brakes	Less likely to skid out	Squeezing one brake
	Keep both wheels on the ground		Squeezing both brakes when body position is too far forward
To Corner in Loose Terrain	Control slide of rear wheel for faster sharp cornering		Failing to make corner, slowing down, losing control of front wheel, turning too hard
	Move weight to inside		
	Pedal through corner		

continued

SKILL	CUE	WHY?	COMMON ERROR
Shifting Under a Load	Anticipate shift	Easier to shift when gears are under-loaded	Waiting before cadence slows before shifting
	Shift front gear first; fine-tune with smaller gears		
	Give pedals a hard push for half-stroke; then ease off and shift		Not easing off pedal prior to shifting

CURBS/OBSTACLES

SKILL	CUE	WHY?	COMMON ERROR
Riding Down Curbs/ Obstacles	Make sure there is enough speed to maintain forward motion	To prevent falling	Going too slow
	Stand up on pedals with both knees slightly bent	Knees will absorb shock	Sitting
	Balance weight over pedals		Weight too far forward may cause you to go over the handlebars
	Keep handlebars straight		Turning handlebars
	Let front tire roll off curb; back wheel will follow		
	Slightly bend elbows and knees	To absorb shock	Keeping extremities stiff
Riding Up Curbs/ Obstacles	Go fast enough to maintain forward motion		Going too slow
	Stand up on pedals		Sitting
	When you're about 3–6 inches from curb, pull up on handlebars to lift front wheels onto curb		Either pulling up too soon or waiting too long

continued

SKILL	CUE	WHY?	COMMON ERROR
Riding Up Curbs/ Obstacles, *continued*	When front wheel has landed, lean forward slightly to get weight off back of bike		Keeping weight back
	Continue to pedal through	So back tire rides right up curb	Stopping pedaling and panicking
Bunny Hop	Use for jumping over large rocks and branches on the trail		
	Go fast enough to maintain forward motion		Going too slow
	Stand up on pedals, knees slightly bent		Sitting
	Before reaching object, bend knees and elbows so back is nearly parallel with ground		Keeping extremities stiff
	Pull up on your handlebars as if you were riding up a curb	To improve forward motion	Not pulling soon enough
	When the wheel is in the air, push the handlebars out forward and down as you leap, or spring with your legs (this will bring the back wheel up)		
	Your front wheel goes through an arc motion as you pull up on the handlebars and then push forward and down		No arc motion

CLEANING THE BIKE

SKILL	CUE	WHY?	COMMON ERROR
Drivetrain	Remove dirt and grease; use oil-based lubricants	Water causes rust and ruins gears	Using water
Cleaning Steps	Turn bike upside down, balance on handlebars to clean		Resting bike on kickstand
Spraying	Spray oil-based lubricant on chain in back cassette while turning pedals backward		Turning pedals forward
	Continue to spray for 3–5 seconds		Spraying longer than 5 seconds
	Have chain in middle of back gears when spraying		Chain on either end
	Wipe off excess oil	Attracts less dirt	
After Spraying	Grab a rag and place it around bottom part of chain in between the two cassettes		
	Continue pedaling backward; change rag to a clean spot; continue pedaling		Pedaling forward
	Change rag until no more dirt or grease comes off on rag		Using dirty rag
	Take rag and run it between gears, remove any excess dirt		
Finish Coat	After removing all dirt and grease, apply a finish coat of dry lube; both are dry-lube-based and will protect chain from collecting dirt while riding		Not applying a finish coat
Spray	Spray dry-lube-based finish coat for one to two complete backward pedal rotations		
Check Chain	Even though a chain looks clean, it usually is not		Not cleaning chain often enough

10

Cycling—Road Biking

INTRODUCTION

Accomplished riders become highly skilled through countless hours on a bike, for there is no substitute for time and mileage. Most have also had some coaching, both formal and informal, which has honed their skills at all levels, especially early in their experience. Additionally, cycling isn't fun if you're not in shape or if you lack technique.

Oftentimes cycling skills are learned by trial and error. For example, you purchase a new road bike, strap yourself in for the first time, and feel a little uncomfortable with the new situation. You take the bike for a spin and find yourself faced with narrow roads, sand, and gravel on roads, hills, different terrain, traffic, corners, new gears, trying to drink from a water bottle, and so on, not to mention rude drivers. Cyclists could benefit from cues to help them feel more successful with techniques and to master the different situations. Another helpful topic is following the rules of the road, which is key to increasing safety when riding a bicycle in motor vehicle traffic.

SKILLS LISTED WITH CUES

The ideas and cues contained in this chapter are concerned with methods of learning to cycle properly, including buying the correct size of bike, developing correct body position on the bike, pedaling for effective energy transfer (pedaling action, revolutions per minute, and riding in a straight line), cornering (braking, anticipating turns, sharp corners), climbing hills, and the transition from climbing to descending a hill.

TIPS

Practice bunny hops, corners, and turning.

Equipment Tips

1. Purchase road bikes that weigh less than 24 pounds (Figure 10.1).
2. The first road bike should cost about $700 to $900.
3. Clipless pedals are easier to twist out of (twist sideways) than strapped pedals and are more energy efficient.
4. It is harder to get feet out of strapped pedals. Coast to 5 mph; then practice pulling feet out of pedals. Caution: The rider will tip over sideways if the foot is not pulled out in time. Adjust the pedal tension as needed.
5. Purchase riding shoes that are comfortable and have stiff soles. The bottom of the foot is like a platform that gives you more energy transfer.
6. Have the bicycle set up (e.g. seat height) or fit by an experienced technician of a local bicycle shop.

Safety and Etiquette

See 'Rules of the Road' and 'Eating and Drinking While Riding' in the cue sheets.

TEACHING IDEAS

1. Perform dynamic warm-up exercises before riding and stretch after, especially the hamstrings, quadriceps, and calf muscles.
2. Start slowly and progress. As your miles increase, increase the number of days. Add another day—up to five or six days a week. Take Wednesday and Sunday off. Learn to listen to your body.
3. Each rider is different when he or she starts putting in mileage. Ride for fun! Ride more days rather than taking one long ride.
4. Technical skills: Practice bunny hopping in a parking lot. Use lines in a parking lot to hop the bike or jump with both wheels over an obstacle. Lift up on the handlebars, and jump or bunny hop over the line by raising both wheels. This drill helps the rider when faced with an unexpected pothole or other obstacle in the road. Also, learn to ride with a group; doing so improves technical skills and enhances intensity of the workouts.

FIGURE 10.1 Equipment Tips

5. When spinning, choose a cadence and keep it constant.

6. Spin to win! Try to keep the same pace on long rides. For example, if you are laboring and spinning too slowly, drop from 8th gear to 6th gear for a 10-speed bike, and 16th gear to 12th gear for a 20-speed bike. Spinning faster causes less pressure on the legs, but allows the rider to maintain the same speed.

7. Practice positioning as you ride down hills. Tuck down and stay behind the handle bar.

8. Practice sprinting: Come up out of the saddle into a standing position, with your hands hanging onto the brake hoods and handlebars. Rock the bike from side to side, keep the wheels in line, and stay in a straight line or hold your line. Avoid zigzagging the wheels.

9. Hydrate your body before and after each ride.

See "Assessment Ideas" section in Chapter 9.

FYI

For further information and special help, consult the following organizations and resources:

ORGANIZATIONS

USA Cycling
210 USA Cycling Point, Suite 100
Colorado Springs, CO 80919-2215
Phone: (719) 434-4200
Fax: (719) 434-4300
Website: www.usacycling.org

USA Cycling provides the rules of the trail and a free 40-page book. This organization is especially useful to newcomers who want to get started right on a bike.

Bicycling Magazine
New Rider Network
Box 6075
Emmaus, PA 18098

WEBSITE

www.bicyclesource.com

BIKE SIZE

SKILL	CUE	WHY?	COMMON ERROR
Selecting a Bike	Proper bike size is critical when purchasing a bike	Safer; more comfortable, bikes are expensive to replace if you get the wrong size	
	Stand straddling bike with 1–2 inches of groin clearance	Safer to get on and off bike	No clearance or too high: 3–4 inches off ground
	Get fitted by qualified bike shop	Ensures proper fit	

BODY POSITION

SKILL	CUE	WHY?	COMMON ERROR
Become More Aerodynamic (Figure 10.2)	Decrease frontal area; keep back flat	Faster, more efficient on bike	Body is big, like a sail
	Wear tight clothing	Reduces drag	Wearing baggy clothing
	It takes practice to become comfortable; work 5–10 minutes at a time in biking position		Not holding position
	Hands should hold bar lightly	Reduces arm fatigue and allows the rider to steer smoothly	White knuckles, gripping too tight
	Bend at waist		Back vertical
	Eyes glance ahead	Allows the rider to better anticipate obstacles and turns	People do not look ahead, and they run into things or the head stays down

PEDALING FOR EFFECTIVE ENERGY TRANSFER

SKILL	CUE	WHY?	COMMON ERROR
Pedaling Action	Spin; pedal in circles, not squares	More efficient; less energy used	Mashing and stomping pedals
	Downstroke motion, like scraping mud off your shoes		Pushing hard at bottom of stroke will not do any good, just attempts to lengthen crank arm
			Dead time at 6:00 or bottom of pedal stroke
Revolutions per Minute (rpm)	80 rpm: adults 90–120 rpm: racers	Reduces the loads placed on the knees and minimizes injury	Pedaling too slow; lugging motor
Riding in a Straight Line	Keep eyes on road 10–15 yards ahead	Prevent crashing	Not looking ahead causes one leg to fight the other and creates a rocking or bouncing motion that depletes energy
			Keeping eyes focused on front wheel
	Ride straight		Wobbling

SKILL	CUE	WHY?	COMMON ERROR
Braking	Assess the speed and do most braking entering corner or curve	Prevents crashing	Applying brakes while leaning through a corner or curve will cause handling problems
Anticipating Turn	Start wide and head for inner tip or point of turn	More efficient and faster	Not turning until well into the corner, which slows you down and can be dangerous
	Visualize the line or path you will travel through the curve and follow it		Following a jerky, changing path
	Lean bike and carve your line through the turn		
(Figure 10.3)	Keep outside pedal down; stand on it to lower center of gravity	Prevent crashing	Leaning too far into curve; hitting ground with inside pedal; crashing
Sharp Corner	Raise inside pedal to top of pedal stroke	Prevents pedal from making contact with ground and crashing	Making sparks while cornering with pedal
			Dragging pedal

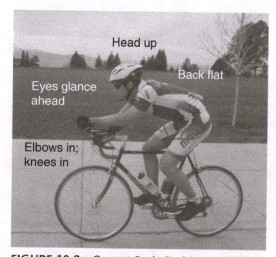

FIGURE 10.2   Correct Body Position on Bike

FIGURE 10.3   Cornering

SKILL	CUE	WHY?	COMMON ERROR
Breathing	Breathe from stomach, like blowing into an instrument	Exchange of O_2 better helps cardiac functions	Breathing in chest; short, gasping breaths
Sitting Climb	Push butt into saddle and push back on handlebars (squeeze saddle with butt like a leg press)		
	Scoot back on seat; sit hunkered down; helps to use your glutes more	Distributes power from quadriceps to gluteal region	Sitting on seat too hard and not standing on pedal
	Choose easy gear	Easier to go up hills	Gear too tight
	Try to relax arms	More efficient	Wasting energy with the upper body
	60 rpm or greater; spin if you can, uphill	Minimizes joint loads	Low rpm makes poor recovery
	Get into *your* rhythm		Trying to match someone else's pace
Standing Climb (Figure 10.4)	Stand, lean forward, pull up and down on bars, and rock the bike		
	Make sure your line stays straight		
Transition from Climbing to Descending	Accelerate near top of hill, pick up speed fast	Faster	Trying to recover at top of hill
			Decelerating at crest of hill
	Recovery occurs after descending speed is reached		

FIGURE 10.4   Standing Climb

FIGURE 10.5   Body Position for Descending

DESCENDING			
SKILL	**CUE**	**WHY?**	**COMMON ERROR**
Position for Fast, Steep Descent	When you cannot pedal fast enough, you spin out	Faster	
Grip	Hands on end of handlebars		Grip the handlebars near the stem, hands right next to each other
Body Position (Figure 10.5)	Back flat, feet at 3:00 and 9:00 position	More streamlined, less air current, faster	Chest up
	Distribute the weight evenly between the pedals, bars, and seat	The bike will be more stable	Weight on arms, knees out

RULES OF THE ROAD			
SKILL	**CUE**	**WHY?**	**COMMON ERROR**
Ride on the Right	Always ride on right; go with flow of traffic	Predictable, legal	Riding in middle of road; going against traffic
	Be predictable; maintain a straight line; change direction without swerving	Prevents crashing	Swerving back and forth

continued

SKILL	CUE	WHY?	COMMON ERROR
Hand Signals	Use hand signal when turning, same as motorist; when making a right turn, use your right arm to point	Predictable	Not using hand signal when turning
Stay Alert	Obey all traffic laws, pay attention	Prevents crashing	Breaking traffic rules, wearing headphones
	Use your eyes and ears as warning devices alerting you to potential hazards	Safer	
	Assert yourself	Safer	Letting vehicles creep by, forcing biker into parked cars or curb
	Ride defensively	Safer	
	Expect a car to pull out from side street or turn left in front of you; if you anticipate the worst, it will rarely happen	Safer	Daydreaming
What to Wear	Be visible, wear bright colors, and put reflectors and reflective tape on your bicycle	Cyclists are more visible to vehicles which can cut down on accidents	Wearing light colors in daytime
	Wear light colors at night		Wearing dark clothing at night
	Put reflective tape on your bicycle		Not putting reflective tape on bicycles
Warning Signal from Cyclist	Shout or use bell, it's the quickest way to let motorists know you're putting them in danger or to warn inattentive pedestrians you are approaching	Alerts pedestrains	Not giving a warning signal
Feet Strapped or Connected to Pedal	Loosen strap, twist foot out of pedal		Leaving foot strapped or not twisting foot out of pedal

SKILL	CUE	WHY?	COMMON ERROR
Rule of Thumb	Drink before you're thirsty and eat before you're hungry	To get hydrated or else you won't get fuel to muscles	Not drinking or eating before ride; eating too much
Hot, Humid Weather	Take a big swig from water bottle every 15 minutes	Constant hydration	Not drinking during ride
Most Popular Food	Banana	A banana provides 105 calories of carbohydrates and replaces potassium, an important element lost via sweating	
Storing Food	Best place: rear pocket of jersey		
5–20 Miles; Less than 90 Minutes	Eat a pre-ride meal with lots of carbohydrates	Provides quick energy	Eating too much and not waiting 30 minutes for food to digest
15–50 Miles; 45 Minutes–3 Hours *Avoid Bonking*	Do not allow glycogen stores to become depleted; this happens when ride is 2 hours or longer; drink sports drinks	To avoid fatigue	Not eating premeals or snacks
Avoid Dehydration	Carry a sports drink, one bottle	Loss of body fluids results in fatigue	Not drinking water or sports drinks
	Carry water, one or more bottles depending on distance		
50–100 Miles; Over 4 Hours	Eat lots of carbohydrate-rich foods in days preceding the event		Failing on long rides due to poor eating habits
Premeal	Eat a big meal a couple of hours before the big ride		Not eating a premeal
Snack During Ride	Bananas, sandwiches with jam, honey, apple butter, and so on		
	Nibble through ride		Eating too much at once
Water During Ride	Four water bottles		Three or fewer water bottles

11

Field Hockey

INTRODUCTION

Field hockey is one of the oldest organized team sports played in the United States. It is a team game played on artificial turf or grass in which players use a curved stick to drive a hard ball into the opposing team's goal. The tactics are similar to soccer, a more commonly played game in the United States.

Modern field hockey evolved in England in the early nineteenth century. Originally the game was played exclusively by men. Today the game is played by both men and women on six continents. More than 70 countries are members of the International Hockey Federation. In the United States and Canada, field hockey is primarily considered a women's sport.

Field hockey was introduced in the United States in 1901 by Constance Applebee, an English field hockey player. Field hockey became an Olympic event for men in 1928, and an Olympic event for women in 1980.

SKILLS LISTED WITH CUES

We provide cues for the following skills: grip, dribbling (moving with the ball), push pass, receiving, hitting and shooting, aerials (flick throw, low lift), and defense skills—dodging, marking, covering, tackling, and goaltending.

TIPS

Equipment Tips

1. Shin guards, mouth guards, and goggles are mandatory at the high-school level.

2. Sticks are composed of either wood or composite, depending on whether the players' level is beginner or advanced.

3. Height, weight, and toe style of the stick are dependent on the height of the athlete and the position played.

Safety

1. If available, students should wear shin guards or use a modified, softer field hockey ball.

2. Close supervision is essential to the success of a class.

3. The "no-contact" rules and use of the specified game ball are important to playing a safe game.

Etiquette

1. No body-to-body contact.

2. No stick-to-body contact.

TEACHING IDEAS

1. Running with the ball (dribbling) is the first skill that should be taught. It is best taught with competitive relays using obstacles and with small games where everyone has a ball and moves the ball constantly.

2. Next, passing and receiving should be taught together. You cannot pass to a teammate unless the teammate is ready to receive.

3. Hitting should be taught only after the preceding skills have been mastered to some degree. In early games, hitting should not be allowed.

4. Field hockey can be played in physical education class and should be played in small groups (4–7 players on each side).

5. A full game consists of two 30-minute halves with 11 players on each side, including a goalie and various combinations of players depending on their skills. The most traditional lineup for field hockey would be five forward, three midfield, two defense, and one goalkeeper. Many other player lineups are used (4, 3, 2, 1, 1; 3, 3, 3, 1, 1; etc.). At the introductory level of play, smaller games should be incorporated into the teaching session. Small games open up the space, provide more opportunity to play the ball, and make tactics easier to master and see.

6. Training sessions should follow this format:
    *   Light jog
    *   Stretching
    *   Running skills for better movement
    *   Ball-control skills
    *   Technical skills (passing combos, two-against-one concepts, etc.)
    *   Games, cool-down, stretching

Mini-Games

1. 4 Goal: Make two fields by splitting the field down the middle from the 25-yard line to the end line. Each team has two goals that they can score on. The distance between the two goals should be far enough to encourage

changing direction. For a penalty, have the players self-pass and try to transfer the ball to the other side.

2. King of the Circle: Each student has a ball in the center circle of the field. The objective is to be the last player in the circle with a ball. Players try to knock other player's balls out of the circle. Players who are out stand along the parameter of the circle and try to jab or tackle the remaining player's balls.

GAME PLAY

Rules

1. Only use the flat side of the stick.
2. The ball cannot touch any part of the body.
3. A goal only counts if it's scored from within the scoring circle.
4. When in the vicinity of others, the swing and follow-through of a hit must be below waist height.
5. No stick-to-stick contact is allowed (hacking).

Strategies

1. Play the ball, not the opponent. All players must be free to move, as in soccer and basketball.
2. Keep it simple and have fun!
3. Have extra game balls ready to put into play.

Indoor Field Hockey Rules

(Played on basketball court)

1. The same five basic rules as outdoor field hockey apply.
2. Use the basketball key area for the crease area.
3. Honor the crease. Shots at the goal must be taken outside of designated crease area. No players are allowed in designated crease area at any time.

FIGURE 11.1 Field Hockey Field

4. Shoot to score. Scoring is possible only when the attacking team has the ball over the center line.

5. Penalty shots are taken behind the center line.

6. No body or excessive stick-to-stick contact is allowed.

7. If six players are on each team, then only four offensive players are allowed on the offensive side at a time. If there are more than four offensive players on the offensive side at once, an offside foul occurs.

Scoring

Players earn one point when the ball crosses the goal in the cage; the ball has to be inside the circle for the point to count.

ASSESSMENT IDEAS

1. Drag Counter: Place two cones a stick length apart, and use one ball. For 30 seconds, the players move the ball from cone to cone, using the fore and reverse stick. Another student counts the amount of controlled taps for the 30 seconds.

2. Cone Passing: Partners are separated across from one another with two cones, making a passing lane between them. Players must hit the ball through the cones to score a point. Each student gets ten opportunities and counts their own scores.

3. Goal Corner Shooting: Markers are placed in each of the four goal corners, approximately one foot from the goal post. Players start at the stroke mark and try to shoot the ball between the marker and goal post. Each player gets 12 chances and three balls for each corner.

4. Back and Forth: Two cones are set about two yards apart. Players dribble the ball back and forth between the two cones without taking their hands off the stick.

5. Crossing Test: Three balls are placed at each cone two yards apart. The player starts with a ball from the left cone, runs to the second cone, and hits the ball on the move toward the target. Then, when the ball has crossed the line, the player can start with the next ball, but this time he or she has to run with the ball to the left cone and hit it at the target. Six cones are placed on the side lines at different lengths apart: 2 yards, 3 yards, 4 yards, 3 yards, and 2 yards. The players must hit the ball between the cones from the opposite side corner hash. A player scores 3 points by hitting the ball between 2 yards, 2 points between 3 yards, and 1 point between 4 yards.

FYI

For further information and special help, consult the following organizations and resources.

ORGANIZATIONS

USA Field Hockey
Strategic Partnerships
120 Somers Court South
Moorestown, NJ 08057
Website: www.usafieldhockey.com

STX Inc.
1500 Bush Street
Baltimore, MA 21230
Phone: (410) 837-2022
Toll Free: 800-368-2250
Website: www.stx.com

For additional games, visit www.sportplan.com

GRIP

SKILL	CUE	WHY?	COMMON ERROR
Position	Lay stick parallel to feet	Ball control	Hands together
	Point to the right		Pointing to left
	Pick up with left hand		Using right hand
	Right hand halfway down stick	Stick control	Left hand halfway down stick
	Hold stick firmly but comfortably	Can be rotated without losing control	Holding stick too loosely
Left Hand	Left hand is the holding hand/turns stick	Top hand	
Right Hand	Right hand is the pulling and pushing hand	Bottom hand	Turing stick with the hand

DRIBBLING

SKILL	CUE	WHY?	COMMON ERROR
Moving with the Ball (Figure 11.2)	Ball "glued" to stick	Able to control ball	Ball far in front of stick
	Use small taps for grass play	Ball can get caught in the grass	Hitting, not tapping
	Keep ball outside and ahead of right foot for grass play	Avoid kicking the ball	Right foot behind ball
	Keep ball on the right side at 3:00 position vision for turf play	Must have full field	Wasting dribbles
Strategy	To run with ball		
Indian Dribble	Left hand tight, right hand loose	Easier to rotate the stick	Both hands tight
	Continuously move the ball from forestick to reverse	Harder for the defense to tackle	Keeping the ball on one side
	Eyes up	See entire field and open teammates	Eyes down
	Keep ball close to stick	Ball control	Ball too far in front of body

Use small taps for grass play

Ball "glued" to stick

Keep ball outside and ahead of right foot

FIGURE 11.2 The Dribble

Left wrist pulls stick back

Firm right hand

Push ball with stick
Stick on ball

FIGURE 11.3 The Push Pass

Hands together on top of stick

Hip-to-hip swing like a pendulum

Contact ball opposite left foot

FIGURE 11.4 Hitting

PASSING AND RECEIVING

SKILL	CUE	WHY?	COMMON ERROR
Push Pass (Figure 11.3)	Push ball with stick		Wide backswing
	Stick on ball; no contact noise	Prevents defense from stripping the ball	Stick off ball, tapping or hitting ball
	Firm right hand	Ball control	Relaxed right hand
	Left wrist pulls stick back		Stiff left wrist
	Short, accurate passing	Not a powerful hit	
	Push ball off the left foot	More power and accuracy	Pushing off right foot is advanced move
Strategy	No time to hit or shoot		
Receiving	Angle stick slightly forward to deflect ball down	To trap ball	Stick flat
	Stop ball on stick	Gain control	Bouncing off stick

HITTING AND SHOOTING

SKILL	CUE	WHY?	COMMON ERROR
Hitting (Figure 11.4) *Grip*	Slide right hand up stick	Better ball speed	Forgetting to slide hand up
	Hands together on top	Produces power	Hands too far apart
	Contact ball opposite left foot		Contacting ball off same foot
Hit	Left shoulder toward target	Helps direct the ball	Directly facing target
	Head down over ball in line with left foot	Improves accuracy	Ball too far away
	Hands together	More power	Hands apart

continued

SKILL	CUE	WHY?	COMMON ERROR
Hitting, *Hit, continued*	Knees bent shoulder width apart	Helps balance	Feet too close together and standing tall
	Weight shift from back to front	Adds more power from the legs	Not shifting weight
	Connect ball with flat face of stick	Keeps the ball straight and on the ground	Topping or lifting the ball
	Follow through in the direction you want the ball to go	Directs the ball	No follow-through, stopping the stick
Slap Hit	Hands apart	Assists in using a short backswing	Hands together at top of stick
	Ball fairly close to body	Accuracy and control	Ball out too far
	Short backswing	Tight space hit	Big backswing
	Form similar to push pass		
Shooting	Variations	To beat defender	
	Follow shot	To get rebound	
	Must be in circle	Rule	
	Shots must be on ground	To control danger	

SKILL	CUE	WHY?	COMMON ERROR
Flick	Body low with right shoulder dropped	More power to lift	Body upright
	Ball to the side of the right foot	Allows for forward step	Ball in front of foot
	Step forward with left foot past the ball	Transfers weight	Staying even with ball
	Stick face under ball	Leverage	Stick flat against ball
	Throw ball with follow-through	Dictates height – high or low	Ball stays on the ground
Low Flick	Light throw with low follow-through	Pop over defender's stick	
High Flick	Hard throw with high follow-through	Drops ball into space over defenders	
Strategy	Used for shooting at close range, penalty strokes, lifting ball to cover a big distance		
	Used for lifting ball over a defender's stick		

SKILL	CUE	WHY?	COMMON ERROR
Footwork	Balance	To be able to change directions quickly	Feet in close or too far apart
	Drop	Keeps ball in front and body balanced	Feet planted
	Approach attacker with control and balance	Force opponent in the direction you want them to go	Closing space too early
	Break down steps	Prevents running past opponent	Running past opponent, stride too long
	Stick defense at 10:00–2:00 position	Protects lead foot	Stick too flat towards feet
Pressuring Defender *Marking*	Stay between your goal and offensive player	To keep attacker from scoring	Not anticipating soon enough or focusing on defenders
	"Face to face" with your opponent at all times	Know where they are	Tumbling with backside to opponent, losing concentration
Covering *Supporting Defender* *Covering Defender*	Either mark dangerous space or take next dangerous attacker	Take away attacker's options	Leaving opponents open
	Make decisions on dangerous space; decide to make attacks or cover space	Limits options and opens up interception opportunities	Waiting until they are too close to begin covering
Block Tackle	Low body position	Helps balance	Standing upright
	Hands and arms away from body; body low; slide stick in, tackle at 5:00 position	Prevents ball from hitting feet	Arms too close to body, hacking to get ball
	Block ball hand; move away with ball		Staying stationary after obtaining the ball
Jab Tackle	Extend body with side on position	Extends reach	Stepping opposite side of stick
	Poke ball with stick	Loosens the ball from the opponent's stick	Hitting opponent's stick
Goaltending	Stop ball by making a V with ankles—keep knees together	Easier transition to attack	Feet and knees apart
	Cover your angles	Limits the opponents view of the goal	Standing flat against the goal line
	Move by sliding feet across goal mouth	Ball will not go underneath feet	Picking up feet

continued

DEFENSE, continued			
SKILL	**CUE**	**WHY?**	**COMMON ERROR**
Goaltending, *continued*	Always clear ball to sides	Front of cage is dangerous	Clearing ball in front of cage
	Stop ball before clearing	Better control of direction	Hitting ball before clearing
	Use sides or tip of boot when clearing	Control and power	Not focusing on ball

OFFENSE			
SKILL	**CUE**	**WHY?**	**COMMON ERROR**
Dodges	Get out of the way!		Backing into the defender
	Execute dodge outside of defense playing distance	Limits chance of intercepting the ball	Anticipating too late or too early
	Execute dodge right off dribble	Must be able to beat defender with the ball	Stalling
	Accelerate by defender; cut in behind defender		Constant speed and direction
			Head-on collision
Techniques	1. Pull to the right, accelerate	Boxes out the defender	Backing into the defender
	2. Pull to the left, accelerate		Backing into the defender
	3. Spin and accelerate; must move away from defender		Backing into the defender
Triangle Passing	Teammates give flat, through or back pass	Assist ball carrier	Leaving ball carrier on their own
	Flat – even with ball carrier		Too far from the ball carrier that the pass can be intercepted
	Through – straight ahead of ball carrier		
	Back – behind ball carrier		

12

Fitness Equipment Workout

INTRODUCTION

The list of positive health benefits derived from physical fitness is astounding. Physical fitness reduces the risk for type 2 diabetes (Hu et al., 2003), decreases the risk of certain cancers (Lee, 2003), reduces the risk of heart disease (Lee et al., 2001), decreases the risk of osteoporosis (Nelson et al., 1994), and is effective in treating and preventing depression (Dunn et al., 2005), among other positive benefits. Even with all this documentation, only a small percentage of the U.S. population is physically fit enough to enjoy these benefits. Imagine how much healthier we could be if physical fitness was a priority!

The components of health-related physical fitness include cardiorespiratory endurance, body composition, and musculoskeletal fitness, which include flexibility, muscular strength, and muscular endurance (Nieman, 2007). Based on health benefits, cardiorespiratory endurance is arguably the most important component. It is defined as the ability of the body (the circulatory and respiratory systems as well as the muscles) to utilize oxygen to fuel physical activity. Body composition is the amount of fat and lean tissue in the body. Flexibility is defined as the capacity of the joints to move through their full range of motion. Muscular strength is the amount of force a muscle exerts, and muscular endurance is the ability of a muscle to withstand fatigue (Nieman, 2007).

The purpose of this chapter is to review available workout equipment (besides free weights, which are covered in Chapter 22) that will enhance the components of health-related physical fitness. The most important thing to remember when trying to improve physical fitness is for the individual to choose something that he or she can enjoy and incorporate into their lifestyle. While this chapter focuses on workout equipment, numerous chapters in this book focus on fitness-enhancing activities from biking (Chapters 9 and 10) to yoga and pilates (Chapter 29).

To be successful and continue being active for a lifetime, you must choose something you enjoy—the choices are seemingly endless. Another important aspect of improving fitness is to start out slowly and tailor the activity to suit your fitness level. If you have not been active at all, you may need to start out slowly. The body is an incredible machine; but unlike mechanical machines, it improves when you "run" it. A car engine wears out faster the more it is used, but our bodies adapt to the stress of physical activity and will work better and be more healthy as we become more active.

SKILLS LISTED WITH CUES

Cues are provided for the following exercises using fitness equipment: cable weights for upper body (bench press), cable weights for a variety of exercises (Cable Cross), treadmill walking or running, upright cycling, recumbent cycling, Incline Trainer walking, and elliptical training. There are too many ways to use the Cable Cross to outline as part of this chapter, so the cues will not be specific to certain exercises.

TIPS

Equipment Tips

1. Have disinfected wipes available for students.
2. Make sure you purchase commercial grade equipment and not home grade equipment.
3. Make sure you have appropriate lighting in the facility.
4. Make sure you have appropriate air circulation in the facility.

Safety

1. Arrange equipment so that it is spaced far enough apart and placed in a safe place (not by windows to avoid injuries if someone fell off the machine while it was still moving).
2. Be sure there is adequate range of motion for all exercises.
3. Keep other students away from exercise equipment that is in use. There are many moving parts that may present a hazard to unsupervised students.
4. The facilities should provide warning signs related to exercise and heart rates.
5. The facilities should provide appropriate air circulation.

Etiquette

1. Clean off machines with a disinfected wipe after each use.
2. Give adequate space and time for individuals to finish lifting weights and using workout equipment.
3. Be respectful to others: Avoid being loud, obnoxious, or boisterous, and don't ridicule others while they are working on machines.
4. Avoid teaching others how to work out unless you are the teacher or personal trainer.

TEACHING IDEAS

Teaching Progressions For Strength Development

1. Warm up before lifting.
2. Each muscle group should be exercised one to three times per week.

3. Start out with low resistance and high repetitions (10–12); if strength increases are desired, increase the resistance and decrease the repetitions gradually.

4. Perform the lift with a slow, controlled movement, breathing in as the targeted muscle group lengthens and breathing out as the muscle group shortens.

5. The greater the extent of muscle fatigue during resistance training, the greater the resulting increases in strength.

6. Strength-training machines should be adjusted to fit the student. Pivot points on machines should correspond with the articulating joint. Cable machines should be positioned so the direction of force is opposite the desired travel direction. Seats can often be adjusted up and down to put the student in the proper exercise position relative to the articulation of the machine.

Teaching Progressions For Cardiovascular Development

1. Warm up slowly for three to five minutes.

2. Cardiorespiratory training should take place three to four times per week.

3. Exercise at a level that is somewhat difficult. A proper level will allow the students to speak a full sentence without inhaling between words.

4. Exercise equipment has adjustments to make the apparatus fit a broad range of students. The seat should be adjusted up or down so that the knee is slightly bent (15 degrees of flexion) when the pedal is in the bottom position. The seat should be adjusted fore and aft so that the knee is directly over the pedal spindle when the pedals are horizontal.

ASSESSMENT IDEAS

Strength Development

1. For motivational purposes, have students chart their progress.

2. Provide resistance-training pictures to help the students learn the lifts, and provide anatomical charts to help the students learn the muscle groups used in different lifts.

3. Monitor heart rate to demonstrate to the students the physiological changes that occur as they increase their cardiorespiratory fitness.

(See Chapter 22 for strength-training cues that include progression, safety, and other concepts.)

Cardiorespiratory Equipment

The overload principle applies to cardiorespiratory equipment, just as it does with strength-training equipment. Overload is accomplished on a treadmill by increasing the speed and/or grade and by increasing the resistance and the revolutions per minute (rpm) on cycle and elliptical trainers.

Stations

1. Have students work at each station starting for one to two minutes. They can rotate through 10 machines or non-machine exercises (for example, sit-ups and pushups on mats). Rotate through the stations once.

2. Increase the time by 10–30 seconds, and increase their speed or weights at each station by individual fitness levels.

3. Advance to complete the stations two to three times.

For further information, consult the following organization.

ORGANIZATION

National Strength & Conditioning Association
1885 Bob Johnson Drive
Colorado Springs, CO 80906
Phone: (800) 815-6826 or (719) 632-6722
Fax: (719) 632-6367
Email: nsca@nsca-lift.org
Website: www.nsca-lift.org

PUBLICATIONS

Dunn, A. L., Trivedi, M. H., Kampert, J. B., Clark, C. G., & Chambliss, H. O. (2005). Exercise treatment for depression: Efficacy and dose response. *American Journal of Preventive Medicine, 28*, 1–8.

Hu, F. B., Li, T. Y., Colditz, G. A., Willett, W. C., & Manson, J. E. (2003). Television watching and other sedentary behaviors in relation to risk of obesity and type 2 diabetes mellitus in women. *Journal of the American Medical Association, 289*, 1785–1791.

Lee, I.-M. (2003). Physical activity and cancer prevention: Data from epidemiologic studies. *Medicine & Science in Sports & Exercise, 35*, 1823–1827.

Lee, I.-M., Rexrode, K. M., Cook, N. R., Manson, J. E., & Buring, J. E. (2001). Physical activity and coronary heart disease in women: Is "no pain, no gain" passé? *Journal of the American Medical Association, 285*, 1447–1454.

Nelson, M. E., Fiatarone, M. A., Morganti, C. M., Trice, I., Greenberg, R. A., & Evans, W. J. (1994). Effects of high-intensity strength training on multiple risk factors for osteoporotic fractures: A randomized controlled trial. *Journal of the American Medical Association, 272*, 1909–1914.

Nieman, D. C. (2007). *Exercise testing and prescription: A health-related approach* (6th ed.). Boston: McGraw-Hill.

CABLE BENCH PRESS			
SKILL	**CUE**	**WHY?**	**COMMON ERROR**
Hand Position (Figure 12.1)	Secure, yet relaxed grip	More control	Grip too tight
Feet Position	Feet flat on ground	Better balance	Weight on heels or toes
Back Position	Back flat against bench	Lessens back strain	Back hunched
Execution	Slow, controlled movement	Develops each muscle group to maximize capacity	Too fast and jerky

FIGURE 12.1 Cable Bench Press

FIGURE 12.2 Cable Cross

CABLE CROSS			
SKILL	CUE	WHY?	COMMON ERROR
Hand Position (Figure 12.2)	Secure, yet relaxed grip	More control	Grip too tight
Feet Position	Have feet far enough apart to be balanced	For balance	Feet too close together

TREADMILL			
SKILL	CUE	WHY?	COMMON ERROR
Focus (Figure 12.3)	Look forward toward console; pull chin in	Helps maintain balance	Looking down or to the side
Hand Position	Beginners should hold rails	Safety: could trip or fall off	Letting go of rail
Running Stride	Stride normally; ball of foot strikes first	No breaking motion	Striking on heel first
	Land lightly on treadmill	Reduces stress on joints	Heavy, noisy foot strikes
Back Position	Back straight	More efficiency in the running stride	Back hunched over

continued

Look forward toward console; pull chin in

Ball of foot strikes first

Land lightly on treadmill

FIGURE 12.3 Running on Treadmill

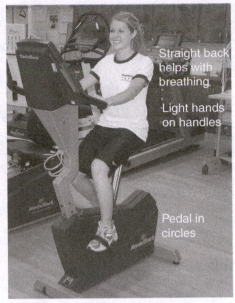

Straight back helps with breathing

Light hands on handles

Pedal in circles

FIGURE 12.4 Upright Cycle

TREADMILL, continued			
SKILL	**CUE**	**WHY?**	**COMMON ERROR**
Arms	Left thumb moves toward the left side of the face and down to the left side of the buttocks, and the right thumb moves similarly on the right side of the body. Arms should stay at 90°.	Fast pace	Cross body with arms
	Brush hips	Slow pace	
Safety	Use safety key	More efficient with energy	
	Teachers should limit max speed	Helps improve posture	.
	Do not stop		

UPRIGHT CYCLE			
SKILL	**CUE**	**WHY?**	**COMMON ERROR**
Hand Position (Figure 12.4)	Light hands on handles	Avoids strain on shoulders and back	Too much pressure on handles
Feet Position	Ball of foot on pedal spindle	More power and control	Heel on pedal
Leg Position	Knees in line with hips and feet	More efficiency, less strain on knees	Knees bent out

continued

FIGURE 12.5 Recumbent Cycle

FIGURE 12.6 Incline Trainer

UPRIGHT CYCLE, continued

SKILL	CUE	WHY?	COMMON ERROR
Movement	Pedal in circles; "scrape off mud" at bottom of pedal stroke	More power; uses more muscles	Stopping the feet at bottom of pedal stroke and not pulling up
Back Position	Straight back	Helps with breathing	Hunched over

RECUMBENT CYCLE

SKILL	CUE	WHY?	COMMON ERROR
Hand Position (Figure 12.5)	Light grip	Conserve energy; less strain on back and shoulders	Tight grip
Feet Position	Ball of foot on pedal	More power, more efficient pedaling	Heel of foot on pedal
Back Position	Flat against seat	Works core	Lean forward
Execution	Pedal circles	More efficient	Pedal slow
Leg Position	Knees in line with hips and feet	More efficient	Knees out of line with hips and feet

INCLINE TRAINER

SKILL	CUE	WHY?	COMMON ERROR
Arm Position	Elbows 90°	More efficient; conserves energy	Arms straight
Back Position (Figure 12.6)	Back straight	More energy	Lean forward
Feet Position	Step on balls of feet	To strike under hip	Heels striking

continued

Back straight

Hold lightly

Knees and hips in the same plane

FIGURE 12.7   Elliptical Trainer

INCLINE TRAINER, continued			
SKILL	**CUE**	**WHY?**	**COMMON ERROR**
Back Position	Straight; be tall	To work core better	Hunched
Execution	Short, high steps	More control	Long steps
Arms/Hands	Brush shorts	Slower pace	Elbows out
	Left arm moves toward the left side of the face, and the right arm moves toward the right side of the face (cheek to cheek)	Faster pace	Elbows out; arms crossing in front of the body

ELLIPTICAL TRAINER			
SKILL	**CUE**	**WHY?**	**COMMON ERROR**
Hand Position (Figure 12.7)	Hold lightly	Conserves energy	Holding too light
	Hold reciprocating arms	More energy used	Not holding arms
	Hold T handle	Reduce upper body involvement	
Focus	Can look around; forward is better	More control; will not fall off	Not focusing on what you are doing
	Heel can come off pedal	More comfortable	
Back Position	Straight	Works core	Back hunched
Leg Position	Knees and hips in the same plane	More efficient	Moving hips and knees off plane
Execution	Comfortable walking stride	To enjoy the machine	Too fast
	Keep weight from shifting	More efficient	Shifting weight from side to side
	Adjust resistance to maintain 60–80 rpm	Seems to be most comfortable	

13

Floor Hockey

INTRODUCTION

Floor hockey is a fast sport because of its transitions, the fact that players are constantly moving from offense to defense, and the speed of the puck or ball. You can substitute players during play without waiting for a whistle. Students have more playing time. Floor hockey develops cardiovascular endurance, core strength, reaction time, hand-eye coordination, foot speed, and agility. Floor hockey also works on skills that transfer to other sports, such as soccer and lacrosse.

Floor hockey is a sport that can be played successfully by all students. There is a role for every student, regardless of physical stature. Each student's personality plays a major role in the cohesion of the team.

SKILL LISTED WITH CUES

This chapter focuses on cues for the following skills: stance, grip, stick position, forehand passing, backhand passing, forehand receiving, backhand receiving, shooting, and goaltending.

TIPS

Equipment Tips

1. Sticks that have a plastic or wood shafts should be used.
2. A plastic puck is recommended for safety reasons because it is easy to control and harder to lift. A plastic ball also works well.
3. PVC net frames, rather than metal net frames, are recommended for safety and durability.

4. Safety equipment for all players includes helmet with face mask, gloves, shin guards that cover from the ankles to the top of the knee, and a mouth guard.

5. The goalie needs a helmet with face mask, catcher and blocker gloves, and shin guards.

6. Colored vests should be worn to identify the teams.

Safety and Etiquette

1. Teach the players to keep the sticks on the floor at all times. This prevents high sticks, which can cause injury. If a player breaks the *sticks on the floor* rule during a game, that player sits out for two minutes, just like in ice hockey. The team plays one player short for the duration of the penalty.

2. Teach the players to watch out for each other. They should avoid hitting another player's ankles, tangling up sticks, or causing a player to fall.

TEACHING IDEAS

1. Make sure players are in a good hockey stance, with their sticks on floor and their knees slightly bent, making a triangle with stick and feet. Emphasize good posture while in the sitting position: head over shoulders, shoulders over hips, and hips over heels.

2. When teaching passing and shooting, make sure to teach students to transfer their weight from the back leg to the forward leg. This increases the power of the shot and helps with the accuracy of the follow-through.

3. When teaching passing and shooting, emphasize the wrist rollover during the follow-through. When these moves are executed properly, the blade of the stick faces down toward the floor. The stick should point to the target and be a foot or so off the floor.

Teaching Progressions

1. When practicing accuracy, have the students stand 10–15 feet from a wall. Each student will pick a spot on the wall or have a target at which to aim, such as a cone. Having a target helps the student focus on rolling the wrist over and pointing toward the target with the stick.

2. Have students stand 20 feet apart with a partner. Work on passing and receiving skills. When students can do this with control, move the partners closer together and have them speed up the passes. The goal of this drill is to improve passing accuracy, receiving speed, and the releasing of a pass.

3. Hang a vest in the upper corners of the goal and/or place cones on the floor in the lower corners. Have three to four students stand in a semicircle. Have each student shoot for the vests. This improves shot accuracy, speed, and power (Figure 13.1).

4. If there is too much contact or games are too physical, have the students play in socks (no bare feet, no shoes). This will reduce the physical nature of the game. Students might resist this initially, but once they try it they will really enjoy the game.

Hang vests in upper corners of the goal

Students shoot for the vests

FIGURE 13.1   Shooting Drill

Mini-Games

Play games of 3 on 3, 4 on 4, or 5 on 5. Set up several mini-games using the width of a basketball court. If a team scores three points, the scoring team stays on the court, and the opponents step off the court. The next team of three comes onto the court and plays a new game. These games keep the players moving. You can also play these games with goalies at each end.

GAME PLAY

Rules

1. Typically, there are six players per team, with only four on offense (past the center line).
2. Due to the physical nature of the game, it is important to abide by a set of rules. Enforcing these rules keeps the sport safe and the game in control.
3. If a player breaks a rule, send him to the two-minute penalty box.
4. Slashing (using a stick to strike another player) is a violation.
5. Tripping (using a stick, knee, foot, arm, hand, or elbow to cause an opponent to trip or fall) is a violation.
6. High-sticking is carrying the stick above the shoulders.
7. Interference with the progress of an opponent who is not in possession of the puck or ball is a violation.
8. Unsportsmanlike conduct, such as overly violent behavior, swearing, teasing, fighting, and so forth, is a violation.
9. Cross-checking—when a player has both hands on his or her stick (off the ground) and uses the stick to shove another player—is a violation.
10. See Chapter 11, Indoor Field Hockey Rules.

Strategies

1. Defensive players send the puck/ball to the side lines.
2. Offensive players hit the puck/ball to the front of goal to gain a shot opportunity.
3. Offensive players move if they do not have the puck to get open.
4. Offensive players should quickly shoot with one or two touches because defense will collapse and protect the goal.

FIGURE 13.2 Creating a Crease

5. Defense players keep your opponent between you and the goal.

6. Goalie should move quickly from side to side of the goal.

7. Goalie stands in front of the line to cut off angles.

Scoring

1. A goal is worth one point.

2. A goal is scored when the puck/ball goes completely across the line.

3. If the puck/ball is kicked in or if an offensive player is inside the crease when the puck goes in, no point is scored (only the stick of an offensive player may enter the crease). Teachers can create a crease on the basketball key by placing a strip of tape from box to box (see Figure 13.2).

ASSESSMENT IDEAS

1. Students play 4 games (5 points for each game = 20 points).

2. Students shoot 5 pucks. Each puck in the goal scores 1 point.

FYI

For further information and special help, consult the following organization and resources.

ORGANIZATION

Olympic training ground for the Amateur Hockey Association of the United States.

USA Hockey
4965 East Fountain Boulevard
Colorado Springs, CO 80910
Fax: (719) 599-5994

SKILL	CUE	WHY?	COMMON ERROR
Feet (Figure 13.3)	Slightly wider than shoulder width, flat and firm on floor	Stability; balance; ready to move forward, backward, or laterally	Stance too narrow
Knees	Slightly bent, but not over toes	Stability; balance; ready to move forward, backward, or laterally	Legs straight
Hips	Slightly back	Core stability and balance	
		Helps to keep knees from going over toes	Knees too far forward
Stomach/Back	Keep stomach muscles tight and back straight	For core stability	Poor posture
Head	Head up, looking forward over entire floor	Allows you to see entire floor and what is happening	Head down
Holding Stick	Arms in front, holding stick straight out, forming a triangle with feet and stick	Stability, balance, ready for pass	Arms too far back
	Stick blade flat on ground 2–3 feet in front of feet	More surface area on ground to hit puck	Stick blade mostly off ground

Emphasize These Cues

1. Feet firm on floor
2. Hips slightly back
3. Back straight, head up
4. Stick flat on floor; form a triangle with feet

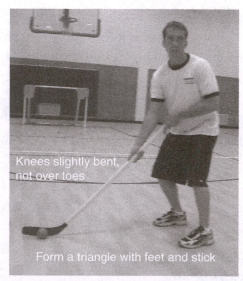

FIGURE 13.3 Hockey Stance

GRIPS

SKILL	CUE	WHY?	COMMON ERROR
Right-Hand Shot	Left hand on top, right hand halfway down shaft	Right hand is power hand	Hands too close together and grip too tight
Left-Hand Shot	Right hand on top; left hand halfway down shaft	Left hand is power hand	Hands too close together
Top Hand	Form a "V" with thumb and index finger; place at the top of shaft	Better control of stick	
Bottom Hand	Form a "V" with thumb and index finger; place about halfway down shaft	Good control of stick; able to utilize more power	
Knuckles of Each Hand	Knuckles of each hand will face opposite direction of each other	Good control; hand halfway down the shaft utilizes flex in stick for harder and faster shot	Hands not facing opposite

STICK HANDLING

SKILL	CUE	WHY?	COMMON ERROR
Stick Position	Hold stick in front of body, forming a triangle with feet and blade	Balance, stability, ready for puck pass	Stick not in front of body
	Blade should be flat on floor 2–3 feet in front of feet		Blade not flat
Stick-Handling Stance			
Stance	Good hockey stance		
Head	Head up; see puck in peripheral vision	Can see the rest of floor and action going on	Head down
Stick Motion	Blade travels parallel to foot line	Control of puck	Blade not travelling parallel to foot line
	Blade rotates toward puck at about 45° angle		
	Blade "cups" puck and pulls it forward and backward	Control of puck	
Wrists	Wrists roll toward puck when you catch it	Control of puck	Not absorbing puck with stick

Emphasize These Cues

1. Keep the puck between your feet (stick on the outside of the puck); thus, you have to pick up the blade and place it on the other side of the puck. Do this while rolling your wrists to get a 45-degree angle.

2. Use soft hands; there should be noise from the puck hitting the stick.

FOREHAND PASSING			
SKILL	**CUE**	**WHY?**	**COMMON ERROR**
Stance	Good hockey stance		
Puck Position (Figure 13.4)	Puck starts at heel of blade and behind back foot	Gives proper spin on puck; control	Not starting puck correctly
	Travels forward to toe of blade and then off blade		Puck leaves from heel of blade
	Puck travels parallel to foot line	Accuracy, power, and speed of pass	Puck does not travel
Stick	Puck stays on floor	Accuracy, ease of receiving pass	Puck bounces
	Sweep puck parallel to foot line		
	Puck is released from blade slightly in front of front foot		Puck is released too far back
	Hands on top of stick and halfway down shaft	Better control of stick	Hands not on top of stick
	Blade "cups" puck throughout motion	Better control of puck	Poor control of puck on blade
	Blade should end up 1–2 feet above floor, with blade pointing toward floor	Better power and safer	Blade too high on follow-through
Head and Eyes	Look at puck position on blade; look at target; look at puck position; pass	Better control	Eyes not on puck
Wrists	Follow puck path to its receiver	Improves follow-through, keeps pass down	Not following puck path
	As you sweep puck forward, roll wrist forward toward target	Puts proper spin on puck, keeps puck down	Not keeping puck down

Emphasize These Cues

1. Weight on back foot (see Figure 13.5a)
2. Puck starts at heel of blade
3. Blade sweeps puck forward with a cupping motion
4. See target, then puck, and pass
5. Roll wrist toward target

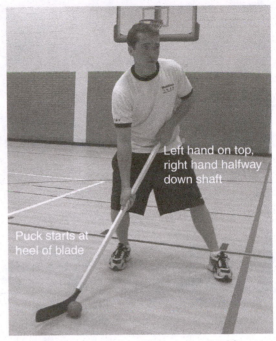

FIGURE 13.4   Passing and Shooting Position

BACKHAND PASSING			
SKILL	**CUE**	**WHY?**	**COMMON ERROR**
Backhand Passing	This motion is the same as the forehand pass; reverse motion		
	Puck starts on back foot	Power and control	Puck starting too far forward
	Weight on back foot	More power	Weight starts forward
	Transfer weight to front foot	More power	No weight transfer

FOREHAND RECEIVING			
SKILL	**CUE**	**WHY?**	**COMMON ERROR**
Stance (Figure 13.5b)	Good hockey stance		
Head and Eyes	Watch puck come all the way into blade until you have control of puck	Ensures you receive puck and maintain control	Not following puck with eyes
Stick Position	Stick path parallel to foot line	Control	

continued

(a) Passing to a Partner

FIGURE 13.5 Stance

(b) Receiving a Pass

	FOREHAND RECEIVING, continued		
SKILL	**CUE**	**WHY?**	**COMMON ERROR**
Stick Position, *continued*	Blade flat on floor, slightly in front of foot	Greater area on floor to receive pass, more time to catch pass	Blade not flat on floor
	When puck reaches blade, pull blade backward to absorb pass	Control	Not absorbing pass
	Blade travels all the way back to back foot	Control	Not having blade travel back
	Blade "cups" puck as it moves backward	Control	Not cupping puck
Puck Position	Initial catch is on toe of blade (front third of blade)	Control; also allows for immediate pass or shot because puck is in proper position	Not having blade touch puck with toe
	As you absorb puck, it should travel forward with heel of blade		Not having heel blade forward
Wrist Position	Wrists roll forward for incoming pass, as stick and hands absorb the pass	Control; soft hands to help absorb pass; wrists in position to immediately pass or shoot	Not absorbing pass

Emphasize These Cues

1. Hockey stance
2. Watch puck into stick blade
3. Absorb puck with blade in a reverse sweeping motion
4. Roll wrist forward when puck meets blade

BACKHAND RECEIVING

SKILL	CUE	WHY?	COMMON ERROR
Backhand Receiving	This motion is the same for a forehand or backhand pass reception; reverse motion		Not absorbing pass
	As puck approaches, weight should be on front foot; as you absorb puck with stick and hands, transfer weight to back foot	This makes you ready to immediately pass again or shoot	

SHOOTING

SKILL	CUE	WHY?	COMMON ERROR
Forehand Wrist Shot (Figure 13.6)	Bottom hand on stick should slide 2–3 inches further down	Power	Not sliding hand
	Weight transfer is very important; drive off back leg	Use of legs and hips aids speed and power of shot	Not driving legs and hips
	Sweeping motion of stick should be faster than a pass		Stick too slow
	Bend knees a little more	To add in weight transfer while keeping good hockey stance	Legs straight
	Roll wrists over and point blade at target	Power	Lack of wrist action
	Height of follow-through affects height of shot		Poor stick control
Backhand Wrist Shot	Same cues as for forehand wrist shot, reverse motion	Power	Lack of wrist action
	Momentum from weight transfer should "pull" shooter onto the front foot only	Natural result of a shot	Lack of weight transfer

Bottom hand should slide 2–3 inches down stick

Sweeping motion of stick should be faster than a pass

Roll wrists over and point blade at target

FIGURE 13.6   Shooting

Emphasize These Cues

1. Good stance
2. Lower hand slides 2–3 inches down shaft
3. Transfer weight from back foot to front foot
4. Roll wrists over and point blade at target

	GOALTENDING		
SKILL	**CUE**	**WHY?**	**COMMON ERROR**
Stance (Figure 13.7)	Head over shoulders, shoulders over hips, hips over ankles, feet shoulder width apart, bend knees at 45° angle	Having good posture allows quick reaction time to stop the ball or puck	
Hand Position	Hold open catching hand off to the side, waist level	Having the open hand off to the side takes up more space, protecting the net even more	
		It also keeps the hand ready to respond more quickly	
	The opposite hand holds the stick so the blade is on the ground in front and makes triangle with feet	Having the stick on the ground in front of the feet provides a barrier between the feet and the puck	
	Blade flat on the ground	It also protects more surface area of the net	

Catching hand
open, off to side

Blade and feet
make a triangle

Blade flat
on ground

FIGURE 13.7 Goalie Stance

Emphasize These Cues

1. Hockey stance
2. Catching hand open, waist-high, and off to side
3. Stick blade flat on floor, making a triangle with feet

Note

1. The goaltender is the last line of defense. The goaltender has one major goal: to stop the puck. The most effective way of goaltending is to take up as much area of the goal plane as possible. The goaltender's body and the stick help to take up this area.

2. To avoid muscle pulls and strains, always make sure that the goaltenders and players are properly stretched before any activity begins. Goaltenders need to be flexible because the position requires a quick reflex time, which could cause injury if the player is not warmed up properly.

3. Before beginning the game, let the goaltender's team take practice shots from a distance at the goaltender. This drill serves the important role of getting the goaltender's reflex time prepared for scrimmage, as well as warming up the rest of the team.

14

Flag Football

INTRODUCTION

When teaching flag football, keep the rules as close to those of the regular game as possible. The students can relate to our national pastime more easily. Football is a huge part of our society. The students will be able to enjoy the game with their family or friends because they will know the skills, rules, and some common plays.

SKILLS LISTED WITH CUES

The cues in this chapter cover the following skills: throwing, catching, punting, catching a punt, snapping the ball, quarterback steps, lateral pass, hand-offs (right and left side), tuck away after catch, running down the sideline, blocking, and in, out, and post running routes.

TIPS

Equipment Tips

1. Use either a leather football, web football, or Nerf multicolor football. The players' skill level determines which ball to choose.

2. Have two spacing dots for each game (line of scrimmage), and make sure they are two different colors (yellow and orange work well).

3. Use colored vests to identify teams.

4. Use flags with Velcro belts for both teams.

5. Have pylon markers (end zones).

6. Flip scoreboards—if players can see a score, it will add excitement to the game.

Safety

1. Do not wear rings, watches, bracelets, necklaces, piercings, or belts.
2. Declare the ball dead on fumbles.
3. Make sure the playing area is free from holes and objects on the field.
4. Players who wear glasses need to wear eye protectors.
5. No hats. Players can wear sweatbands or bandanas to keep sweat out of eyes.
6. No jeans, shorts with belt loops, and shorts with pockets.
7. No metal cleats. Soccer or football cleats are okay to wear.

Etiquette

1. Pull the flag and drop it; do not throw the flag.
2. Do not tie the belt in a knot because then the opponent cannot pull the flag.

TEACHING IDEAS

Divide students into pairs; match highly skilled students with ones with fewer skills. Have them practice the skills together. The highly skilled students can give tips to the other ones.

Teaching Progressions

1. Practice throwing a football with the right and left hands.
2. Practice kicking a football with the right foot and the left foot. Play Philadelphia Football, which is similar to ultimate frisbee (see Chapter 28), except it is played with a football.
3. Practice catching a punted ball with a partner. Challenge the pair to catch 10, 15, or 20 balls.
4. Practice plays with three players. One is the center, one is the quarterback, and one is the receiver. Rotate positions after three balls are thrown. Teach the quarterback steps and centering skills. Add a defender and teach the defensive skill of backpedaling and mirroring the offensive player.
5. Play 4 on 4 (passing plays only).
6. Practice hand-offs and a lateral pass. Play 3 on 3 mini-games with running plays only.
7. Practice a combination of passing and running plays.
8. Let the teams make up their own play patterns and play 4 on 4 games.

Mini-Games

1. Philadelphia Football.
2. Mini-games of 2 on 2 and 3 on 3: These games can be played to practice in, out, and post plays, with a defender on each player.

GAME PLAY

Rules

1. There are seven players on a team.
2. The players use 60–80 yards of the football field for each game (see Figure 14.1).

FIGURE 14.1 Flag Football Field

3. To start the game, flip a coin to determine who will punt, receive, defer to the second half, or decide which direction to go.

4. Three players on both offense and defense must start on the line of scrimmage until the ball is snapped.

5. There is a kickoff from the 20-yard line to start a game and after a score. Kickoffs can be optional since teams running full force at each other can cause injury. Teams can start on 20-yard line to start playing.

6. Put one yellow puck on the line of scrimmage and put one orange puck 1 yard from the line of scrimmage. Defense stands behind the orange puck until the ball is hiked.

7. A fumbled ball is dead when the ball touches the ground. The ball belongs to the team that controlled it last. A loose ball that has not hit the ground may be caught and advanced by either team.

8. Games are divided into two 20-minute halves with a continuous clock. There is 3-minute half-time break. Competitive games stop the clock within the last 2 minutes of play.

9. The offense has 25 seconds to put the ball into play after the official has blown his or her whistle and is ready for play.

10. In order to down a ball carrier, flags must be withdrawn from the waist by a defensive player. The ball carrier is declared down at this point.

11. Any player may hand or throw the ball backward at any time.

12. All players are eligible to receive a pass.

13. Offensive players must set basketball-style screen on defense when trying to get the ball (limits contact).

14. Players must be within 15 yards of the ball before it is snapped.

15. Only one player may be in lateral motion before the ball is snapped.

16. One forward pass is allowed beyond the line of scrimmage.

17. A lateral pass does not count as a forward pass.

18. Each team has four downs to get past the 20-yard line for a new first down.

19. A team may punt on the fourth down by throwing or kicking the ball. Each team must have 4 players on the line. No player is allowed to move until the ball is kicked or thrown.

20. Failure to convert on the fourth down by throwing gives the ball to the other team.

21. The kickoff may be thrown or kicked from behind the 20-yard line.

22. All kicks must be announced. The ball must be snapped. Neither team can cross their scrimmage line until the ball is kicked.

23. It is illegal for a player to deliberately withdraw an opponent's flag unless the player is in possession of the ball.

Violations

All of the following violations result in loss of 10 yards (unless it is inside the 20-yard line, in which case the team loses half of the distance to the goal).

1. No clipping—illegal contact from the back.

2. No diving for offensive players. Why? It increases the risk of head or neck injury.

3. No jumping. Why? It increases the risk of knee or head injury.

4. No spinning with the flags. Why? It increases the risk of knee or head injury.

5. No hurdling any player.

6. No roughing the passer.

7. No flag guarding (holding the flags so the defense can't grab them).

8. No holding of a shirt or shorts when trying to pull flags.

9. No stiff-arming opponents.

10. No defensive use of hands (offensive or defense holding).

11. No illegal offensive screen blocking (too much contact).

12. The defense must stay out of the neutral line of scrimmage zone.

13. Automatic disqualification for: tackling, tripping, or throwing a runner to the ground and intentional tampering with flag belts.

Just by adding 3 rules: no spinning, no diving, and no jumping, Utah State University's intramurals were able to limit injuries by about 60%.

Strategies

Offensive Strategy

1. Players should spread out on offense and make the defenders cover a wide area.

2. Run a variety of intermediate-length routes. It is best to combine routes that cross one another.

3. Have a few set plays that each player knows well.

4. The quarterback should pass the ball as soon as possible.

5. Look to attack the open side of the field.

6. Always look for an available pitch to a teammate before someone pulls your flag.

Defensive Strategy

1. When rushing the quarterback, a player needs to rush the throwing arm. If a right-handed quarterback has to roll to his left, he or she will have a harder time throwing the football with his or her right hand.

2. Never let the offensive receiver get behind you.

3. Make sure that more than one person pursues the ball carrier on each play.

4. Use a good cut-off angle when chasing the ball carrier.

5. Give the receiver a 5-yard cushion to start.

Scoring

6 points for a touchdown

2 points for a safety

1 point = 3 yards from goal line

2 points = 10 yards from goal line

3 points = 15 yards from goal line

ASSESSMENT IDEAS

1. Students throw ball back and forth with partner = 2 points

2. Students hand off on both sides with partner = 2 points

3. Students lateral pass on both sides with partner = 2 points

4. Students pitch the ball on both sides with partner and defender = 2 points

5. Students punt the ball back and forth = 2 points

6. Students run right and left side: in's, out's, post, curl, and fly route = 2 points each route

7. Students play 6 on 6 football games 5 points for each game. Play 4 games.

   20 points for skills

   20 points for games

For further information and special help, consult the following organizations and resources.

ORGANIZATION

Innovative footballs: Tech Tac web footballs and others
   Sportime
   One Sport Way
   Atlanta, GA 30340
   Phone: (800) 283-5700
   Fax: (800) 845-1535
   Website: www.sportime.com

WEBSITES

www.goflagfootball.com
   A rule book is available at this website. It includes passes, the field, equipment, clock, kicks, handling, deflagging, scoring a tie game, substitutions, interference, unfair and unsportsmanslike conduct, fouls and penalties, and a glossary of terms.

www.afafootball.com

THROWING

SKILL	CUE	WHY?	COMMON ERROR
Grip	Grab top of ball like holding a soda can or a fish's head	More surface area on ball, better control	Grabbing middle of ball
	Put 3–4 fingers on the laces, depending on the size of your hand	Better grip	Grabbing all laces or not enough
	Finger pads hold laces	Better release	Palm holding ball
Throwing Action (Figure 14.2)	Stretch arm way back; make an L shape	For better control and to throw the ball farther	Dropping the throwing elbow
Stance and Leg Action	Short to medium step	To get rid of the football fast	Overstriding, high stepping, or taking no steps
Release Point	Release at 2:00 with right hand; left hand, 10:00	Ball will go at correct angle	Releasing too early or too late
	Football points upward	Arch on ball	
Follow-Through Action	Turn palm out on follow-through; ball comes off index finger, thumb finishes down	Ball will fly through the air in a spiral motion	
	Arm should follow through like putting on a seat belt across the body		Throwing arm drops to the side
Left Arm	Pull left elbow up and back; tight package with core left arm and left elbow	Left arm brings core around to create more speed	No follow-through with throwing arm, arm straight at side

FIGURE 14.2   Throwing

CATCHING			
SKILL	**CUE**	**WHY?**	**COMMON ERROR**
Hand Action (Figure 14.3)	Big hands; reach out; shape hands like a diamond	Won't bounce off chest	Hands too close
	Catch ball in diamond	Ball fits best	Catching with chest
(Figure 14.4)	Soft hands	Cushion	Too stiff
Eyes	Pull ball into chest; watch ball into chest	Helps to avoid dropping ball	
Tuck the Ball	Catch with hands, turn ball downward against under armpit	Protect ball	Carry ball with hand only

FIGURE 14.3   Catching Above Waist

FIGURE 14.4   Catching Below Waist

FIGURE 14.5 Punting Stance

FIGURE 14.6 Punting Follow-Through

KICKING A PUNT			
SKILL	CUE	WHY?	COMMON ERROR
Punting (Figure 14.5)	Hold ball with two hands away from body	Ball is more stable	One-hand hold
	Support foot is planted when ball is released	Better stability	
	Pull kicking leg back	More power to send the ball far	
	Drop the ball from waist level	Less chance for error	Dropping from chest or using toss drop
	Swing leg under body	More effective technique	
	Ball makes contact with shoelaces and below knee	More surface area on which to contact ball	Knee bent with contact
	Toes pointed	To get a spiral	
Follow-Through (Figure 14.6)	Kick high, like a scissors kick	Gives more distance to ball	

CATCHING A PUNT			
SKILL	CUE	WHY?	COMMON ERROR
Elbows (Figure 14.7)	Five-point (hand-hand-elbow-elbow-bottom of sternum)	Big area for ball to land	Open arms
	Make a cage with arms about 2–3 inches apart	More surface area to catch ball	Arm and hands parallel to ground

continued

Fingers pointing to sky

Make a cage with arms

Elbows to stomach; pull ball to chest

FIGURE 14.7 Catching a Punted Ball

CATCHING A PUNT, continued			
SKILL	**CUE**	**WHY?**	**COMMON ERROR**
Elbows, *continued*	Fingers pointing to sky	Does not hurt the fingers	Curling fingers into a fist
	Palms toward face	Place for ball to go	Palms facing together
	Elbows to stomach	Keep ball from coming out	Elbows out, ball slides through
Action of Catching	Pull ball toward chest	Ball won't drop to ground	Ball hits too high off chest

SNAPPING BALL FROM THE SIDE			
SKILL	**CUE**	**WHY?**	**COMMON ERROR**
Foot Position to the Ball	Feet behind ball	*Rule:* Feet behind the ball on line of scrimmage	One foot by the ball
Hand Position on the Ball	Hold top of ball with an eagle claw	More surface area on the ball, more control of ball	Grabbing just one end of the ball
Hiking Action with the Arm	Straight arm to the quarterback	More accuracy with this method	Raising arm results in shorter toss
	Put the ball into the quarterback's hands; focus on hands	Gives you a focus on the target	Not watching where ball is tossed
		More concentration and better accuracy	

QUARTERBACK DROPBACK

SKILL	CUE	WHY?	COMMON ERROR
Foot Action	After receiving the snap, turn to side and sidestep	These steps help the quarterback have a fast reaction time	Staying forward and throwing
	Grapevine		
	Slide-slide		
	Plant your back foot and throw	The player has better control of the ball at the time of the throw	Throwing off of front foot

LATERAL PASS

SKILL	CUE	WHY?	COMMON ERROR
Hand Position	Hold ball with both hands	Better control	Holding ball with one hand
	Wide fingers on ball	More surface area on the ball, better control	Fingers together
Throwing Action (Figures 14.8 and 14.9)	Underhand throw	Helps to avoid dropping ball	Side arm throw
	Arms straight	More accuracy	Bending at elbow
Pitch	Lead the runner	So they can keep running with the ball	Ball is thrown behind runner
	Step to runner	Direct the ball	Not stepping
	Flip wrist with thumb finishing downward	Make the ball go end over end	Push ball
Rule	Lateral pass has to go behind or to the side	A forward pass is illegal	Ball going forward is a forward pass

Hold ball with two hands

Underhand throw, arms straight

FIGURE 14.8 Lateral Pass

Flip wrist with thumb finishing downward

Lead the runner

Step to runner

FIGURE 14.9 Pitch

SKILL	CUE	WHY?	COMMON ERROR
To Right Side of Quarterback *Receiver Arm Position*	Inside elbow up with thumb pointing down	Better target area for ball to go in	
	Outside elbow down	Ball is carried with outside arm	Carrying ball with inside arm
	Arms are parallel to each other	Big target	Arms too close to each other
Quarterback Action	Put the ball between the receiver's arms	Target place	Poor aim
Receiver Action	Squeeze the ball	Ball won't fall out	Not squeezing the ball
To Left Side of Quarterback (Figure 14.10) *Receiver Arm Position*	Inside elbow up	The ball fits in the pocket better	Wrong elbow up
	Outside elbow down		Wrong elbow down
	Arms are parallel to each other	Elbow is not in the way	Arms not parallel
Quarterback Action	Put the ball between the receiver's arms	Target place	Poor ball placement
Receiver Action	Squeeze the ball	Ball won't fall out	Not squeezing ball

SKILL	CUE	WHY?	COMMON ERROR
Tuck Away After Catch *Arm Action* (Figure 14.11)	Tuck ball into 4 REEF pressure points:	Ball won't get loose	Ball not on 1 of 4 pressure points
	1. Rib cage (stuff ball into rib cage)	Ball protected	Carrying like a loaf of bread
	2. Elbow (tuck bow in)	Holds the ball in place	Carrying with elbow on top of ball
	3. Eagle claw (spread fingers over point of ball with index finger over tip of ball)	Large surface area means more control of the ball	Poor hand position
	4. Hold ball against the body, so the ball won't bounce out		Poor forearm position

continued

Inside elbow up

Put ball in receiver's arms

Outside elbow down

Arms are parallel

Squeeze ball

FIGURE 14.10   Hand-off

Tuck ball into 4 REEF pressure points:

Rib cage

Elbow

Eagle claw

Forearm

FIGURE 14.11   Tuck Away Ball

BALL-CARRYING TECHNIQUES, continued			
SKILL	**CUE**	**WHY?**	**COMMON ERROR**
Running Down Sideline	SOAP (Switch Outside Arm Position): outside arm on top when switching	Use inside arm to push away defenders	Carrying ball on the inside
Ball Position	Running to the right sideline, carry ball in right hand	If ball gets knocked out, it will roll out of bounds	Ball in wrong hand
	Running to the left sideline, carry ball in left hand	If ball gets knocked out, it will roll out of bounds	Ball in wrong hand

BLOCKING			
SKILL	**CUE**	**WHY?**	**COMMON ERROR**
Stance	Comfortable squat position on the balls of your feet, as if you are sitting on a chair	Good leverage	Putting weight on heels
Arm Action	Arms crossed in front of body, ready to contact the defender	Quicker reaction time	Too much weight on hands
			Stopping feet and lunging
	Feet shoulder width apart	Good base	Feet too wide or too narrow
Strategy	Keep the opponent away from the ball carrier	Keeps you on the opponent	Not keeping with opponent
Body Force	Push with your upper body, using your legs for strength and balance	Legal position on the block	Using any other parts for blocking

Find open area
between defenders

Big hands
for target

Run straight; plant opposite
foot of direction of route

FIGURE 14.12   In Route (Opposite for Out Route)

BASIC RECEIVER ROUTES

SKILL	CUE	WHY?	COMMON ERROR
In Route (Figure 14.12)	Inside foot closest to quarterback in forward in all routes	To create uniformity in all routes	Outside foot is forward
	Run straight, plant outside foot	To fake opponent	
	Cut to the middle of the field at a 90° angle	Get to ball faster and run away from opponent	Rounding out the route
	Big hands for target for the quarterback	More target area for the quarterback to see and the receiver to catch the ball	Chest catch
Out Route (Figure 14.12)	Run straight, plant inside foot at a 90° angle to the outside	To fake opponent	Rounding out the route
	Work your way back to the quarterback	To give quarterback an easier angle to throw the football	Not working your way back to the quarterback
	Run a straight line	Get to ball faster	Not running in a straight line
	Big hands, for the quarterback to have a target	More target area for the quarterback to see, and the receiver has more surface area in which to catch the ball	Not showing target
Post Route	Run straight for 10–12 yards, then cut to one of the goalposts	Fakes defender	Run too flat

continued

SKILL	CUE	WHY?	COMMON ERROR
Stop Route	Run straight	The defender will not know in what direction you will be going	
	Stop as if you had come to a stop sign	The defender will be slow to react to your sudden movement	Take too much time to stop
	Turn around, with your arms and hands ready to receive the ball	Provides a good target to receive the ball	Turning away from quarterback
Curl Route	Run straight		
	Stop as if you have come to a stop sign	To create separation from defender	Not stopping fast enough
	Turn and pivot off outside foot, make a break inside toward the quarterback	To give the quarterback an easier angle to throw	Stop and don't run back to quarterback
	Turn around with your hands and arms ready to catch the ball	Faster reaction time and the release from the quarterback will be fast	Hands not up in position to catch the ball
Hitch Route	Perform first 3 cues for the curl route, but then break to the outside, and have hands and arm ready to catch the ball	To create slow reaction time to defense with different routes	Turn wrong direction toward quarterback
Fly Route	Run straight until you pass the defender	The defender will not know where you are going	
	Don't stop	Run away from the defender	
Slant Route	Start wide from the quarterback	So you do not run into defenders too soon	Start in tight position too close to quarterback
	Start to make your cut within 5 yards	To open yourself up for quarterback sooner	Cutting too late
	Run at a sharp angle across the middle of the field in front of defenders	To run underneath the defenders	A player will float too far uphill off their cut
	Hands come up immediately out of the break	Because of quick release from quarterback, hands need to be ready	Not getting hands up soon enough

15

Golf

INTRODUCTION

"Easy peazzy lemon squeezzy" was a great confidence cue given to Francis Ouimet by his 10-year-old caddy, Eddie Lowery, at the 1913 U.S. Open after he sunk his putt. Ouimet went on to be the youngest amateur ever to win the U.S. Open, beating Harry Vardon, his hero golfer. Welcome to golf: where confidence is of paramount importance and anything can happen. Golf, more than any other sport, challenges the player to pay attention to process rather than results. The golfer's task is to put the best full swing or stroke on the swing or putt, and to give themselves a chance to make a good shot. As soon as a golfer starts thinking about something other than process—whether it be about the lake on their left, winning the hole, or the score—the result is typically poor.

The game of golf is the fastest-growing sport in the world and pulls people in because of the challenge, aesthetics, and social aspects. For students who have played a satisfying round, it is easy to see why it has become so popular. Golf may be the hardest skill game played today, and it definitely cannot be learned quickly. It takes most recreational golfers years to learn the game, even when they are naturally gifted athletes. Keeping this fact in mind, teachers should remember to be patient with students while instructing and encouraging those with a real interest in golf to play as much as possible.

Butch Harmon, teacher to the top golf professionals, recommends practice in the morning by hitting balls using cues and technique, and in the evening by executing shots with no thought process at all. He also states amateurs should spend 80 percent of their practice time hitting golf shots they are not good at and 20 percent of their time practicing maintaining their swing with perfect shots lies. Many amateurs practice what they are good at but do not practice what they are not good at. Professionals spend time practicing what they are good at as much as what they are not good at (game-like situations on the golf course) (Harmon, May 2, 2010).

Three to five demonstrations of a golf stroke, associated with one cue phase, will simplify the learning process and make the skill and stroke more beginner friendly. Make sure to stay with one cue until students are comfortable moving on.

SKILLS LISTED WITH CUES

This chapter presents teaching cues for the following golf skills: three different grips, approach to the ball, and the basic swing for iron shots. Once the students have mastered these skills, additional cues provide information for golf shots, which include specifics for wood shots, putting, and chipping. Also provided are cues on how to handle sand shots, shots on a windy day, and different golf lies, including downhill, uphill, and low shots. These particular cues are designed for beginner-level, right-handed golfers, but they can be adapted for left-handed golfers. Through the use of these cues, you and your students can be more successful golfers!

TIPS

1. It is essential to grasp and ingrain the fundamentals of golf grip, stance, and swing.

2. A strong core, good flexibility, and balance are critical to a good golf swing.

3. Core, stretching, and balance exercises can help the golfer hit the ball longer and with more consistency.

Equipment Tips

1. Ball differences: Premium golf balls are Titleist Pro V1, Pro V1x, Nike 20XI, 20XI-X, ONE RZN, RZN X, Bridgestone Tour B 330 and B 330-s, Callaway Tour i(s), i(z), and Hex Black Tour, and Srixon Z Star and Z Star XV. Premium golf balls do not travel as far as many of the other golf balls, but they have a higher spin rate, which is an advantage in controlling the ball. These balls can cost more the $45 per dozen, and balls that cost less than half that are adequate for most golfers. A PGA golf professional can help you find the best ball to fit your swing.

2. A golfer can legally have a maximum of 14 clubs in his or her bag. A standard set of clubs for men includes a driver; 3 and 5 woods; 3 hybrid or 3 iron; 4 hybrid or 4 iron; 5, 6, 7, 8, and 9 irons; a pitching wedge; 52° gap wedge; 56° wedge; and a putter. A standard set of clubs for women includes a driver; 3, 5, and 7 woods; 4 hybrid or 4 iron; 5, 6, 7, 8, and 9 irons; a pitching wedge; 52° gap wedge; 56° sand wedge; and putter. Wedges can vary in your bag; for example, 3 wedges could include 52°, 56°, and 60°, and 4 wedges could include 50°, 54°, 58°, and 62°.

3. Go to a professional to be fitted for proper club length, proper flex of shaft, and proper lie.

4. Golf shoes with soft spikes help the golfer stay on the ground and prevent slipping. Golf sandals are popular, but bee stings may occur when wearing them; you might want to wear socks.

5. Artificial-turf doormats can be used to hit the ball indoors. These mats protect the floor.

Safety

1. Players should ensure that no one is standing close or in a position to be hit by the club, the ball, or any turf when they make a stroke or practice swing.

2. When teaching the golf swing on grass fields, have players hit balls in a single line like a driving range. Place golf clubs, balls, and tees on grass about 3 yards apart, ready for students.

3. A player should not pick up the golf club until the teacher blows the whistle.

4. Retrieve all balls on the whistle.

5. Stay behind a player when he or she is hitting a ball on the range or on the course.

6. Players should not play until the players in front are out of range.

7. Yell "fore" if you think your ball will hit or come close to hitting someone.

8. Do no throw or bang clubs on other objects.

Etiquette

1. Do not talk, move, or make noise when a player is hitting or putting a ball.

2. Be respectful of other groups.

3. Play and putt in order, starting with the player farthest from the hole.

4. Stay behind and off to the side of the player hitting a ball.

5. Play ready golf. Make sure you are ready to hit when it is your turn. Play at a good pace. Invite faster groups to play through. Avoid taking many practice swings before you hit.

6. The best score tees off first—this is called honors.

7. Keep an honest score.

8. Take care of the course. Replace divots, smooth bunkers, repair ball marks on greens, and put trash in containers.

9. Do not play practice shots on the course.

10. On the putting green, players should not stand on another player's line or cast a shadow over his or her line of during the putt. Also, leave golf bags in position to go for the next hole.

11. Be a positive person on the course. No one wants to play with a sourpuss.

TEACHING IDEAS

Professionals often suggest it is best to learn the game starting from the green. Thus, the order of learning the game should be putting, chipping, pitching, hitting sand shots, hitting fairway woods, hitting the driver, and hitting specialty shots. It is important to learn the mental aspect of the game while learning its physical aspects. The proper mental approach to golf can make a huge difference in a player's success and enjoyment.

Teaching Progressions

1. Choose clubs beginners can have success with. Clubs that are fairly easy to hit with include 7, 8, and 9 irons. These clubs can be used to help ingrain the swing. When a player begins to feel comfortable with the irons, progress to the woods.

2. The driving range is a place for beginners to practice the skills of golf. Beginners can become easily frustrated on a golf course. When the beginner can get the ball up in the air with consistency, it's time to play a round of golf.

3. Putting and chipping require hours of practice. This chapter provides three putting and chipping drills. These drills can be practiced individually on the putting green, at the golf course, or as a class. Remember that putting and chipping is half of a golfer's score.

Spending time practicing these skills will lower scores faster than practicing anything else.

4. Golf is easy to make complex! The simpler we can make it, the better. Stay away from complicated language. Progress happens when staying with the fundamental skills and basic swing.

Mini-Games

1. Setting up a nine-hole golf course on a football field or large grass field is an excellent way to teach scoring and provide a game-like experience (Figure 15.1). Equipment and procedures include the following:

   - Scorecard designed by teacher or picked up at a local golf course
   - Pencils
   - Jump rope and cones to mark tee box
   - For holes, use soccer corner flags, or attach flags to dowel sticks and stand the sticks in the orange cones with holes in top. Place the flag in the center of a hula hoop. The object of the game is to hit the ball in hula hoop.
   - Regulation clubs, white Wiffle balls, and tees
   - Set up nine holes that match the pars on the scorecard.
   - Use a shotgun tournament start: Several players start on each hole and begin on a signal. Have three or four students on each hole. Give each group a 5 iron, a 7 iron, a 9 iron, a scorecard, and a pencil. On the whistle, everybody starts to play.

FIGURE 15.1 Ideas for Modified Golf Equipment and Golf Course

FIGURE 15.2 Early Bird Special Golf Activity

- Students can play games where the teams take the best score on each hole (best-ball tournaments) and other types of contests. Have fun golfing!

2. *Two Team Best-Ball Tournament* (also called Better Ball or Four Ball): Each player records his or her own score for the hole. The best score is recorded. A tournament can be set up with three or four teams. Best ball scoring is the best score of the twosome, threesome, or foursome.

3. *Scramble Tournament*: Each player takes a shot, and the best shot is played by both players from the same spot until ball is holed. Three- and four-person scrambles can also be played using the same rules as above.

4. Have a contest to see who can hit the ball closest to the hole. Tee shots are made from the top of a hill (if hills are not available, tee off level ground) (Figure 15.2).

   - Set up a tee box area and a par 3 hole at the bottom of a small hill.
   - Place a hula hoop about 50 yards out from the tee box with a soccer goal marker or flagstick inside the hoop.
   - Place a blue plastic tarp in front of the hole for a water hazard.
   - Provide 7, 8, and 9 irons for the students to use.
   - Each student tries to get his or her shot closest to the large flagstick. When a student does, a teacher, teacher's aide, or student can mark the spot with a small flagstick.
   - Closest ball to the hole wins the early bird special.

GAME PLAY

Rules

1. Tee ball off between and behind the front of the tee markers. You must tee off within 2 club lengths behind the tee markers.

2. Play your ball as it lies. Do not improve your lie. You cannot move or bend anything fixed or growing.

3. If your ball is in a bunker or water hazard, you cannot touch the ground with your hand or club before the downswing. If you do, it is a 2-stroke penalty.

4. If you accidently cause your ball to move, it is a 1-stroke penalty.

5. If a ball goes out of bounds (beyond the outside border of the white stakes), you play the ball from where your last shot was played with a 1-stroke penalty; the penalty is a stroke and distance penalty, so you will lie 3 after the shot is played again. A provisional ball may be played if you think your ball may be out of bounds or lost (#6).

6. If the ball is deemed lost (after a maximum of 5 minutes of searching), the penalty is the same as a ball hit out of bounds (#5).

7. If a ball goes into a water hazard (beyond the outside border of the yellow stakes) and you deem it unplayable, you have two choices: play the ball from where you last played with a 1-stroke penalty (really a stroke and distance penalty), or drop the ball any distance behind the water hazard, keeping the point of entry into the hazard and the ball in a straight line with the hole.

8. If a ball goes into a lateral hazard (beyond the outside border of the red stakes), you have three choices: the first two are the same as the water hazard (#7), and the third is to drop the ball within two club lengths, no nearer the hole, of the point where the ball crossed into the lateral hazard.

9. On putting green you can mark, lift, and clean the ball. For more details of rules go to: Rules of Golf, USGA, 2012–2015.

Strategies

1. If you don't keep practicing golf, it's easy to lose your skills. Stay with it.

2. To maximize the chance to improve, golfers should spend one-third of their time putting and chipping, one-third of their time hitting range balls, and one-third of their time on the course playing.

3. Try to organize a field trip to the golf course and have students work on each area just listed. Have the golf pro talk about course etiquette and rules.

Scoring

1. When keeping score in golf, *par* is a set number of hits that the golfer is expected to meet within a certain distance. Par is based on distance to the hole:
   - Par 3 distance: 60–250 yards
   - Par 4 distance: 250–475 yards
   - Par 5 distance: over 475 yards

   If the hole is a par 3, the ball should be on the green in 1 stroke and 2 putts.

   If the hole is a par 4, the ball should be on the green in 2 strokes and 2 putts.

   If the hole is a par 5, the ball should be on the green in 3 strokes and 2 putts.

   Here are some possible situations that might occur on a par 3 distance:
   - Hole in one: the golfer puts the ball in the hole in 1 stroke.
   - Birdie: the golfer puts the ball in the hole in 2 strokes.
   - Par: the golfer puts the ball in the hole in 3 strokes.
   - Bogie: the golfer puts the ball in the hole in 4 strokes.
   - Double bogie: the golfer puts the ball in the hole in 5 strokes.

   The scorecard will indicate if the hole is a par 3, 4, or 5 (see Figure 15.3). The scorecard will show the number of the hole, the par of the hole, and

Blue Tees	480	150	565	220	330	395	560	290	362
White Tees	469	135	527	161	289	389	541	287	357
Hole No.	1	2	3	4	5	6	7	8	9
Par (Men's/Ladies')	5	3	5	3	4	4	5	4	4
Red Tees	459	117	467	139	236	389	499	287	357

FIGURE 15.3 Example of a Golf Scorecard for Nine-Hole Course

yardage for the hole for from the different tee (tees markers are often colored). The number of strokes it takes the golfer to put the ball in the hole is recorded on the scorecard in the appropriate box of the "Hole No." column. There are 9-hole or 18-hole golf courses. The total score at the end of 9 or 18 holes is the golfer's final score.

ASSESSMENT IDEAS

1. Play 4 rounds on the field, and have students turn in their scorecards. Each round is worth 5 points, for a total of 20 points.

2. Have a longest drive contest using a driver on a par 5 hole. Choose a prize, such as golf balls, tees, or water bottles.

3. Have a closest to the pin contest on a par 3 hole. Choose a prize, such as golf balls, tees, or water bottles.

4. Play on a regular 9-hole golf course for 3 total rounds.

   5 bonus points for each game with scorecards turned in.

   1 bonus point if score is in the 60s for each 9 holes.

   2 bonus points if score is in the 50s for each 9 holes.
   3 bonus points if score is in 40s for each 9 holes.

FYI

For further information and special help, consult the following organizations and resources.

PUBLICATIONS

George, J. D. (2004). *Let's golf.* San Francisco: Benjamin Cummings.
Hogan, B. (1990). *Five lessons: The modern fundamentals of golf.* New York: Simon & Schuster.
Rotella, B. (1995). *Golf is not a game of perfect.* New York: Simon & Schuster.

WEBSITES

www.nationalclubgolfer.com
www.pga.com (includes video instructional lessons)
www.golfchannel.com
www.taylormade.com

www.callawaygolf.com
www.cobragolf.com
www.peakperformancegolfswing.com
www.Bridgestone.com

BOOK WEBSITE

How to break 80 (go to website www.golf.com)

JOURNALS

Golf Digest
Golf Week

REFERENCE

Harmon, B. (May 2, 2010). Guest Speaker. WAC Conference. Las Vegas, NV.

GRIPS			
SKILL	**CUE**	**WHY?**	**COMMON ERROR**
Overlap (Most Popular)	Little finger of right hand rests between index and middle finger		Gripping too tightly with thumbs
	Last three fingers on left hand and middle two fingers of right hand are the grippers	Control of club	Gripping top of club—instinct is to grip with thumb and index finger
Hand Position	The V of thumb and index finger of each hand points to right shoulder	Accuracy—club face comes through square	Vs point outside or inside of right shoulder
Interlocking	Little finger interlocks with index finger		Little fingers not interlocking
Baseball	Similar to other grips, except all fingers are touching the grip	Control of club and more power	Hands too far apart

Gripping the golf club too tightly while playing a golf game is a common error for many players. Golfers get stressed and tense easily and forget about their grip. "Relax the grip, like you are holding a live bird," is a great cue to say to yourself as you begin your swing or putt. Stress and tension make for a bad golf swing, and it starts in the grip.

GRIP AND STANCE DRILLS

1. Teach students a good grip and stance before teaching the swing.
2. Practice the grip and stance.
3. Students need to develop a routine to follow before hitting the ball. It may be something like—look at the target line from behind the ball, approach the ball and set the club face behind the ball in line with the target, take a proper stance for the target, look at the target and back to the ball, and let it go. A golfer should go through this routine for each shot during a round and should practice the routine with each shot on the range.

SKILL	CUE	WHY?	COMMON ERROR
Stance (See Figure 15.4)	Stand tall	Better core rotation on follow-through	Having feet too wide
	Have feet shoulder width apart		Having feet too close
	Point toes slightly out		Pointing feet straight
Posture Hips	Stand tall	More range of motion for arm swing	Being in sitting position
	Tilt at hips with back straight		Keeping weight back
	Slightly bend knees		Bending knees too much
Arms	Keep arms straight and hanging down loosely	Faster club head swing	Bending arms too far away from body or too close to body
Club Position	Club handle points a little left of midline	Keeping this club position in the best position for striking the ball	Having club handle too far away from body or too close to body
	Keep club handle one hand width from waist	So the arms will swing more freely	Having the club too close to the body
Eyes	Look through the lower part of eyes	Better posture for swing plane	Keeping head and eyes down too far
	Keep your chin up	Helps maintain posture	Chin close to sternum
Head	Keep head still	Keeps body aligned for swing	Moving head
Club Face	Keep club face square to target	For solid, powerful contact	Having club face too open or too closed

FIGURE 15.4   Golf Stance

Tilt at hips—back straight

Look through lower part of eyes

Arms straight and hang down loosely

Routine

- Get 10 feet behind the ball and line up the target.
- Stand by the ball and review the stance cues in your head.
- Keep your feet shoulder-width apart with toes out.
- Tilt your hips, and bend your knees slightly.
- Keep your arms straight.
- Point the club handle toward the left hip, one hand width from waist.
- Check your grip: Vs should point toward your right shoulder.
- Keep your chin up and direct your eyes down as if you were looking through bifocals

SKILL	CUE	WHY?	COMMON ERROR
Backswing Position	Right elbow points down and away from side	Helps keep club face square and club on line	Elbow up or too close to body
	Left elbow wide and arm fairly straight	By pushing your left arm away from head as far as you can there is more time to accelerate speed and power on downswing	Left elbow too bent
	Wide at the top; the longer and wider you make your backswing, the better the swing	Generates more power	Both elbows bent
	Club shaft is parallel to ground at top of swing	Helps for a perfect path and plane line through the face of club	Club shaft is beyond parallel
Head Position on Completion of the Swing	Head stays fairly still until trailing shoulder forces it up	More speed and power through the swing	Keeping head down all the way through swing; don't get as much power

SKILL	CUE	WHY?	COMMON ERROR
Swing Key 1: Low and Wide	Arms wide on the takeaway moved by a big shoulder turn	Foundation of a wide swing arc	Downswing too steep or choppy
	Get the feeling of swinging your left forearm more across your chest rather than up	Facilitates a turning of the shoulders and trunk	Tilting more than turning the shoulders and body
Swing Key 2	Keep your right knee as quiet as possible and in the same position while you turn your shoulders	Allows a base to turn shoulders and body against	Sliding right knee to the right
	Push left hip 2 inches to left		Weight gathered on right foot
	80% of weight on right leg; 20% of weight on left leg at top of backswing	More power from weight transfer; ball will go longer	80% on left leg, 20% on right leg
			Not transferring weight to back leg
	Coil	Emphasizes turn with shoulders and body	Lack of turn
Swing Key 3	Rip it	Promotes acceleration through the ball	Open club face at impact

continued

BASIC SWING—THREE KEYS, continued			
SKILL	**CUE**	**WHY?**	**COMMON ERROR**
Swing Key 3, *continued*	Right forearm rotates over the left	Helps to make sure the club face is squared to target	90% of balls slice or go to right
	"You finish more around your body than up."	Promotes turning through contact	Lack of body rotation

Especially in golf, cues are like aspirin—one or maybe two are useful in a practice session, but don't take the whole bottle.

SWING FINISH CUES			
SKILL	**CUE**	**WHY?**	**COMMON ERROR**
Finish	Use core muscles to turn; have a high finish	Promotes turning through contact	Swinging around too fast
	Hold your pose at the top of swing for 3 or more seconds	Better balance, accuracy, ball control, and longer balls	Getting off balance at the finish of the swing
			Falling forward or backward

SWING DRILL PRACTICE

1. Swing the club with one cue: "Hold your pose at the end of your swing for 3 seconds."
2. In this drill, have students brush the grass and knock the tee out of the ground.
3. When they can accomplish this, have students hit balls with the same routine.
4. Add one swing cue when this is mastered.
5. Keep cues simple: "Check stance, check grip, brush grass, and finish on pose."

SLICE CUES			
SKILL	**CUE**	**WHY?**	**COMMON ERROR**
Slice Ball Goes Right	80 to 90% of balls are sliced		Club face is open at impact
			Forearms rotate too much on the takeaway
			Left wrist is cupped at top of backswing
How to Correct a Slice	You want a flat wrist and a square club face at the top of the backswing		Swing plane is on the outside; no squared club face at the top of the backswing

HOOK CUES

SKILL	CUE	WHY?	COMMON ERROR
Hook Ball Goes to Left			Club face closed at impact
			Lack of body rotation on through swing
			Chin buried in the chest
			Wrist bowed at top of swing
How to Correct a Hook	Flat wrist at top of swing		Swing path is inward to out

WOOD SHOTS

SKILL	CUE	WHY?	COMMON ERROR
Stance (Figure 15.5)	Heel of front foot lines up with ball		Ball lined up with back foot or middle of stance
Tee Ball	Top half of ball or more should be above club face at address		Ball teed up too high or low
(Figure 15.5)	Inside of feet line up with outside points of shoulders	You get more motion in your upper body	
Swing	Tickle grass on backswing		Wood face comes up too soon
	Emphasize low and wide backswing		Hurrying the takeaway swing
	Turn left shoulder under chin		
	Sweep the ball off tee		Hitting at down angle
	Keep club head traveling fairly low to ground after impact	Will promote solid contact	
Follow-Through	Belt buckle faces hole		
	Right knee points to target		Left hip faces hole
	Hold pose at end of follow-through		Swinging too fast; off-balance
Focus of Eyes	Head stays fairly still until trailing shoulder forces it up		Raising head too soon or too late

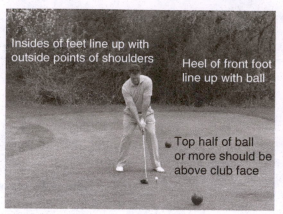

Insides of feet line up with outside points of shoulders

Heel of front foot line up with ball

Top half of ball or more should be above club face

FIGURE 15.5   Wood Shot Set Up

Stand tall—tilt at hips

Hold putter at end of stroke

FIGURE 15.6   Putting

PUTTING CUES			
SKILL	**CUE**	**WHY?**	**COMMON ERROR**
Stance (See Figure 15.6)	Stand tall	Easy to see the path of the ball	Having head down
	Tilt at hips		Bending too far over
Grip	Hold putter lightly, pressure should be 5 on a pressure scale of 0–10	Relieves tension	Holding putter too tightly
Eyes	Position eyes directly over or behind the ball	Helps to hit the ball along the target line	Having eyes too far forward, inside, or outside the target line
Putting Action	Make shoulders and arms do most of the work with a pendulum action	Enables more consistent strokes	Having too much wrist action; putter head passes hands on forward swing
	Pendulum swing		
Follow-Through	Hold putter at the end of the stroke	More consistent results; ball will go straight to target	Retracting putter head
Have a Routine	Always have the same routine when you putt	Develops confidence in pressure situations	Not following a routine
		Enables player to rely on routine	
		Occupies the mind on routine	

EXAMPLE OF PUTTING ROUTINE

Keep the routine simple. Some routines take too long and just waste time.

Steps in Routine

1. Read the putt from behind the ball by standing so that the ball is between the player and the hole, about 5–10 feet behind the ball. You can go to the opposite side of the hole and look at the putt from both directions. This is because sometimes it is easier to see a break from the other side.

2. Step up to ball, and look at the hole. Draw an imaginary line with your eyes from the hole to your ball.

3. Take a practice swing. Hold your putter on the follow-through.

4. Step closer to the ball and visualize the line.

5. Let the putter go. Trust your stroke. Keep your head still through the swing. Hold the putter in your follow-through until the ball drops into the hole.

Potential Problem: Retracting the putter head leads to inconsistent putting.

PUTTING DRILLS

1. First, develop a routine and practice your routine so that it becomes automatic.

2. Practice holding your follow-through until the ball drops in the hole. Practice at a variety of distances and breaks.

3. Take three balls. Select a putt that has a substantial break. Putt the break using three different speeds: easy (ball trickles over front edge of hole), medium, and firm (ball hits back of cup). Practice this drill at a variety of short distances and breaks. This drill develops your sense of touch.

4. Play with a partner. After each putt, take one club-length back from the hole until you make the putt.

5. Play nine holes of golf with your partner. The partner who wins the hole chooses the next hole and distance. The goal is to break 18 putts for nine holes.

CHIPPING			
SKILL	CUE	WHY?	COMMON ERROR
Grip	Hold down on club	Extra control	Holding too high on grip
Club	Use the club you are comfortable with—from a 6 iron to a wedge	Ball can be hit low with all of these clubs	Using a sand wedge for a chip that needs to run across the whole green
Posture	Have an open stance	Able to see the hole's path better	Hunching down on the ball
	Keep shoulders square	Allows club path at the hole	Having open shoulders
Hand Position (See Figure 15.7)	Set hands slightly ahead of the ball	Promotes a downward blow and low shot	Having hands even or behind the ball

continued

Set hands slightly ahead of the ball

Position ball slightly back of center

FIGURE 15.7 Chipping

CHIPPING, continued			
SKILL	CUE	WHY?	COMMON ERROR
Weight	Keep weight on forward foot	Promotes a downward blow and a low shot	Keeping weight on back foot
Ball Position	Position ball slightly back of center	Promotes a downward blow and a low shot	Having ball too far forward
Read the Shot	Choose a spot you want the ball to land	Forms a mental picture of the ball traveling there	No target in mind
Swing Action	Hit down on the back of the ball	Loft of club will produce low flight	Stabbing at the ball
	Accelerate smoothly	Produces consistent shots	Accelerating too fast early
	Keep eyes focused on back of the ball through contact; see the grass where ball was	Promotes less movement during shot	Moving eyes
	Swing is like a long putt with downward action	Keeps the ball low, rolling, and on target	Having a swing too long or too high that does not accelerate

PITCH SHOT			
SKILL	CUE	WHY?	COMMON ERROR
Address and Club Use	Choose a lofted club	Hit the ball high	Hitting the ball low
	Open your stance, aligning your feet left of target lane		Closed stance
	Open club face to increase loft	Hit the ball high	Closed club face
	Play the ball forward of the center of stance	Hit the ball high	Play ball back off your right toe

continued

PITCH SHOT, continued

SKILL	CUE	WHY?	COMMON ERROR
Action Cues	Mini-version of the full swing	Prevents too much body action	Turning too much with the body
	Hips turn slightly back and through	To accommodate the motion of your shoulders, arms, and hands	Turning too much with the body or being too stiff
	Let the club do the work		Trying to force the club
	Slide club head under the ball	For better contact and get the ball airborne	Hitting on top of the ball
	Accelerate through the swing	Smooth acceleration promotes better contact	Allow club head to stop
End of Swing	Club face should be aiming at the sky	Proves that the loft of the club face has been maintained	Club face aiming to the left

SAND CUES

SKILL	CUE	WHY?	COMMON ERROR
Stance (See Figure 15.8a)	Be careful not to touch sand with club	Stroke penalty	Touching club on sand
Feet	Dig feet into sand	Having a solid stance lowers your center of gravity, which makes it easier to hit underneath the ball	Not establishing a solid base
Stance and Club Alignment	Have an open stance and align feet, hips, and shoulders left of target	To swing in line with body	Aligning body to target
	Aim club face at the target	Allows the club head to slide through the sand on the swing	Not aiming club face at target; closed face
	Club face should be open	Increases loft of club face in order to hit high and soft	Having the ball too far back
		Promotes hitting sand first and gives a higher trajectory	
		Slides club through the sand easier because of the bounce of the sand wedge	

continued

Open stance—align feet, hips, and shoulder to left of target

Aim club face at target

Dig feet into sand

(a) Sand Shot Stance
FIGURE 15.8

Hit several inches behind ball

Splash sand on the green

Keep club face flat or open through swing

(b) Sand Shot Swing

SAND CUES, continued

SKILL	CUE	WHY?	COMMON ERROR
Swing (Figure 15.8b)	Make at least $^3/_4$ swing	Hit hard because you contact sand first	Having a short abbreviated swing and follow-through
	Hit several inches behind the ball	Projects the ball in air; lands softly	Hitting the ball first
	Keep club face flat or open through swing; face pointing to the sky	Projects the ball up over lip of the bunker	Closing the face at contact and through the swing
	Accelerate through the ball	Projects the ball out of the bunker	Digging club into sand; no follow-through
	Splash sand on the green	Propels the ball on a cushion of sand	No sand on the green

HILL SHOTS CUES

SKILL	CUE	WHY?	COMMON ERROR
Golf Ball Lies Downhill (Figure 15.9a)	Keep shoulders parallel to the ground	Need to stand level in relationship to the ground	No adjustment for slope
	Choose at least one less club	Ball will go lower	Choosing too much club
	Aim left	The ball has a tendency to go right because there is more weight on the left side	Aiming straight

continued

Aim left

Keep shoulders parallel to the ground

Choose at least one less club

Choose at least one more club

Keep shoulders parallel to the ground

Aim right

(a) Downhill

(b) Uphill

FIGURE 15.9

HILL SHOTS CUES, continued			
SKILL	**CUE**	**WHY?**	**COMMON ERROR**
Golf Ball Lies Uphill (Figure 15.9b)	Keep shoulders parallel to the ground	Need to stand level in relationship to the ground	No adjustment for slope
	Choose at least one more club	Ball will go higher	Choosing too little club
	Aim right	Ball has a tendency to go left because there is more weight on the right side	Aiming straight

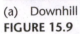

LOW BALLS AND SHOTS INTO THE WIND CUES			
SKILL	**CUE**	**WHY?**	**COMMON ERROR**
Feet	Play ball off your back foot	More control of ball	Playing ball off your front foot
Stance	Put more weight on your left side	Produces lower flight	Keeping weight back
Choice of club	Choose more club	Able to swing easier	Choosing less club
Swing	Make $^3/_4$ swing at $^3/_4$ speed	Produces lower flight	Swinging too hard

16

Lacrosse

INTRODUCTION

"A unique combination of speed, skill, agility, grace, endurance, finesse and historical significance, lacrosse may just be, according to basketball inventor James Naismith, 'the best of all possible field games'" (Lacrosse Foundation, 1994).

Lacrosse is considered to be America's first sport since it originated with the Natives of North America and was adapted by the Canadians. With a history spanning over a century, modern lacrosse is one of the fastest-growing team sports in the United States. No sport has grown faster at the high school level over the last 10 years. Men's professional indoor and outdoor lacrosse leagues are also very popular and have brought the game to national attention.

Lacrosse is played with a stick, the crosse, which the player uses to throw, catch, and scoop the ball. When these skills are mastered, the rest of the game flows. The sport of lacrosse is a combination of basketball, soccer, and hockey. Anyone can enjoy lacrosse because physical size is not important to being successful at the sport. The game focuses on coordination and agility, not brute strength. Lacrosse is a fast-moving and exciting game with rapid scoring. Fast transitions; quick, precise passes; and dodges are common in both men's and women's lacrosse.

Men's and women's lacrosse evolved from the same original game, but today they are played under different rules. Women's rules limit stick contact, do not allow body contact, and; therefore, little protective equipment. Men's lacrosse rules allow some stick and body contact, although violence is not allowed—nor is it in keeping with the culture of the game. Here is a summary of rule differences between men's and women's lacrosse:

- Field dimensions are different (see Figures 16.1 and 16.2), as well as restraining lines.
- Women play with 11 field players and a goalie; men play with 10 and a goalie.
- The men's game allows some stick-to-body contact and body-to-body contact within 5 feet of the ball.

9" Radius

Side Line 110 yards

10 yards | 20 yards

Wing Area

Midfield Line

Wing Area

LIMIT LINE

20 yards

20 yards

6 yards

15 yards

5 yards

Endline
60 yards

FIGURE 16.1 Men's Lacrosse Field

- The women's game allows only stick-to-stick contact within strict guide-lines and no body contact at any time.
- Men wear helmets, shoulder pads, mouth guards, and protective gloves.
- Women wear eye protection and mouth guards.
- Stick pockets may be deeper in the men's game than the women's.

Variations of lacrosse can be added to a curriculum with minimal expense and with such benefits as improved eye-hand coordination, aerobic and anaer-obic fitness, muscular coordination, mental toughness, and competitiveness.

SKILLS LISTED WITH CUES

The tips and cues presented in this chapter are based on co-ed, noncontact play, using soft lacrosse equipment. The skills; however, are directly transfer-able to the traditional men's and women's games.

FIGURE 16.2 Women's Lacrosse Field

If students enjoy the basic skills and tactics of lacrosse learned in their physical education class, they may become acquainted with the standard game of lacrosse—including regulation equipment, protective gear, and rules—by seeking out local playing opportunities. The knowledge and skills gained in physical education class will help them succeed.

TIPS

1. A good drill for catching and throwing is called "wall ball". Find a solid wall with no windows or lights. Using the stick and a ball, practice throwing the ball against the wall. Catch the ball in the pocket with the stick. Follow the throwing, catching, and cradling cues. Spending hours throwing the ball against the wall will lead to mastery of these skills. Pick spots on the wall to aim, or tape an imaginary goal outline to the wall. This will improve shooting, passing, and catching. The goal cage is

6×6 feet. This drill can also be done in a gym. While playing wall ball, make sure to practice alternating hands.

2. Cradling, rocking the ball in the basket of an upright stick, is a critical skill that prevents the player from losing the ball when moving. Have students run at full speed down field with just a ball in their stick, not cradling; then have them cradle as they run down the field. This exercise will reinforce the need for cradling.

3. Body position for passing and catching the ball is important for balance, fluidity of motion, and quick transition to other areas of the game. The ready position consists of a relaxed body with knees slightly bent, holding stick in throwing-ready position (see the cue for ready position).

4. Ground ball position: Bending at the waist and knees and keeping your butt down is critical. Keep your head up, using peripheral vision to locate and scoop the ball. Keep the back hand close to the ground, and make the stick parallel to the ground. This allows the player to have visual contact with his or her own team and opposing players.

5. Develop ambidextrous skills. Perform each skill, alternating right hand and left hand on top.

6. Throwing tip: When developing stick-handling skills, it is important to emphasize wrist and hand flexibility and strength. After instructing the fundamentals of grip and throwing motion, have players practice throwing and catching while in a kneeling position. This isolates the upper body and helps focus on the importance of hand and wrist flexibility.

Equipment Tips

The recommended equipment for teaching lacrosse in the physical education classroom is known as "soft lacrosse" equipment. Soft lacrosse sticks are not gender-specific and differ from men's and women's lacrosse sticks. Soft lacrosse utilizes a larger, softer ball. The U.S. Lacrosse Sports Science and Safety Committee has determined that no protective equipment is necessary to be worn when utilizing soft lacrosse balls or sticks.

Should teachers choose to use standard lacrosse sticks and balls, which is *not* recommended for physical education play, the following statement has been issued by U.S. Lacrosse:

> Any clinic, class, or competitive lacrosse program offered using sticks and/or balls other than the "soft lacrosse" equipment (oversize plastic head and oversized, soft, hollow ball) *must* adhere to players' use of *equipment required* by either the boys' or the girls' lacrosse rules (found at www.uslacrosse.org), depending on which set of rules is chosen for play. Programs using "soft lacrosse" sticks and balls should use the non-contact, "soft lacrosse" rules and may opt to use a form of protective eyewear or other protective safety equipment.

1. Indoor soccer goals, hockey goals, or plastic garbage cans can be used for physical education classes. Soccer balls and volleyballs can be used to teach the tactical skills of the game. Tennis balls may be used as an alternative to lacrosse balls.

2. Men's equipment differs from women's equipment:
   - Men's equipment: Helmet with face mask, shoulder pads, arm guards, gloves, lacrosse stick, lacrosse ball, mouth guard, two goals 6×6 feet, field 110 by 60 yards.

- Women's equipment: Stick, ball, eye protection, mouth guard, gloves optional, two goals 6 × 6 feet, field 120 by 70 yards.

Safety

1. If not using "soft lacrosse" equipment, eye protection and other required equipment must be used.

2. There should be no checking near the head without proper equipment.

Etiquette

1. Keep games clean and fair.

2. Limit physical contact.

TEACHING IDEAS

1. Lacrosse can be played in physical education classes in teams of 5–7 players, each using a smaller goal such as an indoor soccer goal or a plastic garbage can. Lay the can down and throw the ball into the can. This sharpens the shooting skills. The field can be reduced to size available. This provides opportunity for multiple games involving the greatest number of players.

2. Scrimmage once a week with interested students for at least two periods of 15 minutes each on a regulation field. Regulation play requires 10 players for men's lacrosse (1 goalie, 3 defenders, 3 midfielders, 3 attack men) and 12 players for women's lacrosse (1 goalie, 3 defenders, 5 midfielders, 3 attackers).

3. Physical education teachers can teach the tactical skills of lacrosse with a soccer ball or volleyball carried in the hands of a player (instead of a stick). In this scenario, teachers do not need to purchase equipment but can teach the game and rules of lacrosse and present an alternative enjoyable experience. If regular lacrosse goals are not available, hoops or garbage cans can be used.

Teaching Progressions

1. The first skills that should be taught are throwing and catching. Have students do this on their own using a wall. Eventually, have them practice in partners.

2. Scooping (picking up ground balls) is the next skill to learn. Make sure students are bending down low and running "through the ball". A good drill for this is to place students side-by-side and roll a ball between them. Whoever successfully retrieves the ball passes it back to the start. As students progress with this skill, have the person who retrieved the ball be offense and the person who did not be defense.

3. Shooting is the next skill that should be taught. Make sure students are shooting from outside the crease, abiding by national rules. Have students practice aiming for the corners without a goalie. Using a garbage can for a goalie is a good way to prevent students from shooting at the middle of the cage.

4. Body positioning for defense should be taught first without sticks. This forces students to not rely on their stick to force their opponent to the sidelines. Add sticks as skills and concepts progress.

5. Checking, which is dangerous when not done correctly, should be one of the last skills taught. Make sure students know the correct technique and the rules regarding checking in both men's and women's lacrosse.

Mini-Games

1. 3 versus 3: One goal with a crease and one cone opposite the goal are used as the starting position. Each time a goal is scored, offense and defense switch. The objective is to score as many goals as possible. When a goal is scored, the new attack team must restart at the top cone before they can shoot for the goal. The ball must be passed at least once before being shot, and no defender is allowed to stand in front of the goal.

2. 4 versus 4: Set up two goals at both ends of the playing area. This keeps the players spread out because there are two options to score. Start the game from the goal line. Teams must try to score a goal on either one of their opponent's goals. If a goal is scored, the ball is turned over. There must be three passes before shooting is allowed. This game works to create space and to allow passing in the open space.

3. STX Sample Game: STX Ball begins by awarding ball possession to the team in their offensive half of the court (use coin flip to award the first possession). The game then proceeds based on the five basic rules. When a goal is scored, the team "scored on" is immediately given the ball at midcourt of the offensive half of the court. Play should be continuous, using as many "natural boundaries" as possible to keep the ball available for play. Substitution of players may take place at any time and is unlimited. The player leaving the game must go to a designated sideline substitution area and hand the stick to the new player entering the game at that location. Remember: "Keep it simple." The "spirit" of STX Ball is not strength or size, but teamwork, stick work, and fair play. (See FYI for more information.)

GAME PLAY

Five Basic Rules

STX Five Basic Rules—Physical Education Classes

1. Play the ball, not the opponent.
2. Players must keep both hands on their sticks.
3. The ball must be passed to in order to get over the center line.
4. Two passes must be made before you shoot at the goal.
5. Play should be continuous.

Girls' Competitive Lacrosse

1. Stay out of crease.
2. Stay on the sides of the playing area.
3. No body checks are allowed.
4. Provide the shooter with enough shooting space.
5. Players must have the ball in order to check.

Boys' Competitive Lacrosse

1. Keep checks safe.
2. Stay on the sides of the playing area.
3. Keep the sticks legal (width and length).
4. Stay out of crease (circle around the goalie).
5. Keep the correct amount of players on the field at all times.

The first set of rules is for beginning lacrosse or physical education classes that are learning the game. The second and third sets of rules are for advanced girls' and boys' competitive lacrosse games.

Scoring

One point is scored each time the ball goes into the cage. The goal must be shot from outside the crease to count.

ASSESSMENT IDEAS

1. *Four-corner Shooting*: Markers are placed in each of the 4 goal corners approximately $1/2$–1 foot from the goal post. Players start at the 8-meter arc of a women's lacrosse field or 8 meters out of a men's lacrosse field and try to shoot the ball between the marker and goal post. Players receive 12 chances and 3 balls for each corner.

2. *Lightning* (fast-speed wall ball): Players try to see how many times they can catch the ball off the wall in one minute. This assessment can also be done with two players passing between each other.

3. *Scoop and Shoot*: Line up 6 balls on the outside fan of a women's lacrosse field or 12 meters from the goal on a men's lacrosse field. Set up a cone 5 meters from the ball to serve as a starting point. Players run and scoop up one ball, which they then shoot from the perimeter of the 8 meter women's arc or 8 meters outside the men's goal. Once they shoot, they go back to the cone for the next ball. Players score one point for every successful scoop and shot. If a scoop is missed or goal is missed, no point is given. Players are assessed on how many shots they score out of 6 shots.

FYI

For further information and special help, consult the following organization.

ORGANIZATION

U.S. Lacrosse
113 W. University Parkway
Baltimore, MD 21210
Phone: (410) 235-6882
Fax: (410) 366-6735
Email: info@uslacrosse.org
Website: www.uslacrosse.org

MATERIALS AVAILABLE:

1. U.S. Lacrosse Physical Education Curriculum
2. Coaches' Education Program Level 1 outline courses
3. Physical education and youth equipment grants
4. New Team Assistance programs
5. Online store with educational books, videos, and DVDs
6. Men's and women's rules, sports science and safety studies, equipment specs, connections to your local chapter, and the latest in lacrosse news

SKILL	CUE	WHY?	COMMON ERROR
Grip	Soft hands; opposing grip (bottom hand palm down, top hand palm up)	Stick mobility, agility with stick	Hands too loose or too tight
Top Hand	Dominant hand on top, about 6 inches from head	Dominant hand on top provides most success for beginners	Dominant hand too low
	Shaft should lie across fingers of top hand, which curl around shaft	Provides more control	
	Keep handle in fingers and off palm of hand		Death grip on stick; no gap between palm and shaft of stick
Bottom Hand	Gently grips butt end of stick	Provides stability and support; moves in sync with the top hand	Bottom hand not moving in tandem with top hand—windshield wiper action
Throwing Ready Position (Figure 16.3)	Arms up and away	Top hand/arm moves up and behind body at ear level—just like an overhand throw of a baseball, softball, or football; bottom hand points toward target	Elbow of top hand/arm will be tight against body instead of up
	Point with opposite shoulder	Body perpendicular to target by pointing non-throwing shoulder at target	Facing target
Throwing Motion/ Release (Figure 16.4)	Push/pull	Top hand pushes while bottom hand pulls to create a lever action	Dropping stick below the shoulders or throwing sidearm; too much push with the top and not enough pull with bottom (will look like punching) will send ball into the ground
	Step	Like push/pull, step with opposite foot (just like throwing a ball)	Stepping with same side foot; no step
	Follow-through	Trunk rotates through toward target	Not following through to target

Hands are shoulder high

Top hand/arm elbow up

Bottom hand aims toward target

FIGURE 16.3 Throwing Ready Position

Push and then pull

Follow-through

Step with opposite foot

FIGURE 16.4 Throwing Motion/Release

CATCHING, CRADLING, AND SCOOPING

SKILL	CUE	WHY?	COMMON ERROR
Catching	"Ask" for the ball (hold stick out as a target)—should be upright in front of body and shoulder at a 45° angle	Gives thrower a target, exposes largest surface of stick for ball	Not providing a target
	Give/soft hands—as ball enters stick, player should give softly by moving the stick in the direction the ball is traveling, as if cushioning an egg or water balloon	Ball will bounce out of stick if stick is rigid	Ball bounces out of stick—student not giving, or timing the give of the stick incorrectly
	Triple threat—catch motion should finish with stick in the box by shoulder and ear	From this position, the player may either pass, cradle, or shoot	Basket catching—player lowers stick and catches ball as if it were falling into a basket
Cradling (Two-Handed)	Opposing grip (bottom hand palm down, top hand palm up)		Both hands facing up or down

continued

SKILL	CUE	WHY?	COMMON ERROR
(Figure 16.5)	Soft grip—shaft should lie across fingers of top hand, which curl around shaft; bottom hand gently grips butt end of stick	Provides space for the stick to rotate	Death grip on stick; no gap between palm and shaft of stick
	Stick in box—head of stick almost upright near shoulder and ear, facing outward	Positions stick in zone that makes checking difficult	Stick hanging horizontal or below shoulders
	Use top hand to turn the stick head in a semicircular motion, creating centrifugal force of the ball against the pocket. While top hand curls in and out, the bottom hand should allow the shaft to rotate in the fingers.	The two-handed cradle is used by men's and women's lacrosse players to maintain possession and set up faces and dodges. The more adept a player is with the two-handed cradle, the more effective he or she will be in maneuvering with the ball.	Bottom hand out of sync with top hand—causes a windshield wiper effect, and ball will fall out of stick
	"Rock the baby" (to describe both hands working together), "swing the bucket" (top hand motion), "rev the motorcycle" (bottom hand motion)	Keep ball in the pocket with centrifugal force—smooth motion	Jerky wrist movements cause the ball to be lost
Scooping (Picking Up Ground Balls) (Figure 16.6)	Keep stick parallel to the ground, lower arms, bend at the knees, get butt down	Necessary to attain proper positioning	Student bends at waist instead of knees
	Head of the ball		
	Step with same side foot as top hand, even with ball	More extension	Step is too far behind or in front of ball
	"Scrape your knuckles"—push stick under and through ball by pushing bottom hand through	Need to force stick under ball	Student shoves ball along ground as if "vacuuming"
	"Kiss your stick"—raise head of stick to vertical position in front of face	Important for stick protection	Student hangs stick out in front (easy to check in the traditional game, though not allowed in physical education classes)

continued

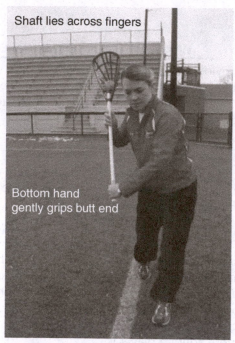

Shaft lies across fingers

Bottom hand gently grips butt end

FIGURE 16.5 Cradling Grip

Get butt down

Lower arms

Bend at knees

Stick parallel to the ground

FIGURE 16.6 Scooping Up Ground Balls

CATCHING, CRADLING, AND SCOOPING, continued

SKILL	CUE	WHY?	COMMON ERROR
Scooping (Picking Up Ground Balls), *continued*	Run through the scoop; begin cradling immediately	Move out of traffic to make a safe pass	Stopping to pick up the ball
	Talk, talk, talk—three things need to be communicated each time a ball hits the ground: 1. "Ball down!"	Lets teammates know a loose-ball situation exists	Not communicating
	2. "Ball!" Communicates your intention to pick up the ball	This allows teammates to concentrate on getting into position or boxing out other players within 5 yards of the ball. Also prevents the situation of multiple players from the same team fighting for the ball.	Too many teammates going for the same ball
	3. "Release!" Announces you have the ball	Allows teammates to stop blocking opponents and move into position to support the pass	

SKILL	CUE	WHY?	COMMON ERROR
Off-Ball Movement: Cutting	Cutting—purpose is to create space, occupy defender, break free to receive a pass	Off-ball movement is essential; quick and even slower, organized motion will create holes in the defense and opportunities for the offense	Standing around watching ball as a spectator
	Watch his or her cut—when opponent's eyes are off you, make a move	It will take longer for them to react to your movement	Not being aware if opponent is watching you
	Backdoor cut—cutting behind the opponent	Harder for opponent to see the cut	Cutting in front of the opponent
	Cut away and then cut to—take defender away from ball, then cut back toward ball carrier to receive pass	Creates space	Moving toward the ball and bringing defender into the area of the ball
	Catch, clear out, or else you clog—three things can happen when a teammate approaches you with a ball: 1. Catch—you cut successfully, get free, make the catch. 2. Clear—you cut successfully but are not the recipient of the pass; move on to make space for the ball carrier or another cutter. 3. Clog—you cut successfully, but don't do either 1 or 2; you will impede the ball carrier's progress by clogging the space.	Sometimes players are forced to leave their player to cover a more dangerous threat. Calling for a slide signals that the other defenders each need to drop in and cover the next open person left by the movement (sliding) of defenders.	Not communicating when player is leaving an attacker
With the Ball *Dodging*	Key principles: deception, change of direction, change of speed, quick feet	Put the opponent off balance	No change of speed or acceleration through dodge—steady pace
	Protect opponent off—get body between stick and opponent	To protect the ball	Hanging stick out, presenting stick to defender when setting up dodge

continued

SKILL	CUE	WHY?	COMMON ERROR
With the Ball *Dodging, continued*	Seal opponent off—get back on a straight opponent as soon as possible (north-south)	Does not allow for easy recovery by opponent beaten by dodge	Finishing dodge parallel or in front of defender instead of behind defender on north-south line
Face Dodge	Shake and bake—dodge performed facing defender; fake to cradling side, pull stick to opposite side, protect stick with body, bring back to cradle side when past defender	Defender will react to the first side you move to	Weak fake to strong side doesn't pull defender off balance
Roll Dodge	Fake to one side, plant foot, roll off defender	Boxes out the defender	Ending the roll in front of or beside defender instead of behind
Tips	Be creative! Try combining moves from the roll and face dodges	Confuses the defender	Be predictable
	Switch hands—try switching hands to protect the stick on the dodge or to create new dodges	Harder for the defender to check	Same side every time

TEAM OFFENSIVE STRATEGY

SKILL	CUE	WHY?	COMMON ERROR
Attack Triangle	Find open space—go where there are limited defenders	Gives the ball carrier two different directions to pass	Hiding behind defenders and not getting into open space
	Flat Player—In line with the ball carrier	Side option	Too far from the ball, carrier making passes easier to intercept
	Through Player—in front of ball carrier	Forward option	Too far from the ball, carrier making passes easier to intercept
Behind the Cage	Quarterback of the attack sets up plays and allows attackers to get open for cuts	Can see all teammates and cuts	No player behind the cage
	Use the crease—hug the crease	Defenders cannot enter the crease, so the ball carrier can roll around the cage	In the crease—illegal

SKILL	CUE	WHY?	COMMON ERROR
Player-to-Player Defense: Individual Positioning	Good defensive stance—knees bent, weight slightly forward on balls of feet not heels, shuffling feet (similar to basketball)	Quick footwork is essential to reacting and dictating where the offense is going	Standing upright, off-balance, lunging after opponent
	Mirror the stick—your stick should mirror the movement of your opponent	Puts defender in position to block, intercept, or force a bad pass	Stick drops to waist and is ineffective
	Goal-side positioning—keep your body between your player and the goal	This strategy slows the attacker down, or forces the attacker away from the goal (similar to basketball)	Letting attacker have a line to the goal
	Stay with your player—maintain a stick length between you and your man		Leaving player to cover another—this leaves your player open for an easy pass
	Slide! Move from your player to a more dangerous, open player	Sometimes players are forced to leave their player to cover a more dangerous threat. Calling for a slide is a signal that the other defenders each need to drop in and cover the next open person left by the movement (sliding) of defenders	Not communicating when player is leaving an attacker
	"Help!" indicates you have lost your player and another teammate must pick up him or her		
	Stick up—if your player does not have the ball, stick should be up in the potential passing lane	Increases chance to block or intercept a pass, makes you seem "bigger"	"Lazy sticks"—arms hanging down around waist
Tips	Communication is essential for good defense		

SKILL	CUE	WHY?	COMMON ERROR
Leading the Team Defense	Goalie controls defense like a soccer goalie: *talk*	Goalies must communicate where the ball is at all times, as well as instruct defenders when and where to move	Lack of communication
	Calls all the passes and movement of the ball; wherever the ball goes, goalie calls the movement ("ball top right"; "ball top left")	Allows all defenders to know where the ball is	Concentration and focus elsewhere
	Goalie needs to have confidence and has to maintain motivation of the team		Getting down on a teammate
	Goalie needs to be always up, mentally tough	Lacrosse is a high-scoring game. Goalies need to know how to bounce back so they can make the next save	Getting discouraged
Playing the Ball	Goalie needs to step to ball		Not stepping out to meet the ball when possible
	Position body between the opponent who has the ball and the goal	Blocks open space making angle difficult	

17

Pickleball

INTRODUCTION

Pickleball is a combination of tennis, badminton, and table tennis that is played on a doubles badminton court (20 feet × 44 feet) with a perforated plastic ball and wooden paddles. The doubles badminton court on the gymnasium floor can be converted to a pickleball court simply by putting the nets at a height of 3 feet. Pickleball can also be played on the inside singles lines on the tennis court.

Many teachers have emphasized how pickleball has been effective in developing the students' reflexes and eye-hand coordination skills, along with quickness and agility. Pickleball is a success-oriented game because after the player strikes the ball, the perforations slow the ball down in midflight, thereby promoting longer rallies and providing an equalizing factor for differences in strength, skill, and athletic ability. Many teachers are adding pickleball to their curricula because students quickly succeed in the game.

SKILLS LISTED WITH CUES

The cues for pickleball skills include the ready position, forehand and backhand swing (grip, stance, and stroke), lob and drive serves, volley and drop shots, topspin, backspin, and the overhead smash. Also provided are cues for, boundaries, scoring, and strategies for both singles and doubles.

TIPS

A pickleball unit can be presented before or after a tennis unit, or on rainy days during a tennis unit. Teachers need not cancel a tennis class at any level because of inclement weather if their school has a gym (Figure 17.1).

FIGURE 17.1 Rainy Day

Equipment Tips

1. Pickleball court (Figure 17.2)

2. Pickleball ball: a specially designed Wiffle ball with a 3-inch maximum diameter (there are both indoor and outdoor models) (Figure 17.3)

3. Wooden paddles: The game was developed to be played with wooded paddles designed for pickleball and that still seems to be the best choice.

4. The length of the paddle makes a difference in performance because it is light in weight and short (see Figure 17.3). Players can feel more control with the racquet, especially with backhand shots (see Figures 17.4 and 17.5).

Safety

1. When playing doubles, be aware of your partner and watch where you swing.

2. When the ball is loose, wait until players end the rally before asking or entering the court for the ball.

Etiquette

1. The server should call the score before serving in order to avoid confusion and arguments.

2. Call balls on your side of the court; use integrity.

3. Do not throw racquets or ball; control your temper.

TEACHING IDEAS

Teaching Progressions

1. For large beginning classes, have players hit the ball against the wall 10 times. This exercise gives them practice with hitting forehands, backhands, and the like by themselves. They progress to the net when they can hit 10 in a row.

2. Use the modified two-bounce-limit rule for beginning classes and less fit players.

FIGURE 17.2 Pickleball Court

3. Have players feed the ball to each other using half-court. This method encourages practicing technique and provides numerous practice trials.

   - A forehand and backhand baseline shot drill provides both forehand and backhand stroke practice. This drill is practiced at the baseline.
   - Dink volley game: Players stand behind the non-volley zone and hit drives back and forth like volley drills in tennis.
   - Hit offensive and defensive lob shots with a partner.
   - Do an overhead smash drill with a partner.

4. Volley the ball in the air with a partner. Your goal is to see how many times you can hit the ball back and forth while keeping the ball in the air. This drill is good for eye-hand coordination.

5. Score on every serve. The side-out rule can be modified so that a point is scored on every serve. One player serves for a total of five serves, then the opponent serves for five serves until one player scores 10 points. If time permits, one player serves 10 serves, then the opponent serves 10 serves until one player scores 11 points. Different numbers of serves can be substituted.

6. Provide challenge drills, games or modified games, or tournaments set up before class. These "early bird specials" encourage the students to come early (Strand, Reeder, Scantling, & Johnson, 1997).

FIGURE 17.3 Pickleball Equipment

Mini-Games

Rally Game:

A. This is a game to help with the transition from hitting a ball that is tossed to actually playing pickleball. It is an extremely versatile formation for a large class and allows each student to maximize the amount of practice with minimal waiting time. It can be set up for any size class; the actual arrangement depends on the class size and the number of courts. It makes better use of the space because the court is divided and two rallies occur at the same time.

B. The following is an example of how to set up the Rally Game with 30 students and 6 courts. Five players are assigned to each court, with one player waiting at the net off the court and two players at each end of the court, behind the baseline. The court is divided along the center line, so that two rallies occur simultaneously. The students play 1 point and then rotate to their left. Players keep track of their own points and continue to play for 5–10 minutes. If you incorporate a rotation with all of the courts, after the 5–10 minutes have ended, the players with the highest points on Courts 2–5 go up, and the players with the lowest points go down. Then, on Court 1, the player with the lowest points goes to Court 2, and the one with the highest points on Court 6 goes to Court 5. So there should be 5 players per court, and each player starts at 0 to begin a new game.

Options:

There are many variations of this basic setup to practice other aspects of pickleball.

• Start the two players on one end at the net, just outside of the non-volley zone.

• Have all of the players at the net, outside of the non-volley zone.

• Have the students play as a doubles team, with all players toward the back, one team up to net, or both teams up to net.

• Have one end of the court hit lobs, drop shots, only forehands, or only backhands.

GAME PLAY

Rules

1. The player who wins a coin toss or spinning the racquet has the option to serve first or choose the side of court.

2. The player not making the first choice has the choice of the remaining options to serve or receive first or to pick the side of court.

3. The server must have one foot behind the baseline without touching the line, serve across the net diagonally, and clear the non-volley zone.

4. A ball landing on any line is considered within bounds.

5. The double-bounce rule indicates that each player or team must play their first shot off the bounce. That is, the receiving team must let the serve bounce once before hitting it, and the serving team must let the return of the serve bounce before playing it. After two bounces have occurred, the ball can be either volleyed or played off the bounce.

6. The hand below the wrist is considered part of the paddle, so shots off any part of it are good.

7. Singles game: The player who starts the game in the right-hand court will always be in the right-hand court when his or her team's score is 2, 4, 6, 8, and 10.

8. Singles and doubles games: Play to 11, win by 2.

9. A ball going out-of-bounds cannot be caught. It is a fault to catch a ball going out-of-bounds.

10. A fault is called when a player is hit by the ball, whether he or she is standing inside or outside the court boundaries.

11. A player who is playing a ball that has bounced in the non-volley zone and then touches the net with the paddle or any part of his or her body shall receive a fault. A service fault occurs when the server swings the paddle with the intent of striking the ball but misses the ball. However, the server may toss the ball in the air and catch it or allow it to fall to the court without penalty so long as he or she does not attempt to deliver the ball.

Strategies

Singles Play

Hit the ball deep into the opponent's court. Try to hit most balls to the opponent's weak side (usually backhand). Hit the ball from side to side to make your opponent move. The server should vary the serves, such as toward deep corners at opponents, hitting the ball hard or softly, etc. The receiver should return the ball to the opponent's deep court. While playing a game, attempt to make deep shots to the sides, play weak sides when possible, and wait for errors before attacking the net. Players can also attempt short volleys followed by deep lobs to keep their opponent off balance, hit right at the receiver, and mix up their shots.

Doubles Play

Players should try to mix up drive and lob serves. Remind players that accuracy is key over power. For front/back play, players should shadow their partner, then attack the net. For side to side play, players should not cross the center line as each is responsible for the ball in their own side of the court. Communication is very important in doubles play; players should remember to call for the ball.

Scoring

Singles Play

Players can score a point only when serving. When the score is zero or even, serve in the right court. When score is odd, players should serve in the left court. The ball must bounce once in the receiver's court as well as once in the server's court on the return; the cue for this pattern is, "Bounce, bounce." Games are played to 11 points and should be won by two points.

Doubles Play

Scoring is similar to singles play, but with these exceptions. Players should serve in this order: One player serves on team A, then both players on team B, then both players on team A. The server switches courts with their teammate if they score a point. Service always starts in the right-hand court.

ASSESSMENT IDEAS

1. Play 6 singles games worth 5 points each.
2. Play 6 doubles games worth 5 points each.

If you win, you earn 1 bonus point.

FYI

For further information and special help, consult the following organization and resource.

ORGANIZATION

Pickle-Ball, Inc. provides a free catalog on request. A rule book, 9-minute videotape for the game of pickleball, textbook, and equipment (paddles, balls, nets, standards, and sets) are also available at this address.

Douglas Smith, President
Pickle-Ball, Inc.
810 Northwest 45th Street
Seattle, WA 98107
Phone: (206) 632-0119 or (800) 377-9915
Fax: (206) 632-0126
Email: info@pickleball.com
Website: www.pickleball.com

PUBLICATION

Curtis, J. (1998). *Pickleball for player and teacher* (3rd ed.). Englewood, CO: Morton.

READY POSITION

SKILL	CUE	WHY?	COMMON ERROR
Stance	Knees bent	Athletic position	Knees locked
	Weight on balls of feet	Ready to react faster	Weight on heels
	Square to net	Ready to move in any direction	Not square with net
Move to Swing	Pivot and step for both forehand and backhand strokes	Better balance	Lack of pivot and step
	Turn shoulders—gets paddle back early	Ready to hit after moving to the ball	No early turn

FOREHAND STROKE

SKILL	CUE	WHY?	COMMON ERROR
Grip	Palm is mostly behind paddle grip	Puts paddle in best position to make contact with ball	Choking the paddle; holding too tight
			Extending first finger behind paddle head
Stance	Pivot and step	Gets player ready to hit	Legs not moving; body is parallel to net
Stroke (Figure 17.4)	Shoulder turn for early racquet preparation	To be ready to hit the ball	Late shoulder turn
	Swing low to high	More power on ball; gives ball topspin	Scooping ball
	Wait for ball to drop	Easier to hit	Hitting the ball too high
	Hit ball in front of left hip	More control	Finishing with paddle flat

Drill:

1. Have partners toss balls to each other.
2. Hit the ball using forehand stroke.
3. Use lots of balls and switch between tossing and hitting.

BACKHAND STROKE

SKILL	CUE	WHY?	COMMON ERROR
Grip	Turn palm a little more on top of paddle grip compared to forehand grip	Small grip change from forehand to backhand to react quickly	Failing to turn paddle
Stance	Pivot and step; turn shoulders early	Gets player ready to hit	Not turning shoulders soon enough
Stroke (Figure 17.5)	Swing low to high	Gives ball power and topspin on ball	
	Wait for ball to drop		
	Hit ball knee-high	Better accuracy	Face of paddle tilted too far up or down

Drill:

1. Have partners toss balls back and forth using backhand stroke.
2. Have partners toss once using forehand stroke, then once using backhand stroke.
3. Use lots of balls and switch between tossing and hitting.

FIGURE 17.4 Forehand Stroke

FIGURE 17.5 Backhand Stroke

SERVING			
SKILL	**CUE**	**WHY?**	**COMMON ERROR**
Lob (Figure 17.6) *Foot Placement*	One foot in front of baseline, other foot in back of baseline		Both feet behind baseline
Toss	Drop the ball, then swing the paddle	Proper sequence	Throwing ball up or not dropping the ball
Swing (Figure 17.7)	Like pitching horseshoes	Promotes low to high swing	
	Follow-through straight up to hit face with biceps	Promotes low-to-high swing	Follow-through too low
	Finish like the Statue of Liberty	Promotes low-to-high swing	Low finish
Drive (Figure 17.8) *Foot Placement*	One foot in front of baseline, other foot in back of baseline		Both feet behind baseline
Toss	Ball held waist high and out in front		Ball held too high or too low
	Paddle is held behind you	Promotes longer swing	Short swing
	Wrist in cocked position	Promotes proper wrist action	

continued

FIGURE 17.6   Serving Position

FIGURE 17.7   Lob Serve

SERVING, continued			
SKILL	**CUE**	**WHY?**	**COMMON ERROR**
Drive, *continued* Swing	Drop the ball, then swing	Proper sequence	Contacting the ball late
	Arm straight at contact	Longer lever	
Follow-Through	Paddle finishes on edge, shoulder level	Promotes longer swing	Short swing

Drill:

1. Have partners serve lots of balls to each other.
2. Have partners play the rally out.

FIGURE 17.8   Drive Serve

FIGURE 17.9   Forehand Volley

FOREHAND/BACKHAND VOLLEY SHOT

SKILL	CUE	WHY?	COMMON ERROR
Ready Position	One foot behind non-volley zone	Rule	Both feet in front of non-volley zone (illegal)
	Paddle at eye level	React faster	Paddle held too low
Grip	Neutral grip	React faster	Extreme grip changes
Legs and Swing Action (Figure 17.9)	Step and make a short swing	Less time	Too long of a swing
	Little or no backswing	More control	Too much backswing
	Turn of shoulders puts racquet in position	Better preparation	Moving arms rather than turning shoulders
	Meet ball in front of you	Better accuracy to place the ball	Letting ball come to you
	Keep paddle in peripheral vision		
Follow-Through	Contact ball in center of paddle	More power	Contacting ball on paddle edge
	Make a short swing	Not as much time for volleys	Swinging too hard
	Limit follow-through	Less time	Too long a follow-through
Strategy	Play just behind non-volley zone	Rule	

Drill:

1. Have feeders toss the ball to their partners behind non-volley zone; then switch roles.
2. Have feeders hit forehand/backhand volleys to their partners; then switch roles.

DROP SHOT

SKILL	CUE	WHY?	COMMON ERROR
Swing	Graze shorts with paddle		Contact to side and front of body
	Slide paddle under ball		
	Love tap/soft touch	More control, softer touch to ball	Hitting too hard
Contact	Open-face paddle	Gives ball backspin	Closing paddle face
	Push, lift, nudge, caress		Fakes opponent because of spin and short

continued

DROP SHOT, continued			
SKILL	**CUE**	**WHY?**	**COMMON ERROR**
Follow-Through	Look in mirror at finish		Paddle is on edge
Strategy	Swing like a ground stroke when opponent is playing deep	To disguise the drop shot	Swinging like a drop shot

Drill:

Have feeders hit forehand to their partners, then hit backhand, and lastly switch roles.

TOPSPINS AND BACKSPINS			
SKILL	**CUE**	**WHY?**	**COMMON ERROR**
Topspin	Swing racket from low to high	Puts topspin on the ball	Swinging paddle level
	Like making a candy cane at end of swing		Finishing with paddle on edge
Backspin	Paddle swings high to low	Puts backspin on ball	Swinging paddle level
	Shave the ball like shaving your face	Imparts backspin	Finishing with paddle on edge
	Cut flat under ball		

Drill:

1. Try backspins against a wall; then have a partner toss to your forehand and then to your backhand.
2. Have a rally, and try to use topspin and backspin naturally.
3. TIP: Follow through with the racquet flat to the net.

SMASH			
SKILL	**CUE**	**WHY?**	**COMMON ERROR**
Position (Figure 17.10)	Get in back of ball	Easier to hit the ball	Too far in front of ball
Contact with Ball	Contact ball in front of body	Better accuracy to get ball down	Contact ball behind head
	Paddle face tilted toward floor	To hit the ball down	Paddle face tilted toward wall

continued

SMASH, continued			
SKILL	**CUE**	**WHY?**	**COMMON ERROR**
Follow-Through	Like a volleyball smash		No follow-through
	Recover quickly to ready position	To be ready for the next shot	Off balance; can't recover to hit opponent's passing shot

Drill:

Have three people hit balls into the air, with the partner returning the ball using smash.

Drill for Singles and Doubles Court (see Figure 17.2):

1. After all skills have been taught, use this drill with three feeders and one hitter.
2. Feeder 1 hits the ball to forehand; feeder 2 hits the ball backhand; and feeder 3 hits short shots.
3. Then the feeders can mix up shots. Hitters move all over court. Rotate hitters every few minutes.

Contact ball high and in front of body

Get in back of ball

FIGURE 17.10   Smash

18

Racquetball

INTRODUCTION

Racquetball is a game that requires agility, speed, and accuracy. One of the great things about racquetball is never having to chase the ball. Racquetball allows the player to practice shots and court movements without an opponent.

Players should work on their forehand and backhand strokes first. Other strokes, such as the ceiling shot, can be developed from the successful use of these strokes.

When learning the forehand and backhand strokes, many players want to hit the ball hard and fast, but hitting too hard causes the player to lose control. Practicing technique and accuracy will help the player progress to the ultimate goal of hitting the ball harder and faster with better control.

Learning to track the ball is another skill players need to develop. A player must watch the angle of the ball coming off the wall to anticipate the next shot. Experience is the best teacher.

SKILLS LISTED WITH CUES

Included in this chapter are cues for the ready position and grips, forehand and backhand strokes, drive and lob serves, corner and ceiling shots, strategy of service return, singles-game scoring and strategy, and cutthroat rules.

TIPS

1. Always wear proper eye protection approved by the United States Association of Racquetball (USAR), no matter what your level of skill is. The ball can travel 80–100 miles an hour.

2. Always warm up adequately and stretch before and after games.

3. If out of position or unsure, play defensively.

4. Concentrate on proper footwork (i.e., body parallel to the side walls for proper forehand).

Equipment Tips

1. Using proper racquet weight and string tension will prevent shoulder and arm pain.

2. Purchase protective eye guards that meets the USAR standards; students should not play in eye gear that does not meet the USAR standards because of the possibility of eye injuries. A list of approved eye guards can be found at www.usaracquetball.com. Do not buy cheap eye guards.

3. Wear proper shoes that provide ankle support and gripping.

4. Be sure that the racquet grip fits your hand comfortable.

Safety

Make sure each player in your class is wearing USAR-approved eye guards before teaching or playing a racquetball game, even if one player is drilling or on the court alone.

Etiquette

1. The player who hits the ball closest to the serving line serves first.

2. Call out the score (servers score first) before each serve; this will avoid confusion and arguments.

3. If a player is uncertain of a call, such as whether a serve is short or the ball bounces twice, and a disagreement arises with no referee, replay the serve.

TEACHING IDEAS

Teaching Progressions

1. Use the modified no-bounce-limit rule when starting with younger students and beginners. Players may allow the ball to bounce as many times as desired before hitting it.

2. Follow this progression: Stop and hit. Step, drop, and hit. Set up off front wall, step, and hit. Continue the rally, step, and hit.

3. One player can toss ball to rebound off wall while the other player hits the ball. This drill can be done with both forehand and backhand strokes.

Mini-Games

1. Use the modified two-bounce-limit rule for older students, junior racquetball leagues, beginning classes, or players who are not physically fit.

2. Play with scoring on each rally. Both server and receiver can score points.

GAME PLAY

Rules

Simple Rules for Playing a Singles Game

1. The server has two serves.
2. The ball must bounce once when serving the ball.
3. The serve must hit the front wall first and can hit a side wall after hitting the front wall.
4. The serve cannot hit the ceiling or the back wall before the ball bounces.
5. The serve must bounce behind the short line to be in play.
6. Players hit the ball alternately.
7. The ball may be hit in the air before it bounces; it must be hit and returned to the front wall before it bounces twice.
8. Only the server can score points.
9. If the receiver wins the rally, he or she wins the serve.
10. Play one game to 15 points. In match play, two out of three games are won. The third game is played to 11 points.

Service Return Rule

1. The receiver may not enter the safety zone (see Figure 18.3) to return a serve until the ball bounces once.

Return Rules

1. After the ball passes the short line and bounces, the receiver must return the ball to the front wall before it bounces twice on the floor.
2. Unlike the serve, the return may hit any number of walls first, as long as the ball hits the front wall before hitting the floor.

Hinders

1. Try not to overswing; it can cause injury to your opponent.
2. Players should always stop their swing if there is any possibility of hitting their opponent.
3. The word "Hinder" should be called out, shortly after the hinder, and rally should be replayed.

Service Rules

Single-Fault Serves

1. Short serve: A serve that, after hitting the front wall, does not cross the short serve line before bouncing on the floor.
2. Long serve: A serve that, after hitting the front wall, hits the back wall before bouncing on the floor.
3. Three-wall serve: A serve that, after hitting the front wall, hits both side walls before bouncing on the floor.
4. Ceiling serve: A serve that, after hitting the front wall, hits the ceiling before bouncing on the floor.

Double-Fault (Side Out) Serves

1. Two consecutive single-fault serves.

2. Any serve that does not hit the front wall first. This includes hitting the front wall and another wall simultaneously (e.g., it bounces off a side wall, the floor, or the ceiling before hitting the front wall).

3. A serve that strikes the server or any part of the server's clothing or equipment.

4. Any serve that leaves the area of the court (e.g., through the observation window).

For additional rules, refer to the cue tables at the end of the chapter.

STRATEGIES

Service Return

Beginner: Keep the ball and self in the center court. Aim for consistency. Try to read the ball and play it accordingly.

Intermediate: Control the rally with return of serve on the defense. Read the serve and place the ball to control the rally.

Advanced: End the rally with the return of serve. Read the serve and place the ball to end the rally.

Singles Game

Hit the ball away from the opponent: the one who is doing the running is doing the losing.

If the opponent is up close, hit a far/passing shot as it is a tough shot to return.

For additional strategies, refer to the cue tables at the end of the chapter.

Scoring

Scoring for a singles game can be found in the cue tables at the end of the chapter.

ASSESSMENT IDEAS

1. Play 6 singles games worth 5 points each.

2. Play 3 cutthroat games worth 5 points each.

If you win a game, you earn 1 bonus point.

FYI

For further information and special help, consult the following organization and resources.

ORGANIZATION

Jim Hiser
Executive Director
USA Racquetball

1685 West Uintah
Colorado Springs, CO 80904
Phone: (719) 635-5396
Fax: (719) 635-0685
E-mail: jheiser@usra.org
      emeredith@usra.org
Website: www.usaracquetball.com

Materials Available

1. Approved list of protective eyewear
2. Videos
3. Training material
4. Racquetball material
5. Clothing
6. Instructional information online

It's not always necessary to join a health club to play racquetball. Facilities are available for use for a nominal fee.

PUBLICATIONS

Edwards, L. (1992). *Racquetball*. Scottsdale, AZ: Gorsuch Scarisbrick.

Norton, C., & Bryant, J. E. (2003). *Beginning racquetball*. Belmont, CA: Brooks/ Cole.

READY POSITION AND GRIPS

SKILL	CUE	WHY?	COMMON ERROR
Ready Position	Knees bent	Ready to move	Standing upright
	Weight on inside of soles of feet in order to push in either direction		Weight on heels
	Forearms on table	Able to move easily to forehand or backhand position	Arms (racquet) to side of body
Forehand Grip	V shape, top of bevel		Gripping too tightly
			Choking up on grip
	Index finger positioned to pull trigger; squeeze trigger finger at impact		Incorrect placement of index finger
	Butt end of racket in palm of hand (for more wrist action)	Creates power	
Backhand Grip	Rotate V one bevel toward thumb	Allows for a more natural arm motion, reducing injuries and creating power	Failing to rotate grip from forehand to backhand
	Turn clockwise		

Like skipping a rock

Elbow extension

Snap wrist on contact

Pull left shoulder through swing

(a) Execution

(b) Contact

(c) Follow-Through

FIGURE 18.1 Forehand

FOREHAND STROKE			
SKILL	**CUE**	**WHY?**	**COMMON ERROR**
Hit Preparation (Figure 18.1a)	Shoulders parallel to side wall		Hitting with body facing front wall
	Set racket first, then step, and then pivot		
	Elbow above shoulder	More power; less arm strain	Rushed and incomplete backswing
Execution (Figure 18.1a)	Like skipping a rock	Low, straight shot	No wrist snap
	Shoulders dictate aim of ball; if shoulders are parallel, hit parallel	Accuracy	Dropping front shoulder; lifting back shoulder
	Okay to contact ball at knee height; ankle is best	The more parallel to the floor and the lower the contact point, the less bounce	Hitting ball at peak of bounce or ascent
	Wait for it to descend		
	Step into hit		Ball too high on front wall; racquet face tilted up
	Shift weight from back to front		
	Hit ball off front foot or close to front foot, depending on shot		
	Watch ball hit strings	Accuracy	Watch target, not ball
(Figure 18.1b)	Elbow extension plus snap wrist on contact	Power	Wrist in a cast

continued

FOREHAND STROKE, continued

SKILL	CUE	WHY?	COMMON ERROR
Execution, *continued*	Follow-through	Accuracy/power	No follow-through
		Less arm strain	
Opposite Arm (Figure 18.1c)	Pull left shoulder through swing	Power	Left arm hanging at side
	Hit and move to center of court	Ready to retrieve opponent's next shot	Standing still, not moving after shot
Ball Position	Be patient to let the ball drop into position—below knees	More accurate and powerful shot	Not waiting for ball to drop into position

BACKHAND STROKE

SKILL	CUE	WHY?	COMMON ERROR
Hit Preparation	Pivot—step—set racquet		
	Shoulders parallel to side wall	Accuracy	Shoulders perpendicular to side wall
(Figure 18.2a)	Elbow pointing to ground		Elbow too close to body
	Hitting elbow about 4 inches away from body		
	Wrist cocked		Wrist not cocked
Opposite Arm	Elbow pulling racquet back	Create power on release	Keeping left hand on racquet
Execution	Shift weight back to front	Body movement creates power	No weight transfer
(Figure 18.2b)	Okay to contact ball at knee height; ankle is best	Low, level shot = less bounce	Hitting ball too high
(Figure 18.2c)	Push belly button to front wall	Power	No hip rotation
	Wait for ball to descend		
	Snap wrist, like backhanding someone	Power	Arm in a cast
	Drive through with hitting shoulder		
	Watch ball hit strings	Accuracy	Watching target or opponent, not ball
	Hit ball off front foot	Accuracy	Hitting ball into floor; hitting off back foot

continued

Racquet elbow pointing to ground

Okay to contact ball at knee height; ankle is best

Push belly button to front wall

(a) Preparation

(b) Execution

(c) Follow-Through

FIGURE 18.2 Backhand

BACKHAND STROKE, continued			
SKILL	**CUE**	**WHY?**	**COMMON ERROR**
Execution, *continued*	Shoulder parallel to floor through swing	Accuracy; shoulders dictate direction of ball	Swinging upward or dropping shoulder and skipping ball
	Follow-through at shoulder level		
	Racquet in "back-scratch position" (allows for more wrist snap in follow-through)		Open stance
	Hit and move to center of court	Ready for opponent's next shot	Hitting and standing still

SERVING			
SKILL	**CUE**	**WHY?**	**COMMON ERROR**
Drive	Visualize bull's-eye on front wall 1–2 feet up	Serve accuracy	Not having a target
Ball Drop	Contact ball between calf and knee		
	Drop ball to allow extension and follow-through or consistent drop	Correct, natural swing	Ball drops too close to body (jamming player)
	Drop—step—drive—move—follow ball		

continued

SKILL	CUE	WHY?	COMMON ERROR
Bull's–Eye	Should be one-third of distance between ball drop and side wall—not more than 1 foot from ground	Aim serve toward the corner—more difficult for opponent to reach	Hitting ball too high
	Hit and move toward center of court	Ready for opponent's return	Inconsistent movement
			Not moving to center after hitting
	Watch ball and know where opponent is		Not knowing where opponent is and not watching the ball
Lob	Firm wrist	Accuracy	Wrist snap
	Elbow extended	Not too much power	
	Like pitching horseshoes		Hitting ball
	Soft touch		
	Like pushing ball instead of hitting ball		
	Contact ball between waist and shoulder		
	High follow-through	Accuracy	No follow-through
	Pull arm to opposite shoulder		
High	Soft touch	Accuracy	Hitting ball too hard
	Contact on rise 15–18 feet—graze side		
Half	10–12 feet—approach opponent at shoulder height	Difficult for opponent to make offensive shot	No follow-through
	Pull arm to opposite shoulder		
	Hit and move to center of court; gain position	Ready for opponent's next shot	Not moving after serve

CORNER AND CEILING SHOTS			
SKILL	CUE	WHY?	COMMON ERROR
Corner Shot (Offensive Shot)	Pinch in corner	Use when opponent is deep in court—ball stays in front court	Hitting too far from corner and too high
	Low shot		

continued

SKILL	CUE	WHY?	COMMON ERROR
Corner Shot (Offensive Shot), *continued*	Pinch—ball hits side wall and then front wall, or vice versa		
	Near side corner	Hit low on front wall so that it bounces twice before reaching the other side wall (otherwise the ball will pop up off the other side wall)	
	Eyes focus on ball 1–2 feet from front		Eyes wandering
	Hit ball hard	Creates a spin and keeps ball in front court	Can't pinch ball if not hit hard enough
Ceiling Shot (Defensive Shot) *(Use when not in position to make an offensive shot)*	Forehand lob to ceiling		
	Volleyball overhand server motion	Accuracy	
	Aim to hit ceiling about 3 feet from front wall, depending on speed of ball	Should land about 4 feet from back wall and less than 4 feet high on back wall—very difficult for opponent to get an offensive shot	Hitting front wall first

SINGLES GAME			
SKILL	CUE	WHY?	COMMON ERROR
Scoring *Server* (Figure 18.3)	Server must stand in the service zone to serve		
	The server must bounce the ball and then hit the ball to the front wall	Rule	Hitting the ball before it bounces
	The server must hit the ball behind the short line to start play	Rule	Hitting the ball in front or on short line
	Only the server can score points	Rule	The receiver scores points
	Servers permitted two serves	Rule	Servers permitted only one serve
Receiver	If the receiver wins the rally, the receiver gains the serve and the opportunity to score	Rule	

continued

Front Wall

15'

Service Line

Service Zone

Screen Line ➞
Doubles Box ➞

5'

40'

Short Line

18" 18" ⟵ 14' ⟶ 18" 18"

5'

Receiving Line

Specifications

All lines are 1.5" wide and solid red in color. No lines are allowed on walls.

15'

Back Wall

⟵ 20' ⟶

FIGURE 18.3 Racquetball Court

SINGLES GAME, continued			
SKILL	**CUE**	**WHY?**	**COMMON ERROR**
Scoring, *continued* *Winning Score*	The first player to win 15 points	Rule	Playing to win by 2 points
	There is no deuce game, overtime, or requirement to win by 2 points		
Match Play	First player to win two games	Rule	
Each Player Wins One Game	If both players win one game, play the next game to 11 points	Rule	Playing to 15 points on third game
	The first player to reach 11 points wins the match	Rule	

continued

SKILL	CUE	WHY?	COMMON ERROR
Scoring, *continued*	Serve in tiebreaker goes to the player who scored the most points in the previous two games	Rule	They do not know who serves first in third game
Singles Strategy Four Square Approach Attack opposite corner of where opponent is	Hit ball to corner opposite of where opponent is	Make opponent leave center court and get out of position	Hitting to where opponent is
	Mix up shots	Be unpredictable	Using same shot
	Mix up serves	Keeps opponent off balance	Using same shot
	Mix up sides of court where you stand to serve	Keeps opponent off balance	Serving only on left side of court

CUTTHROAT			
SKILL	**CUE**	**WHY?**	**COMMON ERROR**
Rules	Cutthroat is played with three players; a server plays against two receivers		
Server	Server has two serves		One serve
	Serve has to hit behind second line		First line
	Must alternate hitting between server and two opponents		All three players hit
Receivers	When the server loses the rally, another player earns the serve		
Advanced Rotation Beginner Rotation: Have the weakest player always positioned on the forehand side or left-handed player always on the backhand side	Rotate clockwise: player 1 trades with player 2; player 2 with player 3; player 3 with player 1	Eliminates one player having to play against another's strong side every time he or she serves	Rotate randomly or in a circle

continued

SKILL	CUE	WHY?	COMMON ERROR
Rules, *continued*	Previous server trades with next server. The other player keeps his or her position. Player 1 trades with player 2, and player 3 remains. Next, player 2 trades with player 3, and player 1 remains. Then, player 3 trades with player 1, and player 2 remains. Repeat.	Keep the receiving even for advanced players	Staying in the same position
	After each serve, player goes to the opposite corner of previous position		
Scoring	Only server can score points		
	Serve against the two opponents		Receivers can score if they win rally
Strategies—Single Player	Hit ball farthest away from opponent		
	Go to middle of court after you serve or hit to be ready for the next ball		
Strategies—Double Players	Player who doesn't receive serve goes to service box to play short shots—receiver stays back for deep shots	Controls all areas of court	Unbalanced position opens court for single player
Serving Rules	The ball may hit only one side wall and must strike the front wall first on the serve		A serve that hits the front wall and then either the back wall or ceiling is a fault
Receiving Rules	The ball must bounce behind the second line before the receiver may return the ball		
After the Ball Passes the Short Line	The receiver must return the ball to the front wall before it bounces on the floor twice		
	The return may hit any number of walls first as long as it hits the front wall before it hits the floor		

19

Recreational Walking, Running, and Hiking

INTRODUCTION TO RECREATIONAL WALKING

Walking for recreation and health has become one of the most popular physical activities enjoyed by adults (Select Marketing Groups of America, 2000). Everyone knows how to walk; it doesn't require any special equipment; it can be accomplished anywhere; and it is a social activity that can be done with a friends. Many people prefer walking over running because it is less strenuous, yet still a healthy activity.

Since walking is such a popular activity for adults, it is important that walking for exercise be taught in the schools so that students learn to value walking as a health-enhancing activity. Physical educators should include some instruction on walking for exercise and give their students an opportunity to walk and be social in their classes. This kind of instruction can teach students that walking and talking together can be valuable and that they don't always have to work at high intensity levels to gain health benefits.

WALKING CUES

Encourage good posture when teaching walking. Arms should be bent, the head up, and the shoulders back. Walking is an even rhythm, with one foot is always in contact with the ground.

1. Head up, eyes forward, pull chin in.
2. Swing both arms.
3. Shoulders back, tummy flat, chest out.
4. Heel to toe.
5. Eyes forward—look for a location in the distance to walk to like a tree, sign, or mailbox.

TIPS

Equipment Tips

1. Wear walking shoes or running shoes—avoid court shoes.
2. Wear well fitting socks that wick moisture.
3. Dress in layers for different weather conditions.

Safety

When you walk at night, you need to wear a reflective vest or light-colored clothing.

Etiquette

1. Walk on the side of the sidewalk farthest from street.
2. Obey traffic signals.

TEACHING PROGRESSIONS

Exercise Guidelines

"The benefits of physical activity depend on three elements: intensity, duration, and frequency of exercise" (Harvard Men's Health Watch, August 2009, p. 2). These benefits follow a classic dose-response relationship that means the greater the dose of physical activity, the greater the benefit.

Because walking is less intensive then running, you have to walk longer and more often, or both to match the benefits of running. The current American Heart Association/American College of Sports Medicine standards call for able-bodied adults to do moderate-intensity exercise (such as brisk walking) for at least 30 minutes on 5 days each week or intense aerobic exercise (such as running) for at least 20 minutes 3 days each week (Haskell et al., 2007, p. 1432; Harvard Men's Health Watch, August, p. 2).

The key aspect to deriving health benefits is to move; that movement can take many different forms depending on the interest and schedules of the individuals. Individuals can realize health benefits from a variety of activities from gardening to hiking to playing raquetball so make sure to do what you enjoy.

ASSESSMENT IDEAS

The Miler's Club

1. Miler's Clubs are popular at schools.
2. Students can count their monthly miles and log them at school.
3. Log miles or convert minutes into miles.
4. The students with the most miles qualify to participate in a race at the end of the year (boys and girls race separately). The top ten of each race earn a T-shirt.
5. Qualifying for the race is a goal that supports the idea that hard work is acknowledged and rewarded.
6. Prizes can be awarded for 5, 10, 15, 20, 25 miles, etc. Prizes could include a keychain depicting a running shoe, etc. Be creative!
7. Miler's club can be used for walking, jogging, or running—see FYI, Dave Watt, American Running Association, to get your school involved.

8. Some schools have been doing this for years—make it a tradition for your school.

9. You can get your elementary and middle schools started!

10. Keep our students fit and stay away from obesity!

National Run-a-Mile Day

"Be a Miler—Run a Mile"

Dates: May 6–8

FYI

For further information and special help, consult the following resources.

REFERENCES

Harvard Men's Health Watch. (August 2009). Walking: Your steps to health. *14*(1), 2. (www.health.harvard.com).

Haskell, W. L. et al. (2007). Physical activity and public health: Updated recommendation for adults from the American College of Sports Medicine and the American Heart Association. *Medicine & Science in Sports & Exercise*. 1423–1434.

ORGANIZATION FOR WALKING AND RUNNING

Dave Watt
American Running Association (ARA)
4405 East-West Highway, Suite 405
Bethesda, MD 20814
Phone: (800) 776-2732; (301) 913-9517
Fax: (301) 913-9520
Email: milerun@americanrunning.org
Websites: www.americanrunning.org
www.amaasportsmed.org

INTRODUCTION TO RECREATIONAL RUNNING

Cross-country Running–1 Mile, 5K, 10K

By far the most popular forms of cardiorespiratory training in the United States are jogging and running. More than 17 million Americans jog or run to develop cardiovascular endurance. Why do Americans participate in these activities? They require no special skills, expensive equipment, or unusual facility, and they can be performed alone (Strand, Reeder, Scantling, & Johnson, 1997).

Another great reason to run is the way it makes you feel when you're done: the brain is clear, the body is physically refreshed, and the feeling stays with you for hours. The key to running injury-free is to wear a good pair of running shoes. Once you have good shoes, it only takes the first step and you're off to a new adventure, experiencing fresh air and different surroundings and letting go of the stress. Start today.

One advantage running has over walking is that a runner can cover a greater distance in a shorter period of time and thus can burn more calories. Jogging is defined as slow running at a comfortable pace at 8–12 minutes per mile. Running is defined as a faster pace of under 8 minutes per mile (Strand et al. 1997).

MISSION AND GOALS OF AMERICAN RUNNING ASSOCIATION (ARA)

Mission

To encourage all people, from youth to adults, to improve their health and fitness by walking and running, and maintaining an active and healthy lifestyle.

Goals

1. To mobilize all Americans to use physical activity as a catalyst to deter and defeat youth obesity.
2. To provide runners with information related to training, nutrition, sport medicine, and fitness.
3. To develop motivational programs to encourage people to begin and maintain active, healthy lifestyles.
4. To support runners by providing advice, motivational and educational programs, and referrals to sports-oriented professionals.

Supporters

1. They are doctors, health professionals, teachers, coaches, CEOs, and other influential people who come together because they believe in the importance of an active lifestyle.
2. The ARA works in coordination with the professional division of the American Medical Athletic Association, which includes running doctors and sport medicine experts who are dedicated to expanding their knowledge in their field.

RECREATIONAL RUNNING SKILLS LISTED WITH CUES

In this chapter, cues have been structured for the following: runner's cues, uphill running, downhill running (short, steep hills; gradual hills), building striders, striders, race course preparation, pre-race routine, start of race, racing strategy, post-performance routines, and senior high-school mileage.

TIPS

Equipment Tips

1. Get a good pair of running shoes. Spend $50 or more and buy a brand-name running shoe. Make sure the shoe is comfortable.
2. Have water available.
3. Wear clothing that is breathable.
4. Dress in layers for cold weather.

Safety

1. Have your runners hydrate well before, during, and after jogs, runs, and races.
2. It has been suggested that side-ache can be related to weak conditioning, weak abdominals, shallow breathing, a large meal before exercise,

dehydration, or excessive exercise intensity. Pain may be relieved by holding the right arm over the head and stretching the side. This condition is not serious, just uncomfortable to the runner (Strand et al., 1997).

3. An important concept in running is that of pacing. In general, pacing means being able to run at a steady pace for a given length of time. Beginning runners have a tendency to start off too fast when given a certain distance to run. Soon they are walking because they have not been able to maintain the speed and have moved into anaerobic training. Instructors need to teach pacing in a jogging class and let students experience what it feels like to run at a steady state for various intensity levels for various lengths of time (Strand et al., 1997).

Etiquette

1. Tie your shoe laces in double knots. If a shoestring comes untied, do not stop abruptly in the middle of the course; move off to the side to tie the laces.
2. Run facing traffic unless instructed by race directors.
3. Remember that cars and other traffic have the right away on the road.
4. Look both ways at intersections before crossing, unless instructed by race director.
5. When running in a group, try to make room for everyone.
6. If you need to spit, spit on the side, avoiding other runners.
7. Do not block runners at any time; move to the side if you slow down or stop.
8. Do not tailgate and follow too close because you could get kicked or spiked. Keep your elbows inside when passing in a group.
9. Do not cut runners off in the race or finish line.
10. Do not stop dead at the finish line. Keep moving so others can finish the race behind you.

TEACHING IDEAS

1. Teachers sometimes get too caught up in the mechanics of running. If they would block out the upper body and see what the legs are doing, they would often find that the runner has good mechanics from the waist down. The runner is doing what feels good to him or her. Remember that the runner is propelled along the ground with the legs, not the arms, head, or hands. Arms are for balance. Reasons that runners may not have perfect mechanics might be a leg length discrepancy, spine curvature, or individual structural difference (people are wired differently). You are fooling around with nature when trying to make major changes in the mechanics of runners. The more they run, the more they will develop an efficient and economical running style. Relaxation and running economy are the keys. It also helps to inherit good genes.

Teaching Progressions

1. *Training for fun runs, 5k, 10k, and up:*
   a. *Warm-up ritual/routine:* Jog about 1 mile with flat shoes, stretch out approximately 10 minutes, jog about 1 mile, building striders (2–4). Make the warm-up similar to race pre-performance ritual/routine.
   b. *Two workouts per day:* Start with daily early morning runs about 2–3 miles during training session at 70–80 percent of the runner's top speed.

c. *M–W–F afternoon workouts:* A hard workout might include a long hard run on Monday, a gradual uphill distance run on Wednesday, and fartlek training (a form of interval training) on a grassy, "hilly" park on Friday.

   T–Th–S: Easy workouts to finish running mileage for week's total.

d. *Hard and easy weeks:* 10–15 miles one week, 20–25 miles the next week. Gradually build up mileage. Avoid overtraining as it causes injuries.

2. See Miler's Club in the walking section.

Strategies

Have a 40–60 minute warm-up before a competition. For example, you can find a quiet spot, make a restroom stop, jog about 1 mile, stretch alone, make a restroom stop, put on spike shoes or racing flats, jog 2–6 building striders, and then walk or jog for 5 minutes. This will allow the runner to get comfortable and relieve stress (getting in the comfort zone) before the competition begins.

For more helpful strategies for before and during a race, refer to the Race Course Preparation, Pre-race Routines/Rituals, and Racing cue tables in this chapter.

ASSESSMENT IDEAS

1. Students enter a 1 mile, 5 K, or 10 K fun run.
2. Enter two races of the same distance and try to better your personal time.

FYI

For further information and special help, consult the following organization.

ORGANIZATION FOR WALKING AND RUNNING

Dave Watt
American Running Association (ARA)
4405 East-West Highway, Suite 405
Bethesda, MD 20814
Phone: (800) 776-2732; (301) 913-9517
Fax: (301) 913-9520
Email: milerun@americanrunning.org
Websites: www.americanrunning.org
          www.amaasportsmed.org

Relax face, neck, jaw, shoulders

Run on forefoot

FIGURE 19.1 Distance Running Relaxation Cues

Belly breathing

Pouch stomach out as you breathe

Brush shorts with fingertips

FIGURE 19.2 Distance Running Cues

RUNNER'S CUES			
SKILL	**CUE**	**WHY?**	**COMMON ERROR**
Relaxation (Figure 19.1)	Work on drills to relax face, jaw, neck, shoulders, arms, and hands	Conserves energy; smoother running technique	Tensing face, neck, jaws, shoulders, arms, and/or hands
	Repeat the word "relax" or other predetermined cues		
Breathing (Figure 19.2)	Belly breathing	Avoids side-aches caused by breathing too fast and high in chest	Side-aches caused by shallow, rapid breathing
	Pouch stomach out as you breathe in	Side-aches also caused by starting too fast when not trained to do so	

HILL RUNNING			
SKILL	**CUE**	**WHY?**	**COMMON ERROR**
Uphill (Figure 19.3)	Short, quick steps	Prevents overstriding	Overstriding
	Quickly get feet back to touching the ground	Faster	

continued

Quickly get feet back to touching ground

Short, quick steps

Run on forefoot

FIGURE 19.3   Running Uphill

HILL RUNNING, continued			
SKILL	**CUE**	**WHY?**	**COMMON ERROR**
Uphill, *continued*	Compact stride contained within oneself		
	Run on forefoot	Faster; quicker transitions	Losing balance if heel strikes first
	May lean forward, depending on steepness of hill		
	Maintain the hill and power over the crest of the hill	Prevents slowing down at the top of the hill and losing momentum	Slowing down at the top of the hill
Downhill *Short, Steep Hills*	Brake to avoid falling and/or gaining too much speed	Prevents falling	Gaining too much speed
	Use a heel-first running stride	Prevents shin splints—pressure on front of legs	Running on balls of feet
	Shorter braking stride		Overstriding
	Short, quick steps		Long strides
	Bring elbows out	For balance	Arms too close to body, elbows cross midline of body

STRIDERS

SKILL	CUE	WHY?	COMMON ERROR
Building Strider *1–50 Meters*	Start from jog; go into a good pace by 50 meters	Warm-up for the race	Sprinting too soon
50–80 Meters	Accelerate to 80% of full speed	Get the muscles ready to race	Accelerating over 80% of full speed
80–100 Meters	Smooth transition to acceleration and then to deceleration		Decelerating too quickly
Strider *Distance 50–100 Meters*	Begin slowly, but by 50 meters athlete is at 80% speed		Athlete is over 80% speed

RACE COURSE PREPARATION

SKILL	CUE	WHY?	COMMON ERROR
Knowing the Course	Go over course before race	Build confidence; you know what to expect	Not taking time to go over course; arriving too late
	Walk or run course alone	Helps them focus on details of the course	Running the course with team instead of individually; good for team unity, but all may not focus on course
	Have a tentative plan	Creates race strategy	No plan
	Know where crucial hills and blind spots are on course	Gives them opportunities to know when to pass a runner	Daydreaming during course

PRE-RACE ROUTINES/RITUALS

SKILL	CUE	WHY?	COMMON ERROR
Pre-race	When countdown starts for the athlete, do not interfere	If the coach's job has been done well, there is no need for last-minute coaching	Pep talks to teams and individuals just before race
	Athlete knows what is expected early in week		
	A shorter warm-up is needed		

continued

PRE-RACE ROUTINES/RITUALS, continued

SKILL	CUE	WHY?	COMMON ERROR
Hot Day Warm-Up	Hydrate well all day	Maintain hydration; conserves energy	Not having enough fluids; warming up in sun or on cement
	Warm-up in shade if possible		
Cold Day Warm-Up	Don't forget to hydrate; a longer warm-up is needed	Keeps body in top performance; prevents energy loss; gets the muscles ready to go	

RACING

SKILL	CUE	WHY?	COMMON ERROR
Start	Both arms down		Both arms up
	Dominant leg back	More powerful start	Weakest leg back
	Most weight on back foot		Weight even or too much on front leg
Leg action	Push off back foot first	Faster start; legs will be in correct running stride	Forgetting to push with back leg first
Arm action	Arms come up	To protect yourself at the crowded start	Left arm forward and left leg forward
Strategy *Beginning of a Race*	Begin race significantly fast in order to gain good position	Gives you a jump start	Getting behind at start
	Maintain good early position	Confidence builder	Going out too fast for too long
	Be near front		
	Control breathing	Conserves energy; a goal to focus on	High, quick breathing; having no goals
	Determine where key runners are and keep them in range		
	Fast and relaxed		
	"I feel strong"	Confidence builder; keeps athlete focused	"Thinking this is hard"; "I'm tired"
	Draw into oneself, the sport, and opponent		Responding to harassment by spectators

continued

Don't get into no-man's-land

Catch someone and pass 'em

Catch someone and beat 'em

FIGURE 19.4 Tactics During a Race

RACING, continued			
SKILL	**CUE**	**WHY?**	**COMMON ERROR**
Tactics During a Race (Figure 19.4)	Catch someone and pass 'em	Provides a specific goal on which the runner focuses	Not focusing on a runner or group of runners ahead of you to pass
	Catch someone and beat 'em	Keeps the mind alert	
	Don't get into no-man's land	Other runners motivate and support you for maximum potential; less likely to give up	Not staying with the pack or another runner
	Don't run alone; stay with group	Motivation and support; direct goal to think about	
	Focus on the runner in front of you by imagining that you are connected with a rope and are slowly being pulled in		
	Accelerate and pass runners after a turn, over a hill, or through trees	Discourages other runners	Don't attack or charge up hills; it's not energy efficient
	Blind spots are effective for 20–50 yards when runners cannot be seen	Surprises runners and stops their momentum	Not knowing the course and where they are to take advantage on the course route

continued

RACING, continued			
SKILL	CUE	WHY?	COMMON ERROR
Tactics During a Race, *continued*	Use of groups is helpful to break opposing groups (extended acceleration of 100–200 yards)	Motivation; power in groups	Bring it alone
Finish Line	Run through the line	A better time	A racer might pass you
Post-performance Ritual	Jogging, easy running (no acceleration, flat terrain, training shoes)	A cool-down helps recovery; gets rid of lactic acid wastes	Could injure legs by overtraining tired muscles

MILEAGE			
SKILL	CUE	WHY?	COMMON ERROR
High School Distance Races	2–3 miles		Overtraining runners
	Cross-country distance is 3 miles (5 kilometers)		School schedules often require two competitions per week. If this is done all season, it may be too much racing.
			Injuries from lack of proper adaptation time

INTRODUCTION TO RECREATIONAL HIKING

It's often thought that hikers are just outdoorsy types. After all, it takes real passion to spend all day trudging to the top of a mountain, only to turn around and come back. However, hiking comes with both physical and mental benefits that can be reaped even from a short evening hike on a local nature trail.

Since you have to walk in order to hike, the health benefits of hiking are comparable to those of walking. Research has shown that "walking may help reduce the risk of age-related conditions like heart disease, insulin resistance and type 2 diabetes, as well as stroke, high blood pressure, and metabolic syndrome" (Upton, 2005, p. 1). Other studies have also shown that adults who walk for 2 1/2 to 4 hours a week "tend to have less than half the prevalence of elevated serum cholesterol as those who do not walk or exercise regularly" (Greenberg, 2004, p. 404).

So, why hike? If there are so many healthy reasons to walk, why not just stick close to home with smooth sidewalks and civilization? Hiking on uneven surfaces may improve balance and blood pressure even more than simply walking on smooth surfaces will. Consider this study from Oregon Health Sciences University: "Participants (all over 60 years old) significantly improved their blood pressure when they walked on cobblestones for half-hour a day compared to those walking on smooth surfaces for three times a week" (Upton, 2005, p. 6). The research was influenced because the study participants used cobblestone walking paths that may stimulate acupressure points on the feet (Upton, 2005, p. 6).

Hiking provides a wide variety of trails and different terrain for any level of hiker. Hiking uphill and downhill can build muscles and strengthen bones ("Hike for good health," 2002, p. 9). The incline of hiking provides a greater cardiovascular workout than walking does. In addition, hiking allows the participant to enjoy nature's fresh air and sunshine, a good source of vitamin D—just remember to wear sunscreen!

Hiking is also a great way to relieve stress. Wherever the hiker goes, there are beautiful surroundings. Hiking can be quiet, peaceful, and renewing; being able to view the beauty of this earth can bring peace to a person's life. Taking a trail that leads to the top of a peak, ridge, or just an overlook leaves the mind and body with a great sense of accomplishment after reaching the destination.

HIKING SKILLS LISTED WITH CUES

The cues contained in this chapter are concerned with methods of hiking properly, including using correct hiking equipment, treating blisters, hiking downhill, hiking uphill, and hiking down steep terrain.

TIPS

Equipment Tips

1. The most important item is sturdy hiking shoes. Shoes don't need to be the top-of-the-line Gore-Tex backpacking boots, but they should have good tread, be broken in (to prevent blisters), and be comfortable.

2. Wear socks that wick away moisture. Wigwam has a Gore-Tex sock. Anything with Gore-Tex will bump up price by 100 percent or more.

3. The company Under Armour offers underwear, T-shirts, and compression shorts that wick moisture and prevent chaffing. They are made from 86 percent nylon and 14 percent elastane.

4. Shirts and pants with nylon that wick moisture away and/or have a UVA rating of 30 percent are ideal. The higher the UVA rating is, the higher the cost of the item will be. Have short- and long-sleeved T-shirts as well as short and long pants available.

5. Sunscreen, hat, and sunglasses are essential for hiking outdoors.

6. A hiking stick helps with balance.

7. Most hiking trails don't have drinkable water, so bring your own. How much depends on the individual person, the location of the hiking area, and how long the hiker plans to be hiking. "Rangers at Grand Canyon National Park recommend 2 gallons per person for a full day of hot-weather hiking ... in cooler climes, you may be able to hike on less than 1 gallon a day. The important thing is that you pay attention: to your body, to your thirst, to your environment, to your map" (Berger, 1997, p. 162). Most short hikes will take a couple of hours, so a whole gallon isn't necessary; a more general rule to follow is drinking 1 liter per hour. Water can easily be dumped, so to be safe, always bring more than you think you will need (Sinclair, 2004, pp. 31–33). There are water bottles with filters—these cost anywhere from $20–$50 a bottle. You can fill the bottle with water from a stream safely for 40–50 times before you have to purchase a new filter. Replacement filters cost less than $10.

8. It is wise to check the weather of the area where you plan to hike before the trek.

9. Get a map or trail guide of the hiking area, as well as a compass. Getting lost is no fun and can easily be prevented by carrying a map and taking frequent inventory of the surrounding area as you progress. For most hiking areas, there are several guidebooks with decent maps in them. For even greater detail, topographical maps can be purchased at the forest station in a hiking area.

Safety

1. Have your hikers hydrate well before, during, and after hikes.
2. Prevent blisters by making sure shoes fit properly. Make sure hikers keep their feet as dry as possible.
3. Go on shorter hikes until shoes break in and fit the feet of the hikers. If necessary, have hikers wear two pairs of socks.
4. If hikers feel an irritation in shoes, have them stop and take care of it. If they wait, the irritation can develop into a huge blister.
5. Have hikers carry a first-aid kit with antiseptic (such as Neosporin), zinc oxide ointment, and moleskin or second skin for blister care and treatment.
6. If a hiker gets a blister, have him or her treat it by doing the following:

   a. If the blister has not opened yet, tell the hiker not to open it to drain it. Putting needles or other objects into the blister only introduces the possibility of infection, whereas the closed blister is sterile.

   b. If the blister has popped and drained on its own, have the hiker cut away the dead skin. Do not peel it away, as this can lead to peeling away live skin.

   c. Make sure the hiker cleans the wound with soap and warm water. He should also use an antiseptic and cover the wound with an antibiotic.

   d. If the hiker is in a clean environment, the wound can be left open to dry out. If the hiker continues to be active, he or she should cover the blister up with moleskin or second skin to help keep it clean. Both items are available at local pharmacies.

   e. The best thing to do is rest and let the blister heal. The more active one is, the more chance there is of infection. If the hiker thinks the blister is infected and notices red streaks or the area getting hot, he or she should see a physician immediately.

Etiquette

1. Stay on marked trails and switchbacks to prevent destruction of natural habitat.
2. Stay to right to let other hikers pass.
3. Pack up all of your trash, and pick up after your dog.

FYI

For further information and special help, consult the following organizations and resources.

WEBSITES FOR HIKING

American Hiking Society
www.americanhiking.org

Hiker's Corner—Hiking and Backpacking Gear
http://hikerscorner.webs.com

Hiking.biz
www.hiking.biz

LifeTips—Hiking
www.hiking.lifetips.com

PUBLICATIONS

Berger, K. (1997). *Everyday wisdom: 1,001 expert tips for hikers*. Emmaus, PA: Backpacker.

Greenberg, J. S., Dintiman, G. B., & Oakes, B. M. (2004). *Physical fitness and wellness*. Champaign, IL: Human Kinetics.

"Hike for good health." (October 2002). *Consumer Reports on Health, 14*, 9.

"Mental Health: 10 ways to keep your brain in top shape." (October–November 2003). *Massage and Bodywork, 18*, 168.

Sinclair, J. (2004). *Cache trails*. Logan, UT: Bridgerland Audubon Society.

Upton, J. (September 2005). "Walk yourself well: EN's step-by-step guide to good health." *Environmental Nutrition, 28*, 1 and 6.

Williams, M. (May 26, 2006). Personal Interview. Athletic Trainer, Utah State University, Logan, Utah.

HIKING PREPARATION

SKILL	CUE	WHY?	COMMON ERROR
Measure a Hiking Stick	Bend elbow with arm parallel to ground; stick should reach hand	Stick is appropriate in height	Using a stick that is too short
Preventing Blisters	Wear shoes that are broken in	Prevents blisters	Wearing sandals, tennis shoes, or street shoes that are flat on the bottom; wearing hiking shoes that aren't broken in yet
	Stop when you feel rubbing	Prevents bigger blisters	Not stopping—blister gets worse
(Figure 19.5)	Carry first-aid kit	To treat blisters and other injuries	Not packing a first-aid kit

FIGURE 19.5 Carry First-Aid to Treat Blisters and Other Injuries

SKILL	CUE	WHY?	COMMON ERROR
Hiking Terrain (Figure 19.6)	Hike on uneven surfaces	Burns more calories; promotes better balance	Hiking on paved trails
Hydrating the Body (Figure 19.7)	Drink plenty of water	Prevents heat exhaustion and heat stroke	Not bringing enough water or running out of water
Resting (Figure 19.7)	Take frequent rests	To conserve energy for a longer hike	Hiking too fast or for too long without rest
Keeping Balance (Figure 19.8)	Use a hiking stick	Provides balance; takes pressure off body back and legs, especially when packs are heavy and terrain is steep and rough	Not using a hiking stick
Relaxation (Figure 19.9)	Pause to enjoy the natural scenery	Provides sense of accomplishment; decreases stress	Being tense
	Breathe in the fresh air	Increases blood flow to the brain	

FIGURE 19.6 Hiking Terrain

FIGURE 19.7 Drinking and Resting

Use a
hiking stick

FIGURE 19.8 Keeping Balance

Pause to enjoy the
natural scenery

Breathe in the
fresh air

FIGURE 19.9 Relaxation

CLIMBING			
SKILL	**CUE**	**WHY?**	**COMMON ERROR**
Hiking Uphill (Figure 19.10)	Step on balls of feet	Conserve energy	Weight on heels

DESCENDING			
SKILL	**CUE**	**WHY?**	**COMMON ERROR**
Hiking Downhill	Short, quick steps	Balance weight transfer; conserves energy	Taking long strides
	Bend knees	Absorb the momentum	Straight legs
	Use hiking stick	For balance	No stick
	Look down	So you do not trip on objects on trail	Looking up
Hiking Down Steep Terrain (Figure 19.11)	Side-step	Prevents falling forward	Feet forward going downhill
	Lean toward hill	Prevents falling downhilll	Lean out away from hill
	Bend knees; back straight—be tall	Keep balance	Straight legs
	Pole on downhill side	Keep balance	

FIGURE 19.10 Hiking Uphill

FIGURE 19.11 Hiking Down Steep Terrain

	TREATMENT OF BLISTERS		
SKILL	CUE	WHY?	COMMON ERROR
How to Treat Blisters	Keep blister covered	Prevents infection—protects the area	Popping blisters causes infection
	Apply ointment with cotton swab	Prevents infection	Not carrying ointment in pack
	Apply large bandage to cover area, or apply moleskin	Protects and pads area	

20

Soccer

INTRODUCTION

Soccer is a game that everyone can play—a game that keeps you fit and challenges you to the max. Soccer has been around for centuries and is played in every country of the world. It has been termed the Sport of the World, and rightly so. In most countries, it is more commonly known as *football*, and here in the United States, it is known as *soccer*. What makes it so exciting is the challenge of a whole team trying to score. Soccer is a simple game, one that all students will enjoy.

SKILLS LISTED WITH CUES

The following soccer skills are included in this chapter: ball control and ball control drills, the dribble and dribbling drills, passing and two-player passing, chipping and two- to three-player chipping drills, the long-pass and two-player drills, trapping and trapping drills, kicking-shooting and kicking-shooting drills, heading, throw-in, goalkeeping, defense, and offense.

TIPS

Equipment Tips

The first thing you need to consider is proper equipment:

1. A 27–28-inch–circumference (commonly referred to as a size 5) ball is appropriate for students of 12 years and older.
2. One ball for every two to four students is recommended to practice skills. The students can work in small groups, with no standing in line to wait for a turn. This maximizes student involvement.
3. Students should wear comfortable clothes.

4. Students should wear comfortable shoes (no sandals); cleats are not needed at a basic level of play. Decide whether cleated shoes will be allowed in class. Be aware that some toes may get stepped on. However, cleated shoes are recommended for recreational soccer teams.

5. Shin guards are important in preventing injury to the anterior compartment of the shin, which is particularly susceptible to injury because there is very little room for tissue and blood. It is recommended that all students have shin guards, especially for games.

6. The field of play can be an actual soccer field or an open, grassy area at the school or a nearby park.

7. Use cones to outline the field. Flags can be substituted for goals. Half cones are great to use in drills. You can make a set of goals 3 feet high × 3 feet wide out of PVC pipe.

8. Use colored vests to divide students into teams.

Safety

1. Shin guards that are covered with socks should be required.

2. Emphasize the importance of playing with control and being aware of others' personal space. Use mini-games to reduce the number of players in a game situation.

3. Be prepared for accidents. Have a first-aid kit available and a first-aid plan.

4. Have plenty of water available during the activity, especially on a hot day.

5. Avoid playing during the heat of the day when possible.

6. Ensure that players are not wearing jewelry, that their shirts are tucked in, and that proper clothing is worn for weather conditions.

7. Have proper warm-up and cool-down periods to prevent possible muscle injuries.

Etiquette

1. Soccer etiquette comes into play when there is an injured player. When a player becomes injured and the referee has not blown the whistle, it is proper etiquette to kick the ball out-of-bounds so that the player can receive medical attention as soon as possible. Once play is resumed, the opposing team should throw the ball into the team that kicked the ball out-of-bounds.

TEACHING IDEAS

Include a warm-up with every class practice. A proper warm-up involves moderate physical activity, such as jogging or a game of keep-away with the soccer ball. This, along with proper stretching, decreases the likelihood of injury. Warm-ups should elevate the heartrate—students should break a sweat. Other ideas for warm-ups include running and dynamic stretching.

Teaching Progressions

1. The recommended teaching progression is to start with dribbling. Dribbling allows the students to become comfortable with using their feet to kick the ball and run with a ball at their feet.

2. After dribbling, it is best to teach passing short and medium distances.

3. After students have mastered passing, it is recommended students learn to receive and trap the ball with the different parts of the body, such as the thigh, the chest, and the head.

4. It is then best to move on to chip drills and long passes because the ball will most likely be received and trapped with the different body parts.

5. Shooting and long passing are very similar, but in shooting the students will be trying to kick the ball very hard. Practicing proper form without kicking the ball as hard should help prevent injuries during shooting drills.

Mini-Games

- 3 vs. 3 can be played on a field whose width is between 15 and 25 yards and whose length is between 20 and 30 yards.

- 4 vs. 4 can be played on a field whose width is between 20 and 30 yards and whose length is between 40 and 50 yards.

- 6 vs. 6 can be played on a field whose width is between 35 and 45 yards and whose length is between 45 and 60 yards.

- 8 vs. 8 can be played on a field whose width is between 40 and 50 yards wide and whose length is between 60 and 70 yards.

- When playing mini-games, you may play with smaller goals (flags or cones to mark the goal) and no goalkeeper. Times can also be varied to suit your schedule.

- Scoring options in these games include 1 point when the ball goes over the endline and 1 point if the ball goes through two cones.

GAME PLAY

Rules

1. A standard soccer game is played with 11 players vs. 11 players on a rectangular field whose width is between 65 and 80 yards and whose length is between 100 and 120 yards. The length of the game consists of two 45-minute halves, including a halftime that does not exceed 15 minutes.

2. Play is started with a kickoff at half field—a direct kick. The ball must go forward on the first kick.

3. If the ball goes out-of-bounds over a goal line, restart with a goal kick if the ball was last touched by attacking team, or a corner kick if the ball was last touched by defending team.

4. If the ball goes out-of-bounds over a sideline, restart with a throw-in.

5. A direct kick occurs when the person kicking the ball can score directly off of the free kick. Fouls that result in a direct kick include kicking, tripping, pushing, holding, and deliberate hand balls. The defending team must be 10 yards away from the free kick, and the ball does not have to touch an additional player.

6. An indirect kick is a free kick in which the ball must touch a person in addition to the kicker before going into the goal for it to count. Fouls that result in an indirect kick include dangerous play (e.g., too high of a kick and playing the ball while lying on the ground) and offsides (if a player is closer to his or her opponent's goal than the second-to-the last defender). Players cannot be offsides on a throw-in or if they are on their own half of the field. The defending team must be 10 yards away from the free kick. Games with 3 vs. 3, 4 vs. 4, 6 vs. 6, and 8 vs. 8 must be 10 yards away from the defending team.

7. A penalty kick is awarded if any direct free kick infraction occurs in the penalty box.

8. In order for a goal to be scored, the entire ball must go over the goal line. A goal counts for one point.

9. After a goal is scored, play starts with the team that got scored on taking a kick-off.

10. A goalkeeper is the only player allowed to use their hands, but is restricted to doing so only inside their team's penalty box.

Strategies

Offensive

1. Use the width of the field to help spread the defense out.

2. Use quick passes to move up the field; passing is faster than dribbling.

3. As the ball moves closer to the goal, try to move it to the middle of the field for a better shot on goal.

Defensive

1. When on defense, get compact and protect the middle of the field.

2. Put pressure on the ball as soon as possible to delay attack and create a turnover—when in doubt, clear the ball up the field as quickly as possible.

Scoring

1. A goal is scored when the ball has completely crossed over the goal line.

2. A goal is worth one point.

3. During a penalty shot, the ball must completely cross the goal line and is worth one point.

ASSESSMENT IDEAS

Assessment can include dribbling drills, mini-games, and shooting drills. When using mini-games, students receive points for playing and then bonus points for winning. When using dribbling and shooting drills to assess skill performance, use a clearly defined rubric and grading scale.

FYI

For further information and special help, consult the following organizations.

ORGANIZATIONS

American Youth Soccer Organization
12501 S. Isis Avenue
Hawthorne, CA 90250
Phone: (310) 643-6455
Fax: (310) 643-5310
Website: www.ayso.org

U.S. Soccer Federation
1801 South Prairie Avenue
Chicago, IL 60616
Phone: (312) 808-1300
Fax: (312) 808-1301
Website: www.ussoccer.com

Ball Control Drills

Juggling the Ball: Try to keep the ball in the air, using only the feet, for as long as you can. The goal is to make 2 touches in a row before it hits the ground, then 3, then 4. Players who can do between 5 and 10 have good ball control.

CUE: Strike the ball with the top of the foot—point the toe toward the ground. This drill increases ball touch and familiarity with the ball, thus increasing ball control skills.

Experimenting with Ball (Partner Drill): Players strike the ball on the five surfaces listed above.

Kick bottom of ball   Ball goes up like pop-up in softball

FIGURE 20.1 Ball Control

BALL CONTROL/BALL CONTROL DRILLS

SKILL	CUE	WHY?	COMMON ERROR
Ball Control			
Knowing the Ball	Kicking the ball	To get familiar with the ball and how it works	
Kicking Top of Ball	Ball goes down (ball stays low)	Keeps ball low and in control	
Kicking Middle of Ball	Ball goes straight		
Kicking Bottom of Ball (Figure 20.1)	Ball goes up (like a pop-up in softball)	For chipping and defensive clears	
Kicking Left Side of Ball	Ball goes right		
Kicking Right Side of Ball	Ball goes left		

DRIBBLE/DRIBBLE DRILLS

SKILL	CUE	WHY?	COMMON ERROR
Dribble Technique	Caress ball in stride	Keep the ball close to your body	If you push the ball too far ahead, a defender can easily steal it away
Dribble Ball with Different Surfaces of Foot (Figure 20.2)	Inside, outside, sole, or laces		
	Push firmly		

continued

Caress ball
during stride

Keep ball close   Push ball firmly

FIGURE 20.2 Dribble

Dribble Drill:

Using six or seven cones for each small group, have students dribble through cones in a weaving pattern.

CUE: Use both the inside and outside of the foot.

This helps the student learn how to keep control of the ball while dribbling, and the cones help players control the ball. The goal is for the player to stay close to the cones while dribbling.

DRIBBLE/DRIBBLE DRILLS, continued

SKILL	CUE	WHY?	COMMON ERROR
Dribble Technique, *continued*	Head up; pull chin back	See where you are going and see where the defense is	Head down, looking at ball
	Arms out; elbows bent for balance		
Action of Dribble	Depending on the situation, change pace and direction		

PASSING/PASSING DRILLS

SKILL	CUE	WHY?	COMMON ERROR
Passing *Push Pass*	Pendulum swing with the foot (like on a grandfather's clock)	For easy, quick passes to a teammate	
Foot Position	Ankle firm	Creates power	
Inside	Strike ball with instep of foot		
Outside	Strike ball with outside of foot		
Laces	Strike ball with laces	Control	Using toe
Striking the Ball Action	Knee over ball	To have more control so the ball won't go flying up in the air	Body leans backwards

Two-Player Passing Drills:

Five- to Ten-Yard Passes: Pass back and forth to partner, using different surfaces of the foot.

This drill allows the student to gain familiarity with the technique of the push pass. Kicking with both the right and left feet gives you an edge over the average player, who can't pass with both feet.

Passing Accuracy: Player 1 stands with legs shoulder-width apart while player 2 tries to pass the ball through partner's legs; then switch positions.

CHIPPING/CHIPPING DRILLS

SKILL	CUE	WHY?	COMMON ERROR
Chipping the Ball *Eyes*	Focus on the bottom part of the ball	Clears the ball out of the defense, or for a pass over the opposing team to one of your teammates	
Approach	Approach the ball straight on		
Action	It's a quick, hard stab under the ball (like a shovel)		
	Bring your knee toward your chest		

LONG PASS/LONG-PASS DRILLS

SKILL	CUE	WHY?	COMMON ERROR
Long Pass		Used for crosses and shooting	
Ankle	Ankles firm (no floppy feet)—toe pointed	Stronger, more controlled pass	Toe connects ball first
	Take a slightly angled approach		
Non-kicking Foot	Place it next to the ball	Helps create greater velocity in kicking foot	
	Toe is pointing at target	Increases accuracy of pass	
Kicking Foot	Strike the ball with laces and inside of foot	More foot surface is on the ball; better control	Striking the ball with the toe
Used for Corner Kicks and Clears	Follow through with the foot pointed and leg toward the target		

continued

SKILL	CUE	WHY?	COMMON ERROR
Long Pass, *continued*	Strike the ball where the ball touches the grass; keep your ankle locked when striking; your leg kicks up and into the ball with a good follow-through	Follow-through increases power and accuracy	

Two-Player Drill:

At Least 20 Yards Apart: Player 1 passes to player 2; they pass back and forth. Have players take a step backward each time they do a successful pass at that distance.

	RECEIVING/RECEIVING DRILLS		
SKILL	**CUE**	**WHY?**	**COMMON ERROR**
Receiving		To gain quick possession of uncontrolled ball	
Trap	Absorb the ball and soften the hit by moving your body away slowly	Controls the ball, brings it right to your feet	
Different Surfaces	Cushion the ball; stop the ball as if catching an egg	Keeps ball close to body	Stiff body with no cushion causes ball to bounce away
Foot	Trap ball with soft feet		
Thigh (Figure 20.3)	Trap ball with upper front of thigh		
Chest (Figure 20.4)	Trap ball with breastbone		
Head	Trap ball with forehead		
Receiving the Pass	Present the trapping surface to the ball; take the pace off the ball by withdrawing the body part as soon as the ball is received		

Receiving Drill:

Each Player Has a Ball: Have the player throw the ball up in the air, and practice using the different surfaces of the body to trap the ball.

This drill helps the player practice the skills of trapping.

FIGURE 20.3   Thigh Trap

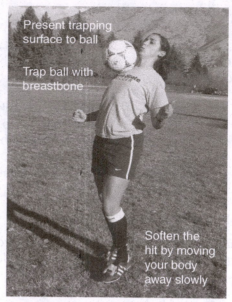

Present trapping
surface to ball

Trap ball with
breastbone

Soften the
hit by moving
your body
away slowly

FIGURE 20.4   Chest Trap

KICKING-SHOOTING AND KICKING-SHOOTING DRILLS

SKILL	CUE	WHY?	COMMON ERROR
The Kick (a striking action executed with the feet—e.g., the long-pass kick, corner kick, goal kick)	Body is stationary and leg is straight, with little flex at the knee; there is minimal movement of the arms and the trunk; concentrate on the ball; hold arms out for balance		
The Shot *Non-kicking Foot*	Place the non-kicking foot alongside the ball, toes pointing at the target	Ball goes where the toes point	Having non-kicking foot behind ball or too far to the side of the ball
Leg	Like firing a cannonball: pull back the kicking leg; have it pointing at the target		
Kicking Foot	After shooting, follow through. After the follow-through, land on the kicking foot (not the non-kicking foot).	Puts more power and control in the stroke	Stopping follow-through to stay on non-kicking foot
Ankle (of Kicking Foot)	Ankle is firm; toes are pointing down	Creates more power and accuracy	
Head	Keep head down and chest over the ball	To keep the ball low	Head up—body leans back

SKILL	CUE	WHY?	COMMON ERROR
Head	Strike ball with top of forehead (where the hairline meets the forehead)	It doesn't hurt when heading on the hairline; more control	Using top of head
Eyes	Keep eyes open—watch the ball meet your forehead	See where the ball is	Close eyes
Upper Body	Draw upper body back (pull shoulders back)	It will provide more power in the header	
Chin	Pull chin in		
Follow-Through	You strike the ball—do not let the ball hit you	No power in the header if you let it hit you	
Torso	Snap the upper body forward to meet the ball (whip the body through the ball)	Most of the power comes from here	
Offensive Header	Head downward toward goal	Use offensive header for passing and shooting	
Defensive Header	Head upward	Used to clear the danger area	

THROW-INS

SKILL	CUE	WHY?	COMMON ERROR
Throw-Ins	When the ball crosses the sideline into out-of-bounds, it is thrown back onto the field (which is the only time a field player may touch the ball with the hands), stand where the ball crossed the line and throw from behind the head (USSF rules)		
The Throw (Figures 20.5 and 20.6)	Face the field		
	Use both hands		
	Start behind the head, and throw over the head (follow-through with both hands)		

continued

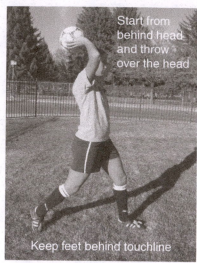

Start from behind head and throw over the head

Keep feet behind touchline

FIGURE 20.5 Soccer Throw-In (Hand/Arm Position, Side View)

Both feet have to stay on the ground

FIGURE 20.6 Soccer Throw-In (Hand/Arm Position, Front View)

Arms throw outward

Follow through with both hands

Body snaps through the throw

FIGURE 20.7 Soccer Throw-In (Follow-Through)

THROW-INS, continued			
SKILL	**CUE**	**WHY?**	**COMMON ERROR**
The Throw, *continued*	Keep both feet behind the touchline; both feet must stay on the ground	It is the rule	Pick up back foot, violating the rule
	Arms throw outward		
Follow-Through (Figure 20.7)	Body snaps through the throw	More power in the throw	
Short and Close Throw	Snap (arms snap down, hands and palms down)		
High and Low Throw	Snap up! Throw up and over		

GOALKEEPING			
SKILL	**CUE**	**WHY?**	**COMMON ERROR**
Positioning	Stay 2 or 3 yards off the goal line	Allows you to cover more of the goal with less diving	Standing on goal line or retreating into the goal
	Move in semi-circle with the ball	This allows you to cover more angles of the goal	Moving straight across the goal line

continued

SKILL	CUE	WHY?	COMMON ERROR
Receiving Balls Crossed Into the 18-Yard Box	Call for ball by saying "keeper"	Allows the defenders to know where the goalie is coming from	No communication, resulting in goalie and defender running into each other
	Attack the ball	Going toward the ball assures that an opposing player will not get to it first	Waiting for the ball to reach you
	Catch ball at highest point you can then bring into body	The goalie's hands can reach higher than most players' heads can	Trying to catch ball at chest level, which gives opposing team chance to knock the ball loose
Handling Balls on the Ground	Get behind ball	If you miss the ball with your hands, it will hit your feet instead of rolling in	Reaching out to the side
	Put feet together or knee on the ground	Keeps ball from going between legs	Feet spread, allowing the ball to roll in between your feet
	Hand position in the "M." Palms up, pinkies together	This creates a pocket for the ball to roll into	Hands spread apart, allowing the ball to get through
Catching Balls Below the Waist	Get behind the ball	If you miss the ball with your hands, it will hit your body instead of going into the goal	Reaching to the side; if you have to reach to the side, you should always use the diving form to be safe
	Put forearms together	Ball will hit your forearms	Trying to catch the ball with your hands, which are weak in the "M" position
	Scoop ball to chest	It secures the ball and keeps it from bouncing off your forearms	Not securing the ball against chest and letting it bounce off your forearms

Big hands
Lunge and cover
lots of area

FIGURE 20.8 Goalie Dive

Reach out with hands,
catch ball, and pull in
Land on outer thigh,
hip, and side of body

FIGURE 20.9 Goalie Dive Landing

GOALKEEPING			
SKILL	CUE	WHY?	COMMON ERROR
Catching Balls Above the Waist	Hand position the "W." Thumbs touching, fingers spread	The thumb and fingers spread creates a pocket for the ball	Thumbs are not touching and far apart, which makes it easier for hard shots to get through hands.
	Bring ball into body	Protects the ball for opposing team; whenever you are near players, ball should be held close to chest	Loosely holding the ball, which gives chances of opposing players to knock it loose
Diving (Figures 20.8 and 20.9)	Lunge forward	The forward lunge makes it so you do not have to dive as far	Lunging to the side or backwards, which makes it so you have to dive farther to protect the goal
	Reach out with big hands	This helps cover more ground when you swing your arms out	Trying to catch ball against your chest, which makes it hard to control and you cannot dive as far
	Land on the outer part of hip and side of body	Landing on your side covers more of the goal and creates a pocket for the ball to go into; it is also easier to get up	Landing on your stomach or knees, which makes it harder to control the ball
	Have one hand on top and one hand behind the ball	The hand on top keeps the ball from bouncing up and the hand behind keeps it from rolling past you. You want to pin the ball into the ground for control	Having one hand on top and one hand on the bottom of the ball is less stable when hitting the ground

continued

SKILL	CUE	WHY?	COMMON ERROR
Diving, *continued*	Bring ball into body	This protects it from opposing players who are trying to kick it out of your hands	Leaving the ball exposed and away from your body
Punching to Clear the Ball	Create fist with two hands at center of chest	This will give you more surface area to punch the ball	Trying to punch with one fist, which lessens accuracy
	Extend fist from chest to reach ball at highest point	This will give you power to clear the ball away from the goal	Not putting power on the punch; the ball is not cleared from potential danger
	Punch ball up the field and to the sidelines	This clears the ball from the defensive zone and gives the defense and goalie time to rest	Punching toward the middle of the field, where the attacking players want the ball to be
Punching to Deflect Ball Over Goal	Create fist with one hand	One fist will allow you to reach the ball. You do not need power on this, just to deflect the ball	Not creating a fist and trying to deflect the ball with one hand. On hard shots, deflecting with one hand does not work
	Redirect ball high and slightly backward	Punching the ball high will make sure the ball clears the goal and punching only slightly backward helps assure that you are not punching it into the goal	Punching straight backward, which punches the ball straight into the goal
Distributing the Ball	Balls can be distributed by punting, rolling, or throwing	Punting clears the ball from the goal while rolling and throwing give you more control of where the ball is going	Not reading the field and using the wrong method of distributing the ball which leads to turnover
Rolling (10 Yards or Less)	Rolling a bowling ball	The ball will not bounce, which makes it easier to control	Holding the ball too loosely and trying to roll the ball side arm, which makes the ball bounce
	Roll ball in front of player or directly to players feet toward sideline	The ball is easier to control and the players momentum is not stopped	Rolling the ball up the middle of the field or behind players
Throwing (10 to 20 Yards)	Throw ball with backspin on it	The backspin will help decrease how much the ball bounces	No spin on release makes the ball bounce and difficult to receive

SKILL	CUE	WHY?	COMMON ERROR
Tactics	Team gets compact	To give attackers very little room to play in	Team is spread out in front of goal, creating space for attackers to exploit
	Players in front of goal will be close together, closing down goal-scoring options for attackers		Defense posture is loose, allowing goal-scoring opportunities
	*Stagger the defense for depth and support		Players are caught in a straight line across the field, allowing for penetration with a single pass
	*Delay opposition as far away from goal as possible to allow players to recover		Team in possession allowed to freely advance forward
	†Players closest to ball must provide immediate pressure		Closest individual defender does not delay attacker
	†Keep playing space narrow for opponents by channeling toward touchline or supporting defenders		Defending with body square to attacker allows for options to the sides or through legs
	†Keep balance of team organized through communication		Confusion and disarray in defense through lack of communication
	If ball cannot be won directly from challenge, clear ball away from danger area either upfield or over touchline	Players in their defensive third of the field attempt to advance ball under extreme pressure and lose possession, possibly creating goal-scoring opportunity for opponent	
	*Once ball has been recovered, offense begins immediately	While defense is on its heels	Slow transition from defending to attacking

continued

*Important when the defense brings the ball up; supports the offensive attack.

†Important in an attacking situation on defense.

SKILL	CUE	WHY?	COMMON ERROR
Tactics, *continued*	Results can be achieved through man-to-man marking, zonal marking, or a combination		
Objectives	Regain possession		
	Deny penetration		
	Slow down attack		
	Stop shots		
Stance	Bend knees slightly; bend elbows (ready for action); eyes on the ball and the opponent		
Tips	Keep on the goal side of your opponent		
	Be first to the ball		
	Defend the ball, not the player		

OFFENSE			
SKILL	CUE	WHY?	COMMON ERROR
Tactics	*Offense begins immediately when ball has been won	To have many options that the defenders must contend with	Delay in transition may result in loss of possession
	*All players are involved in offense from point of recovery		Player fails to move into offense, limiting options
	*Create options by utilizing width of field (spread the field out)		Attacking players squeezing in toward center of field closes down space for players in possession
	†Quickly move ball into defensive half through quick, short, crisp passes to open players, directly to forward target, or by dribbling	To open up more space for the attackers to play in	Delay in advancing ball allows defense to recover

continued

*Important when offense begins an attack.

†Important when offense is attacking and trying to score.

SKILL	CUE	WHY?	COMMON ERROR
Tactics, *continued*	† Forward movement of offensive players not in possession creates dribbling or passing opportunities for player with ball		Lack of movement provides few options for player with ball
	Vary focus and method of attack		Team becomes predictable and easy to defend
	Creativity and imagination in final offensive third of field are vital to creating chances for scoring		Lack of imagination and creativity stifles attack
	† Taking risk in front of opponents' goal is encouraged as loss of possession does not create immediate danger	The ultimate objective in soccer is to score goals; therefore, always attempt to end attack with a shot or goal	Without taking risk in front of defensive team's goal, scoring will become difficult
			Teams that play so as not to lose, rather than to win develop players who find the game to be dull and boring
Dribbling	Keep head up; look for a pass		Body forward and erect
Off the Ball	Get on the goal side of the opponent		
	Penetrate the defense		
	Move into empty space, always creating chances		Standing around

*Important when offense begins an attack.

†Important when offense is attacking and trying to score.

21

Softball, Fast-Pitch and Slow-Pitch

INTRODUCTION

"Safe!" yells the umpire as the runner slides into home. The crowd goes wild as the home team wins the tournament.

One of softball's unique features is that it is a hometown game that pulls a community together. Recreation departments accommodate people of different ages and provide opportunities for them to join youth, coed, female, and male leagues. Nearly every town, small or large, has a ball diamond where residents gather to enjoy the cool evenings and chat with neighbors while watching the game. Opportunities to teach softball skills begin in middle school and continue through high school and college.

SKILLS LISTED WITH CUES

Softball requires a variety of skills: throwing, catching, windmill pitching, hitting, sacrifice bunting, base-running, runner-on-base techniques, the catcher, sliding (straight-in slide), and slow-pitch skills. The use of these organized cues and progressions can be very beneficial.

TIPS

Equipment Tips

1. An outfielder's glove is longer for more range, while an infielder's glove is shorter for more speed. Use a batting glove under either glove to help pad it.

2. Batting gloves can also be used to protect the hand when diving back to base, when sliding into base, or when hitting for bat grip.

3. Boys, girls, women, and men should use a bat light enough to control and swing for speed. Start with a 22-ounce bat for young girls and boys, and go up to a 25- to 28-ounce bat for college-age athletes.

4. Sliding shorts, knee and elbow pads, and sweatbands are especially good for sliding drills to avoid scratches and abrasions.

5. Steel cleats add speed and agility for defense, running base paths, and preparation for sliding.

6. Make sure that all softball equipment is comfortable and functional.

Safety

1. Do not dive headfirst into home plate; you might slam into the catcher and his or her gear.

2. Before throwing the ball to a player, make sure he or she looking at you.

3. Wear a helmet when batting; use a glove when fielding.

Ettiquette

1. Respect umpires—no arguing.

2. No foul play—for example, a pitcher trying to hit someone on purpose.

3. Keep all walkways clear of equipment.

4. No throwing equipment, including bats, helmets, gloves, etc.

TEACHING IDEAS

Teaching Progressions

1. Warm-up arm: First throw short distances (emphasize correct throwing technique); then move to longer distances.

   a. *Progression drill:* Have a partner throw 10 ground balls to the backhand side, 10 on the glove-hand side, and 10 ground balls that need to be charged so that ground-ball technique and defensive movements are emphasized.

   b. *Short-hop drill:* Have a partner throw the ball at the receiver's feet or glove when in a defensive position, so that the player can't catch it in the air.

   c. *Short underhand or overhand lob drill:* Use correct technique for close and long pop-ups. Do 10 short hops and always catch with two hands. Do 10 pop-ups: call them, move your feet, communicate when the ball is "mine," and move with the glove tucked.

2. Quick-hands partners drill: Catch the ball with two hands, rotate the glove to see the ball, grip it, and get rid of it as quickly as possible. The goal is to see who can get rid of the ball the fastest while still keeping the fundamentals in mind.

3. Soft-toss drill against a fence: Pair up. Pitchers stand on a bench or chair, then drop the ball straight down. Hitters work on quick hands and ball contact.

4. Throw the ball to fielders; progress to side-by-side then up-and-back, always hitting the ball with the bat.

5. Lateral drill: All players line up at third-base position. The coach hits the ball to the first player in line. That player fields the ball and then throws home; moves to the shortstop position and fields the ball, throws home; moves to the second-base position, fields the ball, and throws home; and finally moves to the first-base position, fields the ball, throws home. That player stops at first base and waits until last fielder goes. The fielders in

line repeat the same drill. Everyone goes back around. All players in line should encourage the fielder who is up.

6. Base-running and defensive strategy drills are best taught without batting to permit more offensive and defensive plays (repetitions).

7. Give players opportunities to play all positions.

Mini-Games

1. Move the Runner: The goal of this drill to practice moving the runner. So the drill includes laying down bunts, hitting to the right side, or hitting a long fly ball.

2. Home Run Derby: Everyone gets 5 pitches to see how many home runs they can hit.

GAME PLAY

Rules

1. Three strikes and the batter is out.

2. Three outs lead to a new inning.

3. Nine players allowed on defense; ten can be in the lineup because one player can be a designated hitter.

4. All batters must wear a helmet.

5. All fielders must wear a glove.

6. A ball hit on the foul line is good. A ball out of the foul line is not in play.

7. If you catch a fly ball that is in or out-of-bounds, the batter is out.

8. On a pop-up, a runner needs to tag the base they were on after the ball is caught, then proceed to the next base.

9. A bad throw goes to the dugout; all runners are rewarded one base.

10. If the batter tries to bunt with two strikes and the ball is foul, the batter is out.

11. You can't block the base unless you have the ball.

Strategies

1. Bunt to advance the runner.

2. Hit to the right side with the runner in scoring position.

3. Steal bases.

4. Suicide squeezes—bunt with runner on third base.

5. Sacrifice fly balls.

Scoring

1. One point is scored for player touching home plate.

2. If a run scores before the third out is made, the run counts.

ASSESSMENT IDEAS

1. Use a radar gun for pitchers and for players throwing a ball.

2. Measure time spent running on the bases.

3. Playing scrimmages is more game like.

FYI

For further information and special help, consult the following organization and resource.

ORGANIZATION

ASA (Amateur Softball Association of America)
2801 NE 50th St.
Oklahoma City, OK 73111
(405) 424-5266
www.asasoftball.com

PUBLICATION

Kneer, M. E., & McCord, C. L. (1995). *Softball: Slow and fast pitch*. Dubuque, IA: Brown and Benchmark.

See Throwing cues in Chapter 2.

FIELDING A GROUND BALL

SKILL	CUE	WHY?	COMMON ERROR
Glove (Figure 21.1)	Put fingers of glove in dirt	So balls don't go under the glove	Glove too high
	Keep glove hand palm up, throwing hand with palm down as a shield (a.k.a. Venus flytrap)	Protects from bad hops hitting your face	
	Keep glove in front of body	Won't lose track of the ball	Glove off to side or behind body
Body	Keep body square to ball		Body too high off the ground and stiff
	Keep a good stance	Maintains balance	
	Keep buttocks down, like sitting on a stool	Allows for position readjustment if needed	Standing tall
	Stay behind ball		
	Keep knees flexed		
	Head/chin down		Pulling head
	Eyes on ball		
Action	Call for the ball		
	Give target with both hands	Tells where you want the ball thrown	
	Reach out with hands, pull ball in		Hands too close to body

continued

Glove on ground;
catch with two hands

Spread fingers
over ball

Watch ball go into glove

FIGURE 21.1   Catching and Fielding a Ground Ball

FIELDING A GROUND BALL, continued			
SKILL	**CUE**	**WHY?**	**COMMON ERROR**
Action, *continued*	Give with ball		Not pulling ball in
	Spread fingers over ball		
	Catch with both hands	Decreases the chance of balls popping out	
Focus of Eyes	Watch ball go into glove or fingers		Taking eyes off ball; not tracking the ball

FIELDING FLY BALLS			
SKILL	**CUE**	**WHY?**	**COMMON ERROR**
Glove	Out in front of body		Palm up or glove to side
	Raise glove toward ball		Glove down
Body	Square to ball		Side to ball
	Point fingers upward, thumbs together		Fingers down, hands apart
	Fingers toward sky; thumbs touch		
	Stay behind ball but keep your momentum forward	Forward momentum puts more power behind your throw	Not getting behind ball
	Block out sun	Don't lose the flight of the ball	
	Get feet in throwing position after catch		

continued

FIELDING FLY BALLS, continued			
SKILL	**CUE**	**WHY?**	**COMMON ERROR**
Action	Soft glove		
	Give with catch		Arms stiff
	Cover ball with throwing hand	Balls don't pop out	Catching with one hand
	Catch ball with both hands		
Focus of Eyes	See ball all the way into glove		Looking away too soon in haste to make throw

FIELDING			
SKILL	**CUE**	**WHY?**	**COMMON ERROR**
Hard Hit	Catch ball as if it were an egg (a.k.a. soft hands)		Body stiff and hands hard
	Give with ball; funnel into waist		
	Glove down		
	If you can, get in front of ball	Getting in front of ball gets you in better position to throw afterward	
Slow Hit	Get behind ball		
	Charge slow balls		Waiting for ball
	Scoop ball as if with a shovel, but keep glove down		
Rolling Ball	Pick and throw on the run	Saves time for speedier runners	Using the glove to "pick" and then throwing
	Use hand to pick and throw if there's little time		
Focus of Eyes	See ball all the way into glove	Don't lose path of ball	Looking away or looking at runner
Chin	Keep head down with chin on chest as you go down	Keeping head down and chin down decreases chance of getting hit in throat, face, or chin	Pulling head up too soon
Throwing Hand	Place above glove hand like a Venus flytrap for protection		Hand prevents bad hops from hitting one's face

WINDMILL PITCH

SKILL	CUE	WHY?	COMMON ERROR
Stance	Square to target	Proper presentation of ball	Perpendicular to target
	Keep front heel and back toe on rubber		No contact with rubber
Grip	Three-finger grip (thumb and three fingers)	Ball control	Holding ball in palm of hand
	Hold ball in fingers, without palm touching ball		
	Keep ball in glove or hand, waist high		Ball too high or too low
			Ball not in glove
Arm Swing (Figure 21.2)	Raise hand above head		Bringing arm to side
	Momentum should go back to front		
	Back-circle to release point		
Release (Figure 21.3)	Release ball at hip	Pitch's path is level	Releasing in front or behind hip
	Keep weight back		
	Turn belt buckle to target	Hips give the power behind the ball	Letting arm do all the work
	Make sure to rotate hips		
	Snap wrist on release	Wrist snaps put the spin on the ball	Keep wrist stiff
	Keeping wrist relaxed		
	Follow through after wrist snap		Bending elbow as hand finishes up by head
	Point toe at catcher	Push-off puts final momentum on ball	Not striding directly at plate
	Push off rubber with back foot		

FIGURE 21.2 Arm Swing for Windmill Pitch

FIGURE 21.3 Release for Windmill Pitch

HITTING

SKILL	CUE	WHY?	COMMON ERROR
Stance	Stand sideways	Allows rotation of hips and shoulders	Standing forward
	Feet slightly wider apart than shoulder width		Feet too far apart or too close together
	Weight on balls of feet		Weight on heels
	Heels lightly touching the ground		
	More weight on back leg (80%/20%)	Weight back decreases the chances of lunging toward the ball; more power to hit ball	Weight on left leg during the swing
	Front shoulder slightly lower		
Arm Swing	Hitter should think "shoulder to shoulder" (start swing with chin on front shoulder; finish swing with chin on back shoulder), a.k.a. "Ike to Mike"		Moving head during the swing, head too tense

continued

SKILL	CUE	WHY?	COMMON ERROR
Hip Rotation	Snap or rotate back hip at pitcher, drive body through ball; take photograph of pitcher with belly button	Rotating hips provide the power; keeping 80% on back leg provides more power	No rotating hip
	Throw hands through softball: "Slow feet, quick hands"		Using arms instead of wrists
Focus of Eyes	Watch ball all the way into catcher's mitt	Middle-ball contact is solid contact	Not seeing ball hit bat
	Watch spin and delivery of ball	Pitch detection	
Step	Step 3–6 inches (stride should be more of a glide)		Overstriding causes bat to drop during swing (jarring step)
	"Step to hit"		Hitter "steps and then hits"
	Step toward catcher with weight on ball of foot	So your upper body doesn't fly open	Stepping "in the bucket"
	Keep front shoulder level		
Follow-Through	Top hand rolls over bottom hand; bat goes all the way around the body		
	Take your right palm to the pitcher; draw a straight line through your chest with left thumb	Leads to quicker hands	

Teaching Progressions

Teach these cues in the order given (first three); then add others as needed. Remember the four basic steps to hitting:

1. Coil your weight on the back leg.
2. Stride.
3. Pivot.
4. Pop.

HITTING FOR INEXPERIENCED BATTERS

SKILL	CUE	WHY?	COMMON ERROR
Checkpoints for Coaches	If the batter is not gripping, standing, or holding the bat correctly, coach should correct the player individually.	Personal feedback is always more beneficial	Don't use these cues unless a player needs assistance; give one at a time
Grip	Hold bat in base of fingers (this technique allows wrist to roll freely and generates bat speed)	Holding bat in palm of hand; squeezing too hard	Loose grip allows for greater wrist rotation/ extension and relaxes forearms
	Align knuckles		
Closed Stance	Place feet shoulder width apart; then move front foot toward plate (helps untrained hitter step toward pitcher)	Keeps hips in control	Stepping back; flying open
Bat Position	Bat held armpit high and far enough away from the body that both of the player's fists could fit between chest and fists	Bat up allows you to stay above the ball	
	Front elbow should resemble an L shape		
	Back elbow held away from body (a.k.a. "the box")		Holding bat too close to shoulder
Bat Angle	Straight up in air or up and angled slightly over back shoulder		Cradling bat around head; bat pointing back toward pitcher

SACRIFICE BUNT

SKILL	CUE	WHY?	COMMON ERROR
Grip	Grip bat lightly with thumb and two fingers		
	Pinch the bat		
Action	Pivot with back foot toward pitcher; square body to pitcher	Presents the bunt	Keeping side toward pitcher
	Bend knees	Allows hitter to go up or down with pitch rather than one's bat	Legs straight

continued

SACRIFICE BUNT, continued

SKILL	CUE	WHY?	COMMON ERROR
Action, continued	Slide top hand up to the bat trademark; keep bat at a 45° angle	45° angle helps to push ball to ground and not in the air when contacted	Not keeping bat at 45°
	Place bat in front of plate at top of strike zone	Increases the likelihood of ball being fair	Keeping bat behind body
	See ball all the way in	Easier to make contact	Take eyes off ball
Contact	Play catch with ball	Softens bunt, deadens ball, allows for ball/ bunt placement	Dropping bat to ball
	Give with the ball (a.k.a. soft hands)		Swinging at a ball
			Going for a pitch out of a strike zone
	Bunt strikes!!!		

BASE-RUNNING

SKILL	CUE	WHY?	COMMON ERROR
Running to First	Push off with back leg	Legs provide power	Swinging arms wildly
	Run through base, then brake down	So momentum doesn't slow	Pointing toes out
	Dig, dig, dig		Shortening or lengthening stride
	Full acceleration		
	Run with form and run relaxed		Leaping at base, which leads to injury
Extra Base	Make loop midway to base	So that you are in position to advance to the next base	Looking at base, cutting too early or late
	Hit inside of base	Shortens base path	Hitting outside of base
	Round bag hard and jog back if necessary		Looping too wide
	Always look for the extra bag	Aggressive base-running is the difference between winning and losing	

SKILL	CUE	WHY?	COMMON ERROR
Ready Position	Square body to next base		Keeping body perpendicular
	Take stagger start	Allows for better push-off from base	Keeping feet together
	Keep right foot a stride behind base		
	Push off left foot, stride with right		
Break	Find the pitcher's rhythm	Helps to establish when to lead off	
	Start stride at top of pitcher's windup	Gives you a good jump	Leaving before pitch is released; however, early is better than late
	Push off at release or a little sooner		
	Rock 'n' go, back-front	Adds to momentum	
Approach	Pump arms with stride	To run faster	Little arm action
	Round base and look for coach	To see if you are supposed to advance	Not looking for coach

SKILL	CUE	WHY?	COMMON ERROR
Stance	Crouch over balls of feet	Proper stance allows for good reaction time, especially on toes	Body held erect with weight over heels or down on knees
	Align right toe with left heel, toes out (slightly staggered stance)		
	Keep weight over balls of feet		
	Keep knees flexed, butt down		
Glove	Hold glove out as target in front of body	Big glove target gives pitcher an idea where you want the ball	Holding glove to one side or the other and not far enough in front of body
	Relax hands; give steady, big target		Arms and hands stiff

continued

SKILL	CUE	WHY?	COMMON ERROR
Glove, *continued*	Runner on: Keep bare hand alongside (slightly behind) glove. No runner on: Keep bare hand behind back.	Hand by glove with runner on increases the transition time from receiving to throwing	
Receiving	Pitch above waist: Fingers up		
	Pitch below waist: Fingers down		
	Frame pitch by catching outside of ball	Framing increases your strikes-to-ball ratio	
	Block ball in dirt with body while pulling head down		Trying to catch ball in dirt
	Relax hands and draw body in	Relaxed hands give with the ball, which means fewer bobbled balls	Arms and hands stiff, unable to cushion ball
	Keep weight on the balls of feet		Being caught on your heels
	Move body over to get in front of and receive inside or outside pitches	Decrease the chances of passed balls	Standing still and trying to reach to one side or other to catch, which leads to passed balls
	Let ball come to you; don't reach		
Throwing	Get up quickly but keep body low, explode forward, drive with legs	Body low keeps ball on direct path to target	Sitting on heels and not getting into throwing position
		Body low is quicker and puts more power behind throw	Standing straight up, which leads to many overthrows
	Push off ball of back foot, step directly toward target with front foot	Fewer overthrows	Looking at the runner or covering person
	Keep eyes directly on final target		
	Trust your throw!		

SKILL	CUE	WHY?	COMMON ERROR
Approach	Inside corner of base on infield side of base (ball is in outfield)	Sliding to the corners of bags positions you to avoid the tag	Sliding straight into plate, which may injure lower extremities
		It is the difference between safe and out	
	Outside corner of base on outfield side of base (ball is in infield)		
Sliding Action (Figure 21.4) *Leg Action*	Lead with top leg straight, bottom leg bent under (looks like the number 4)	Number 4 with legs increases your momentum toward the base	Not bending bottom leg under, sliding on the knee
	Slide on outside of calf, thigh, and buttocks		
Torso Action	Sit down		Sitting straight up
	Lean back; relax back	Leaning back keeps your slide momentum forward	Body tense
Arms	Touchdown signal	Arms above head (prevents injuries)	Dragging arms and hands slows slide, so keep them up
Head Position	Back with closed fists	Eyes on play lets you know where the ball is, for you may not need to slide	Keeping head up, resulting in a tag in face or head
	Eyes on play		

continued

Touchdown signal with arms

Number 4 with legs

Stop scooter with heel, sole up

FIGURE 21.4 Straight-In Slide

SKILL	CUE	WHY?	COMMON ERROR
Sliding Action, *continued* *Base Contact*	Lead with heel, like stopping a scooter or slide, sole up	Soles up decreases the likelihood of injury and doesn't slow movement toward the base	Soles down and getting cleats stuck in dirt
	Straight leg, but don't hyperextend		Straight leg doesn't give when base is contacted

SLOW-PITCH SOFTBALL DIFFERENCES

1. There are 10 or 11 players, rather than 9 players as in fast-pitch.
2. The tenth player is extra on defense and is called the short fielder or rover; they can play anywhere on the field.
3. The eleventh player, the extra hitter (EH), may not be used on defense. The EH is not allowed in coed slow-pitch.
4. Leading off and stealing bases are not allowed.
5. Bunting is not allowed.
6. Slow-pitch batting requires a lot of patience if you are used to fast-pitch. Basically, wait longer for the ball, let the ball come to you, and don't reach for the pitch.
7. The pitched ball must travel through an arc between 6 and 12 feet high.

SLOW-PITCH STRATEGIES

1. Pitch the ball so it is as close to 12 feet high as possible when coming close to the batter.
2. Make the ball drop quickly as it crosses the plate. Placing a forward, backward, or sideward spin on the pitch is also a commonly used, legal strategy. One foot must be in contact with the pitching plate when the pitch is released.

SLOW-PITCH SKILLS			
SKILL	CUE	WHY?	COMMON ERROR
Underhand Slow Pitch *Grip*	Like throwing a ball normally		Gripping the ball too tightly
Setup	Ball in front of chest	Allows for proper presentation of ball	
	Both feet parallel on mound		
	Feet not quite shoulder width apart		

continued

SKILL	CUE	WHY?	COMMON ERROR
Underhand Slow Pitch, *continued* *Arm Action*	Pendulum swing	Allows for the pitch's momentum	
Stepping Action	Step with foot opposite to throwing arm	Enhances ball arc, spin, and momentum	
Releasing the Ball	Release ball out in front of you at belt height		
Batting *Batting Action*	The key to slow-pitch batting is waiting for the ball	Let the ball travel to you until it is in your power zone; then explode!	Swinging too soon
	Be patient and relaxed		Swinging too soon
	Focus eyes on ball spin	To detect the ball's movement and inside or outside pitch recognition	Eyes wandering
	Swing level	Level contact equals solid, line-drive contact	Reaching too high
			Trying to hit the ball like a golf swing

22

Strength Training with Free Weights

INTRODUCTION

Training with free weights allows you to activate major muscle groups as well as smaller ones that help stabilize joints. There are many training methods, tools, and subcategories within strength training that include: barbells, dumbbells, kettle bells, resistance bands, free moving straps, weight plates, medicine balls, and your body as the resistance for certain exercises.

In addition, there are several strength sports tied directly to weight training with free weights: weight lifting, power lifting, strongman, and body building. It is important to put together a well-balanced training program that addresses all areas of the body. Depending on your training focus (strength sports, athletics, general fitness, or weekend warrior), the possibilities are endless as far as exercise ideas and training protocols. With all free weight exercises, you should start with very light weights and/or instructional tools such as PVC pipes, sticks, etc. As the student learns sound technique, they can progress with weight and follow different workouts and training progressions. Various methods to progress training are: progressive overload, linear periodization, undulating periodization, concurrent sequencing, conjugate periodization, and block periodization. All these methods vary intensity, volume, means, and the layout of your training days/weeks/months. As your training with free weights progresses properly over time, you will experience many positive outcomes—you will increase your muscle mass, metabolism, strength and power, self-esteem, athletic performance, and the ability to face and overcome challenges.

SKILLS LISTED WITH CUES

The following are coaching cues and pictures on these specific strength-training free-weight exercises: lower body-free squat, parallel box squat, front squat, trap bar dead lift, upper body-bench press, overhead press (anterior), and chin-ups. These are just a sampling of several free weight exercises that recruit more muscle mass than machine weights. By no means are these the only exercises you should perform. Yet having some of these as a staple in your training programs will help create body balance and strength, as well as build muscle to help support other exercises and training variations.

TIP

Hand chalk can be used to help secure your grip during all training exercises and activities.

EQUIPMENT TIPS

Barbells:

1. Always make sure your grip is even and that your body positioning is centered under the bar (when appropriate).
2. If using an older bar, purchase a metal barbell brush to help clean off dirt, rust, and other debris.
3. Replace a general strength/exercise bar or training bar (not an Olympic lifting bar) if it starts to rotate too much.
4. Replace the bar if the knurling starts to wear completely away due to years of use.

Dumbbells:

1. Always make sure that the ends of the dumbbells are secure before use. If they are loose, tighten them with an Allen wrench or another appropriate tool.
2. A metal brush can be used to keep dumbbell and barbell handles clean.
3. Replace dumbbells if their parts frequently loosen and/or if the knurling grips are loose.

Kettle Bells:

1. Frequently look for cracks or other hazards before use.

Medicine Balls:

1. Based on the type of medicine ball, check frequently for cracks and/or tears.
2. Based on the exercise, purchase a ball with grip, rather than a leather version.

Free-Moving Training Straps (for example, TRX):

1. Make sure that the straps are properly attached to a sturdy and fixed object in your weight room or on your lifting rack.
2. Frequently check for broken pieces of the strap, and replace it when needed.

Resistance Bands (Various Types):

1. Frequently check for tears or rips in the bands.
2. Have several resistance options available as you gain strength and for various exercises where resistance levels can change often.

Weight Plates:

1. Frequently check for cracks in plates.
2. Make sure your grip is secure when holding them.

Body Weight Exercises:

1. Make sure you are properly warmed up specifically around the joints used in the exercises.
2. Secure your grip or hand/foot position before performing all exercises.

Safety

1. Before any workout, training session, or physical activity, make sure you properly warm-up the body through a mixture of general calisthenics, mobility exercises, muscle activation exercises, and some stretches.
2. Always make sure that you have a safe and clean training area (free of all clutter) in all parts of your weight room and or training facility.
3. Always have spotters present, attentive to the lifter's needs, and in the proper positioning for each exercise where a spotter can be used.
4. Utilize weight/bar collars when they are needed to keep weights from sliding or falling off the bar.
5. Know your training limits.
6. Utilize appropriate breathing technique: inhale during the eccentric portion and exhale during the concentric portion at the hardest point of exercise. Keep your core musculature tight.

Etiquette

1. Give positive encouragement to all training partners.
2. Help coach others on proper lifting technique; fill your weight room with as many coaches as possible.
3. Be open to coaching feedback from others.
4. Put your weights and training materials away in the proper locations when done.

TEACHING IDEAS

1. Have students chart their progress either on their lifting sheets and/or on a class/team record board.
2. Use training pictures and/or videos to help remind participants of proper lifting techniques and coaching tips.
3. Match people up by strength levels.
4. Create various recognition and/or reward systems not only for strength and power, but also for technique, peer coaching abilities, and other quantifiable training items.

Teaching Progressions

When progressing instruction on all exercises and training programs, here are some simple suggestions to follow:

1. Start athletes out with light resistance and lots of coaching and instruction.
2. Always start athletes out with full range-of-motion exercises, and then over time, you can progress to more advanced/sport-specific trainings.

3. Begin all exercises with controlled movement patterns. You can also incorporate some sub-maximum eccentrics (timed lowers, ex. 3 seconds down) or isometric pauses (1–5 seconds) to reinforce technique. As your training progresses, you can start working on faster movement patterns and varying the lifting/training techniques.

4. Over the course of your training week, give the muscles you work time to recover. Larger muscles will need 48–72 hours to recover, whereas smaller muscles will only need 24–48 hours. Always follow the rule: If it is sore, let it rest. Weekly sessions can be laid out in various patterns. Some examples are:

   a. 3 total body days a week (Monday, Wednesday, & Friday)

   b. 4 training days that alternate upper & lower body (Monday, Tuesday, Thursday, & Friday)

   c. 3 training days with 2 upper body days & 1 lower body day (Monday, Wednesday, & Friday)

   d. 3 training days with 2 lower body days & 1 upper body day (Monday, Wednesday, & Friday)

5. Remember to include core work in all training sessions. Your core is the central power base of the body. It constitutes your abdominal muscles, hip flexors, spinal erectors, and glutes.

6. Remember to address individual and group weaknesses throughout training. A common weakness is posterior body strength compared to anterior body strength. Another could be mobility at major body joints (ex. ankle, hip, and shoulder).

Mini-Games

The following are a few examples of games and competitions that you can utilize when training students. By using your imagination and creativity, your possibility for weight-room training games and competitions are endless.

1. Team Totals: You can divide your students into even teams. Have the best weight lifted for the day on your main movements added together for best total pounds lifted. You want to make sure that all lifts adhere to range of motion requirements and are not spotter-assisted. You can have team boards posted in the weight room or locker rooms for motivation and recognition.

2. Technique Wars: Around the weight room, you want to post signs with the 3 main cues for all your main lifting/training movements. Create a point system (ex. 1 to 3 with 3 = great, 2 = good, 1 = poor), then rate technique. At the end of the lift, add up team scores for the training group with the best technique. You can have team or individual boards posted, similar to the team totals game.

3. Time Trials: Every now and then, you can pick barbell or dumbbell exercises at below maximum weights and/or strap, band, or bodyweight exercises, and put them together in a circuit fashion. Put your students together in teams and see what team finishes the workout challenge first. Prizes can be as simple as picking the next circuit when you do that challenge again. Have some kind of board or sheet ready to chart progress through the workout. An example of a workout for this game is:

Push-Ups = 100 total

Chin-Ups = 50 total

Resistance Band Pull Aparts = 100 total

Dips = 100 total

Sit-Ups = 100 total

ASSESSMENT IDEAS

When evaluating your training programs, you have several options:

1. You can chart progress on overall weight lifted for any amount of reps on your main training movements in your lifting program.

2. You can chart progress in number of reps per set at a certain training weight per certain exercise.

3. You can chart speed and power improvements through test such as the 10-, 20-, 30-, or 40-yard dash; pro agility shuttle; 60-yard shuttle; L-Drill; vertical jump; broad jump; or any self-designed test you feel is suitable for your students.

4. Take pre- and post-training cycle photos.

5. Body part size measurements and/or body fat percent testing.

FYI

For further information and special help, consult the following organizations.

ORGANIZATIONS

National Strength & Conditioning Association (NSCA)
www.nsca-lift.org
Collegiate Strength & Conditioning Coaches Association (CSCCA)
http://www.cscca.org/

FREE SQUAT			
SKILL	**CUE**	**WHY?**	**COMMON ERROR**
Free Squat (Figure 22.1a)	Line body up with the center of the bar	Balances the weight on bar on the back	Balance of the bar can be off, making the lift harder
Grip	Set an even grip on the bar	Builds a shelf for the bar to sit on that will help to evenly distribute weight	Can't hold bar comfortably and balance is off
Upper Body	Pull body under the bar to set up lift	Initiates lift	If set up is not tight, it increases the chance of not holding lift posture
	Pull shoulder blades tight together	Builds shelf for the bar to sit on, supports upper body lift posture	Back can round if not tight (can't hold lift arch)
	Push your chest out	Ensures proper lift posture	Back can round if not tight (can't hold lift arch)
	Drive head back into the bar	Creates a counter force into the bar to help upper body posture	Back can round if not tight (can't hold lift arch)

continued

FREE SQUAT, continued			
SKILL	**CUE**	**WHY?**	**COMMON ERROR**
Lower Body (Figure 22.1b)	Walk bar out of rack	Clears J-hooks on the rack	Possibly hit J-hooks while descending or ascending
	Set feet up for squat stance (shoulder width or wider)	Puts legs and rest of body in proper lift positioning	Too narrow of a stance could cause trouble keeping feet (heels) on the floor. Too wide of a stance and it is hard reaching proper depth
	Angle toes slightly out	Naturally opens up hip joint to allow lifter to reach proper depth easier	Can't reach proper or desired depth
	Break at hip and knee joint and sit into squat hole	Allows for proper squat and to keep the knee behind the toes—lowers stress on knee joint	Knees come too far forward over toes, increasing stress on knee joint

The free squat is a multi-joint leg movement that works quadriceps, hamstrings, glutes, hips, abductors, adductors, lower back, and abs.

BOX SQUAT			
SKILL	**CUE**	**WHY?**	**COMMON ERROR**
Box Squat (Figure 22.2)	Line body up with the center of the bar	Balances the weight on bar on the back	Balance of the bar can be off, making the lift harder
Grip	Set an even grip on the bar	Builds a shelf for the bar to sit on that will help to evenly distribute weight	Can't hold bar comfortably and balance is off

continued

(a) Top Position

(b) Bottom Position

FIGURE 22.1 Free Squat

SKILL	CUE	WHY?	COMMON ERROR
Upper Body	Pull shoulder blades tight together	Builds a shelf for the bar to sit on, supports upper body lift posture	Back can round if not tight (can't hold lift arch)
	Push your chest out	Ensures proper lift posture	Back can round if not tight (can't hold lift arch)
	Drive head back into the bar	Creates a counter force into the bar to help upper body posture	Back can round if not tight (can't hold lift arch)
Lower Body	Walk bar out of rack	Clears J-hooks on the rack	Possibly hit J-hooks while descending or ascending
	Set feet up for squat stance (shoulder width or wider)	Puts legs and rest of body in proper lift positioning	Too narrow of a stance could cause trouble keeping feet (heels) on the floor. Too wide of a stance and it is hard reaching proper depth
	Angle toes slightly out	Naturally opens up hip joint to allow lifter to reach proper depth easier	Can't reach proper or desired depth
	Break at hip joint first and sit/shift body back to sit on box. Your knees should make a 90° angle when seated	Allows for muscle activation of posterior chain (low back, glutes, and hamstrings) and takes stress off the knee joint	Lifter doesn't sit far back enough and stresses anterior muscle chain too much
	Once seated, pause for 1 second, then explode up standing as fast as possible using posterior chain and hip musculature	Allows a static and dynamic action with a strong contraction of hips and posterior chain muscles	Lifter doesn't control sit onto box, pause is too short

FIGURE 22.2 Box Squat

The box squat is a multi-joint leg movement that works the hips, lower back, glutes, hamstrings, adductors, abductors, and abs.

SKILL	CUE	WHY?	COMMON ERROR
Front Squat (Figure 22.3)	Line body up with the center of the bar (anterior side)	Balances the weight on bar on the shoulders	Balance of the bar can be off, making the lift harder
Grip	Set an even grip on the bar (clean grip)	Secures the bar onto the shoulders and serves as a breaking system to hold the weight steady	Bar can slip off the shoulders and shift while lifting
Upper Body	Pull the body under the bar to set up the lift	Initiates lift	If set up is not tight, it increases the chance of not holding the lift posture
	Pull shoulder blades tight together	To get a strong upper back at contraction to hold posture	Back can round if not tight and can't hold lift arch
	Push your chest out	Ensures lift posture	Back can round if not tight and can't hold lift arch
	Keep head neutral to slightly up	Helps stabilize the bar on the shoulders to help upper body posture	Back can round if not tight and can't hold lift arch
	Drive elbows in and up	Allows you to hold upper body posture and stabilize bar	Bar can fall off shoulders or lifter could round forward
Lower Body	Walk bar out of the rack	Clears the J-hooks on the rack	Possibly hit J-hooks while descending or ascending
	Set feet up for squat stance (shoulder width or narrower)	Puts legs and rest of body in proper lift position	Too narrow of a stance could cause trouble keeping feet (heels) on the floor. Too wide of a stance and it is hard reaching proper depth (want to stress anterior chain)
	Angle toes slightly out	Naturally opens up hip joint to allow the lifter to reach proper depth easier	Can't reach proper or desired depth
	Break at hip and knee joint	Allows for proper squat and keeps knee behind toes, lowers stress on knee joint	Knees come too far forward over toes increasing stress on knee joint

Break at hip and
knee joint

Elbow drive
(in and out)

Angle toes
slightly out

FIGURE 22.3 Front Squat

The front squat is a multi-joint leg movement that works the quadriceps, hips, lower back, glutes, hamstrings, abductors, adductors, and abs.

TRAP BAR DEAD LIFT			
SKILL	**CUE**	**WHY?**	**COMMON ERROR**
Trap Bar Dead Lift (Figure 22.4)	Stand in the center of the bar with feet hip width apart or slightly wider	Balances weight of bar around your frame and to prevent the legs hitting the bar from too wide a stance. Also activates the posterior and anterior chains as you complete the lift.	Body is off center making the lift off balance. Legs hit bar during ascending portion of lift. Body is rounded forward if legs are too wide apart.
Grip	Grip handles in the center of the grip	Evenly distributes weight on the bar during lift	Grip is uneven and makes the lift harder or off center
Upper Body	Pull body into an upright position with head neutral or slightly up. Pull upper back muscles tight with chest pushed out.	Allows for a tight upper body posture to help isometrically support the weight of the lift	Upper body can round forward causing an incomplete lift or low back injury
Lower Body	Drive through heel hard into floor, keeping the whole foot flat on the ground	Creates balance during the lift and activates the posterior chain muscles.	Heel comes up from the ground and transfers all stress to the anterior muscle chain. Can cause lifter to lose balance forward
	Initiate lift thorugh the legs	Activates the biggest muscles in the body and maintains proper lift position. Keeps abs tight	Lifting with arms first and getting off balance, causing a missed lift. Can also put too much strain on the low back/ posterior chain

continued

The trap bar dead lift is a multi-joint leg movement that works the glutes, hamstrings, low back, quadriceps, hips, and abs.

Pull body into an upright position, chest/back tight

Grip handles in center of bar

Stand in center of bar

FIGURE 22.4 Trap Bar Dead Lift

TRAP BAR DEAD LIFT, continued			
SKILL	CUE	WHY?	COMMON ERROR
Lower Body, *continued*	Stand tall, driving through the heels, squeezing the glutes, keeping upper body musculature tight and upright	Completes lift as safely as possible and activates the muscles in the proper sequence	Missing the lift or rounding too far forward

BENCH PRESS			
SKILL	CUE	WHY?	COMMON ERROR
Bench Press (Figure 22.5)	Lie on bench and set up body arch by pulling together the shoulder blades, pushing the chest up, and firmly driving the heels down and out into the floor	Stabilizes the body, protects the shoulder joints, and creates a leg drive while keeping your glutes in contact with the bench	Body stays flat on the bench increasing the pressing distance and no leg drive is used. Leg drive is performed wrong and glutes come off the bench
Grip	Take an even grip on the bar (width based on injury history and training goal)	Secures grip and makes sure the bar is even in the hands and the weight is balanced	Uneven grip, weight feels unbalanced, could drop bar
Upper Body	Take the bar out of the rack; get lift off keeping arch tight	Initiates lift	Bar taken out or lifted off too high and arch position is lost
	Lower bar to high point of chest/sternum. Keep elbows in at a 45° angle.	Completes eccentric portion of lift, lowers stress on shoulder joints	Bring bar down either too high on the chest or too low on the sternum making it harder to press up and could impinge shoulder joint

continued

Lower bar to high point of chest/strenum.

Take ever grip on bar

FIGURE 22.5   Bench Press

The bench press is an upper body multi-joint movement that works the chest, shoulders, triceps, and lats.

BENCH PRESS, continued			
SKILL	**CUE**	**WHY?**	**COMMON ERROR**
Upper Body, *continued*	Press bar off the chest, pressing body away from bar and drive heels outward	Completes lift, creates a total body drive to put more force into the bar, and creates a more natural bar path with the chest and shoulder muscles	Don't use the whole body to press the bar
	Rack bar	To complete lift	Missing and causing the bar to fall off the rack

OVERHEAD PRESS			
SKILL	**CUE**	**WHY?**	**COMMON ERROR**
Overhead Press (Figure 22.6) **Grip**	Take an even grip on the bar, shoulder length or slightly wider	Avoids putting too much stress on the shoulder joint due to hand position and gives an even grip	Grip too wide—increased shoulder pain Uneven grip—unbalanced weight
Upper Body	Squeeze bar tight and brace abs/core to lift the bar off	Stabilizes the body to stay upright when lifting and readies the body to receive the weight	Body too relaxed, can't stabilize the bar when trying to lift
	Take bar out of rack	Performs lift	Rack is set too high or low, makes setting up for the lift harder than needed

continued

The overhead press is an upper-body, multi-joint movement that works the shoulders, triceps, and abs.

FIGURE 22.6 Overhead Press

OVERHEAD PRESS, continued			
SKILL	**CUE**	**WHY?**	**COMMON ERROR**
Upper Body, *continued*	Press par initially in a straight line clearing the face, then back overhead driving your head through, squeezing your shoulder blades together	Performs concentric portion of lift maximizing ROM in shoulder joint and scapular stability. Working joints' natural ROM	Squeezing shoulder blades tight causes an unstable bar overhead and shoulder pain. If pressing the bar away from the body the lifter can lose lift forward
	Lower bar under control in reverse fashion of pressing it (squeeze lasts on way down for stability)	Returns bar safely to start position and completes lift	Lowering the bar too fast and hitting it on the clavicle and/or applying negative stress too low on the back
	Rack bar	Finish lift	Missing hooks

CHIN-UPS			
SKILL	**CUE**	**WHY?**	**COMMON ERROR**
Chin-Ups (Figure 22.7) **Grip**	Take an underhand grip on a chin-up bar at shoulder width	Sets up lift and lowers stress on shoulder and elbow joints	Grip too wide and/ or not tight/strong enough
Upper Body	Hang with arms straight, gripping the bar tight with every finger, thumb wrapped around tightly	Maximizes ROM on lift and ensures maximum muscle activation through grip	Grip too loose or ROM used is not full
	Pull with a tight/strong grip in a straight line, driving elbows back toward ribs until chin is above or equal to the bar	Performs concentric portion of the lift through a full ROM and maximizes back activation	Pulling body away from bar making the lift harder, stopping the lift short of full ROM

continued

Take an underhand grip

Pull with nice strang grip, until chip is above of equal to bar

FIGURE 22.7 Chin Ups

Chin-ups are an upper-body, multi-joint movement that works the back and biceps.

	CHIN-UPS, continued		
SKILL	**CUE**	**WHY?**	**COMMON ERROR**
Upper Body, *continued*	Lower body back down to start position in a straight line using a tight grip and squeezing lats for control	Controls eccentric movement to a full ROM finish and finishes rep	Not lowering all the way down and not letting the muscles fully stretch and get to a full ROM point and/or dropping too fast causing no muscle activation
	Step or get down from bar safely	To stop lift	Dropping from bar and landing on something/ hurting lower body

23

Swimming and Water Polo

INTRODUCTION

Swimming has a rich history that dates back as far as human records can take us. Swimming began in lakes and streams and has slowly transformed into a recreational, competitive, and healthy way of life. This increased interest in water, however, has also brought with it an increase in risk associated with water. Learning to swim is the best way to understand those risks and to get the most out of the aquatic experience in a safe and enjoyable way. Swimming is a low-impact, high-energy sport, as well as all-around good fun. Learning proper stroke mechanics and safe swimming procedures will give anyone lessons that will last a lifetime.

SKILLS LISTED WITH CUES

Swimming strokes include the front crawl, back crawl, butterfly, sidestroke, breaststroke, elementary backstroke, trudgen, trudgen crawl, and double trudgen. Swimming skills include the rotary kick, treading water, front and back open turns, swimming underwater, breaststroke and butterfly turns, speed turns, surface dives, and diving.

TIPS

Equipment Tips

1. Goggles help beginning swimmers enjoy the water and open their eyes underwater; they also prevent the eyes from burning when a person swims laps in a chlorinated pool.
2. Kickboards.
3. Fins, buoys, hand paddles.
4. Water polo ball for gutter ball.

Safety

1. Walk on the deck; do not run.

2. Do not dive into 9 feet water or less.

3. Do not prolong holding your breath; you can pass out.

Etiquette

1. In lap swimming, if there are 2 swimmers sharing a lane, each swimmer should swim either on the right side or left side.

2. In lap swimming, if there are 3 swimmers sharing a lane, all swimmers should swim on the right side of the lane and circle the lane, staying on right side. Pass a slow swimmer on their left side.

TEACHING IDEAS

Teaching Progressions

1. The following is a suggested teaching progression for the five basic swimming strokes: front crawl, back crawl, elementary backstroke, breaststroke, and sidestroke. The sidestroke should be taught after the whip kick has been mastered because of negative transfer with the scissors kick.

2. Front Crawl: If students have erratic breathing habits or body twists, have them breathe on the opposite side. This tactic helps them relearn correct breathing patterns.

3. Sidestroke: Have students learn sidestroke on both sides.

4. Breaststroke Coordination: When teaching the breaststroke to beginners, have students practice only one stroke. Once they master the one stroke, add two strokes, three strokes, and so on. This method helps to develop coordination and gliding for the stroke.

5. Kickboard Drill: The purpose of the drill is to have students flutter kick without making noise with their feet. This drill conserves energy and makes them more streamlined and efficient in the water.

6. If a student is having trouble breathing in the front crawl stroke, have them put on a pair of fins. The fins help maintain streamline position by creating momentum in the water, which can make it easier to breathe.

7. Have students use buoys to help with arm pull.

8. Have students use pull paddles to create resistance in the water.

9. Snorkel Drill: The purpose of this drill is to improve the timing of the pull and to help the breathing organize around the stroke, versus the other way around. Use a buoy and an ankle band with the swim snorkel if possible, and swim a longer set.

Mini-Games

Wet Base (a modified game) is a new water game that is played like baseball in the water. Instructions for the game follow.

Equipment

1. One kickboard used for the bat

2. One lightweight, plastic, 8-inch ball

3. Four hula hoops used for the bases

4. Four ten-pound weights to keep hula hoops secure (optional)

Rules

1. Create two teams with 4–10 players on each team.

2. Bat like you bat in baseball. Swim underwater through the hula hoop to first base, then to second base, and so on. Award 1 point for making it back to home plate.

3. A ball that goes out on the deck is a foul ball.

4. Outs are made just as they are in baseball.

5. The batter stands in the shallow end of the pool and bats to the deep end of pool. The pitcher pitches the ball underhand, with no more than three pitches.

ASSESSMENT IDEAS

1. Each student swims the length of the pool: front crawl, backstroke, side-stroke, elementary backstroke, and breaststroke. Use a 10-point scale each stroke, and take the best 4 strokes, with 40 total points possible.

2. Award 5 points for individual skills, such as performing a dive, treading water for 5 minutes, etc.

3. Encourage students to swim 300 yards, which is six laps of a 25-meter pool (this is the distance for a sprint triathlon). Time them for this distance.

4. Have the better swimmers set goals to complete 1, 3, 5, 7, 10, 12, 15, etc. miles outside of class. Have a certificate for each mileage goal reached.

5. Have students complete $1/4$, $1/2$, $3/4$, or 1 mile during your class time, depending on skill level. Have students set a goal for themselves, and test them at the end of the swimming unit.

FYI

For further information and special help, consult the following organization and resources.

ORGANIZATION

Your local American Red Cross
  National Headquarters of the American Red Cross
  430 17th Street Northwest
  Washington, DC 20006
  Phone: (800) RED-CROSS
  Website: www.redcross.org/hss

PUBLICATIONS

American Red Cross. (2009). *Swimming and water safety*. Washington, DC: American Red Cross.

American Red Cross. (2009). *Water safety instructor's manual*. St. Louis: Mosby Life.

SKILL	CUE	WHY?	COMMON ERROR
Body Position	Be a superhero	More streamlined through the water	Hips and shoulders sway
	Proud shoulders	Reduces crossover on arm entry	Crossing midline
Head Position	Water level at crown of head	More efficient in the water	Head too far under the water
		Best for streamlined body position	Head too high (creates a drag)
Arm Pull	Early catch	Creates power	Straight arm pull
	Thumb to middle of leg		Head-first recovery
	Keep arm between midline and shoulder throughout pull	Keeps pull moving forward	Crossing arm across midline under water
Arm Recovery (Figure 23.1)	High elbow recovery	More energy efficient	Dragging elbow in water
		Prevents elbow drag in water, which slows you down	
	Drag thumb lightly along the water		Straight arm recovery
			Hand is higher than elbow during recovery
Hand Entry	Reach forward with arm outside of water	Better streamline longer stroke to pull better	Hand entering water too soon
	Reach when arm enters water (two reaches—one out of water and one inside of water)		
	Hand enters before elbow	Keeps elbow upon entry and underwater	Dropping elbow after the reach
	Spear a fish that is 2–3 inches below the water and in front of you	Gets the arm in position for greater pull under the water	Palm enters the water first
	Flat hand entry and relaxed	More water to pull creates more power in the stroke	Thumb first causes crossover
Leg Action	Point toes like a diver	Reduces wave drag to swim faster; more streamlined	If feet are flexed stiff, swimmer does not move forward; can even go backward in the water
	Kick heels to the surface	Less wave drag	
	Feet relaxed, like throwing a fishing line		

continued

FRONT CRAWL, continued

SKILL	CUE	WHY?	COMMON ERROR
Leg Action, *continued*	Kick generated from large muscles of buttocks and thigh give more power		Bending too much at the knees
Breathing	Follow the elbow back; look through window	Creates way for air, efficient breath	Head too far under the water (causes exaggerated roll)
		Keeps body streamlined	
	Roll chin to shoulder	Less wave drag	
	Rotate body on skewer	Less drag	
	Hum while face is in water	More efficient air exchange	Water gets in mouth
	Exhale through nose	Avoids getting water in mouth	
	One eye in and one eye out of the water (spot only the side of the pool)	Pocket for breath and keeps good position	Over rotation of head—looking too high

BACK CRAWL

SKILL	CUE	WHY?	COMMON ERROR
Body Position	Iron rod down back	Less wave drag	Hips and shoulders sway
	Eyes look at toes splashing water		
Head Position	Lie down, as if head is on a pillow, water touching ears	Less wave drag	Head is too far back, eyes looking at the ceiling
Hand Recovery (Figure 23.2)	Thumb leads coming out of the water as if a string is pulling the thumb up	Specific goal for swimmer to heed	Fingers lead coming out of the water
	Thumbs up, making the OK sign	More streamlined; more efficient to cut through the water	
Shoulder Recovery	Lead with shoulder; straight arm	More streamlined	Arms are bent
	Raise hand to ask question	More efficient for best power position	
	Graze your ear with your arm		
	Skim the ear		

continued

FIGURE 23.1 Front Crawl

High elbow recovery

Boil the water
Only heels break surface

Spear a fish that is 2–3 inches below water

FIGURE 23.2 Back Crawl

Graze ear with arm

Thumb leads coming out of water
Raise hand to ask question

Pinkie finger leads going into water

BACK CRAWL, continued

SKILL	CUE	WHY?	COMMON ERROR
Hand Entry	Pinkie finger always leads going into the water	More efficient	Arms enter too far out to the side of the body
	Palms facing away	Less splash	Hand or elbow enters first
Arm Pull	Make a question mark with each arm pull	Creates power to move body forward	Straight arm pull
		Less stress on shoulders	
Leg Action	Point toes like a diver	More streamlined; move through the water faster	Flexed, stiff feet; swimmer does not move forward well; knees and heels break the surface of the water
	Kick toes to the surface	More efficient	
	Make water boil	Less drag	
Body Rotation	Hip to sky	Keep body streamlined	
	Rotate body on skewer	More efficient	

BUTTERFLY STROKE

SKILL	CUE	WHY?	COMMON ERROR
Arm Pull	Draw an hourglass with high elbow pull	More power	Straight arm pull
	Push arms; explode out of the back of stroke; touch thigh with thumb		
	Stay low		
Arm Recovery	Elbow is being pulled by string upward	Gets arms ready for power phase, more efficient stroke	Elbows stay in water on recovery

continued

BUTTERFLY STROKE, continued

SKILL	CUE	WHY?	COMMON ERROR
Arm Recovery, *continued*	Thumbs drag along the water to keep elbows high		Arms drag along the water
	Pinkies exit first		
Hand Entry	Catch the water with hands		
Leg Action	Legs are together, like a mermaid	Gets legs in position for power phase	Legs too far apart
	Two strong kicks		Whip kick or frog kick
	Make kick like a metronome		
Coordination	Lead with head	Better coordination of stroke	
	As hands enter in front, chest is down, buttocks up		
Breathing	Keep chin near the water when breathing	Easier to take the breath	
Body Roll	Body roll through a relatively narrow band of water at the surface	Body is streamlined to move through water	
	No deeper than 1–2 feet	More efficient	

SIDESTROKE

SKILL	CUE	WHY?	COMMON ERROR
Body Position	Lay head on arm	Keeps body streamlined to move through water more efficiently	Ear and head too far above the water
	Lower ear is in water		Lying on stomach
Arm Pull	Tie a big knot	Creates best power from the arms	Both hands start above head
	Pick an apple from a tree and put it in your pocket	Keeps upper body above the water	
Arm Recovery	Rest the top hand on the top leg during glide	Keeps body streamlined and aerodynamic to move through the water	Top arm pushes too far past the leg
Leg Action	Draw both heels toward buttocks	Legs in best power position	Whip or frog kick used
	Tuck the knees, flex the top foot, and point the bottom foot		

continued

SKILL	CUE	WHY?	COMMON ERROR
Leg Action, *continued*	Do the splits	Gets body ready for power phase	Legs too close together when trying to make the splits; legs go up and down, not sideways
	Splits done sideways		
	Legs do not pass each other when kick is finished	Keeps swimmer on side and streamlined	Legs pass each other on the kick
	Avoid up-and-down splits; close legs like scissors	More efficient	
Coordination	Stay streamlined	Rest	
	Count to 3 on glide		
	Stay parallel with side	Keeps body aerodynamic in water	Roll or lie on stomach

BREASTSTROKE

SKILL	CUE	WHY?	COMMON ERROR
Body Position	Arch back to bring shoulders out of water		Body vertical in water
Head Position	Eyes focused on wall	Streamlined to move through the water more efficiently	
	Crown at water level		Hair submerged in water
Arm Pull/Arm Recovery	Make a small upside-down heart; start at the point of the heart, trace it with hand, then split it in half with hands	Creates power in the stroke	Heart shape is too wide or long
Arm Glide	Fully extend arms and count to 3 before starting to pull	Creates better aerodynamics	Starting to pull too soon
Leg Action (Whip Kick)	Kick buttocks with heels	More power	Knees too far apart
	Try being knock-kneed		Frog kick
	Knees a fist apart		
	Keep knees closer together than ankles		
	Draw circles with heels		Knees outside ankles
	Push feet/squeeze legs		

continued

BREASTSTROKE, continued

SKILL	CUE	WHY?	COMMON ERROR
Breathing	Lift chin, not head, to breathe	Easier to breathe	Head too far out of water
Coordination	Pull, breathe, kick, glide	Saying these words helps you coordinate the stroke	Gliding when arms are at waist

ELEMENTARY BACKSTROKE

SKILL	CUE	WHY?	COMMON ERROR
Body Position	Ears in the water	Helps streamline body to move through water more efficiently	Head too far out of water
	Arms down at sides		
Arm Recovery	Tickle sides with thumbs all the way to the armpit	Creates more pull for power	Hands do not come to armpits, half stroke
Arm Pull	Palms out	More power	Hands and arms come too far above head
	Make a T		
	Make a snow angel	Creates more pull for power	
Leg Action (Whip Kick)	Drop feet straight down	Requires less energy	Buttocks drop, knees bent to chest
	Make penguin feet	When knees come up, body sinks	
	Try being knockkneed	Gets legs in position for power phase	Knees are outside of ankles
	Feet outside knees	Action with feet faster	
		More power	
	Upper legs form a table		Knees come out of water
	Draw heels toward buttocks		
	Try drawing circles with your heels	Action phase more powerful	Scissors kick with one or both legs
	Push feet, then squeeze legs		
Coordination	Recover the arms first, kick and pull, then glide		Arms and legs start at the same time

TRUDGENSTROKES

SKILL	CUE	WHY?	COMMON ERROR
Trudgen	Front crawl with scissors kick		Breathing on both sides
	Roll hips to side	Creates power	Whip kick, staying on stomach
	Scissors kick when breathing	Help with timing to breathe	Kicking when head is in water
Trudgen Crawl	Front crawl with scissors kick and flutter kick		
	Roll hip to side		Hips flat
	Scissors kick when breathing; flutter kick when face is in water	Create more power in the stroke	Forgetting to flutter kick
	Breathe on one side		Breathing on both sides
Double Trudgen	Front crawl with no flutter kick		
	Scissors kick—scissors kick	Creates more power	Kicking on only one side
	Roll hip to each side when performing a scissors kick on each arm stroke		Not rolling hips
	Breathe on one side only		Breathing on both sides
	Head stays in water on one arm stroke and one scissors kick; keep head in water	Helps with the coordination of the stroke	Turning head right and left
	Try to keep arms moving and in sequence with each scissors kick		

SWIMMING SKILLS

SKILL	CUE	WHY?	COMMON ERROR
Rotary Kick (Figure 23.3)	Sit on horse, back straight		Standing straight up
	One foot rotates clockwise, the other foot counterclockwise like being on a barrel and riding a bike		Legs going same direction

continued

FIGURE 23.3 Rotary Kick

	SWIMMING SKILLS, continued		
SKILL	**CUE**	**WHY?**	**COMMON ERROR**
Rotary Kick, *continued*	Eggbeater		
	"Wax on! Wax off!" with your feet (as in the *Karate Kid* movie; same motion, but use feet)		
Tread Water	Look over fence		
Arms	Figure 8 with hands, palms up, palms down; or like spreading butter with sides of hands		Hands pushing down
Legs	Scissors/breaststroke/rotary		
Body Position	Relaxed		Body too rigid, not relaxed
			Too much energy, too tight
Front Open Turn	Drop one shoulder, meet hands above head		Grab wall with both hands
	Knees tuck against wall; submerge in water		Not tucking
	Spring off wall		Not pushing
	Stay submerged	More streamlined	Staying on top of water, not submerging
Back Open Turn	Drop one shoulder, meet hands above head		Arms by side
	Spring off wall		Not tucking
	Be a torpedo	Creates power	No power

continued

SKILL	CUE	WHY?	COMMON ERROR
Sidestroke Arms and Coordination	See sidestroke cues		
Swimming Underwater	Be a submarine	Body is streamlined	Swimming on top of water
	Scrape a big bowl with hands	More power; more efficient pull	Straight arm pull
Butterfly Arm Stroke and Coordination	See butterfly stroke cues		
Breaststroke Turn	Drop shoulder, hands meet above head; submerge	Gets body underwater for more efficiency	Shoulders level
	Superhero looking over city underwater	More streamlined	
Sidestroke Turn	Touch wall with leading arm		Touching wall with both arms
	Drop one shoulder		
	Spring off wall		
Speed Turn and Pull Out for Breaststroke	Drop one shoulder, meet hands above head	Gets body in streamline position	
	Spring off wall		Not tucking
Arms	Draw light bulb to thighs (feel water move down legs to toes)	More power	Shallow pull
Legs	Whip kick and stretch	More power	Kicking too quickly after pull
Flip Turn for Front Crawl	Front somersault (one stroke from edge of pool)	Gets body in ready position to be more efficient during turn	Body stays flat, too far from, or too close to wall
	Bend at waist; be a hinge		
	Put buttocks in air		Not tucking
	Throw legs out of water	More power	
	Find wall with feet		Finding wall with buttocks, too close to wall, finding gutter instead
	Put footprints on wall	More power to push off	

continued

SKILL	CUE	WHY?	COMMON ERROR
Flip Turn for Backstroke	Turn on stomach one stroke from edge	Won't run into wall	
	Do a front flip turn		
	Push off on back like a torpedo, arms above head	Creates better control and power in push off	
Pike Surface Dive	Swim with continuous motion into pike; pull water up; drive your head down	Creates momentum to get body down	No power into pike
	Hands touch toes		Body stays flat
	Be a hinge or break like a pencil at hips		Stay in bent position
	Shoot legs up or put pencil back together as you dive down	Creates energy to get down to bottom of pool	
Tuck Surface Dive	Swim front crawl with continuous motion		No power put into swim
	Drive your head down; pull water up	Creates momentum to get body down fast	
	Swim and roll into ball or cannonball		Head remains up
	Cannonball explodes, shoot feet up in air	Gets body in a straight position to go down	
Feet-First Surface Dive *Arm Action*	Start in T position		Starting with hands at side
	Perform jumping jack action with arms	Gives body momentum	Keeping arms down at sides
	Arms and hands push down like a jumping jack and push back up like a jumping jack; or push arms back up like a referee's signal for touchdown	More power to get down, keeps body streamlined	

DIVING

SKILL	CUE	WHY?	COMMON ERROR
Safety Rules	Dive in deep water (9 feet or more)	To prevent serious permanent injury	Diving in less than 9 feet of water can cause spinal or head injuries
Side-of-Pool Dive			
Kneeling Position	Kneel on one knee; grip pool edge with other foot	If head is up, you will flop in the water	Kneeling on two knees
	Head between arms and fingers pointing to water		Hands and arms moving to front of body
	Focus on target on bottom, 4 feet out; or surface 1–2 feet from side		Not focusing on target (causes a belly flop)
Action of Dive	Lean forward, try to touch water		Jumping in water with head lifted
	Push with front foot		Somersaulting in
	Keep hips up and dive over barrel	Keeps diver from falling into water	Hips down
	Straighten legs		Legs bent
	Push downward in water with hands	Breaks water with hands, not head	Pushing upward
		Does not hurt the head	
Compact Dive	One foot forward, one foot back		Staying on knee
	Kneel and rise		Staying on knee
	Head between arms, point fingers at water		Head not between arms
	Hips up, stretch, and touch surface of water	Reaching for water gets body into position to go head first	Hips down, hands in air
	Lose balance, push off toward water	Gets students going in head first	
	Ankles together on water entry		Legs apart
Stride Dive	Walking stance		Legs together
	Front toes grab edge		Foot is not at edge

continued

SKILL	CUE	WHY?	COMMON ERROR
Side-of-Pool Dive *Stride Dive, continued*	Head between arms		Head is up
	Bend at the waist like breaking a pencil		Body is straight
	Kick back leg up, hips up	Correct body angle for water entry	Not kicking leg
	Once body is underwater, point fingers to surface of water		Fingers pointed down
Long, Shallow Dive	Push and stretch		Falling in or plopping in
	Spear into the water		Pointing fingers to bottom of pool
	Over the barrel and through the hoop		
	Hands enter through doughnut hole	Helps divers dive out, not deep	
	Go through the tunnel just below surface of water		
Diving from the Board	Hips up, arms stretched, fall forward; focus on target in water		Hips down
Approach Hurdle	Lift knee like a tabletop or a stork position	Gets diver up in the air	Keeping knee down
	Arms back, like pushing ski poles		
	Arms up to touchdown position		Arms staying down
Jump Off Board	Use approach hurdle position		One or two steps in approaching hurdle
	Arms back like a back arm circle	Gives diver power to get up—not out	
	Land on both feet and push off board	Balance and control	
Jump, Tuck Position	Use approach hurdle position		
	Jump off board		
	Lift knees to chest in fetal position; straighten back up in spear position		Not getting in a tuck position
Tuck Dive	Use approach hurdle position		

continued

	DIVING, continued		
SKILL	CUE	WHY?	COMMON ERROR
Diving from the Board, *continued*	Jump in tuck position		
	Lift hips		Hips down
	Drive heels into ceiling	Keeps body straight at entry point	
	Push hands into water, above head		Hands down
Pike Dive	Use approach hurdle position		
	Hips up	Power	Hips down
	Break the pencil		Bending at hips
	Fingers to toes	Gets in pike	
	Drive heels into ceiling	Keeps body straight at entry point	

WATER POLO

INTRODUCTION

Water polo is an exciting sport that is fast-paced and requires the players to know both the offensive and defensive aspects of the game. Water polo involves a tremendous amount of swimming and treading water, and it is an extremely physical sport. It is a great way to become physically fit and have fun at the same time.

TIPS

Equipment Tips

1. One water polo ball per two players (men, women, and youth sizes)
2. Two water polo cages
3. One water polo cap per player

Safety and Etiquette

If you get pinched, let go.

GAME PLAY

Water polo is played in a 30 × 20 meter pool with seven players on each team: six field players and one goalie (see Figure 23.4).

FIGURE 23.4   Offense and Defense Set-Up
for a Water Polo Game

Basic Rules

Minor Fouls

1. Pushing the ball underwater (even if you are forced to do so by a defensive player)
2. Touching the ball with both hands
3. Coming into contact with the arm of a player who has the ball
4. Hitting the ball with a fist
5. Throwing the ball out-of-bounds
6. Pushing off of the pool side, pool bottom, or another player

Major Fouls

1. Intentionally holding the player with the ball
2. Interfering with a free throw
3. Pushing another player underwater (called "sinking the player")
4. Swearing
5. The player with the ball intentionally pushing another player (think "offensive foul" in basketball)

Brutal Fouls

1. Hitting another player
2. Kicking another player

Strategies

See Figure 24.4 for how to set up the offense and defense for a game.

Scoring

One point is scored for a goal.

SKILL	CUE	WHY?	COMMON ERROR
Passing	Keep body in tripod form (non-shooting hand sculling and both legs eggbeater) (see rotary cues)	Keeping one hand underwater sculling and both legs eggbeater (forming the tripod); will keep your body in good shooting and passing form	Having legs straight down and hand out of the water
	Keep eyes on target		
	Keep elbow up slightly behind the ball	Keeping the elbow up will allow for proper shoulder rotation and follow-through	Elbow dropping low and decreasing power and control
	Make hand follow through to water	To improve accuracy and velocity	Not following through and allowing the ball to go high and out of control
Shot	Keep body in tripod	Keeping one hand underwater sculling and both legs eggbeater, forming tripod; will keep your body in good shooting and passing form	Having legs straight down and hand out of the water
	Keep eyes on target		
	Make hand follow through to water	To improve accuracy and velocity	Not following through and allowing the ball to go high and out of control
	Keep elbow up slightly behind head	Keeping the ball up will allow for proper shoulder rotation and follow-through	
	Aim for corners	To get ball past the goalie	Not aiming or aiming at the goalie
	Know where the goalie is	To be able to shoot around the goalie	
Dribbling	Keep elbow high	Maintains ball control	
		Protects the ball from the defender	
	Strong flutter kick	Helps to move you through the water	Having a weak kick or not kicking at all
	Keep head straight forward	Keeps your body in line	Swinging head side to side

SKILL	CUE	WHY?	COMMON ERROR
Defensive Sculling			
Hips	Keep hips at the surface of the water	Avoid offensive grab and defensive foul	Dropping hips and allowing referee to call an offensive foul
Hands	Wax on, wax off	Helps propel body backward	
Legs	Eggbeater	Helps keep hips at the surface	
Defensive Position	Stay between the offender and the cage	To not allow offender behind the defender and give an open shot	Allowing offense to get behind and get one-on-one with the goalie
Lunge for Steal	Keep eyes on the ball	Defender knows when the ball is coming to your offender	Staring at the offensive player
	Keep head on a swivel	Keeps track of where the ball is and where the offensive player is	Focusing on the ball and losing track of the offensive player
	Use a breaststroke kick	Propels body in direction of the pass to intercept the ball	Using a flutter or scissors kick
	Reach with hand for the ball	Takes possession of the ball	
Center Defense	Keep hips at the surface of the water	Prevents offensive center from grabbing and moving	Playing defense with hips down
	Try to stay between the offensive player and the ball on the perimeter	Prevents entry pass to offensive center	Playing offensive center directly behind them
	Commit foul on entry pass	Stops the shot opportunity of the offensive center	

24

Team Handball and Indoor Hybrid Ball

INTRODUCTION

Team handball is a dynamic sport that is fun to play and exciting to watch. Natural athletic skills such as running, jumping, throwing, and catching provide the action for the game. Players and spectators alike enjoy the fast, continuous play, body contact, and goalie action. First-time spectators describe team handball as soccer with your hands, but they also notice elements that remind them of basketball, water polo, and ice hockey.

SKILLS LISTED WITH CUES

The cues listed for team handball include passing and catching (overhand pass, catching on the run), individual movement in attack (piston movement and sidestepping), shooting (general principles, set shot, jump shot), goalkeeping, defense (basic stance, individual tactics, shot blocking, small-group tactics, team defense: 6–0 zone), and offense (attacking the gap, small-group tactics, team offense: fast break, 3–3 formation).

TIPS

Equipment Tips

1. Regulation indoor court, 20 meters × 40 meters, approximately 65 feet × 131 feet, one-third larger than a basketball court.
2. Indoors with limited space, that is, only a regulation or smaller basketball court:
   a. Try to maintain a 18- to 20-meter width by using extra space outside the basketball court.
   b. Small basketball court: Have no sideline boundaries, and play balls off the side walls. Reduce the number of players to five plus a goalie.

c. After a goal is scored, the goalie puts the ball back into play with throw-off from the goal area, rather than restarting from the center of the court. The goalie cannot leave area or shoot.

3. Marking the court: The most essential lines are the arced 6-meter goal area line and the 7-meter penalty-throw line. Use gym floor tape, the basketball court's three-point line, cones, rope, "chalk dust," paint, or white flour on grass to create these lines. The dashed free-throw line is optional (see Figure 24.1).

4. Modified goals, 2-meter × 3-meter opening: Tape on a wall, portable standards made with rope or old volleyball nets, large crash mat against wall, field hockey or indoor soccer goals, or goals built from PVC pipe.

5. Team handballs (about 23 inches in circumference): For safety reasons, the official men's or women's leather ball is not recommended for beginning players or coed classes. Use Sportime's "Supersafe Elite" handball, a dense foam ball, or a slightly deflated volleyball.

Safety & Etiquette

1. Each player has to be an arms-length from other players.

2. A player cannot shoot the ball from within the crease because it is dangerous to the goalie.

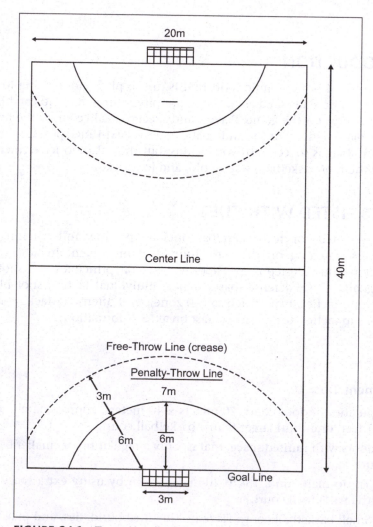

FIGURE 24.1 Team Handball Court

3. Using a regulation volleyball to play the game helps to minimize injuries.
4. This is a non-contact sport, so no body-to-body contact is allowed.

TEACHING IDEAS

Teaching Progressions

1. Teach non-contact, basketball-style defense. The official handball rules do allow some body contact, but it is not recommended for beginning players.
2. Use the "teaching rules" during scrimmage to encourage players to develop passing and shooting skills along with increasing goalie safety:

   a. Three passes before the team can shoot.

   b. No dribbling or a limited number of dribbles.

   c. Without a goalie, you can shoot only bounce shots or use targets in the goal corners, such as towels, cones, hoops, and the like. Only the designated goalie can go into goal area and put ball into play after a shot.

GAME PLAY

Rules

1. A player is not permitted in the goal area. A player can jump into the crease but must release the ball before landing.
2. Start the game with a jump ball.
3. A player is permitted 3 steps when they have possession of the ball.
4. A player can hold the ball for 3 seconds.
5. A player can have a 3-step dribble to encourage passing.
6. If the ball goes out-of-bounds, possession goes to other team.
7. A defender needs to be an arms-length from the offensive player with the ball.
8. If there is a foul within the 3-point line, a penalty shot is awarded.
9. The goalie cannot leave the goal area when in possession of the ball.
10. Goal Throw: The ball is blocked and recovered in the goal area, or the ball goes over the end line.
11. The goalie needs to be inside the goal area on a goal throw.

Strategies

For offensive and defensive strategies, see the cue tables.

Scoring

A goal is scored when the entire ball crosses the goal line inside the goal. A goal may be scored from any throw (free-throw, throw-in, throw-off, or goal-throw).

ASSESSMENT IDEAS

1. Shoot from behind the 3-meter arc 5 times and award 1 point for each goal.
2. The way to learn the game is to play games. Each game is worth 5 points.

For further information and special help, consult the following organization and resources.

ORGANIZATION

Available resources for sale include: team handball basic rules sheet; team handball rule book; videos; suggestions: *Introduction to Team Handball*, Olympic games, and international games (designate men's or women's).

USA Team Handball
P.O. Box 58-1486
Street Address:
2330 W. California Ave.
Salt Lake City, UT 84158
Phone: (801) 463-2000
Email: info@usateamhandball.org
Website: www.usateamhandball.org

PASSING AND CATCHING

SKILL	CUE	WHY?	COMMON ERROR
Overhand Pass	Pass with one hand, catch with both	Accuracy, distance, and control	
Preparation	Fingertip grip		Holding ball in palm of hand
	Lift ball up and back with elbow flexed at 90°		Elbow too close to body—ball too close to head
	Weight on back foot		
	Shoulders perpendicular to target		
Throwing Action	Step toward target	Transfers weight	Standing stationary
	Rotate and square shoulders to target		No shoulder rotation—always facing target
	Lead with elbow; whip forearm and snap wrist	More velocity on ball	The ball is pushed from shoulder and hand, and ball leads
Catching on the Run (Figure 24.2)	Maintain running rhythm		Stopping to catch the ball
Preparation			
Position	Hands up; form a triangle with thumbs and forefingers almost touching	Provides a target for the passer	

continued

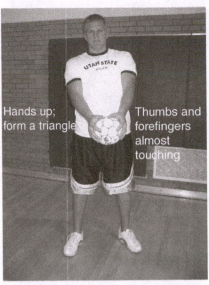

FIGURE 24.2 Catching on the Run

SKILL	CUE	WHY?	COMMON ERROR
Catching on the Run, *continued*	Push off one leg, extend arms toward ball		
Receiving Action	Soft hands—catch while flexing elbows to give with ball		Ball rebounds off hands
	Land on other foot		

INDIVIDUAL MOVEMENT IN ATTACK

SKILL	CUE	WHY?	COMMON ERROR
Piston Movement	Fundamental movement of backcourt players; sum of three actions similar to up-and-down motion of a piston in a motor cylinder		
The Three Actions	1. Run to receive; catch ball while running toward goal		Standing in one spot to receive pass
	2. Use three steps to attack goal; rules—allow three steps with ball (i.e., a right-hander should step left-right-left); on third step, shoot or pass, throw off foot that is opposite to throwing arm		Throwing off foot on same side as throwing arm, or passing ball while backing up

continued

SKILL	CUE	WHY?	COMMON ERROR
Piston Movement, *continued*			Poor timing
	3. Back up quickly; prepare to attack again		Forgetting to back up and staying too close to defense
			Watching for action; not moving
Sidestepping	Fundamental movement for circle runners along or near 6-meter line		
Position	Balanced position; knees bent, feet shoulder-width apart, hands open ready to catch		Standing upright with hands down, not ready to catch
			Not creating own space
Leg Action	Step sideways using quick, small steps without crossing feet; maintain balanced position		Bringing feet together or crossing feet
			Off balance; poor footwork

SHOOTING

SKILL	CUE	WHY?	COMMON ERROR
General Principles	Shoot on move— piston movement	Movement adds deception	Shooting while stationary
	Watch goalie and shoot for open corners of goal; may choose to bounce ball when shooting low	Harder areas for the goalie to defend	Shooting at the center of the goal
	Take shots between 6 and 9 meters; avoid severe angles	Learn to dive into circle to improve angle	Shooting a set shot from a wing position
	Shoot only when there is an opening (shoot over and between defenders)	Higher chance of scoring	Charging into a defender or carelessly shooting a ball that hits a stationary defender
Set Shot *Preparation*	Run to receive and attack using three steps	Adds speed to the shot	Standing still when shooting

continued

SKILL	CUE	WHY?	COMMON ERROR
Set Shot, *Preparation, continued*	Weight on back foot (same as shooting arm)	Transfers weight	Shooting off same foot as shooting arm
	Elbow flexed at 90° or greater		
	Shoulders perpendicular to goal		Facing target, shoulders square to goal
	Head up and eyes on goalie, shoot to open corner; equals "cobwebs"	Harder to defend	Shooting at the center of the goal
Follow-Through	Momentum continues forward and arm motion continues across body	Gives more force to the shot	Stopping arm at the moment of release
Jump Shot	Use jump shot to shoot over a defender, or when jumping into the goal area to score		
Preparation	Run to receive and attack using three steps	Adds momentum to the jump	
Jumping Action (Figure 24.3)	To jump: plant foot opposite throwing arm and drive other knee up (changing forward momentum into upward momentum)		Charging into defender; not reading spacing properly
	Raise shooting arm up and back; make an L		
	Rotate shoulders square to goal while whipping throwing arm forward (elbow, shoulder, forearm, wrist)		
Throwing Action	Pike slightly at waist and land on takeoff foot		Shot lacks velocity, all power coming from strong upper-body action; poor mechanics

Raise shooting arm
up and back;
make an L

Drive knee
up

Plant foot opposite
throwing arm

FIGURE 24.3 Jump Shot

Stand tall

Arms and legs spread,
like a jumping jack

FIGURE 24.4 Basic Position of the Goalie

	GOALKEEPING		
SKILL	**CUE**	**WHY?**	**COMMON ERROR**
Basic Position (Figure 24.4)	Stand tall with knees slightly flexed, weight on balls of feet, hands up, eyes on ball (like a jumping jack)	Makes the body bigger to block more of the goal	Bending at waist with hands low, similar to basketball defensive position
Movement in Goal	Step out about $^1/_2$ meter from goal line and follow ball by moving with quick shuffle steps, keeping body aligned with the ball	Limits open angles	Standing in middle of goal and not moving
	Get stable prior to shot; be ready to block shot	Better body control	Feeling off balance when shot is taken
	Protect near post		Poor balance
			Mechanics
Blocking High Shots *Footwork*	Take small step in direction of ball, push off leg farthest from ball, and leap in direction of shot		Leaning, reaching for ball rather than moving body
			Poor mechanics
			Fatigue

continued

GOALKEEPING, continued			
SKILL	**CUE**	**WHY?**	**COMMON ERROR**
Blocking High Shots, *continued* *Blocking Action*	Extend arm(s) in path of ball and attack the ball; block ball, don't try to catch it		Ball goes through hands when trying to catch it
			Taking eye off ball
			Weak hands
			Fatigue
Blocking Low Shots *Footwork*	Take small step in direction of ball, push off leg farthest from ball	Adds length and momentum	
Blocking Action	Extend opposite leg and arm(s) in path of ball to block	Strength, balance, and flexibility	Shot goes over leg— failing to block with both leg and arm(s)
Blocking Wing Shots *Position*	Stand tall close to goal; place weight on goal-side leg		
	Goal-side arm up, elbow bent about 90° with forearm in front of face, other hand out to side, bent about 90°		
Footwork	As shooter jumps into the goal area, take one step out from the goal and move with quick shuffle steps to keep body aligned with ball		
Blocking Action	Block high shots with arm(s) and low shots with leg and arm(s)		

DEFENSE			
SKILL	**CUE**	**WHY?**	**COMMON ERROR**
Individual Basic Stance	Feet shoulder width apart, knees slightly bent, weight forward on balls of feet, body upright, arms out, hands up		Upper body bent forward, hands down, like basketball defensive stance

SKILL	CUE	WHY?	COMMON ERROR
Individual Defense Tactics *Movement*	Shift along 6-meter line in direction of ball		
	See ball and direct opponent at all times		
	When your opponent attacks, step out from 6-meter line to meet attack—play basketball defense, no contact		Attacker is able to get a shot off from 7 or 8 meters
	Wing defenders should not step out, as a set shot or jump shot is not likely to be successful from such a bad angle		Attacker drives around player and jumps into goal area for a shot
	Stay between opponent and goal		
	When opponent passes the ball, recover to the 6-meter line		Leaving space for circle runner to run behind you
Shot Blocking *Action*	From basic stance, extend one or both hands into path of ball		
	Attack ball similar to volleyball blocking		Ball goes through hands toward goal
Small-Group Defense Tactics	Help triangle—when player steps out, two adjacent players squeeze in slightly for help on both sides		Big open space is left along 6-meter line
	Communicate—each defender should know who is stepping out, who is staying back to help	Good offensive	Two players step out to meet one attacker, or no one steps out to meet attacker
Team Defense *6–0 Zone*	All six defenders take positions along 6-meter line, forming movable wall in front of goal		
	Shift as a unit in direction of ball movement		

continued

SKILL	CUE	WHY?	COMMON ERROR
Team Defense *6–0 Zone, continued*	Each defender is responsible for attacker in his or her area of zone—each attacker should be accounted for by one defender	Good offensive	One defender guarding two attackers, or an attacker left unguarded

OFFENSE

SKILL	CUE	WHY?	COMMON ERROR
Individual Offense Tactics *Attack Gap: Space Between two Defenders*	Use fakes to get in a gap		
	Create a workable space from defense		Attacking too close to defenders; causing free throws, which interrupt flow of attack
	Be a threat to score; look to shoot first, then pass		Not maintaining proper passing
	Break through gap for a shot from 6-meter line		
	Create overload by drawing two defenders and passing to an open teammate		
Small-Group Offense Tactics	Two or three players work together to create scoring opportunity		
Basketball-Type Tactics	Give-and-go		
	Pick-and-roll		
	Crossing splits or scissors		
	Screens		
Three Phases of Team Offense *Fast Break*	Primary—long pass from goalie to breaking wing		

continued

SKILL	CUE	WHY?	COMMON ERROR
Three Phases of Team Offense, *continued*	Secondary—goalie shoots outlet pass, and team moves ball up floor quickly		
Organize into 3–3 Offense Formation; Move Ball in Support Points	Three players near the 6-meter line: left wing (LW), right wing (RW), circle runner (CR)		
	Three players outside 9-meter line in backcourt: left backcourt (LB), center backcourt (CB), right backcourt (RB)		
	Move ball with short, quick passes, wing to wing		
	Run to receive, play in good timing with teammates		
Execute Small-Group Tactics	Play with patience; wait for good scoring opportunity		Trying to score too often one-on-one

INDOOR HYBRID BALL

Introduction

What sport might LaBron James, Cristiano Ronaldo, Russell Wilson, and Gary Hines play if they all got together? They'd probably play indoor hybrid ball! This sport has elements of basketball, soccer, American football, and team handball combined. Hybrid ball allows players of each of these sports to interact and bring their personal styles to the game. While experience in any one of these sports may prove an advantage, it can also be a disadvantage if players cannot expand and learn skills other than those of their preferred sports. Best of all, the sport is simple enough that students can play it on their first day, while also being challenging enough to continue playing it for weeks in a physical education curriculum.

Randy Webb in Knoxville, Tennessee invented indoor hybrid ball. The sport was first played in the physical education classes in Knoxville. Since its inception, indoor hybrid ball has been played in numerous physical education and recreational settings. The sport has increased in popularity because of its unique characteristics, the options to score, the variety of athletic skills utilized, and the cardiorespiratory fitness it develops.

Skills Used in the Game

Skills used in hybrid ball include throwing, catching, basketball and soccer passing, basketball dribbling, soccer dribbling, soccer trapping, kicking, punting, team handball goal shot, soccer goal shot, and goalie skills. Skill development appears to be accelerated when students have the opportunity to practice a sport that incorporates multiple sports within the context of one.

TIPS

Equipment Tips

Hybrid ball requires an 8" web ball, a volleyball, or a ball that can bounce but not hurt players when it is thrown into the goal. One ball is needed for every two students in the class for warming up, as well as 8–10 mesh vests to field two teams and a scoreboard.

Safety and Etiquette

The safety and etiquette for indoor hybrid ball are the same as team handball.

Teaching Progressions

Gamelike Warm-Up

1. Throw the ball to a partner 10 yards away.
2. Basketball dribble the ball with the right hand and left hand, alternating hands.
3. Soccer dribble the ball to a partner 10 yards away. Same drill soccer pass.
4. Three-point zone passing with 3–4 players.
5. Three-point zone passing with 3–4 players. Add defenders.

Goal Warm-Up

1. Three-step approach: Throw the ball into the goal from behind the 3-point line with the right hand. Repeat the same drill using the left hand.
2. Throw the ball into the goal from behind the 3-point line. Repeat the same drill but also add the goalie.
3. Soccer kick the ball into the goal from behind the 3-point line. Repeat the same drill but also add the goalie.
4. Throw the ball in from the end line to outside the 3-point line, pass, and shoot. The shooter becomes the goalie and rotates through the line.
5. Punt from behind the centerline, aiming for the basketball backboard. As a class, work for five goals. When playing the game with large classes, rotate teams every 6–10 min. Students who are not playing can keep the time and the score.

Game Play

One indoor basketball court is needed. The court or playing area has one basketball hoop and one indoor soccer goal at each end of the court. The goals do not need to be full size. If the basketball court has a mat on the back wall, the mat can be used as a target to score with two orange cones placed on the end lines of each free-throw sideline. If indoor soccer nets or mats are not available, place tape on the back wall, making a box the size of a soccer goal, and place two orange cones on the basketball end line—one on each side of the free throw sidelines (see Figure 24.5).

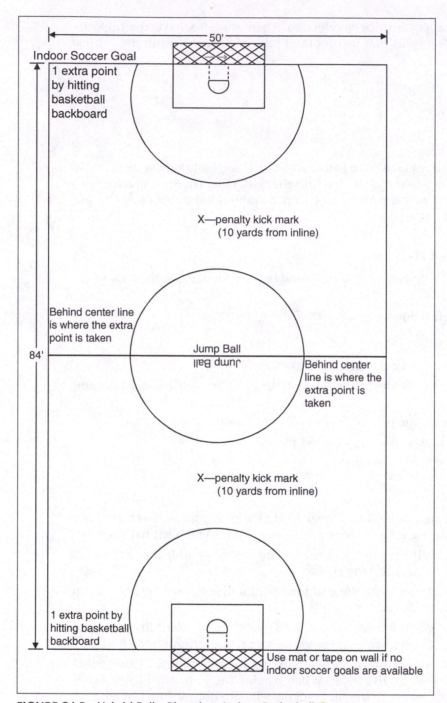

FIGURE 24.5 Hybrid Ball—Played on Indoor Basketball Court

Time

- Four 8-minute quarters, 1-minute time-outs, and 10-minute halftime for the middle school level
- Four 10-minute quarters, 1-minute time-outs, and 5-minute halftime for the high school level
- Two 20-minute halves and 5-minute halftime for collegiate level

Start of the Game

Begin the game with a jump ball, similar to basketball, at the center line.

Rules

1. A player can use a basketball dribble or soccer dribble to move the ball down the court.
2. A player can throw the ball to a teammate.
3. A player can kick the ball to a teammate.
4. A player can pick up the ball off the floor.
5. A player cannot double dribble, like in basketball.
6. A player cannot travel, like in basketball.
7. A player cannot run or walk with the ball.
8. A player cannot place a foot in front of the 3-foot line before releasing the ball for a goal.
9. No offensive players are allowed in the key on a free ball.
10. Goalies can switch after each point scored.
11. Offensive players can cut through the 3-point line, except on a loose ball.

Rule Violations   If a violation occurs, the ball goes to defending team from the sideline. A player throws the ball into play.

Fouls

- Pushing, tripping, hitting, tackling, kicking, or charging a player.
- Having more than minimal body contact.

Foul Violations

1. The first offense on a player results in a penalty kick from the 10-yard line.
2. For the second offense, the player goes to penalty box for 2 minutes, and a penalty kick is awarded from the 10-yard line.
3. For the third offense, the player is disqualified, and the opposing team gets a penalty kick from the 10-yard line.

Penalty Kick Rules

1. The ball is placed on the 10-yard line.
2. The goalie has to stand on the end line and cannot move until the ball is kicked. Every offensive and defensive player has to be outside the 3-point line at the time of the kick.
3. If the penalty kick is missed, play continues immediately.

Offside Player Violations

1. Only one goalie and one defender are allowed inside the basketball 3-point line when a shot is taken.
2. Offensive players can cut through the key.

Out-of-Bounds Rules (optional for middle school and high school, but not college)

1. If the ball goes out-of-bounds, the other team throws the ball from the sideline into play, like basketball.

2. If the ball goes over the end line off of an offensive player, the goalie can throw or kick the ball into play from behind the free-throw line.

3. If the ball goes over the end line off of a defensive player, the offensive goalie can kick or throw the ball into play from behind the free-throw line.

Game Modifications   Play the game with no out-of-bounds. The game moves faster, especially for the collegiate level.

Strategies

Scoring and Points

1. Two points for a throw into the goal from behind the 3-point line.

2. Two points for a kick (not a punt) into the goal from behind the 3-point line.

3. One extra point is awarded when any offensive player kicks the ball from behind the centerline and the ball hits the basketball backboard. The players start behind the centerline but can finish in front of the centerline.

4. Two points for a penalty kick from 10 yards away.

What to Do After the Score

1. When a goal is scored, a player kicks the ball for an extra point.

2. If the extra point is made, the goalie takes the ball and kicks or throws the ball to a teammate from behind the free throw line.

3. If the extra point is not made, it is a free ball.

ASSESSMENT IDEAS

1. Shoot from behind the 3 meter arc 5 times, awarding 1 point for each goal.

2. The way to learn the game is to play games. Each game is worth 5 points.

FYI

For further information and special help, consult the following organization.

ORGANIZATION

Indoor and Outdoor Hybrid Ball Rules and Game

Randy Webb
3508 Maloney Road
Knoxville, TN 37920
Phone: (865) 984-6367
Email: randywebb1954@yahoo.com

You can email, write, or call Randy Webb. He will send you information on indoor and outdoor hybrid ball rules and game.

25

Tennis

INTRODUCTION

No one can describe the stress, intensity, and exhilaration one goes through when stepping up to the line to serve for the big point in tennis. No other sport can match the beating the body receives during a three-hour match played in 105-degree weather. No other feeling can top the desire to scream a forehand past your opponent after a rally that has made your legs burn. You know it's all up to you. No other game can be as exciting, different, and rewarding for each individual point. No other situation can be as maddening, frustrating, and absolutely glorious as a match of tennis. It gets better every time you step out on the court.

Tennis is not only a sport for a lifetime, but it also helps build character. It teaches you about speed, endurance, agility, anticipation, and quick reaction time. Tennis also tests your mental skills. You learn to control your temper and stay mentally tough to earn those big points that determine who wins the match. To be successful, you must be creative in combining mental and physical skills. Once you are able to do this, you will learn to construct points. It is gratifying to put the different shots and strokes together to earn a point. The satisfaction comes when you hit a great shot. You keep coming back to the court for more.

The more you play, the more fun it gets. You can always reach for the next level. That is why tennis is one of the most enjoyable sports.

SKILLS LISTED WITH CUES

This chapter presents cues for the following tennis skills: grip, set position, volley, forehand, teaching progressions for forehand stroke, backhand, teaching progressions for backhand stroke, teaching progression for the serve, serve receive, backspin, overhead smash, and singles, doubles, and tiebreaker scoring.

TIPS

Equipment Tips

1. Tennis rackets: Unless a player is really young, go with the full-size racket because children grow out of them so fast.
2. Balls: The teacher needs at least 10 tennis balls per student.
3. Clothing: Tennis shoes and comfortable clothing are recommended.

Safety

1. Use quality rackets that are light.
2. Students should wear court shoes.
3. Make sure that the tennis courts are clean.
4. Make sure that students are careful when they swing their rackets.
5. Do not have students stand in front of a student who is hitting the ball.
6. Try to match up students of similar abilities during class.

Etiquette

1. Have a positive attitude.
2. Treat others as you would like to be treated.
3. Treat equipment well.
4. Do not talk or make loud noises in the middle of a point.
5. Announce the score before serving.
6. If you cannot tell if a ball is in or out, call it good.
7. If your ball goes on another court, wait until they are done with their point before asking for it back.

TEACHING IDEAS

Teaching Progressions

1. Teach grip and ready position. Next move to forehand and backhand: first hitting balls with forehand stroke only, then hitting balls with backhand stroke only. The next step is to alternate the forehand and the backhand. Then do the same progression with forehand and backhand volleys. Teach the tennis serve last.
2. Try not to hit in the *doughnut hole* area—the center—of the court. Why? Because your opponent can stand there, hit the ball back and forth, and move you all over the court.
3. When working on positioning, imagine two magnets. One magnet is centered behind the baseline, while the other is at the center of the court, about one to two steps from the net. Have the magnets draw you to one of these two spots on the court. The goal for the receiver is to stay out of the doughnut hole, which is in the middle of the court. Players can pass you easily by hitting a shot deep into the court.
4. See the teaching progressions after each skill.

5. Bounce-Hit Drill: The instructor or another player feeds the ball to a player. Before hitting the ball, the player watches the ball and shouts out loudly, "Bounce, hit."

   a. Alternate feeding the ball to the right and left sides.

   b. Have the players rally back and forth, each time calling out, "Bounce, hit."

   c. Play a game so that each player calls out, "Bounce, hit."

   This drill helps the player with timing and hitting the ball. A player focuses on the ball when the ball bounces, which gets them into ready position faster. This drill also works on the mental aspects of the game by clearing the player's mind to concentrate on only one thing: the ball.

Mini-Games

1. Quarter-Court Games (see Figure 25.1):

   a. Play games inside the service area using volleys so that points are quickly scored.

   b. The game is started with the ball on top of the net. Drop the ball and play it out.

   c. Players begin to volley the ball back and forth.

   d. Whoever has the ball can start the point.

   e. Play games to 7 points and switch sides.

2. Ground-Stroke Points:

   a. To put the ball in play, bounce the ball and hit it underhand anywhere in the opposite court.

   b. Use singles court lines for singles games and doubles court lines for doubles games.

   c. The ball can bounce only once in your court.

   d. Whoever has the ball can start the point.

   e. Pick a total, such as 11 points, and the first one to reach the score wins. You can play the best of three or best of five, and rotate with your neighbors.

   f. This drill is great for learning how to put points together.

FIGURE 25.1 Quarter-Court Games

3. Half-Court Games:
    a. Two players play on a half-court.
    b. The rules are the same as a ground-stroke game.
    c. Play games to 7 points.
4. Five Misses:
    a. Four players play on a court at a time with "alternates" at the net post. (There can only be one player at the net post.)
    b. Players play out a ground-stroke point together, and whoever misses goes to the net post.
    c. One at a time, the alternates replace the misses.
    d. As soon as a player has five misses, the game is over and you form new teams.
    e. You can also play this game with a feeder in one of the posts. The feeder tosses the ball in the court to start play.
    f. Players rotate after each point, with alternates at each net post.
5. Regulation Tennis Game, One Serve: Only hit a second serve.
6. Regulation Tennis Game, Two Serves: You can hit a harder first serve.

GAME PLAY

Rules

To start a game, the server starts behind the baseline and to the right of the center line. The server is given two serves to get the ball into the right service court of the opponent (see Figure 25.18). Whoever wins the rally earns the point.

> "Love–15" would be the score if the receiver won the first point (Love is equal to zero in tennis).
> "15–Love" would be the score if the server won the first point.

The server then moves to the left of the center mark behind the baseline and serves to the opponent's left service court (see Figure 25.2). The server continues to alternate service courts each time a point is scored by either the server or the opponent. The progression of scoring goes 15, 30, and 40. After 40, the next point wins the game. If score is 40–40, it's deuce; players continue playing until someone wins 2 points in a row.

After a game is completed, the opponent serves. Alternate serving games until one player has won six games. See the scoring cue boxes in the following tables for more information.

SCORING

Singles Scoring

For scoring information, see the cue table on page 336.

1. Playing a Set: Players should change sides on the odd-numbered games (1, 3, 5, 7, etc.). The winning player needs to win a total of six games and win by two games. If each player wins six games, a tiebreaker is played.
2. Match Play: A player must win two out of three sets.

Doubles Scoring

For scoring information, see the cue table on page 337.

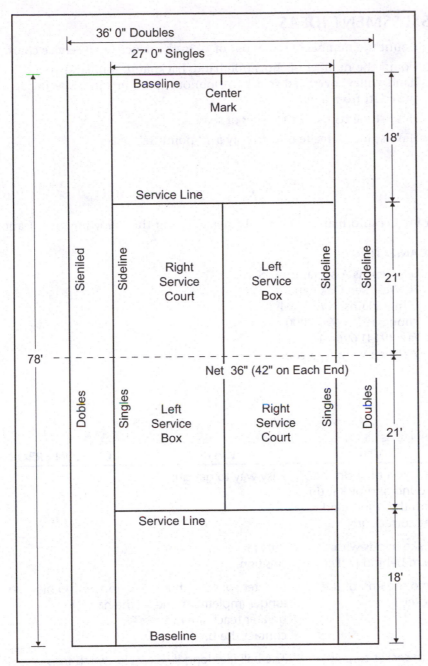

FIGURE 25.2 Tennis Court

Tiebreaker

12-point Tiebreaker: Service begins with the player who received in the 12th game. Players don't call zero "love" in a tiebreaker (1-zero). Player A serves the first point to deuce (right) court for 1 point. Player B serves to ad (left) court first and then to deuce (right) court for points 2 and 3. Player A (or C in doubles play) serves to ad (left) court first and then to deuce (right) court for points 4 and 5. Player B (or D in doubles play) serves to ad (left) court first and then to deuce (right) court for points 6 and 7. Players should change ends after every 6 points, but they cannot stop and take a break. The first player (or side) to score 7 points and win by 2 wins the tiebreaker.

ASSESSMENT IDEAS

1. Count the number of serves out of 10 in the deuce or ad service court.
2. Count the number of shots (forehand, backhand, forehand volley, backhand volley, overhead smash, or lob) out of 10 hits in a specific area of the court from a fed ball.
3. Have students recite the order of scoring.
4. Have students recite how to play a 12-point tiebreaker.

FYI

For further information and special help, consult the following organization.

ORGANIZATION

U.S. Tennis Association (USTA)
70 West Red Oak Lane
White Plains, NY 10604
Phone: (914) 696-7000
Fax: (914) 696-7167
Website: www.usta.com

GRIPS

SKILL	CUE	WHY?	COMMON ERROR
Forehand Grip (Right-handed) (Figure 25.3)	Lay racket flat on the ground and pick it up with the right hand to get correct grip	Easy way to get grip	
	Shake hands with palm behind racket	Puts racket in proper position	
	Hold the end of the racket	Greater speed with a longer implement and greater reach area to contact the ball	Gripping too high on the handle
Backhand Grip (Figure 25.4)	Turn racket so palm is more on top of racket	The ball flies long if you don't rotate your grip. Remember: "Grip wrong, ball long"	No switch from forehand grip
Two-Handed Backhand Grip (Right-handed)	Same cues for regular backhand—dominant hand more on top of racket	Puts racket face in proper position	No switch from forehand grip
	Keep left hand up to anticipate hitting a backhand	More power with both hands	Left hand not in position
	Grip left hand above right hand on racket	Proper racket position	

Lay racket flat

Palm is behind handle

(a)   Placement

Hold the end of
the racket

(b)   Grip

FIGURE 25.3   Forehand Grip

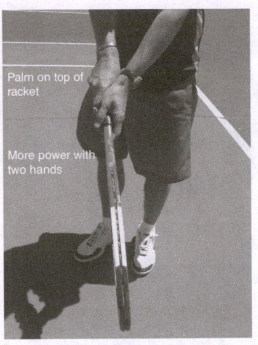

Palm on top of
racket

More power with
two hands

FIGURE 25.4   Two-Handed Backhand Grip

VOLLEYS

SKILL	CUE	WHY?	COMMON ERROR
Forehand Volley	Grip is not as extreme as ground-stroke grips—somewhere between forehand and backhand.	No time to change much for quicker reaction time to ball	Having a ground-stroke grip
(Figure 25.5)	Turn shoulders to get racket ready	Positions racket to move straight forward	No turn
	Move racket straight toward target	Better control and power	Moving racket around body
	Firm wrist, firm grip	Prevent the racket from coming out of hand, especially if the ball is hit hard into the racket	Dumping the head of racket down
	Keep racket head up	Firm contact when you hit the ball; better control and accuracy	Having racket head too low
	Contact ball in front of body	Easier to hit solidly	Contacting ball late
	Be aggressive; in this shot, go get the ball, don't wait for the ball to come to you	Places the opponent on the defensive	Waiting too long for the ball
	Bend at the knees, not at the waist		
Backhand Volley (Figure 25.6)	Same as forehand volley cues, just hitting on backhand side		

Make a
short swing

Turn shoulder to
get racquet ready

Point strings
where you want
the ball to go

FIGURE 25.5 Forehand Volley

Make a short swing

Contact ball in
front of body

Point strings
to where you
want the ball
to go

FIGURE 25.6 Backhand Volley

FOREHAND STROKE—RIGHT HAND			
SKILL	**CUE**	**WHY?**	**COMMON ERROR**
Grip	Palm is behind handle	The ball does not go high and you can get under the ball	
Preparation (Figure 25.7)	Turns shoulders early	Early preparation allows for contacting ball in front of body	Turning late
Footwork	Turning shoulders causes a pivot on the back foot and a step toward net	More power	Allowing the ball to come to you, rather than taking a step in as you hit
Stroke Action	Turn body to face net as racket goes from low to high	Enhances power	Staying sideways to net
Contact Point	Contact point, racket is in vertical plane	Accuracy	Not keeping head still
(Figure 25.8)	Hit ball even with front hip	Easier to see and hit solidly	Hitting late

continued

FIGURE 25.7 Forehand Stroke Preparation

FIGURE 25.8 Forehand Stroke Contact Point

FOREHAND STROKE—RIGHT HAND, continued			
SKILL	CUE	WHY?	COMMON ERROR
Finish and Follow-Through (Figure 25.9)	Swing low to high and finish with belly button facing net	Using body creates power	Pulling up too quickly on follow-through
	Point elbow toward the opponent when done	To get good topspin; ball will not go out of bounds	Swinging too slow using topspin; the ball needs to be hit aggressively
	Kiss your biceps	The friction created with "over-the-ball" motion will give more powerful topspin	
	Bend knees and get low	Ball will not go into net if you get low and bend your knees	Ball goes into net

Swing racquet from low to high

Point elbow toward opponent when done

Finish with belly button facing net

FIGURE 25.9   Forehand Stroke: Finish and Follow-Through

TEACHING PROGRESSION FOR FOREHAND

Check Grip First—Always, Always, Always

To practice the grip, have students bounce the ball with their racket, using the appropriate grip. Have students count how many times they can bounce the ball up and down in a row.

1. Have players stand 1 to 2 feet away from the tennis fence. Start with the racket head back, and in closed position, swing the racket to the contact point. Make sure the racket is vertical. On the follow-through, the racket should go over the opposite shoulder, and the elbow should point toward the opposite court. Swing from low to high and finish "kissing the biceps." Step 5 feet away from fence, drop the ball, and hit it into the fence.

2. When the students' stroke is done with control, move to the court. Drop-hit a ball over the net. Give them a target to aim for—for example, hit down the alley.

3. Next, teach students how to toss to a partner. One student tosses a ball underhand so that it bounces 5–8 feet in front of his or her partner. Toss a ball back and forth until they have good accuracy. The ball should bounce at least waist high.

4. When they're ready, have students toss the ball to their partners. The tosser stands off to the side of the net and tosses balls to his or her partner, who is standing at the service line, ready to stroke the ball (see Figure 25.10).

(a) Step 1   (b) Step 2

FIGURE 25.10 Partner Forehand Drill

5. The tosser is on one side of the net and tosses balls to his or her partner, who is standing on the baseline, ready to stroke the ball. Encourage students by saying it doesn't matter where the ball is landing, but stress the importance of good form on their stroke. When they have some accuracy, allow them to hit forehands back and forth with their partner.

TWO-HANDED BACKHAND—RIGHT HAND			
SKILL	CUE	WHY?	COMMON ERROR
Grip	Right palm more on top of handle	Puts racket face in proper position	No change from forehand
	Left hand up early, grab racket	Reaction time	
Preparation	Turn shoulders early	Early preparation allows for contacting ball in front of body	Twisting late
Footwork	Shoulder turn causes a pivot on back foot and step toward net		Not taking a step into the court as you hit
Stroke Action (Figure 25.11)	Bend at knees, back vertical	Better shot accuracy	
	Turn shoulders early	Better power, better accuracy	
Contact Point (Figure 25.12)	Contact point vertical and off the front hip	So ball will land in court	Not leading with the left hand
Finish (Figure 25.13)	Follow through high and finish over opposite shoulder	To achieve topspin	
	"Kiss your biceps"		

Turn shoulders early

Racquet up

Bend knees

FIGURE 25.11 Backhand Stroke Preparation

TEACHING PROGRESSION FOR BACKHAND

1. Demonstrate the backhand grip. Line students along the fence, and have them shadow-swing from low to high, following the cues.

2. Have partners drop-feed the ball to each other and hit it into the fence.

3. When they feel comfortable with the stroke, line students on the baseline and partner-feed. Give them a target to hit the ball, such as in the court, down the line, or across the court.

4. When the students are ready, pair them up. Have one student stand off to the side of the net and toss balls to his or her partner, who is standing at the service line, ready to stroke the ball.

5. Have partners feed ball from the other side of the net.

6. Rally backhand to backhand.

7. Have partners toss the ball to alternating sides: forehand, backhand, forehand, backhand, etc. This drill makes players change their grips, move their feet to the ball, and learn how to hit backhand in a game-like situation.

8. Teach a ground-stroke game. It incorporates all of the skills students have learned, and gives them game-like practice with many repetitions.

GAMES FOR LEARNING FOREHANDS, BACKHANDS, AND VOLLEYS

1. See "Rally Game" in pickleball (Chapter 17).

Contact ball off the front hip

FIGURE 25.12 Backhand Contact Point

Follow-through from low to high

Racquet finishes over opposite shoulder

Belly button faces net

FIGURE 25.13 Backhand Stroke Finish and Follow-Through

SERVE—RIGHT HAND			
SKILL	**CUE**	**WHY?**	**COMMON ERROR**
Grip	Move toward backhand grip as player develops	Accuracy and control	Holding racket too tight
Foot Placement (Figure 25.14)	Point left foot toward right net post; if left-handed, point right foot toward left net post	This allows for good shoulder rotation and power	
	Left foot 4 inches from baseline	Prevents foot fault	Foot too close to the baseline
	Back foot comfortable position	Stability and balance	
Toss	Hold ball in fingertips	Control of ball	
	Hold the ball down by leg	Control and accuracy of toss	
	Gently toss the ball high	Timing for serve	Tossing too high hurts power and rhythm
(Figure 25.15)	Keep arm straight all the way up	Accuracy of toss	

continued

Point foot toward right net post

Back foot comfortable

Front foot about 4 inches from line

FIGURE 25.14   Serve Set-Up

Hold tossing arm up until ball contacts racquet

Keep tossing arm straight all the way up

FIGURE 25.15   Serve Toss

SERVE—RIGHT HAND, continued			
SKILL	**CUE**	**WHY?**	**COMMON ERROR**
Stroking Action (Figure 25.16)	Hit high and in front of you	Power and good contact point	Ball hit too low and behind body
	Racket motion is like throwing a ball	Creates a powerful serve	
Follow-Through (Figure 25.17)	Arm action comes across the body	Completes the motion of your serve and power isn't lost	
	The shoulder of the arm that hits the serve rotates to where the other shoulder was	The movement naturally provides more power as body weight goes into serve	
Let	Ball hits top of net, goes over net into court; serve is taken over again		Calling it a fault or double fault (on first or second serve)
Ace	Serve is in, and receiver cannot touch it		
Double Fault	Neither of two serves goes into court		

TEACHING PROGRESSION

1. Teach the ball toss first. Place the racket on the ground at a 30-degree angle and place your foot at the end of the handle. Toss the ball up and try to hit the strings of the racket.

2. Have students throw a ball into the service box. If they can throw it into the box, they can serve it into the box.

3. Teach the entire serve.

Hit high and in front of you

Racquet motion like throwing a ball

Arm action comes across the body

The shoulder of the arm that hits the serve rotates to where the other shoulder was

FIGURE 25.16   Serve Stroking Action   **FIGURE 25.17**   Serve Follow-Through

4. If a student has difficulty with the serve, have him or her start the serve with racket up behind the head first.

5. Allow beginners to serve closer to the net and then move back to the baseline when they are ready.

RECEIVING SERVES			
SKILL	**CUE**	**WHY?**	**COMMON ERROR**
Powerful Serve	Shorter swing like a volley	Better control of ball	Bringing racket too far back
	Watch ball go into racket		Looking to the target early
Less Powerful	Hit ball into court like a typical ground-stroke	More time to react	Too short of a swing

SPIN AND SMASH SHOTS			
SKILL	**CUE**	**WHY?**	**COMMON ERROR**
Topspin	Racket swings low to high		Swinging level
	Candy cane swing		
	Racket starts knee-high and finishes nose-high		
Backspin (Slice) (Figure 25.18)	Racket swings high to low		Swinging level
	Cut through ball		
	Watch ball hit strings		

continued

FIGURE 25.18 Backspin

SPIN AND SMASH SHOTS, continued			
SKILL	**CUE**	**WHY?**	**COMMON ERROR**
Overhead Smash	Hit like the serve		
	Left foot in front; power with left foot		Power comes from both feet or back foot
	Point elbow to ball with left hand		Misjudging ball by losing focus of ball

SINGLES SCORING			
SKILL	**CUE**	**WHY?**	**COMMON ERROR**
Rules	First score is the server's score	Traditional	Saying receiver's score first
	In this game, *love* means zero		
	Love (0), 15, 30, 40, game 15–0 = 15–love 0–15 = love–15 30–30 = 30 all 40–40 = deuce		
	Win by 2, deuce and ad		
	Scoring is used for game, set, and match		

continued

SINGLES SCORING, continued			
SKILL	**CUE**	**WHY?**	**COMMON ERROR**
Rules, *continued*	*Ad in:* server's advantage		
	Ad out: receiver's advantage		
	Or in "no ad": 1–2–3–game		
	No ad after 3–3		
	Next point is game point		
	Receiver chooses side on which to receive serve in "no ad" scoring		

DOUBLES SCORING			
SKILL	**CUE**	**WHY?**	**COMMON ERROR**
Rules	Partner A1 serves one complete game		
	After the set you can serve two in a row (at the end of first set and beginning of second set, the team whose turn it is to serve chooses which partner starts)		
	Partners always serve from opposite sides of court		
	Opponent B1 serves one complete game		
	Partner A2 serves one complete game		
	Opponent B2 serves one complete game		
Doubles Receiver	*Deuce court* is the right side		Switching during set
	Ad court is the left side		
	At beginning of set, each player chooses which side to receive—deuce or ad court		
	Must stay in that court to receive serve		Receiver's teammate stepping into server's box
	Change ends of court every odd-numbered game		

26

Track and Field Events

INTRODUCTION

How can I go over the hurdle faster? How do I improve my sprint time? What's the best way to exchange the baton? In track and field, students and athletes might ask questions such as these. Are you ready to answer without giving them too much technical information?

An effective way to teach track and field skills is to provide teaching cues that are simple and to the point. Good visual teaching cues help athletes create visual images for better concentration and consequently help to perfect techniques. For example, when teaching the use of starting blocks, have students make a check mark with their hands at the starting line. The check mark cues the student to establish the correct hand position. As another example, when teaching the long jump, a coach should say, "Mark, I really liked how you arched your back like a C in the air; however, be sure to close the jackknife on your landing a little sooner."

Giving students and athletes visual teaching cues can make a significant difference in the outcome of a race or event. A tenth of a second faster time or a 1-inch difference in a throw or jump could mean advancing to regionals and then state competition.

SKILLS LISTED WITH CUES

Teaching cues in this chapter include the following: pillar, sprinting form, skills and drills, relays, hurdles, jumping events (long jump, triple jump, high jump), and shot put.

Each event is broken down into its component phases, and cues are provided for each phase of the skill. The cues can be used in teaching the beginner or in helping experienced athletes perfect their technique.

TIPS

Equipment Tips For Running Events

1. Starts: Blow a whistle to replace a gun, and use toilet paper for the finish line (see Figure 26.1).

Equipment Tips For Jumping Events

1. High jump: Use elastic surgical tubing as a crossbar (see Figure 26.1).
2. Use grass for long jumps and triple jumps for large classes (see Figure 26.2).

Equipment Tips For Throwing Events

1. Use lightweight, safe substitutes for competitive implements. If you don't have enough equipment, introduce the event as a station activity.
2. Shot put: Use tennis balls filled with lead shot and bound in tape, or use soft softballs.

Safety/Etiquette

1. Be aware of the sprinters who are using the blocks.
2. Do not cross the track in front of the sprinters.
3. Runners should stay out of the throwers' sectors.
4. Throwers and jumpers should stay off of the track. Be aware of other athletes.
5. Do not argue with the officials.
6. Follow the rules.

FIGURE 26.1 Equipment Ideas for a Track and Field Unit

FIGURE 26.2 Teaching Long Jump to a Physical Education Class

TEACHING IDEAS

1. Have all students practice long jump and triple jump together, shoulder to shoulder on the grass, instead of one at a time in the pit, until they gain some proficiency in the sport. Everyone will get more practice, and students may be less self-conscious than they might be when jumping in front of their peers.

2. For the long jump, place a low hurdle or cone in sand. Have students jump over the object. Place the hurdle or cone farther out or higher up to challenge students.

3. For the triple jump, place three hula hoops equidistant on the runway. Have students place a foot in each hula hoop as they run down the runway. Gradually lengthen the distance of the hula hoops to challenge the students.

4. Let students roll the discus on the ground, making sure the discus is coming off their index finger. See how far they can roll a discus before it falls over. Release is like slipping a bar of soap.

Teaching Progressions

Warm-Up

Start the warm-up with a 1- to 3-minute jog, and then move to dynamic stretches.

Dynamic Stretches

Dynamic stretching is a method of warm-up for explosive, high-speed activity. Dynamic stretches stimulate the body's ability to move faster by promoting more efficient nerve firing and more blood flow to deeper muscle tissues. Dynamic stretching is thought to be superior to static stretching because of the positive effects on the nerves. Static stretches are thought to dampen nerve firing. Dynamic stretches move the limbs through a full range of motion. Basically, the joint is moving continuously through various coordinated and sport-specific motor executions (Winkler & Schexnayder, 1998).

It is important to start gradually and then progress to greater speed and muscle recruitment. Warm-up the large muscles first and then go to smaller, more specific muscles. Most of the following progressive exercises can be performed while jogging, skipping, running backward, or zigzagging (Pfaff et al., 1991, p. 50).

1. Big Arm Circles: Move the arms forward, backward, swimming backstroke, front crawl, and windmill type of motion—alternating one arm forward, the other arm backward. Use your imagination to create ways to move the arms while also moving the legs.

2. Bend-Over Sweeps: Bend over at the waist, swing the arms left and right, and move to a cross-swing.

3. Torso Twist: In a standing position, straddle the legs and twist the torso from side to side.

4. Leg Swings: Stretch by swinging the leg in front, back, and to the side of the body. Extend one hand to balance against a wall or partner's shoulder.

5. Speed-Skater Stretch: Slowly lean in squatting speed-skater position and do a stretched lunge to right and left sides.

6. Slow Forward Leg Lunges: Take slow, long lunge steps while moving forward.

7. Ankling: Roll from the heel to toe, alternating each foot. Place the heel next to the instep of the opposite foot, rolling forward with half-steps. Swivel the hips while moving forward heel-to-toe.

8. Ankle Rolls: Draw the alphabet with your toes so that the ankle rotates.

9. Inverted Scissors: Lie on your back and roll up on your shoulders. Hands and forearms are flat on the ground or floor. Move the legs above your head in a scissors motion, forward and backward, side to side, and crossing the legs.

10. Inverted Bicycles: Lie on your back and roll up on your shoulders. Keep your hands and forearms flat on the ground or floor. Move your legs like you're riding a bicycle.

11. Calf Stretches (three steps and bend over to pull up).

12. Ski Jumps (hopping side-to-side as if parallel skiing).

13. Backward Run: Run backward with both short steps and long steps.

14. Skipping Arm Swings (exaggerate arm swing while skipping).

15. 3-Point, 4-Point Stance: Get into 3-point or 4-point stance. Explode out and run for 10 yards, then go again for 10 yards.

As a rule of thumb, be creative and have fun. As long as you stay in continuous motion, you are stretching or moving dynamically.

All elite, explosive athletes, including sprinters, warm up in this dynamic manner because of its positive effect on nerve firing. These same high-level athletes avoid static stretching while warming up for high-speed performance because of its negative effects on nerve firing. This does not mean that static stretching is bad, only that it is inappropriate as a warm-up for high-speed performance (Winkler & Schexnayder, 1998).

Core Exercises

Before and during the teaching of sprinting technique, emphasize exercises that develop the core of the body from mid-torso to mid-thigh. Core exercises develop the ability to stabilize the core into a pillarlike configuration. The core can be strengthened with exercises requiring the use of core musculature in any or all planes. A general fitness block that includes extensive core development would be appropriate to teach before beginning a skill block that includes sprint technique. See the strength training chapter (Chapter 22) for more details on the core and exercises.

Mini-Games

Acceleration Drills/Reaction Time Drills/Fitness Fun Drills

Make two lines:

```
    xxxxx    x  ................................................ 20 yards
           T
    xxxxx    x  ................................................ 20 yards
```

1. Have two students lie on their stomachs, with their hands behind the line. The teacher stands behind them. On the teacher's clap, the students get up quickly and sprint 20 yards.

2. Have two students lie flat on their backs, with their heads on the starting line. The teacher shouts "right" or "left," and students move accordingly. The students turn over, get up as quickly as they can, and sprint 20 yards.

3. Have two students lie flat on their stomachs, with their hands behind the line. The teacher shouts "right" or "left." The students get up quickly, make a complete right or left turn (whichever the teacher shouts), and sprint 20 yards.

4. Have two students stand up and face the teacher. The teacher will move his or her right or left thumb, and the students will turn in that direction and sprint 20 yards.

5. Have two students sit on the ground and cross their legs. The teacher claps. The students get up without touching the ground with their hands and sprint 20 yards.

6. Have two students get into push-up position, with their hands on the line. When the students hear a clap, they do one push-up and then sprint 20 yards. Make sure students do the push-up correctly.

7. Have two students perform one squat thrust and then sprint 20 yards.

8. Have two students perform one squat thrust, jump, and then sprint 20 yards.

9. Students get in the on-your-mark position. The teacher says "set." The students quickly switch their front legs from right to left, then get up and sprint 20 yards.

10. Teachers and students can design their own drills to make them fun and creative.

GAME PLAY

Rules

Block Start Rules

1. Hands must be behind the starting line.
2. Once set, do not move the block.

100-/200-/400-Meter Dash

1. Stay in lane.
2. Stepping on the line for 3 consecutive steps results in disqualification.

Hurdles

1. Stay in your own lane.
2. Keep your trail leg in tight so that you don't hit the hurdler in next lane over.
3. Keep your trail arm in tight so that you don't hit the person in next lane over.

Relay Rules

1. Exchange the baton in hand-off zones only.
2. Stay clear of other athletes who are racing, and stay in your own lane.

High Jump

1. Jump off only one foot.

Long Jump

1. Jump from behind the board.
2. Jump off only one foot.
3. Walk out the back of the pit.

Triple Jump

1. Jump from behind the board.
2. The jumping sequence is: one foot to same foot to opposite foot into the sand.
3. Walk out the back of pit.

Shot Put and Discus

1. Enter the ring wherever.
2. Stay in the ring until the shot put or discus hits the ground.
3. Exit out from the back half of ring only.

ASSESSMENT IDEAS

Mini Skills Meet: Students choose 3 to 5 of the following skills for competition.

1. Jog 1 mile or 5K (timed).
2. Sprint 40 yards or 100 yards (timed).
3. Throw right side and left side for speed using a radar gun, or throw for distance.
4. Underhand throw right side and left side for speed using a radar gun.
5. Punt for distance, or use goal posts at 10 to 25 yards for accuracy.
6. Kick 5 to 10 balls into a soccer goal from 12 to 25 yards.
7. Do a standing vertical jump.
8. Do a standing horizontal jump.

FYI

For further information and special help, consult the following organization and resource.

ORGANIZATION

USA Track and Field
RCA Dome, Suite 140
Indianapolis, IN 46225
Phone: (317) 261-0500
Fax: (317) 261-0481
Website: www.usatf.org

PUBLICATION

Carr, G. (1999). *Fundamentals of track and field* (2nd ed.). Champaign, IL: Human Kinetics Publishers.

SKILL	CUE	WHY?	COMMON ERROR
Pillar (Sprinting Posture)	Critical for many sport skills	Foundation of correct body posture in most sport skills	Bent at hips
Head Position	Head over shoulders	Creates more efficiency in runners' sprinting technique	Bent at neck
Shoulder Position	Shoulders over hips	Best, most comfortable postion	Arched back and shoulders back
Hip Position	Hips over feet	Balance	Hips bent and back
	Make a pillar with your torso when performing sprinting drills and sprinting	Easy and no wasted motion	Bent at hips, leaning over

SKILL	CUE	WHY?	COMMON ERROR
Toe Action (Figure 26.3)	Toe up	To allow foot contact	Pointed toes
		To be as close under the hips as possible—allows for sprinting to be a pushing action, instead of a pulling action	
		Decreases time spent on the ground and places the foot in an optimal position to come up under the hip; eliminates "dangle time"	
Heel Action	Heel up	To shorten the lever as quickly as possible by bringing the heel directly under the buttocks; avoids dangle time	Leg extended behind you after it leaves the ground
Knee Action	Knee up	Increases stride length	Knee does not reach parallel to ground

continued

SKILL	CUE	WHY?	COMMON ERROR
Knee Action, *continued*	Thigh parallel to ground	Increases stride frequency	Thigh not high enough
	Knee at a 90° angle	Control, stride length increased	Knee at less that 90° angle
Arm Action	Hold arms at 90° angle; fingers come to the eye on the front side	No wasted motion	Arms extended beyond 90°
	Don't pass the hip on the back side ("cheek to cheek")	Control and balance— no wasted motion	Arms go too far back (past hips)
	Shoulder joint only joint to move	Power generation, no wasted motion	Moving at elbow joint
	Fingers "eye to hip"	Elbows stay at 90°	Elbow extension
Pillar	Run tall and make a pillar with torso: head over shoulders, shoulders over hips, hips over feet, abs like an accordion	Prevents upper body from leaning back	Leaning back or forward

FIVE PROGRESSIVE SPRINT DRILLS

Drill 1: Walking A's

Walking A's are similar to the pawing action. Begin by standing in the start position (knee parallel to ground, toe flexed, and heel to buttocks). Perform the pawing action one leg after the other and begin moving forward. Emphasize the cues of toe up, knee up, and heel up, arms "cheek to cheek," and keeping core tight (Figure 26.3).

Drill 2: Skipping A's

This drill emphasizes the powerful snap of the leg to the ground under the hip. A skip is performed. The student focuses on the cues: thigh parallel, toe up, and heel up, in addition to placing the foot in the optimal position under the hip upon contact with the ground (Figure 26.4). Arm action should be cheek to cheek.

Drill 3: Running A's

Sometimes known as "High Knees." Running A's puts all the drills together and emphasizes frequency of contacts with the ground, not distance traveled. The student focuses on the same cues as the walking and skipping A's, emphasizing a stable core (stand tall but push abdominal wall toward spine).

Knee and thigh parallel to ground

Toe up

Heel up

FIGURE 26.3 Walking A's

1. Perform a step

2. Ball of foot lands under hip

3. Toe up, knee up, heel up

FIGURE 26.4 Skipping A's

Drill 4: Running C

1. Take the instep of the right foot and follow up the opposite leg to the knee or above the knee.

2. Stay tall in both the shoulders and the hips.

Drill 5: Single Fast Leg

1. Start out in a jog, explode a single leg, do a C, move to doing an A, and finally paw the ground under the hips.

2. Take 3 or 5 steps, and do the same leg or alternating legs.

SPRINT DRILLS

Strides

1. This drill is for warming up the body muscles for sprinting. Start out in an easy jog, and get in a good mechanical, technically sound running form.

2. Hold this form for 60 to 85 meters. Do this drill 3 to 5 times.

Build-Ups

1. This drill is meant to move the body at a faster speed. This drill reminds the body what to do when sprinting full speed. Start out slowly; gradually build up speed to top controlled speed and mechanics.

2. Build-ups should last for 90 to 100 meters. The runner should hit the top speed at about 80 meters and hold the top speed until 90 to 100 meters.

3. Do this drills 2 to 3 times.

SKILL	CUE	WHY?	COMMON ERROR
Sprint Accelerations (Initial 15–30 meters)	Push back into the track on balls of feet	More time needed on the ground during the initial acceleration phase to obtain a faster top-end speed	Hit heels
	Angle of body at 45°	Creates power	No angle
	Low heel recovery (heels don't come above the opposite knee)	Puts power into the ground faster	Take too long of steps
	Toe up	So toe doesn't catch and you fall	Pointed toes
Transition (through 50 meters)	Uniformly progress from an emphasis on pushing to a "pawing action"	Allows sprinter to maintain speed that has been generated from the acceleration phase	Leaning back, reaching out too far, and striking with heel
	Foot contact gradually becomes upright under hip	Maintains speed	Keep low foot recovery
	Toe up, heel up, knee up	When the knees drop, deceleration occurs; the longer a sprinter can keep the knees up, the longer he or she will maintain full speed	Pointed toes, thigh does not reach parallel to ground
	Body must be a "pillar," stand tall	Remains in proper technique	Bent at hips
	Transition from low heel recovery to high heel recovery (heel under buttocks)	To continue gaining speed	Slow down stride while lengthening stride

SKILL	CUE	WHY?	COMMON ERROR
Full Speed	Toe up, heel up, knee up!	When knee drops, deceleration occurs; the longer a sprinter can keep the knees up the longer he or she will maintain full speed	Knees drop
	Maintain knee parallel to ground	To maintain full speed	Knees do not reach parallel

continued

SPRINTING, continued

SKILL	CUE	WHY?	COMMON ERROR
Full Speed, *continued*	Hold arms at 90° angle	Less wasted motion	Bent at elbows
	Fingers "cheek to cheek"	Keeps arms at 90°	Bent at elbows
	Make a pillar with your torso (hips up, abs tight)	Prevents students from leaning back when running	Leaning back, bending at hips, leaning forward
	Run tall	Keeps good form	Leaning back or forward
	Ball of foot lands under hip	To continue gaining speed, control over body	Striking with heel
Initial Block Setting	Front block 2-foot lengths from start line	Strongest position from which to push	Feet too far apart or too close together, or front foot is too close to or far from back foot
	Back foot at 3-foot lengths from start line	Comfortable position, better push from blocks	Feet too far apart or too close

STARTING BLOCKS

SKILL	CUE	WHY?	COMMON ERROR
"On Your Mark" (Figure 26.5)	Back into blocks; do the same routine every time	Get ready for race routine	No routine, no order, no sequence
	Toes barely in contact with track	More power into the starting blocks	Ball of foot in contact with ground
	Hands make a bridge with fingers and thumb (behind starting line)	Raises center of gravity	Weight on thumb and knuckles
	Shoulders over hands	Engages forward momentum	Weight back, shoulders behind hands
	Weight forward	Fall out of blocks	Weight back
	Eyes looking down	Keeps head neutral	Dropping the head
	Head in neutral position	No wasted motion to see where you are going	Looking around
	Sit in blocks	Ready for next call	Twitching or moving
"Set" (Figure 26.6)	Buttocks up in one motion	Less stress on supporting arms	Coming up too slow, buttocks lower than head

continued

Weight forward on hands
Hands make a bridge on finger pads, form a check mark

Eyes looking down

FIGURE 26.5 "On Your Mark"

Shoulders lean over line

Eyes back at starting line

Front leg at 90° angle

FIGURE 26.6 "Set"

STARTING BLOCKS, continued

SKILL	CUE	WHY?	COMMON ERROR
"Set", *continued*	Lean until you are just about ready to fall	Gets you ready for the 45° angle of your body	Buttocks too high or low
	Shoulders over line	Fall out of blocks	Leaning back
	Body still like statue	So gun can fire	Moving body
	Front leg at 90° angle	Most power	Too big or small of an angle
	Back leg at 120° angle	Most power	Too big or small of an angle
	Both feet pushing back hard into pedals	Gives sprinter tension in legs	Only using one leg to push
"Gun"	Drive opposites (right arm, left leg or left arm, right leg)	Helps extend body while coming out of blocks	Right arm and right leg come out of blocks first (or left arm and left leg)
	Drive arm out and up	To get momentum going	Not using arms
	Push both legs equally hard	More power	Stepping with forward leg first
	Explode out of the blocks at 45° angle	Helps sprinter push back into track, rather than pulling	Standing straight up
			Pulling motion
	Short, quick steps	Powerful steps	Long, slow steps
	Feet contact track directly under hip	Power generation	Stride too far out

SKILL	CUE	WHY?	COMMON ERROR
Racing Form *Hip-Torso Action*	Tall, as if being picked up by the hair	Allows sprinter's knees to come up to 90°	Hips turned down
	Tummy flat	Tight core	Bending at hips
	Make a pillar with the hips and torso	Tight core	Bending at hips
	Buttocks tucked under	Keeps hips turned up	Arched lower back
Arm Action	Sharp elbows	Keep elbows tight at 90°	Arms crossing midline of body
	Back arm stays at 90°; "cheek to cheek"	Proper technique, more power	Bending at elbows
Hand Position	Hold a potato chip	Keep hands soft	Fists clenched, breaking chip
Leg Action	Heel to buttocks	Proper technique to maintain speed	Not enough knee flexion
	Step over opposite knee	Keeps technique and speed	Knee lift too low
	Thigh parallel to ground	Maintains full speed	Knees not high enough
	Point toe to sky	Keeps toe up and prevents tripping	Pointing toe to ground before contact
	Claw ground with foot	Generates power	Not clawing ground with foot
	Snap leg down	Generates power	Not snapping leg down
	Ground contact with ball of foot directly under hip	Energy efficient	Stopping foot on contact with ground

SKILL	CUE	WHY?	COMMON ERROR
Receiver's Arm Position (Figure 26.7)	Slam the door directly behind you, keeping arm straight	Gives the passer an accessible target	Arm extended outward
	Thumb in toward backbone; make check mark toward ground	Place for baton, opens hand	Hand not open

continued

SKILL	CUE	WHY?	COMMON ERROR
Receiver's Hand Position	Steady hand and arm	Good hand-off	Hand and arm moving
Passer's Arm Position (Figure 26.7)	Hit the palm with underhand delivery	Prevents passer from missing receiver's hand	Trying to pass before target appears
	Focus eyes on hand; hit target	Good hand-off	Miss target, drops baton
Passer's Code	Tape mark for takeoff	Exact spot to leave from	Leaving too early or too late
	Leave when incoming runner crosses tape with body	Get best hand-off	Leaving too early or too late
Exchange (Figure 26.8)	Passer yells "hit," a signal for the receiver to lift arm back	Minimizes the time of the exchange	Passer is too fast
	Receiver and passer at full speed when exchange takes place	Best exchange	Receiver is not at full speed

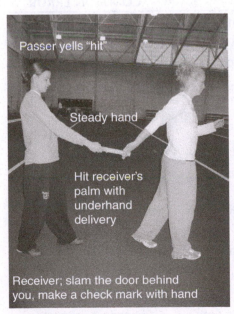

FIGURE 26.7 Relay Hand Position

FIGURE 26.8 Relay Passer's Code Drill

SKILL	CUE	WHY?	COMMON ERROR
Receiver	Turn head back over left shoulder toward passer; judge incoming runner's speed	To be able to match passer's speed, minimizing the time of exchange	Taking off too soon or too late
	Take two accelerating steps, then turn	Best speed for hand-off	Passer runs into receiver
	Point hand at incoming runner with palm up and elbow down	Best hand-off	Hand not pointing in proper direction
	Take the baton from the incoming runner like you're taking the money and running	Decreases the chances of dropping the baton	Dropping the money (baton)
Passer	Put baton in receiver's hand, arm fully extended at shoulder level	Decreases the chance of dropping the baton	Watching other competitors
	Full speed until receiver has baton	Fastest hand-off	Slowing before pass

SKILL	CUE	WHY?	COMMON ERROR
Receiver's Arm and Hand Position	Arm and hand parallel to ground	Easy hand-off placement	Hand bent up at wrist
	Elbow facing up	Can get hand parallel	Arm and hand too low
	Make a check mark with palm facing up	Creates a big target	Making a small check mark; hand facing down
Passer's Arm Position	Punch baton into target	Minimizes chance of passer missing the hand	Passing the baton from above shoulders coming down
	Piston-type motion	Easy hand-off more control	Passing baton before target appears
	Focus eyes on hand	Focuses on target	Eyes wandering
Passer's Code	Tape mark	Know when to run	Leaving too early or too late
	20–30 steps; leave when incoming runner hits tape	Minimizes the time of the exchange	Too soon or too late

continued

SKILL	CUE	WHY?	COMMON ERROR
Exchange	See target before pass	Controls hand-off	Passer is too fast, receiver not at full speed
	Passer yells "hit," the signal for the receiver to put arm back	Lets receiver know when to put arm back	Not yelling word

LOW HURDLES

SKILL	CUE	WHY?	COMMON ERROR
Body Position *Before Hurdles*	Short last step	Best speed to push into hurdle	Long last step
	Pawing action (like a bull)	Prevents hurdler from going high over hurdles	Sitting, planting drive leg in front of hip
Over Hurdles	Exaggerated sprinting form over the hurdles	Maintains hurdler's speed over hurdle and in between	Jumping over hurdles
Between Hurdles	Dive into hurdle	Creates aggression, assists in lead leg power snap	Staying tall
	Snap lead leg down	Get back on the ground	Floating over hurdle
	Sprinting form between hurdles	Accelerate between hurdles	Not sprinting between hurdles
	Heel to buttocks, toe up	Sprinting form	Short step, long step, short step
	Thigh parallel to ground	Sprinting form	Knee does not reach parallel
	Body erect, tall	Sprinting form	Bent at hips
Trail Arm	Drive elbow back	Arms in close to body	Swings back too far
	Stay in running form	Controls body	Elbow extension
Lead Leg (Figure 26.9)	Upper leg flexed	Fast lead leg	Straight lead leg
	Heel to buttocks	Running form	Heel stays low
	Extend like a switchblade	Extension for power snap	Slow lead leg
	Snap foot downward and backward	Aggression to sprint	Toe contact too far forward of hips
	Ball of foot lands under hip	Sprinting form	Landing on heels

continued

Keep trail leg/
arm in tight
to body

Dive into hurdle

Snap lead leg down

FIGURE 26.9   Going Over Low Hurdle

LOW HURDLES, continued			
SKILL	CUE	WHY?	COMMON ERROR
Lead Leg, *continued*	Vigorous pawing action	Get back on ground as fast as possible	Floating over hurdle
	Hips stay level	Conserves energy	Moving hips
Trail Leg	Hips parallel to hurdle	Fastest way to get to ground	Hips not parallel
	Lead with knee and bring knee back to parallel	Helps maintain speed throughout race	Leading with thigh
	Picking toes up	Prevents hitting hurdle	Toes pointed down
	Foot flexed	Prevents hitting hurdle	Foot loose
	Snap foot down "quick"	Gets to sprint faster	Slow trail leg

LONG JUMP			
SKILL	CUE	WHY?	COMMON ERROR
Approach	Start with takeoff foot forward	Easier to count steps	Changing starting/ jumping foot
	12–18 strides; fewer strides for younger athletes; more strides for faster athletes	Get tired easily	Too many strides
	Accelerate to maximum usable speed	Consistency	Changing speed of approach
	Same approach every time	Makes runway accurate	Changing speed or technique
	Knees up and tall in last strides as if being lifted by the hair	Full speed	Changing speed

continued

364   Track and Field Events

SKILL	CUE	WHY?	COMMON ERROR
Takeoff	Last two steps, like a layup in basketball—long-short	Ensures last step will be under hip	Last step too long
	Jump up and out	Best distance	Only jumping out
	Drive up knee and opposite arm vigorously	Provides better leverage	Not driving up free knee and opposite arm
	Overemphasize knee lift and arm drive	Power off ground to go up and out	No power
Action in the Air (Figure 26.10)	Body makes a curve, like a half-moon	Sets jumper up for a landing	Upper body ahead of hips
	Arch back like a C	Proper landing	Staying stiff
	Knees and feet behind hips	Best possible form	Knees and feet out front
	Arms above head and behind shoulders	To make the C stretch	Arms are in front
	Close jackknife	Brings legs up higher in air to allow for greater distance	Little or no leg action
	Extend legs and throw arms past knees	Greater distance	Arms are not thrown past knees
Landing	Collapse buttocks to heels upon landing	Greater distance	Feet apart
	Arms thrust forward	So you do not land on your back	Arms stay back
	Feet together	Greater distance	Feet apart

FIGURE 26.10 Long Jump

SKILL	CUE	WHY?	COMMON ERROR
Approach	Start with jumping foot forward	Easier to count steps	Changing starting/ jumping foot (takeoff foot)
	12–18 strides; fewer strides for younger athletes; more strides for faster athletes	They tire easily	Too long or too short of an approach
	Knees up and tall in last 5 or 6 strides, as if being lifted up by the hair	Keeps full speed	Overstriding or sitting
	Maximum speed at board	Best jump	Last step too long
	Same approach every time	Makes runway accurate	Changing speed and technique
	Last two steps like a layup in basketball— long-short last two steps	Ensures last step will be under hip	Long last step
Hop	Take off and land on same foot	The rule	Landing on the opposite foot
	Tall upper body	Knees come up better	Leaning forward at waist
	Head and eyes level	Keeps body posture correct	Looking down at ground, head down
	Look ahead	Keeps body posture correct	Looking down or up
	Knee up, toe up	Power off the ground	Straight leg
	Snappy, pawing action	Gets jumper ready for next phase	No pawing action
	Active landing	Best distance	Leg does not snap down
Step	Long step, as if stepping over mud puddles	Keeps momentum and speed	Hopping again
	Take off and land on opposite foot	Legal and best way	Wrong foot
	Tall upper body	Knee comes up better	Leaning forward at waist
	Head and eyes level; look ahead	Keeps good posture	Looking down at the ground, head down
	Split in air	Power	Short steps

continued

SKILL	CUE	WHY?	COMMON ERROR
Step, *continued*	Wide thigh separation during step	Best "step" phase	Low thigh recovery
	Landing—snappy, pawing action	Gets jumper ready for next phase	No pawing action
	Active landing	Preparation for jump	Passive landing
Jump *Arm Action*	Reach for the sky; drive arms upward	Provides better leverage	Not driving arms upward
Head and Eye Position	Head and eyes level; look ahead	Good body posture	Looking down
Body Action	Close jackknife	Best jump distance	No hips
	Extend legs from hips	Best distance	Only extending from knees
	Throw arms past knees, as if driving ski poles back at the start of the race	Allows for greater distance	Reaching hands to feet
	Collapse buttocks to heels upon landing	Greater distance	Straight-leg landing on buttocks
Ground Contact	Even cadence throughout jump	Greater distance	Uneven cadence
	Even rhythm	Controllable	Uneven rhythym
	Feet make "ta–ta–ta" sound (even–even–even step)	Even and control for power	Feet make "taaa–ta–ta" sound (long–short–short step)

HIGH JUMP

SKILL	CUE	WHY?	COMMON ERROR
Approach	Start just on the outside of the standards	Allows for better curve	Too close or too far away
Running Stride	Make a J	Centrifugal force for best run	Running straight at the bar
	10-step total approach	Easy and controllable	Too long or too short
	Get speed in run first	Speed helps jump	Too slow
	The last four steps start the turn for the J	Curve creates power	Running straight at the bar
Body Position	Lean into curve	Centrifugal force	Standing tall in curve
	Inside shoulder a little lower than outside shoulder	Centrifugal force to jump up	Outside shoulder too low

continued

HIGH JUMP, continued

SKILL	CUE	WHY?	COMMON ERROR
Running Stride continued	Last three steps medium, long, short	Ensures last step will be under hip	Last three steps too long or too short
Takeoff *Legs*	Take off from outside foot	Best jump technique	Inside foot used to take off
	Foot placed parallel to bar	Be able to jump straight up	Not parallel to the bar
	Takeoff foot down quickly, as if stepping on a bug	More power	Take off with both feet
	Plant power leg, active landing	Aggression to jump up	Failing to plant power leg, no power in run or jump
	Drive the lead knee vigorously up	Provides for greater leverage	Not driving knee up
Arms	Drive both arms up	Provides for greater leverage	Using legs only
Flight *Body Position*	Arch like a banana	Makes better arch	Flat back
	Head back	Arch back	No arch
Arm Position	Jump arm up and back	Create arch	Flat back

SHOT PUT

SKILL	CUE	WHY?	COMMON ERROR
Enter/Exit Position	Enter ring from same place everythime	Develop routine	Inconsistent in where entering the ring
	Exit from rear	The rule	Not exiting out the back
Hold Shot	Cradle shot	Allows for better release	Dropping the elbow and having the shot roll into palm
	Hold shot on finger pads	Best elastic release	Holding with palm
	Push shot firmly against neck	Control over shot	Shot falls out
	Elbow up	Power, control	Throwing like a baseball
Release of Shot	Push shot through head		Throwing like a baseball
	Shot leaves from neck, a "put" not a throw	Power, control	

continued

	SHOT PUT, continued		
SKILL	**CUE**	**WHY?**	**COMMON ERROR**
Release of Shot *continued*	Release is fast like a punch and at a 45° angle	Best flight angle for maximum distance	Punch is horizontal
Start of Glide	Bend support knee	Best power	Hurrying start and keeping weight back
	Kick backward and down with nonsupport leg	Best power	Trying to throw before reaching power position
	Land both feet simultaneously still facing back	Position for greatest power	Facing sector after throw
	Hips open up quick like a baseball swing	Power	Not opening hips
	Free arm swings up as if slapping a giant	Creates torque	Not slapping high enough
Explosion of Glide	Push with both legs	Makes throw more powerful	Legs collapse on thrower
	Keep shot back last	Best power	Shot goes first
	Release shot at 45° angle	Best angle for maximum distance	Releasing too low or too high
End of Throw	Slap and pull with free arm	Shorten lever to speed rotation	Do not use off hand

27

Ultimate Frisbee and Disc Golf

INTRODUCTION

Ultimate Frisbee originated in Maplewood, New Jersey, in 1968. It uniquely combines high competition with the spirit of the game. "Spirit of the game" means no referees, honest playing, and positive spirits on and off the field. "Spirit" means ultimate athletes need not waste time faking out officials. Instead, efforts are focused on high performance and going all out. In all other sports, players are allowed to do anything until an official informs them that an activity is illegal. (In basketball, it isn't a foul unless it is called as such.) Combining skills from sports ranging from soccer to Frisbee to basketball, ultimate Frisbee is a fast-paced, highly energetic, noncontact sport that isn't for the lazy or pessimistic.

SKILLS LISTED WITH CUES

The cues in this chapter include the following skills: backhand throw, forehand throw (sidearm), and catching.

TIPS

Equipment Tips

1. Use lots of Frisbees (175 grams is official weight for a Frisbee).
2. Have students wear rubber cleats if available.
3. Use cones, lines, or flags to mark end zones and boundaries.
4. Field dimensions should be 40 yards wide × 70 yards long, with end zones that are 25 yards long.
5. Have students wear colored vests.
6. Use a scoreboard.
7. Disc golf discs. For advanced there is a driver, mid range, and putter.

Safety

1. No earrings, rings, jewelry, or piercings.
2. Avoid contact with other players.
3. Do not wear belts or pockets.

Etiquette

1. The "spirit of the game" means no referees, honest playing, and positive spirits on and off the field.
2. A certain level of maturity, trust, and honesty are required for the spirit of the game.
3. "Spirit" means ultimate athletes need not waste time faking officials, but rather focus on high performance and effort.
4. Encourage the students to call their own violations. This is one of the few games where you call your own violations. Students can develop integrity in game situations.

TEACHING IDEAS

Teaching Progressions

1. Have the students practice throwing and catching. Let them find their own personal space and give them plenty of room.
2. Do side-to-side partner throws: one partner throws, and one partner receives. The receiver will start in the middle. The thrower will choose which side to throw it to, and the receiver moves to the side, catches the disc, and throws it back to his or her partner. The thrower should throw to both sides in order to keep the receiver moving from side to side. When the players master this drill, add a defender.
3. Ready, Aim, Fire: Give each student a Frisbee. Line up all the students arms-length apart on a field. Quickly check their grip and stance. Review the cues: say "Ready, aim, fire!" The students run to get their disc, form a line, and get ready to throw back across the field.

Mini-Games

1. Play mini-games of 4 on 4, 5 on 5, and 6 on 6 on any flat, open space available with a fairly well-marked end zone.
2. Disc Golf: Set up one golf courses. Determine a par for each hole. Have students aim their Frisbees at hoops, buckets, etc. Maximize participation with small groups.
3. Rules: Throw disc and set marker where disc lands. Throw from marker. The player farthest from the basket throws first.
4. Count number of throws for each hole (similar to golf). Each hole has a par and to finish the hole, the disc has to be in the basket, in the chains, or on top of the apparatus to end the hole for a score.

GAME PLAY

Rules

1. There are usually seven players per team. The game can be played with as few as four players per team on any flat, open space available that has a fairly well-marked end zone.

2. The game starts with both teams standing on opposite end lines. The disc is thrown to the other team which is called a pull. The player throwing the pull yells "Ultimate." Players move the disc down the field by throwing it to one another. If the Frisbee hits the ground or goes out-of-bounds, the other team gains possession.

3. You must stand at least one Frisbee width from the player with the disc. You count stalling with "1, 2,…8, 9, 10." If the thrower still has the disc after the marker says "10," a turnover is called, and the other team gains possession.

4. The disc may never be handed—it must always be thrown.

5. While in possession of the disc, a player may pivot on one foot in any direction, as in basketball.

6. The disc may be thrown in any direction.

7. No more than one player may guard a thrower. Double-guarding equals a free pass on the spot.

8. Use both legs and hands to guard or knock down the disc.

9. The defensive team gains possession of the disc whenever the offensive team's pass is incomplete, intercepted, knocked down, or goes out-of-bounds.

10. Out-of-bounds throws are taken over by the opposing team at the point where the disc went out-of-bounds.

11. If a disc goes out-of-bounds after crossing the goal line, the opposing team may throw in from either corner of the end zone at the goal line.

12. No hand slapping to knock the disc down or out of the hand is allowed.

13. A player must stop within 3 steps after receiving disc.

14. No running with the disc is allowed.

Strategies

1. Handlers (three players) are the first players to take a "pull" (similar to the kickoff in football). Generally these players are the most accurate throwers of the seven players on the field.

2. Mids (two players) are players who generally have good cutting and maneuvering skills. They provide constant "flow" of the disc downfield with back or side cuts.

3. Longs (two players) are players who have the ability to run fast, long back cuts into the end zone or at least downfield. Longs should have good field sense and accurate catching skills.

4. Substitute when players get tired; keep a fresh crew. Only when one team scores can a substitution be made.

Scoring

1. One point is scored if a player catches the disc in the end zone (both feet must be inside the end line). The opposing team must walk to the far goal line and await the pull or throw-off from the scoring team.

2. A player cannot run in the end zone with the Frisbee to score.

3. Play to 21 points, with a victory margin of 2 points. Informal games can be played to other point totals or for a specified time.

4. After each point, the player throwing the pull yells "Ultimate", which will alert the offensive team that play is to begin.

ASSESSMENT IDEAS

1. Playing many games of ultimate Frisbee is a great cardiovascular workout. Each game can be worth 5 points.

2. Have a Frisbee throwing contest for longest distance thrown. Award bonus points for the longest throws.

FYI

For further information and special help, consult the following organization.

ORGANIZATION

USA Ultimate offers the following teaching materials: videos, discs, publications, rules, how to start teams or leagues, college starter kits, and how to teach ultimate Frisbee.

USA Ultimate
4730 Table Mesa Drive, Suite I 200C
Boulder, CO 80305
Phone: (800) UPA-GetH
Website: www.usaultimate.org

THROWING

SKILL	CUE	WHY?	COMMON ERROR
Backhand (Figure 27.1)	Stand sideways		
Grip	Pinch disc's edge with thumb and forefinger	To control the flight of the disc	
Throw	Throw frisbee as if there was a glass of water on top of disc	Disc will go farther and straighter	Releasing with disc at too much of an angle
	Release like snapping a towel	Accuracy and specific target to focus on	
	Pivot, windup, step, snap, release	Power on the disc	Using too much arm motion
	Point finger at target after follow-through		
	Step at target	Keeps disc level	Letting the arm drop to the side at release of the throw
	Keep Throwing arm parallel to ground on follow through		
Forehand (Sidearm) *Grip* (Figure 27.2a)	Thumb holds inside of disc	To generate a spinning disc	
	Middle finger is pivot finger		Incorrect grip
Throw (Figure 27.2b)	Outside rim of disc lower than inside	Keeps disc flat while in the air	Too much arm motion
	Step (same side) to target, snap towel	Throw farther	Incorrect release angle will cause disc to dive into ground

continued

Pinch disc edge with thumb and forefinger

Release, as if snapping a towel

FIGURE 27.1 Backhand Grip and Throw

Middle finger is pivot point

Roll off middle finger

(a) Forehand Throw (Sidearm)

Elbow on hip—wrist snap

Snap towel

Step to target

(b) Forearm Pass (Hand Position)

FIGURE 27.2

THROWING, continued

SKILL	CUE	WHY?	COMMON ERROR
Forehand (Sidearm), *continued*	Elbow on hip—wrist snap		Throwing like a baseball
	Try not to use arm for strength on this toss		
	All wrist action		

CATCHING

SKILL	CUE	WHY?	COMMON ERROR
Sandwich Catching	Watch disc come to hands	Keeps eyes focused on target	Looking away, incorrect timing
	One big hand on top of disc, one big hand on bottom	Big hands gives bigger surface to hang onto the disc	Not using both hands
	Clap before you catch		
	Hands like a clam	More surface area on the disc for better control	
	Spread fingers		

OFFENSE

SKILL	CUE	WHY?	COMMON ERROR
Movement	Cut, circle away, cut, circle—keep moving!	Avoids same-speed movements	Same-speed movements
	Fake and sharp cut	Keep the defensive players guessing	

continued

FIGURE 27.3 Defensive Marking

OFFENSE, continued			
SKILL	**CUE**	**WHY?**	**COMMON ERROR**
Movement, *continued*	Look while pivoting; fake, pivot, fake; anticipate!	The goal is to get open	No faking movements, standing still
	Lead teammate with throw	Better option to catch the disc	
	Throw to area, not to person, on long throw		Not giving player enough lead on throw

DEFENSE			
SKILL	**CUE**	**WHY?**	**COMMON ERROR**
Marking (Figure 27.3)	Stick like glue	Not letting an opposing player get open for a throw	Lack of conditioning
			Going for steal and losing opponent
	Play the annoying little brother— opponent cannot get rid of you		
	Watch midsection		Watching head and feet—getting faked out
			Overrunning opponent
	Keep hands low		
	Count to 10 slowly; thrower has only 10 seconds to throw before a violation is called		

28

Volleyball

INTRODUCTION

Teachers and coaches face a monumental task when preparing instructional methods for teaching motor skills. They make many decisions regarding content, method, class organization and control, evaluation, and methods of grading. When planning for content and method, the teacher should be able to answer the following questions: Why did you teach that skill the way you did? Why was the instruction sequenced as it was? Why did the group practice like that? Why did you have them use instructional aids? Why did you say what you said to them?

Most, if not all, of these answers should be based on empirical evidence rather than on opinion, tradition, or the teacher's whim. Researchers have found that modeling facilitates motor-skill learning. Magill (1985) states, "Selecting the correct cues is one of the most important elements that an instructor includes in the teaching process."

In addition to focusing a student's attention on essential elements of the model, meaningful cues reduce the amount of information that is given. Because students attend to a limited amount of new material for a limited time, such a routine will enhance learning. For example, when teaching the block, the two cues are "Hands up" and "Make Mickey Mouse ears." These cues provide the "hooks" on which to hang memories of the instruction. Some teachers find that years later students can remember many of the cues they received in their volleyball classes.

SKILLS LISTED WITH CUES

This chapter presents the cues for the following skills: ready position for forearm pass, forearm pass, overhead pass, setter's position and signals, serves (underhand and overhand—topspin and floater), jump serves, spiking, blocking, preparation for dig, forearm pass dig, and dig (sprawl, pancake, overhead, fist).

TIPS

After each drill, have players perform a set number of push-ups and sit-ups. This allows for a more efficient use of time with the added benefit of increasing strength.

Equipment Tips

1. Leather balls are better than rubber balls in preventing arm soreness.

2. Lower the nets, or have students work back to the baseline on serving drills.

3. Use a blackboard and chalk to record competitive drills and the like.

Safety and Etiquette

1. Diving/Digging: Stay low to the ground and land on stomach.

2. Hitting: Watch for balls rolling under the feet of the hitter. If the set is tight to the net, be safe—do not jump into the net. Do not cross the line under the net, and do not jump into or touch the net.

3. Serving: Watch for balls rolling under the feet of the server. Aim for the court—not for people.

4. Passing: Call the ball loudly three times. The first time nobody listens, the second time gets their attention, and by the third time, the other athletes know to move out of the way. This helps to avoid collisions.

5. If you see someone about to get hit by the ball, call "heads" three times to get their attention.

6. If someone is hitting or serving, and you see a ball about to go under their feet, call "ball" three times so they know not to jump.

TEACHING IDEAS

1. When possible, perform drills that contain the playing sequence—that is, "pass, set"; "serve, pass, set, hit"; "dig, set, hit"; and so on.

2. Drills should always have a specific goal (i.e., targets, scores, hit a certain number in a row perfectly, create competition with score 13–13, hit until you lose, etc.).

3. Always end drills on a positive note.

4. Games take 20 to 40 minutes to play. Some drills need to be as long as game time.

Teaching Progressions

Forearm Pass

1. *Throw, Hit, Catch:* A player tosses the ball to a partner, and the partner passes back. The ball is caught and tossed again. Repeat 10 times.

2. *Toss, Pass, Pass:* Two players start with a toss and keep passing back and forth until 20 passes have been tossed (see Figure 28.1).

FIGURE 28.1   Forearm Pass Drill, Toss-Pass-Pass Drill

3. *Line of Three:* Three players line up. Player A passes to player B, who passes behind his head to player C, who passes long to player A. Rotate after 10 passes. Switch the person in the middle to give each player a chance to pass the ball backward over his or her head.

4. *Triangle:* Three players pass the ball in a triangle. This allows the passer to practice facing the ball and angling the arms. Switch after 12 passes.

Overhead Pass

1. *Throw, Hit, Catch:* A player tosses the ball to a partner, and the partner passes back. The ball is caught and tossed again. Repeat 10 times.

2. *Toss, Pass, Pass:* Two players start with a toss and keep passing back and forth until they have made 20 passes.

3. *Line of Three:* Three players line up. Player A passes to player B, who passes behind his or her head to player C, who passes long to player A. Rotate after 10 passes. Switch the person in the middle to give each player a chance to pass the ball backward over his or her head.

4. *Triangle:* Three players pass the ball in a triangle. This allows the passer to practice facing the ball. Switch direction of the pass after 12 passes.

Overhead Serve

1. Serve at the wall.

2. Serve from the attack line with a partner and move back.

3. Serve and chase the ball.

4. Serve to opponents, who try to catch the ball.

5. Serve in a game situations, such as 3-on-3 games and games played on half-courts.

Spike

1. You Go, I Throw: Players begin their approach, and you toss the ball as if they have performed the proper approach. The players need to come to you. Toss the ball as they jump, a couple of feet from the net and directly in front of you.

2. I Throw, You Go: You toss the ball to the outside. The hitters start off the court and behind the line.

Block

1. Have players practice the two-step move with an opposing partner across the net.

2. Have players block against hitters in the spiking drill. Be careful of spikers who run under the net. Blockers tend to come down on spikers' feet and sprain their ankles. Encourage setters to set the ball off the net (not tight). This decreases the possibility of injury.

Mini-Games

1. If court space is available, play 2-on-2, 3-on-3, or 4-on-4 games.

2. Queens: Play games to 7 points and make new teams. Split athletes into teams of three. One team serves to the "Queen" side. If the "Queens" win, they stay on that side of the court; if they lose, then the "Queens" are off, and the other team becomes the new "Queens." Points are only awarded if the team stays on the "Queen" side; points are not earned for going over to the "Queen" side. In Queens, you can also use two permanent setters—one on each side.

GAME PLAY

Rules

1. The first server of the set is in the right, back position.

2. A live ball is in play from the moment the ball is legally contacted by the correct server until a dead ball occurs.

3. A live ball becomes dead when:

   a. The ball touches the net antennas or does not pass entirely between the net antennas and passes completely beyond the plane of the center line extension.

   b. The ball lands out-of-bounds.

   c. The ball contacts the ceiling or an overhead obstruction and is not legally played next by the offending team.

   d. The ball becomes motionless in the net.

   e. The ball touches the floor.

   f. The ball passes completely under the net.

4. A contact is any touch of the ball by a player.

5. A team shall not have more than three hits before the ball crosses the net into the opponent's playing area or is touched by the opponent.

6. Legal contact is a touch of the ball by any part of a player's body that does not allow the ball to visibly come to rest or involve prolonged contact with a player's body.

7. Successive contacts of the ball are two or more separate attempts to play the ball by one player with no interrupting contact by a different player between the two plays. A player shall not have successive contacts of the ball unless:

   a. There is simultaneous contact by teammates.

   b. There is simultaneous contact by opposing players.

   c. There are successive contact by a player whose first contact is a block; then the second contact shall count as the first hit by the player's team.

8. Multiple contacts are more than one contact by a player during one attempt to play the ball. Multiple contacts are permitted only:

   a. When the first ball over the net rebounds from one part of the player's body to one or more other parts in one attempt to block.

   b. On any first team hit, whether or not the ball is touched by the block. A player cannot touch the in line until after the ball is contracted on the serve.

9. An attack includes any action other than a block or a serve that directs the ball toward the opponent's court. A team's third hit is always considered an attack. A completed attack occurs the instant the ball completely crosses the vertical plane of the net or is legally blocked.

10. A block is the action of a player(s) close to the net that deflects the ball coming from the opponents by reaching higher than the top of the net or the net extended.

11. Back-row players, while positioned behind the attack line, may contact the ball from any position inside or outside the court above or below the top of the net.

12. A player may touch the floor across the center line with one or both feet/hands, provided a part of the foot/hand remains on or above the center line. Contacting the floor across the center line with any other part of the body is illegal.

13. A player shall not contact a ball that is completely on the opponent's side of the net, unless the contact is a legal block.

14. Blocking a served ball is not permitted.

15. A net foul occurs while the ball is in play and a player contacts any part of the net, including net cables or net antennas.

16. A libero is a defensive specialist and shall not:

    a. Complete an attack from anywhere if, at the moment of contact, the ball is entirely above the height of the net.

    b. Set the ball using overhand finger action while on or in front of the attack line extended.

    c. Block or attempt to block.

    d. Rotate to the front row.

Strategies

1. Call the ball three times.
2. Call the ball in or out.
3. Hitter calls the set they want to hit during the rally.

Team Strategies

Offense: Stress passing and serving over all other skills because a good pass means that players will be able to then hit and spike the ball well. Players should use all three contacts if possible, or the other team will, giving them an advantage. Players should only attempt technically what they can do physically. Do not attempt to do too much; have the players work up to a skill. The most important and most athletic player on the team is the setter. Their sets must be high in order to achieve a successful attack. Players should talk to each other when passing, hitting, and moving around the court, as communication is key to good team play.

Defense: Players in the front should funnel the attack to back-row players. The defensive side should first do offense, and then play defensively. Front-row players should stay close to the net and should never reach back for a dig—they might punch a teammate in the face. When playing defense, players should stay low, with a good center of gravity.

Individual Strategies

Offense: Front-row hitters should stay away from the net so that they can successfully execute a three- or four-step approach. Staying back will give them more time to get to the ball and hit hard. When hitting, keep the ball in front of you. Try to hit around the blockers, even if it means you cannot hit as hard. Above all, try to anticipate what will happen before it happens.

Defense: Be ready for anything all the time and try to anticipate attacks. Keep your weight on the balls of the feet, not your heels. If you intend to pass or dig a ball, call for it so that your teammates know. Use phrases like "I go" or "Mine!" Communication is key to good team play.

Scoring

1. One point is earned for each rally won.
2. There are 25 points in a game, won by 2.
3. The winning team must win 3 out of 5 games.
4. The 5th game is to 15, won by 2.

ASSESSMENT IDEAS

1. Athletes need to forearm pass and overhead pass 20 times in a row.
2. Serve 10 balls and keep track of how many were inbounds.
3. Play a game, and have players keep track of points. More points allow teams to move up a court, while fewer points moves teams down a court. This game will separate the better athletes from the not-so-experienced players.

For further information and special help, consult the following publication.

PUBLICATION

McGown, C., Fronske, H., & Moser, L. (2001). *Coaching volleyball: Building a winning team*. Boston: Allyn & Bacon.

PASSES

SKILL	CUE	WHY?	COMMON ERROR
Forearm *Ready Position*	Arms extended in front of body; keep low to ground	Ready to come up and pass the ball when it comes to you—you can get under the ball	Weight on heels instead of balls of feet
	Bent at hips—bend knees	Better ball control	Knees locked straight
Execution	Wrists and hands together—thumbs down	Keeps you from standing up	Keeping thumbs up
	Lifelines together	Makes a nice flat and strong surface for the ball to contact	Elbows held at sides, arms too close to body
	Forearm contact with ball		
	Hide your chest		Hitting ball on wrists
	Fat part of arms hits ball		Hitting ball on wrists
	Elbows straight and simple	This provides a smooth surface to bounce the ball off straight	
(Figure 28.2)	Make a flat surface with the forearms		Bending elbows, moving arms up and down to add power
(Figure 28.3)	Face ball, angle arms		
	Shuffle		
	Pass over lead leg		Facing target
	Beat ball to the spot	Better accuracy	
	See the server, see the ball		
Overhead (Figure 28.4)	Big hands	Big hands allow you to cover a wide surface area of the ball, which gives you more control and accuracy	

continued

Elbows straight and flat

Thumbs down

Hands in front of knees

FIGURE 28.2 Forearm Pass (Hand Position)

Face ball, angle arms

Platform out early and under ball

Pass over lead leg

FIGURE 28.3 Forearm Pass (Foot Position)

	PASSES, continued		
SKILL	**CUE**	**WHY?**	**COMMON ERROR**
Overhead, *continued*	Hands form a Hershey kiss	Shoots the ball farther	Fingers pointing to sky
	Bend knees—keep arms in scrunched position		
Execution (Figure 28.5)	Shape early	Gives you more time to prepare to receive the ball. This is a key for correct performance. Not shaping early is the biggest cause of failure of this skill. Over-emphasize to your players to have their hands up extra early	Hands down at sides
	Soft hands—use finger pads		
	Hands up at hairline	Better ball control	
	Extend arms	More power on ball	
	Like a basketball chest pass; elbows straighten		Ball staying in contact with hands too long—violation

continued

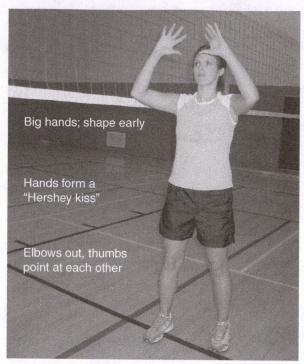

FIGURE 28.4 Overhead Pass (Ready Position)

FIGURE 28.5 Overhead Pass

PASSES, continued			
SKILL	**CUE**	**WHY?**	**COMMON ERROR**
Overhead, *continued*	Follow-through position like superman	More power on ball	Only using arms to push ball
	Face target		
	Over lead leg		Setting over right or left shoulder, sideways

SETTER'S POSITION			
SKILL	**CUE**	**WHY?**	**COMMON ERROR**
Technique	Right shoulder to net	For consistent sets to spike	Not looking at pass early enough
	Stand next to or as close as possible to the net	Helps control ball	Trying to pass a serve
	Right side of court, front row		
	Shape early	Helps set the ball at hairline—not chin or chest	
	Extend	More power	

continued

SETTER'S POSITION, continued			
SKILL	**CUE**	**WHY?**	**COMMON ERROR**
Technique, *continued*	Face target	More accuracy	Overarching the back, telegraphing the set, and lowering the point of contact
Back Set	Hips forward, extend the arms behind the head	Helps push setting base backwards, so setter can push body weight and momentum into a reverse set	Extending the arms forward or straight up
	See setter's signals		

SERVES			
SKILL	**CUE**	**WHY?**	**COMMON ERROR**
Underhand *Leg Action*	Step toward net with foot opposite to throwing arm	More power to the ball	Stepping forward with same leg as stepping arm
Hand Position	Palm up, make a fist	Bigger surface area for ball to contact; better control of ball	
	Thumb rests on side of index finger		
	Arm close to body, brush shorts	Better efficiency	
	Elbow straight	Helps with the follow-through	Elbow bent
	Hit ball out of hand	Greater control of ball	Tossing ball into air
	Like pitching horseshoes		Arm action stops at ball contact
	Follow-through toward target		
Overhead *Ready Position* (Figure 28.6)	Bow-and-arrow action	Keeps elbow high and ready to hit ball	
	Stand sideways; left foot points at target	More power to serve the ball	
		Weight transfer from back to front foot	
	Hold ball in one hand; ball in left hand and up in front of hitting shoulder	Simplifies the serve; eliminates extra movement and allows accurate and consistent contact with the ball	

continued

SKILL	CUE	WHY?	COMMON ERROR
Overhead, *Ready Position, continued*	Hitting elbow up	Timing to contact ball is more efficient	
Toss (Figure 28.7)	Precise toss	Simplifies timing and decreases decision making	
	Toss it (step, toss, hit)		Rotating shoulder forward, elbow stays back
	Toss in front of serving shoulder		
	Heel to target		Hitting behind or on top of ball
(Figure 28.8)	Contact ball at top of toss		
	Have a routine you do each time, like basketball free-throw routines		
Floater Serve	Low, controlled toss	Easy to time the contact; server can make contact at the peak of the ball toss, where the ball has neutral energy; server can prevent the ball from spinning after contact	Throwing too high and getting poor contact (harder to time a falling ball)

continued

FIGURE 28.6 Overhead Serve (Ready Position)

FIGURE 28.7 Overhead Serve Toss

FIGURE 28.8 Overhead Serve (Contact)

SKILL	CUE	WHY?	COMMON ERROR
Floater Serve, *continued*	Toss the ball in front of the shoulder at 11 o'clock	Ideal position to get a flat contact with the ball without putting spin on the ball	Tossing the ball directly above shoulder, more likely to put topspin on the ball
	More front-on stance, with left foot slightly forward	Encourages a balanced and stable body position that is optimal for producing a flat contact	Side-on stance encourages body rotation through the ball, gives the ball a right-to-left spin
	Abbreviated follow-through	A short follow-through reduces the chance of putting spin on the ball	Following through usually puts backspin on the ball
	Fire abdominals	Puts power into the serve; the abs should be fired vertically rather than horizontally to avoid putting body rotation into the contact	Relying on the arm can lead to injury eventually
	Contact with a flat, solid hand	Encourages a short contact, less likely to put spin on the ball	Loose hand contact gives a longer contact
Topspin Serve	Toss with topspin	Makes it easier to generate a powerful topspin serve if you are hitting with the spin	
	Toss over shoulder, hit at 12 o'clock	At the point of contact, the hand is traveling upward and forward (ideal for hitting a powerful topspin)	Contacting the ball out in front of the shoulder, where the hand is falling from its peak; makes it harder to put topspin on the ball
	Step into the contact	Helps generate power	Lack of transfer puts pressure on the shoulder; more chance of injury in the long run
	Fire the abs	Vertically and horizontally to help generate power	
	Snap the wrist over the top 1/3 of the ball	Helps to create the maximum amount of topspin	
		Encourages a long contact, which helps to control the direction of the ball	

continued

SKILL	CUE	WHY?	COMMON ERROR
Topspin Jump Serve	It is a topspin serve conducted in the air	Helps young athletes new to the serve break the skill down into two skills they can already do (learn topspin serve first)	Overcomplicating the process
	Toss with the right hand high out in front with a flick of the wrist to spin the ball forward—for right-handed servers	Gives player time to hit the ball	
	Take a step with the left foot and then alternate right, left and right, left	Gives more momentum to get up in the air	
	Arm and hand action is the same as the topspin serve		

OFFENSIVE HIT

SKILL	CUE	WHY?	COMMON ERROR
Used for Balls Off of Net (Figure 28.9)	Elbow back, hand above head, rotate elbow forward, and reach up with an open hand	Rotation increases torque and translates into a faster, harder hit	
	Hit ball at highest point of reach with the heel of the hand and follow through after contact at the intended target	Increases control of the direction of the ball	
	Similar to a throwing action, with the hand above the head		
	Contact ball on bottom third	A higher contact increases the probability of the ball going over the net	
	Watch the ball hit hand	Decreases the probability of missing the ball	

continued

Hand above head

Elbow back

Watch the ball

FIGURE 28.9 Offensive Hit (Ready Position)

OFFENSIVE HIT, continued			
SKILL	**CUE**	**WHY?**	**COMMON ERROR**
Used for Balls Off of Net, *continued*		Increases the chance of a solid hit	
Hitting Action	Step under the ball, with the foot opposite of hitting arm	More power in the hit; lining up the hitting arm with the ball is critical for the ball hitting the hand squarely or solidly	
	The hitting arm should be lined up directly under the ball		

SPIKING			
SKILL	**CUE**	**WHY?**	**COMMON ERROR**
Execution	4-step approach: R-L-R-L if right-handed; L-R-L-R if left-handed	Carry momentum and power into spike	No approach; starting approach too close to net
(Figure 28.10)	Arms forward-back-forward	Able to jump higher	Jumping off only one leg like a basketball lay-up
	Bow and arrow action; elbow back and high	Increases power and speed of the hitting arm	

continued

SKILL	CUE	WHY?	COMMON ERROR
Execution, *continued*	Fingers apart		Fist
	Hand open and firm	Increases surface area of the contact, which aids in control	
	Hand in shape of ball	To control ball and apply spin	Hand is flat, or fist, or like jelly
	Wrist somewhat stiff	Ensures firm contact	
Timing	First step when ball is set		Running too far forward; ball goes over attacker's head
	Stepping and setting		
	Trust eyes; do not guess		
(Figure 28.11)	Contact ball high and in front of you at 11 o'clock	To hit downward on ball	Contacting ball too low or behind head
	Powerful wrist snap	Controls the ball and puts spin on ball so it will go down into the court	No wrist snap
	Fast arm swing	Make a positive, decisive motion	Slow swing leads to poor timing and poor contact

Arms back shoulder high

Watch the ball

FIGURE 28.10 Spike (Ready Position)

Contact ball high and in front of you

FIGURE 28.11 Hitting Execution

SKILL	CUE	WHY?	COMMON ERROR
Setup (Figure 28.12)	Keep hands up at eye level	Shorter distance to travel to cross net	Bringing hands and arms below net, straight legs
	Knees bent, ready to jump	Preparation to react quicker to setter	
	Seal the net with body	Prevents ball from coming down on your side of net	Body too far from net
	Chin down for peripheral vision		
Arm Action	Hands up as if playing a piano		
	Fingers are firm and spread—Mickey Mouse ears		Fingers close together and not firm
Timing	Ball, setter, ball, hitter	Aware of all opponents' attacking options	Hands down at sides
			Watching only the ball
	Lead step		

continued

FIGURE 28.12 The Block

SKILL	CUE	WHY?	COMMON ERROR
Setup, *continued*	Three-step move		Moving with hands down at waist
	Get over		
	Penetrate		
	Angle hands into opponent's court as if diving into a swimming pool		Being too far away from net
	Reach over		

DIGS

SKILL	CUE	WHY?	COMMON ERROR
Dig Preparation	Anticipate spike		
	Feet apart, arms ready	Balanced position to move	Weight back on heels, standing straight up
	Ball, setter, ball, hitter; watch hitter's shoulders and head	Can adjust to ball better	Watching ball, not hitter
	Knees bent	Can move quicker	Flat-footed, rooted to spot
Forearm Pass/Dig Pass	Arms like a wall; don't swing arms	Swinging arms adds energy to the ball and makes it harder to control the direction	Swinging arms
	Absorb shock of spike; like a sponge	Absorbing energy of ball to keep in play	
	Platform underneath ball	Directs the ball up— allows teammate to get ball	Arms too close to body
Sprawling	Anticipate spike; be stopped when hitter contacts ball	Anticipate ball speed better	Still moving when hitter contacts ball
	Big step toward ball	More efficient	No tennis hop
	Close to floor, chin up	Lessens impact when you hit the floor	
	Hit ball, then sprawl	First things first	Falling over instead of moving feet
	Helping hand	Helps support your weight	
	Turn knee out	Prevents knee from getting hurt	

continued

SKILL	CUE	WHY?	COMMON ERROR
Pancake	Big step toward the ball	Efficient movement	Not moving feet fast enough
	Close to floor	Lowers your center of gravity, increasing the distance you can travel and lessening the impact as you hit the floor	Diving up and down means you can't reach as far—more likely to hurt yourself
	Helping hand	Use your hands to help support your weight as you hit the floor	
	Turn knee out	Keeps knee from directly hitting floor	
	Slide hand close to the floor	Prevent friction burns	Sliding the hand across the floor can slow you down and lead to friction burns on the heel of the hand
Overhead	Tomahawk action	Solid contact to be legal and push ball upward	Contact between ball and hands is too long to be legal
	Deflection or rebound back toward net	Gives team second chance; targets middle of court	
Fist	Flat surface		

SETTER'S SIGNALS

SKILL	CUE	WHY?	COMMON ERROR
Setter	Quarterback of team signals with fingers to spiker and team		Other players call the signal
	Calls the set signal by using a hand signal to notify players of type of play		
Height of Set; Spiker on the Court	4 3 3 2 ———1———net 5 4 3 2 1 A B C Setter		

continued

SKILL	CUE	WHY?	COMMON ERROR
Spiker's Court Position on Net	Setter signals for first number or letter Examples: 1–1 short set 5–1 long short set		Not listening or looking for signal from setter
Height of Ball Number	Setter signals for second number Examples: 5–4 high set C–4 high back set		Confusing the numbers
Short Sets	"You go, I throw"		
1–1, 3–1, A–1, C–1	Spiker watches ball go over shoulder		Not watching ball; moving too late or too early
	Correct timing takes practice		
	As soon as ball passes shoulder, chase the ball to net; stay with it		Becoming frustrated and quitting
Medium Sets *1–2, 3–2*	When the ball leaves setter's hands, go!		
High Sets	"I throw, you go"		Leaving too soon
5–4, C–4	Watch where ball is set		
	Go when the ball leaves the setter's hands		Not watching the ball leave the setter's hands

SETTER'S HAND SIGNALS			
SKILL	**CUE**	**WHY?**	**COMMON ERROR**
End of Play *Setter's Responsibility*	Setter gives signal before ball is served	Setter gives signal at side of leg to prevent opponent from seeing it	
Hitters' Responsibility	Hitters look for setter's signal as soon as play is over		Forgetting to look for setter's hand signals

continued

SETTER'S HAND SIGNALS, continued			
SKILL	**CUE**	**WHY?**	**COMMON ERROR**

End of Play, *continued*	Move with setter on calls
	net _____
	    S S
	   H H
			Not looking for setter's hand signals

	Everybody watch pass, move accordingly		
During Rally *Hitters' Responsibility*	Hitters can call signals 1–5–C	Communication critical between hitter and setter	
Front Sets	Thumb, index, and middle fingers used for front sets		
Short Set	Index finger = 1 − 1		
	Index and middle finger = 1 − 2		
Middle Front Set	Thumb, index, and middle finger = 3 − 2		
	Four fingers = 4 − 4		
Long Set	Five fingers = 5 − 4		
Back Sets	Pinkie and ring finger used for back sets		
Short Back Set	Pinkie finger = A 1		
Middle Back Set	Pinkie finger and ring finger = B2		
High Back Set	Make letter C = C4		

29

The Practice of Yoga

INTRODUCTION TO YOGA

We offer people something extremely important when we teach yoga in this day and age. Although yoga today is often taught and practiced as a pursuit for health and fitness in a changing world, its spiritual roots still nourish authentic yoga teachings. We have Americanized it and turned it into a workout, so it is important that we as teachers make it restorative and rejuvenating, not miserable!

Yoga can be defined as "mindfulness," or the process of directing the attention toward whatever we are doing at the moment. Through the practice of various yoga techniques and postures, we are continually moving the attention toward the present moment using the breath. In doing so we learn to feel the action from the postures, or *asanas,* from deep within.

The practice of yoga is teaching the mind to steady or to become calm, without distraction, fixed gently on the sound and quality of our breath. Yoga ability grows with time. Some days are easy, the mind is calm, and the physical body is light and responsive; on other days, you may find that the mind is very busy and the body feels like heavy sand.

Why is yoga, an ancient practice, becoming so popular? Perhaps it is because the practice addresses so many modern concerns. In our fast-paced lives, we are always multitasking, rarely making decisions carefully and one at a time. The practice of yoga can benefit all types of people—from children to older adults, from athletes to couch potatoes. Yoga tones the muscles, sculpts the body, improves flexibility, builds muscular strength and endurance, and increases lung capacity while calming the nervous system and mind. It creates the range of motion needed to therapeutically work and heal all areas of the body. It heals, detoxifies, electrifies, and regenerates both body and mind at the deepest levels. One of yoga's greatest advantages is to assist in preventing injury. It is also a helpful tool for recovering from injury and for restoring loss of mobility or range of movement and loss of strength.

As teachers, we create safe environments in which students can approach the practice of yoga, including its different or awkward aspects. For example, we ask students to be barefoot, and to get into funny positions. We ask them to wear fitted clothing and to investigate what they feel. To facilitate this growth, it is crucial to attend to the environment and the attitude with which we encourage students to approach practice. The hallmark of the yoga practitioner is moderation. So as teachers, we remind ourselves and our students that the pose/posture should never take precedence over the person. We also set up appropriate boundaries (e.g., regarding touch) to support safe environments, and we encourage our students to attend to boundaries they need in order to relax. Around the world, thousands of people have benefited from yoga. Practicing with awareness, common sense, and a little basic knowledge can help ensure that yoga is a safe and healing experience for many more.

YOGA SKILLS LISTED WITH CUES

This chapter presents cues for the following: Sun Salutations A and B, standing postures/asanas, seated postures/asanas, and modified closing sequence.

TIPS

Equipment Tips

1. Consider playing quiet yoga music during instruction or using a guided relaxation (see FYI section).

2. Wear clothing that is comfortable and fitted; avoid baggy clothing.

3. Practice barefoot, without socks.

4. Use a clean yoga sticky mat, preferably one's own mat. Mat wipes or spray may be used to clean mats between users if mats are going to be shared. Note that these mats are thinner than the usual aerobics mat; using thick or cushy mats can create severe stress on the wrists and ankles.

5. For modification of poses, have props available—such as blankets, blocks, or straps.

Safety

1. Stomach and bowels should be empty; practice 2–3 hours after a meal.

2. To avoid injury, do not force the body beyond its capacity. Practice at "the edge," with enough effort to create sensation and keep you engaged, but with less effort than will create pain or an inability to breathe. Discomfort is different from pain; it should disappear once the pose is released. Even among very fit people, weaknesses will become visible during the practice—this is ok! If a pose is causing pain, try a modification or a less strenuous pose until the body is strengthened and the original pose can be performed more comfortably.

3. If there is any persistent pain, it is a sign of incorrect practice of some physical problem. Consult with a qualified teacher.

4. Hold the postures only as long as the proper alignment can be maintained. The length of time spent in each pose will increase along with strength, flexibility, and endurance.

5. Elongate the spine before bending to maximize disk space. Normal curves keep the spine healthy. The spine bends forward and backward most easily in the lumbar region, so we tend to overwork the lower back. Forcing the spine into forward bends is one of the most dangerous things you can do in all of yoga. It is important to always return the spine to neutral.

6. Go into Child's Pose for a break if your body is telling you that you need one.

Etiquette

1. Clean your mat with hot water and soap after each use.
2. Take your shoes off outside of the room.
3. Respect other students' space; do not walk on others' mats.
4. Enter and settle in quietly, and keep conversation to a minimum to maintain the serenity of the room.
5. Do not skip Savasana (final relaxation pose).

TEACHING IDEAS

1. Alignment principles:
   a. Scoop the tailbone under and lift the chest (telescope the ribs) to create space in the vertebrae.
   b. Draw the shoulders back, in, and down with the lower portion of the blades curling under toward the heart. (A good visual is having the arms lifted shoulder height and bent at a 90-degree angle. Draw only the elbows forward, and feel how the blades curl under toward the heart).

2. Engage the internal locks, or *bandhas*, lightly throughout the practice.
   a. *Mula bandha*, or root lock, located at the perineum approximately $1/2$ inch in from anus. Drawing the pelvic floor up will help the tailbone scoop under.
   b. *Uddiyana bandha*, or navel lock, is performed by exhaling fully and then drawing the lower belly inward and upward while simultaneously lifting the diaphragm.
   c. Children under 13 should not engage the *bandhas*.

3. Use a focal point, or *drishti*, to reduce distraction. Keep eyes softly focused on this gazing point while practicing; may be off the fingers, toes, nose, or middle of the forehead. Alternatively, one may choose to focus the gaze on a spot on the floor approximately 3 feet ahead, or lift the gaze slightly to a point on the wall.

4. Breathing techniques, or *pranayama*, aid concentration. In yoga, the breath is viewed as a sacred bridge between the tangible body and the intangible mind.
   a. Breathe in and out through the nose.
   b. Fully expand the lungs on inhalation; fully contract on exhalation. Pay attention to the exhale, and allow the inhale to simply happen.
   c. Create an audible breath, called *ujjayi pranayama*, which sounds similar to ocean waves gently crashing. While contracting the back of the throat and keeping the mouth closed, inhale making a "hsss" sound and exhale with a "hammm" sound.
   d. Use the breath as an indication of appropriate effort level. Try to keep the breath smooth…pause slightly between breaths and restore an even, flowing breath.

5. Value students' opinions; praise and encourage them. Teach respect and compassion through example. Give them options or choices, and help them to see possibilities. Teach them to accept their limitations and where they are at this moment in time. Be playful and loving.

6. According to Sri K. Patthabi Jois, Master Yogi, the Primary Series in Astanga Yoga may be taught to ages 9–11. Those over 12 can begin a more serious study of this type of power yoga. Younger children generally can concentrate only for up to 40 minutes, while older ages can practice up to 60 minutes. Do not overwork children.

7. Teach Child's Pose and Knees into Chest first (see Closing Sequence). Encourage students to use these poses, or Downward Facing Dog, as resting poses if they become lightheaded, short of breath, or too tired during the practice.

Teaching Progressions

1. Breath: *Pranayama* (life current/life force) (pg. 5)
2. Internal locks: *Mula bandha, Uddiyana bandha* (pg. 4)
3. Alignment principles (pg. 4)
4. Sun Salutations A and B (pg. 7–9)
5. Postures (pg. 16–17, 22–25)
6. *Vinyasa*: a unique linking of one posture to the next in a dynamic flow (pg. 25)
7. Closing sequence (pg. 27–28)
8. Final relaxation: *Savasana* (pg. 28).

Mini-Games

1. Use the familiar figure of Darth Vader to introduce the breath technique of *ujjayi pranayama*. Bring hand to mouth and act as if you are steaming up a mirror to get the effect of abdominal breathing. Be playful and do not force students to participate; have fun with this.

2. Use animals and nature to portray the postures. For example: Eagle, Down-dog, Cat/Cow, Stork, Frog, Bug, Cobra, Mountain, Half-moon, Tree, etc. Be playful and creative.

3. As students become more familiar with the poses, invite them to choose a pose their body is calling for. They can practice individually during the closing sequence before going into relaxation. Offer appropriate calming poses for them to consider, such as Child's Pose or Spinal Twist.

ASSESSMENT IDEAS

1. Teacher will come and move body into proper alignment if student is holding a pose incorrectly.
2. Students are making progress if they can hold the pose longer or can move deeper into the pose.

For further information, consult the following organizations and resources.

ORGANIZATIONS

Hugger Mugger
www.huggermugger.com

Barefoot Yoga
www.barefootyoga.com

PUBLICATIONS

Iyengar, B. K. S. (1989). *The tree of yoga*. Boston: Shambhala Publications, 1989.
Feuerstein, G. & Payne, L. (1999). *Yoga for dummies*. IDG Books Worldwide.

SUN SALUTATION A SEQUENCE/WARM-UP

This sequence is designed to produce heat in the body so that muscles and joints are prepared for the physical work to follow.

SKILL	CUE	WHY?	COMMON ERROR
Mountain Posture (*Tadasana*)	Stand with both feet together (big toes touching), legs active, spine long; engage the *bandhas;* breathe deep	Builds awareness of feet, ankles, alignment of spine; strengthens feet, ankles, quads, hamstrings, core, and back	Pressing back into knee joint to "lock" knees. *Modification:* Lift/pull up with quads to bring legs straight.
Upward Hand Pose (*Urdhva hastasana*)	**Inhale.** Raise both arms (lungs should be full just as the hands touch); gaze at the thumbs; chest upward	Lengthens spine, shoulders, and arms; strengthens hips, legs, and feet	Collapsing in low back. *Modification:* Even if a slight backbend is desired, lengthen from tailbone, lifting up from waist.
Full Forward Fold (*Uttanasana*)	**Exhale.** Fold forward, taking the chest toward the knees; look toward toes. *Note:* Every Full Forward Fold *must* be done with bent knees.	Lengthens hamstrings and back; strengthens quads and abs	Not folding enough. *Modification:* Pull belly button back toward spine, allowing torso to come closer to legs and protecting low back.
Look Forward	**Inhale.** Lengthen the spine, draw the chest away from belly; lengthen back of neck, look forward	Lengthens spine, neck, and hams; strengthens quads and abs	Overworking back by forgetting to use legs. *Modification:* Keep legs engaged as in Mountain Posture; keep abs engaged as in Forward Fold.

continued

SKILL	CUE	WHY?	COMMON ERROR
Four-Limb Stick (*Chaturanga dandasana*)	**Exhale.** Step back, lower from plank to four-limb stick while gazing forward. *Modification:* Drop knees, uncurl toes; elbows beside ribs if possible; hover or lie flat on the floor	Total core stability; increases strength in wrists, shoulders, triceps, quads, and hams	Collapsing in low back. *Modification:* Pull in abs to help support, but also rely more on arms. To do so, make sure hands are placed right under shoulder, with fingers widespread and middle fingers pointing forward.
Upward Facing Dog or Cobra (*Urdhva mukha svanasana*) (Figure 29.1)	**Inhale.** Straighten the arms or slightly bend at the elbows and roll onto the tops of the feet; knees lifted or dropped to floor; toes pointed; lift chest high; scoop tailbone	Increases strength in upper body; increases flexibility of chest and abs	Hyperextending elbows. *Modification:* Turn arm muscles to make the inner elbows face each other.
Downward Facing Dog (*Adho mukha svanasana*)	**Exhale.** Push hips up away from floor toward the intersection of the ceiling and the wall behind; press heels toward the floor and lift the kneecaps; gaze at navel; engage the *bandhas;* remain here for three to five breaths	Increases arm, shoulder, quad, and ankle strength; increases flexibility in spine, hams, calves, and achilles	Resting weight on toes. *Modification:* Lengthen along back of legs from hips to heels, allowing heels to descend toward floor; balance weight between hands and feet.
Walk or Jump Forward	**Inhale.** Walk or jump the feet forward in between hands; lengthen the spine, take gaze forward	Strengthens core and arms; lengthens spine	Not trying jumping— try it! It's not as hard as it looks.

FIGURE 29.1 Upward-Facing Dog

continued

SKILL	CUE	WHY?	COMMON ERROR
Full Forward Fold (*Uttanasana*)	See cues on page 400		
Upward Hand Pose (*Urdhva hastasana*)	See cues on page 400		
Mountain Posture (*Tadasana*)	**Exhale.** Lower arms in preparation for next Sun Salutation A or *vinyasa*	Returns the body to a neutral alignment	

SUN SALUTATION B SEQUENCE

SKILL	CUE	WHY?	COMMON ERROR
Mountain Posture (*Tadasana*)	Stand with both feet together (big toes touching), legs active, spine long; engage the *bandhas;* breathe deep	Builds awareness of feet, ankles, alignment of spine; strengthens feet, ankles, quads, hamstrings, core, and back	Pressing back into knee joint to "lock" knees. *Modification:* Lift/pull up with quads to bring legs straight.
Fierce Posture (*Utkatasana*)	**Inhale.** Bend knees (coming into a squat) and raise both arms to the sky; fill lungs fully; gaze toward thumbs	Stretches shoulders and arms; lengthens spine; strengthens quads, hams, abs, and chest	Staying too upright. *Modification:* Move hips back behind heels as though sitting in a chair.
Full Forward Fold (*Uttanasana*)	**Exhale.** Fold forward, taking the chest toward the knees; look toward toes. *Note:* Every Full Forward Fold *must* be done with bent knees.	Lengthens hams and back; strengthens quads and abs	Not folding enough. *Modification:* Pull belly button back toward spine, allowing torso to come closer to legs and protecting low back.
Look Forward	**Inhale.** Lengthen the spine, draw the chest away from belly; lengthen back of neck, look forward	Lengthens spine, neck, and hams; strengthens quads and abs	Overworking back by forgetting to use legs. *Modification:* Keep legs engaged as in Mountain Posture; keep abs engaged as in Forward Fold.
Four-Limb Stick (*Chaturanga dandasana*)	**Exhale.** Step back, lower from plank to four-limb stick while gazing forward. *Modification:* Drop knees, uncurl toes; elbows beside ribs if possible; hover or lie flat on the floor.	Total core stability, increases strength in wrists, shoulders, triceps, quads, and hams	Collapsing in low back. *Modification:* Pull in abs to help support, but also rely more on arms. To do so, make sure hands are placed right under shoulder, with fingers widespread, and middle fingers pointing forward.

continued

SKILL	CUE	WHY?	COMMON ERROR
Upward Facing Dog, or Cobra (*Urdhva mukha svanasana*)	**Inhale.** Straighten the arms or slightly bend at the elbows and roll onto the tops of the feet; knees lifted or dropped to floor; toes pointed; lift chest high; scoop tailbone	Increases strength in upper body; increases flexibility of chest and abs	Hyperextending elbows. *Modification:* Turn arm muscles to make the inner elbows face each other.
Downward Facing Dog (*Adho mukha svanasana*)	**Exhale.** Push hips up away from floor toward the intersection of the ceiling and the wall behind; press heels toward the floor and lift the kneecaps; gaze at navel; engage the *bandhas;* remain here for three to five breaths	Increases arm, shoulder, quad, and ankle strength; increases flexibility in spine, hams, calves, and achilles	Resting weight on toes. *Modification:* Lengthen along back of legs from hips to heels, allowing heels to descend toward floor; balance weight between hands and feet.
Warrior I Pose, Right Side (*Virabhadrasana I*) (Figure 29.2)	**Inhale.** Bring right foot forward between hands and flatten back foot in 30° angle, heel away from little toe. Bend forward knee, bringing knee directly over ankle; raise hands over head with arms straight until palms touch; gaze at thumbs (this should be done in one inhale)	Increases strength in gluteals, legs, core, back, shoulders, arms, ankles, and feet	Forgetting to breathe! If necessary, take an extra breath.

continued

FIGURE 29.2 Warrior I Pose

SKILL	CUE	WHY?	COMMON ERROR
Four-Limb Stick (*Chaturanga dandasana*)	Exhale; see cues on page 402	See cues on page 402	
Upward Facing Dog or Cobra (*Urdhva mukha svanasana*)	Inhale; see cues on page 403		
Downward Facing Dog (*Adho mukha svanasana*)	Exhale; see cues on page 403		
Warrior I, Left Side (*Virabhadrasana I*)	Same as Warrior I, Right Side, but use left side instead	Increases strength in gluteals, legs, core, back, shoulders, arms ankles, and feet	
Four-Limb Stick (*Chaturanga dandasana*)	Exhale; see cues on page 402		
Upward Facing Dog or Cobra (*Urdhva* mukha *svanasana*)	Inhale; see cues on page 403		
Downward Facing Dog (*Adho mukha svanasana*)	Exhale; see cues on page 403; remain here for three to five complete breaths		
Walk or Jump Forward	Inhale as you walk or jump feet toward hands; lengthen the spine while gazing forward	Core stabilization; increases strength in arms; stretches spine	
Full Forward Fold (*Uttanasana*)	Exhale; see cues on page 402		
Fierce Posture (*Utkatasana*)	Inhale; see cues on page 402		
Mountain Posture (*Tadasana*)	Exhale, lower your arms and straighten the legs in preparation for the next Sun Salutation B; gaze straight ahead	Brings spine back into neutral alignment	

Hold all standing postures for multiple breaths, work up to 3–5 minutes per pose.

SKILL	CUE	WHY?	COMMON ERROR
Big Toe Posture (*Padangusthasana*) *Base: Full Forward Fold*	From Mountain Posture, jump feet hip width apart. **Inhale.** Lift gaze toward sky. **Exhale.** Fold forward, clasp the big toes with middle and index fingers of each hand.	Strengthens quads and shoulders; increases flexibility in hamstrings	If cannot reach toes, clasp ankles, bend knees, bring ribs to thighs
Hand Under Foot Pose (*Padahastasana*) *Base: Full Forward Fold*	From Mountain Posture, exhale; place hand under foot with toes to wrist	Counterstretch for wrists; increases flexibility in hams; strengthens quads and shoulders	If cannot reach under feet, bring fingers to toes, or blocks, and bend knees
Extended Triangle Pose (*Utthita trikonasana*) (Figure 29.3)	From Mountain Posture, walk feet one-leg length apart; turn right foot out and left toes in slightly. **Exhale.** Raise arms to shoulder level; shift hips to left while lengthening torso to right; rotate arms as windmill, bringing right hand to shin. **Inhale.** Come up slowly. Repeat on other side.	Strengthens quads, hams, calves, back, and abs; lengthens intercostals, waist, hip flexors, and inner thighs	If hand does not come to shin, use a block. If hand goes below shin, try to take hold of big toe.
Revolved Triangle Pose (*Parivritta trikonansana*) *Base: Extended Triangle Pose*	From Mountain Posture, step feet one-leg length apart, front to back. **Exhale.** Turn right foot out, left toes in; square hips to the right, place right hand on sacrum; reach left arm forward, descend to shin or outside of right little toe; spiral around, open left shoulder to sky, reach up. **Inhale.** Come up slowly. Repeat on other side.	Stretches hams and hips; lengthens spine; strengthens quads, shoulders, and arms	If feet are too narrow, the pose will be wobbly. Make sure feet are at least hip width apart; may also help to shorten length of stance. Try to keep sacrum level.

continued

SKILL	CUE	WHY?	COMMON ERROR
Extended Side Angle Pose (*Uttihita parsvahonasana*) *Base: Extended Triangle Pose*	From Mountain Posture, step feet 3–4 feet apart, arms outstretched; turn right foot open and left foot in approximately 45°. **Exhale.** Bend right knee directly above heel, lower right hand to the floor outside the right foot (inside of foot for beginners); extend left hand up to sky. **Inhale.** Come up slowly. Repeat on other side.	Lengthens torso, outer side leg, ribs, and intercostals; strengthens hams, quads, calves, and shins	If hand does not reach floor, bring right forearm onto right thigh; place left hand on sacrum (reverse for left side)
Prayer Twist (*Parivritta parsvakonasana*) *Base: Extended Side Angle Pose*	Turn right foot out, stay up on left toes. **Exhale.** Bend right leg, knee above heel; left elbow to outside of right knee; place left and right hand into prayer position. **Inhale.** Come up slowly. Repeat on other side.	Rotation of torso; lengthens spine, groins, inner thighs; strengthens hams, quads, shins, and calves	If pose is wobbly, drop knee to floor
Expanded Leg Pose (*Prasarita padottanasana*)	From Mountain Posture, step feet 3–4 feet apart; outer edges of feet parallel, hands on hips, drawing elbows back toward each other; scoop tailbone, contract quads, telescope ribs, lift chest, and look up. **Exhale.** Fold forward, hands stay on hips, keep legs active. **Inhale.** Come up slowly.	Increases flexibility in inner thighs and outer shins; strengthens back and abs	
Hand to Big Toe Pose (*Utthita hasta padangusthasana*)	From Mountain Posture, raise right knee; grab big toe with index and middle fingers; straighten leg; hold for 3 to 5 breaths; open to right side; hold for three to five breaths	Strengthens hips, feet, and knees; stretches hams and opens groins; develops balance	If leg cannot straighten while toe is held, hold onto bent knee; may open bent knee to outside

continued

SKILL	CUE	WHY?	COMMON ERROR
Tree Posture *(Vrksasana)* (Figure 29.4)	From Mountain Posture, **inhale.** Lift right foot with both hands. **Exhale.** Place foot on upper-left thigh, bring hands to prayer position. Repeat on other side.	Strengthens hips, legs, and core; opens hips; increases balance	If foot cannot comfortably stay on opposite upper-left thigh, bring foot to opposite calf
Warrior I *(Virabhadrasana I)*	**Inhale.** Bring right foot forward between hands and flatten back foot in 30° angle, heel away from little toe. Bend forward knee, bringing knee directly over ankle; raise hands over head with arms straight until palms touch; gaze at thumbs (this should be done in one inhale).	Increases strength in gluteals, legs, core, back, shoulders, arms, ankles, and feet	Forgetting to breathe! If necessary, take an extra breath.
Warrior II *(Virabhadrasana II)* *Base: Warrior I*	From Warrior I, **exhale** and open arms parallel to floor and in line with legs. Left leg should remain at 90° angle, right foot flat at 30° angle; left knee over heel; gaze over the left middle finger. **Inhale.** Come up slowly. Repeat on other side.	Strengthens feet, ankles, knees, quads, spine, and shoulders; increases flexibility in groin, legs, and feet	

FIGURE 29.3 Extended Triangle Pose

FIGURE 29.4 Tree Posture

SEATED POSTURES SEQUENCE

Hold all seated postures for multiple breaths; work up to 3–5 minutes per pose.

SKILL	CUE	WHY?	COMMON ERROR
Staff Posture *(Dandasana)*	Sit with legs extended in front of body, feet and knees touching. **Exhale.** Drop chin to chest; keep legs active, spine long, arms straight, hands pressing down with palms flat and back of knees pressing down.	Lengthens spine; strengthens shoulders, arms, and hands	Lifting heels off ground
Intense West Posture *(Paschimottansasana)* *Base: Staff Posture* (Figure 29.5)	From Staff Posture, raise arms up, telescope ribs, scoop tailbone. **Exhale.** Fold forward, clasp big toes with middle and index fingers, gaze at toes; keep feet and knees together; contract quads.	Increases flexibility in the hamstrings and the back; increases strength in the biceps and chest	Rounding in low back. *Modification:* Straighten spine by pulling abs in and up. May keep arms at side to help lift torso.

continued

SKILL	CUE	WHY?	COMMON ERROR
Intense East Posture (*Purvottanasana*) *Base: Staff Posture*	From Staff Posture, place hands flat on the floor behind hips, pointing fingers toward toes. **Inhale.** Drop head back, push hips up to sky. Keep legs straight and active with feet touching and soles of feet on the floor; keep arms straight and fully engaged.	Increases flexibility in the front of the body; opens anterior shoulder	Dropping hips. *Modification:* Lift from waist so body is like one plank; push into hands, and spread fingers wide.
Single Leg Forward Bend A (*Janu sirasana A*) *Base: Staff Posture*	From Staff Posture, extend left leg straight, bring right foot to inner left thigh, right knee should be at 90° angle. **Exhale.** Fold forward, clasp left foot with both hands. **Inhale.** Come up slowly. Repeat on other side.	Increases flexibility in hams; opens hips	If knee of bent leg is off floor, support it with a blanket. If cannot reach foot, may use strap around foot or clasp shin.
Seated Twist (*Marichyasana C*) *Base: Staff Posture*	From Staff Posture, bend right knee and bring right foot flat near right sitting bone. **Inhale.** Lengthen spine and take hold of right knee with left hand. **Exhale.** Begin spiraling to right and place right hand on the floor behind back. With each inhalation, lengthen spine; with exhalation, invite body to twist further. Release slowly. Repeat on other side.	Increases flexibility in back; increases range of movement in torso	"Hanging out" in pose. *Modification:* Move deeper in twist with a deeper variation: place left outside elbow on outside right knee, hand up, fingers spread, and use the knee to push against.
Boat Posture (*Navasana*) *Base: Staff Posture* (Figure 29.6)	In Staff Posture, **inhale.** Lift and straighten both legs and feet together, toes spread at eye level; gaze at toes; arms straight, parallel to floor with palms facing each other.	Strengthens core, especially transverse abdominals	Collapsing in low back. *Modification:* May bend knees and hold behind them to lift out of low back; much better to start with modified version; as one develops strength to hold spine straight, work on extending legs.

continued

FIGURE 29.5 Intense West Posture

FIGURE 29.6 Boat Posture

SEATED POSTURES SEQUENCE, continued			
SKILL	**CUE**	**WHY?**	**COMMON ERROR**
Bound Angle Posture (*Baddha konasana*) *Base: Staff Posture*	From Staff Posture, bring soles of feet together in front of groin; hold feet with fingers on top of foot (with thumbs on the soles), keeping outer edges of feet on floor; lower knees toward floor.	Increases flexibility in adductors	Ignoring knee pain. *Modification:* Try elevating hips by sitting on edge of rolled blanket or on block. Use blankets to support legs if knees are up in the air, allowing muscles to relax.
Hero Posture (*Virasana*)	Kneel on floor; bring knees and feet together, then sit on your feet	Stretches quads and outer front shin	Again, ignoring knee pain! *Modification:* Try placing rolled blanket on calves and sit back. For deeper variation, allow feet to separate just wider than hips, and sit down between feet (or on rolled blanket placed between hips).
Seated Angle Posture *Base: Staff Posture*	From Staff Posture, open feet wide, legs straight; hold feet with hands. **Inhale.** Lengthen the spine and gaze forward. **Exhale.** Release deeper into pose.	Increases flexibility in adductors	Collapsing in lowback. *Modification:* Imagine doing Expanded Leg Pose while seated. If hands do not reach feet, use straps around feet, or place hands on shins.

SEATED POSTURES SEQUENCE, continued

SKILL	CUE	WHY?	COMMON ERROR
Child's Pose (*Balasana*)	On all fours, knees apart, bring glutes back and down toward heels; lengthen arms over head, forehead down on mat, abdomen between thighs; breathe deeply	Restores and rejuvenates whole body and mind; excellent rest pose. Also increases flexibility in back and hips.	
Spinal Twist	Lie flat on back; draw left knee into chest, extend right leg out; hook left toes on right quad, right hand on outside of left knee; bring left knee down toward floor on right side of body. Extend left arm with palms down on floor, allowing left shoulder to drop toward floor; look over left shoulder.	Increases flexibility in rib cage, intercostals, glutes, and lower back	

MODIFIED CLOSING SEQUENCE

End your practice with this sequence to return the spine to neutral and the body to its basal metabolic rate. Rest in Final Relaxation for a minimum of 5 minutes; 10–15 minutes is recommended. These restorative poses are actually the most important and beneficial of all.

SKILL	CUE	WHY?	COMMON ERROR
Knees into Chest (Figure 29.7)	Lie flat on back; draw both knees into chest, wrap the arms around the knees and gently roll in a circular motion	Releases lower back, gently massages back; preparation for final relaxation	
Knees into Chest Twist	From Knees into Chest, open arms to side with palms facing down; draw shoulders down into sockets, drop both knees to right side, look over left shoulder. Repeat on other side.	Releases residual tension in the lower back, spine, gluteals, intercostals, and lats	

continued

FIGURE 29.7 Knees into Chest

MODIFIED CLOSING SEQUENCE, continued			
SKILL	**CUE**	**WHY?**	**COMMON ERROR**
Final Relaxation/ Corpse Pose (*Savasana*)	Lie flat on back; allow feet to flop open and let arms extend along floor at 45°, palms up. Release all muscles, dissolve all tension; close your eyes and completely relax.	Allows heart rate and breath to slow to a natural, soothing rhythm; revitalizes and rejuvenates whole body and mind	

When coming out of this sequence, wiggle fingers and toes to return to awareness. Then roll onto your right side in a fetal position. When prepared, place both hands on the floor and push yourself up to a comfortable position and maintain seated lotus or any comfortable position to keep the spine tall. Take three slow breaths in and out. *Breathe in slowly.* Now the body has been cleansed and the mind is relaxed, ready to meet the rest of the day with energy and vitality!

Namaste, everyone! (My light salutes your light!)

References

Christina, R. W., & Corcos, D. M. (1988). *Coaches guide to teaching sport skills.* Champaign, IL: Human Kinetics.

Coker, C. (1998, January/February). Performance excellence: Making the most of natural speed. *Strategies, 11*(3), 10–12.

Docheff, D. M. (1990). The feedback sandwich. *Journal of Physical Education, Recreation, and Dance, 64,* 17–18.

Fronske, H., Abendroth-Smith, J., & Blakemore, C. (1997). Critical overhand throwing cues help 3rd, 4th, and 5th grade students achieve efficient throwing patterns and increase their distance. *The Physical Educator, 54*(2), 88–95.

Fronske, H., & Birch, N. (1995). Overcoming road blocks to communication. *Strategies, 8*(8), 22–25.

Fronske, H., & Collier, C. (1993, September). Cueing your athletes on good jumping events. *Journal of Physical Education, Recreation, and Dance, 64*(7), 7–9.

Fronske, H., Collier, C., & Orr, D. (1993, February). Cueing your participants in on track events. *Journal of Physical Education, Recreation, and Dance, 64*(2), 9–10.

Fronske, H., & McGown, C. (1992, October). Visual teaching cues for volleyball skills. *Journal of Physical Education, Recreation, and Dance, 63*(8), 10–11.

Fronske, H., & Wilson, R. (2002). *Teaching cues for basic sport skills for elementary and middle school students.* San Francisco, CA: Benjamin Cummings.

Lacrosse Foundation. (1994). *The Lacrosse Foundation's parent's guide to the sport of lacrosse.* Baltimore, MD: Lacrosse Foundation, Inc.

Lawther, J. D. (1968). *The learning of physical skills.* Englewood Cliffs, NJ: Prentice-Hall.

Lockhart, A. (1966, May). Communicating with the learner. *Quest, VI,* 57–67.

Mack, G. (2001). *Mind gym.* Chicago, IL: Contemporary Books.

Magill, R. (2003). *Motor learning: Concepts and applications* (7th ed.). Blacklick, OH: McGraw-Hill.

Masser, L. (1993). Critical cues help first grade students' achievement in handstands and forward rolls. *Journal of Teaching in Physical Education, 12,* 301–312.

McGown, C. (1988). [Motor learning]. Unpublished lecture notes. Provo, UT: Brigham Young University.

Pfaff, D., Myers, B., Light, R., Freeman, W., & Winkler, G. (1991). *USA Track & Field Level II. Coaching education program: The jumps.* Indianapolis, IN: The Athletic Congress, TAC, USA.

Rink, J. (2000). *Teaching physical education for learning* (5th ed.). Blacklick, OH: McGraw-Hill.

Strand, B., Reeder, S., Scantling, E., & Johnson, M. (1997). *Fitness education: Teaching concepts-based fitness in schools.* Scottsdale, AZ: Gorsuch Scarisbrick.

Winkler, G., & Schexnayder, I. (1998, July). *Level three coaching seminar.* Baton Rouge, LA: United States of America Track & Field.

Winkler, G., Seagrave, L., Gambetta, V., Orognen, J., Jolly, S., & Rogers, J. (1986). *Coaching Certification Level II: Sprints and hurdles.* Indianapolis, IN: The Athletic Congress, TAC, USA.

Index

Page references followed by *f* indicate figure.